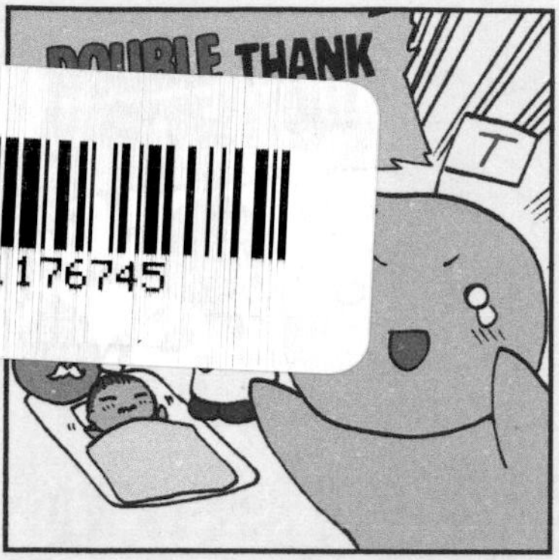
THANK
T

This is Tsutsui!

This is volume 10! It's a dream come true:
we're finally in the double digits!

Thank you so much for supporting the series all the way into a realm of numbers so high they take both hands to count!

I'm also excited to share that I've become the father of a second child. Two digits, two children! I'm deeply grateful to be twice as lucky! And I'm determined to work harder than ever on this manga!

So, whether or not you're brimming with your own motivation, I hope that every now and then, you'll pick up this romantic comic and enjoy some R & R!

• Taishi Tsutsui •

We Never Learn

We Never Learn

Volume 10 • SHONEN JUMP Manga Edition

STORY AND ART **Taishi Tsutsui**

TRANSLATION Camellia Nieh

SHONEN JUMP SERIES LETTERING Snir Aharon

GRAPHIC NOVEL TOUCH-UP ART & LETTERING Erika Terriquez

DESIGN Shawn Carrico

EDITOR John Bae

First published in Japan in 2017 by SHUEISHA Inc., Tokyo.
English translation rights arranged by SHUEISHA Inc.

Printed in the U.S.A.

Published by VIZ Media, LLC
P.O. Box 77010
San Francisco, CA 94107

10 9 8 7 6 5 4 3 2 1
First printing, June 2020

VIZ MEDIA
viz.com

SHONEN JUMP
shonenjump.com

RATED T+ OLDER TEEN
ratings.viz.com

PARENTAL ADVISORY
WE NEVER LEARN is rated T+ for Older Teen and is recommended for ages 16 and up. This volume contains mild language and sexual themes.

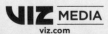

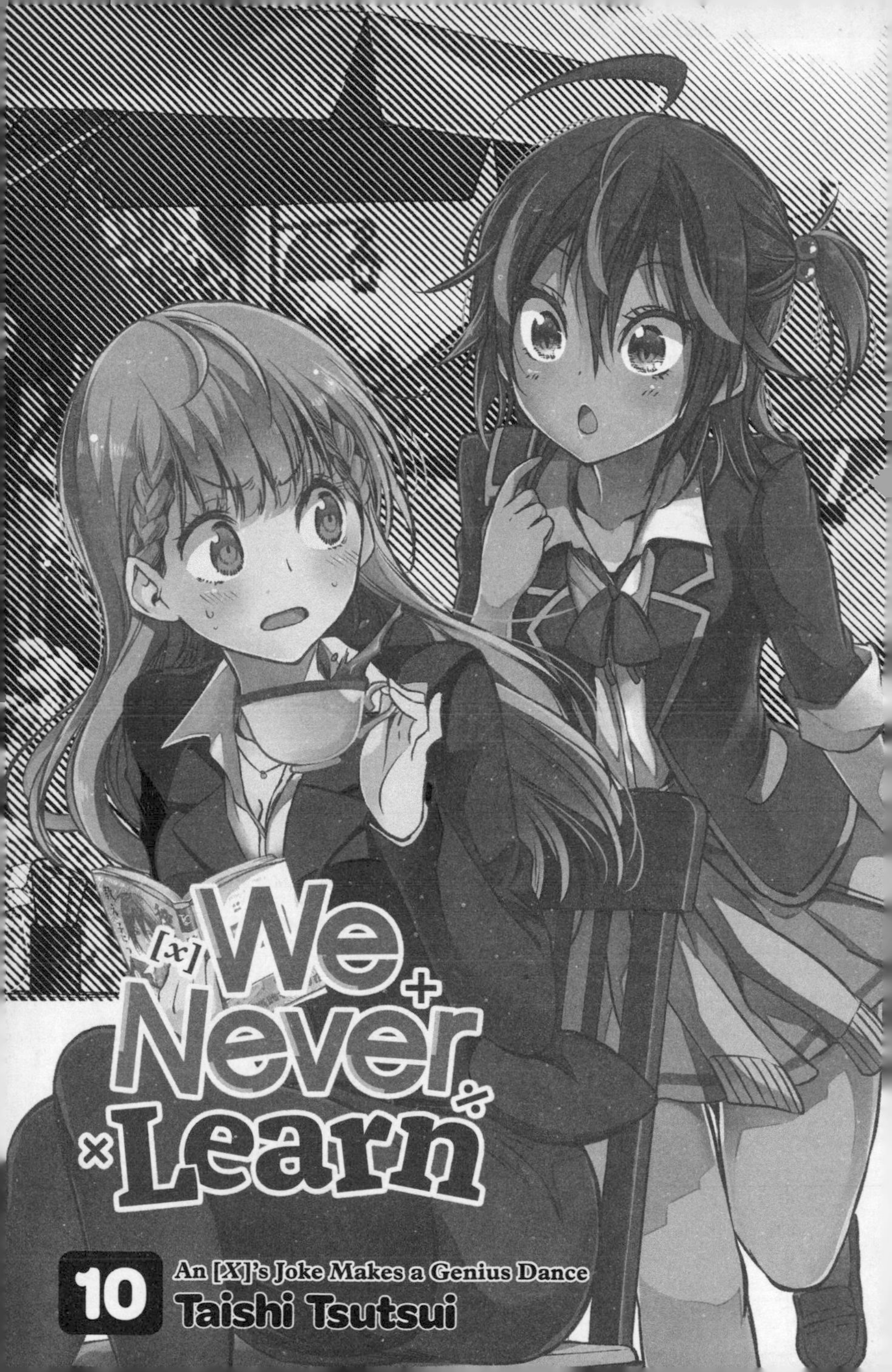
[x] We Never Learn
10
An [X]'s Joke Makes a Genius Dance
Taishi Tsutsui

We Never Learn

Characters & Story

Nariyuki Yuiga and his family have led a humble life since his father passed away, with Yuiga doing everything he can to support his siblings. So when the principal of his school agrees to grant Nariyuki the school's special VIP recommendation for a full scholarship to college, he leaps at the opportunity. However, the principal's offer comes with one condition: Yuiga must serve as the tutor of Rizu Ogata, Fumino Furuhashi and Uruka Takemoto, the three girl geniuses who are the pride of Ichinose Academy! Unfortunately, the girls, while extremely talented in certain ways, all have subjects where their grades are absolutely rock-bottom. How will these three struggling students ever manage to pass their college entrance exams?!

At the school festival, Nariyuki runs himself ragged dealing with everything. When he goes on stage during a play wearing a full-body costume and mask, he ends up receiving a kiss from Fumino. Later, Nariyuki takes someone's hand during a romantic fireworks display. What could happen next?!

NARIYUKI YUIGA

CLASS:3-B

☺ Liberal Arts
☺ STEM
☹ Athletics

A bright student from an ordinary family. Nariyuki lacks genius in any one subject but manages to maintain stellar grades through hard work. Agrees to take on the role of tutor in return for the school's special VIP recommendation.

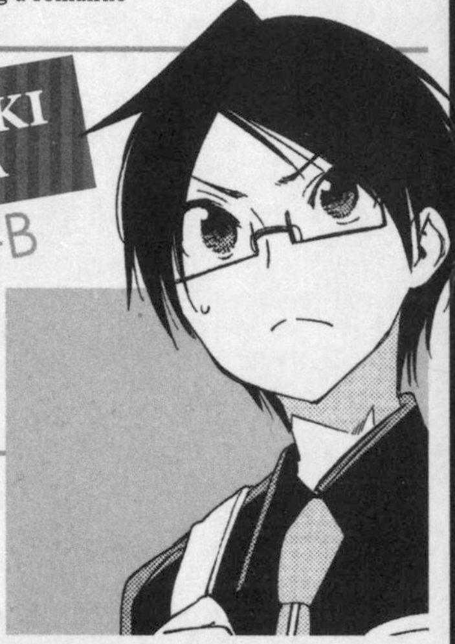

The Yuiga Family

A family of five consisting of Nariyuki, his mother and his siblings, Mizuki, Hazuki and Kazuki.

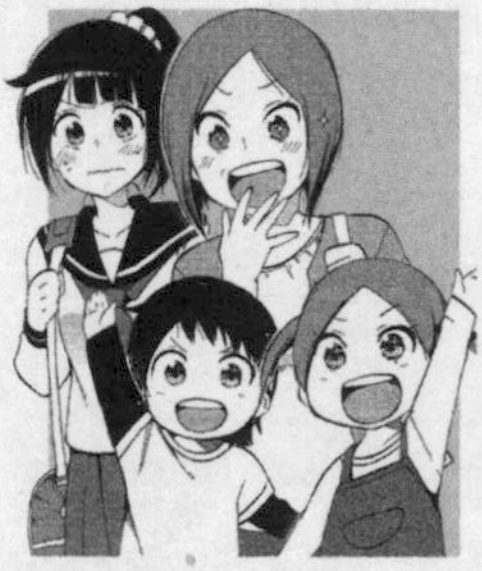

Kobayashi and Omori

Nariyuki's friends.

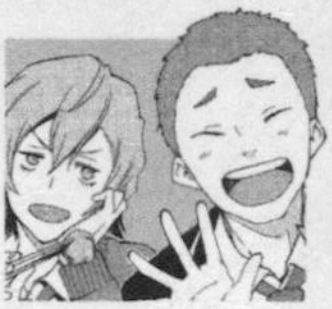

Sawako Sekijo

The head of the science club and a rival of Rizu's, who in fact adores Rizu.

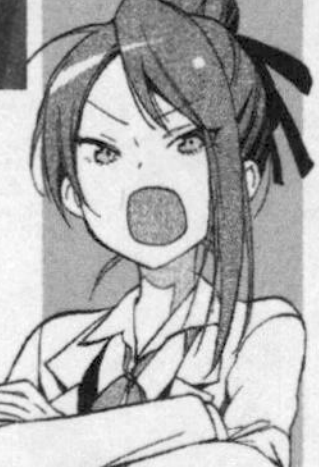

Kawase and Umihara

Uruka's friends.

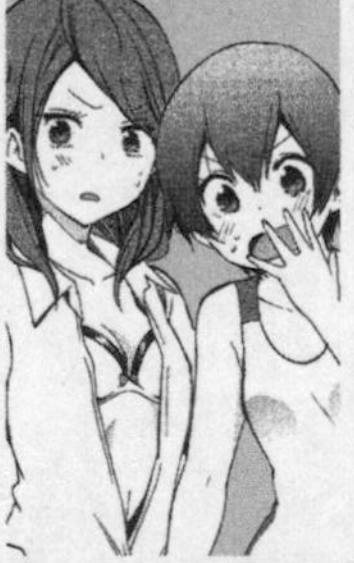

Machiko

Asumi's coworker at the maid cafe.

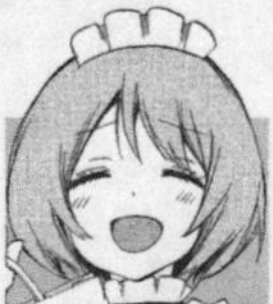

RIZU OGATA

Known as the Thumbelina Supercomputer, Rizu is a math and science genius, but she's a dunce at literature, especially when human emotions come into play. She chooses a literary path to learn about human psychology—partially because she wants to become better at board games.

CLASS:3-F

☹ Liberal Arts ☺ STEM ☹ Athletics

FUMINO FURUHASHI

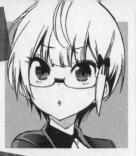

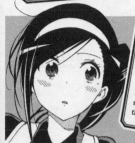

Known as the Sleeping Beauty of the Literary Forest, Fumino is a literary wiz whose mind goes completely blank when she sees numbers. She chooses a STEM path because she wants to study the stars.

CLASS:3-A

☺ Liberal Arts ☹ STEM ☺ Athletics

URUKA TAKEMOTO

Known as the Shimmering Ebony Mermaid Princess, Uruka is a swimming prodigy but is terrible at academics. In order to get an athletic scholarship, she needs to meet certain academic standards. She's had a crush on Nariyuki since junior high.

CLASS:3-D

☹ Liberal Arts ☹ STEM ☺ Athletics

MAFUYU KIRISU

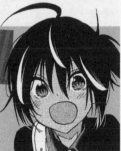

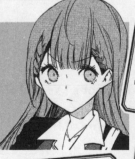

A teacher at Ichinose Academy, and Rizu and Fumino's previous tutor. She believes people should choose their path according to their talents.

TEACHER

☺ Pedagogy
☹ Home Economics

ASUMI KOMINAMI

A graduate of Ichinose Academy. Works at a maid cafe and attends cram school in order to get into medical school and take over her father's clinic one day.

OG

☹ Science
☺ Service

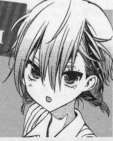

TITLE

We Never Learn

CONTENTS

VOLUME 10 An [X]'s Joke Makes a Genius Dance

NAME **Taishi Tsutsui**

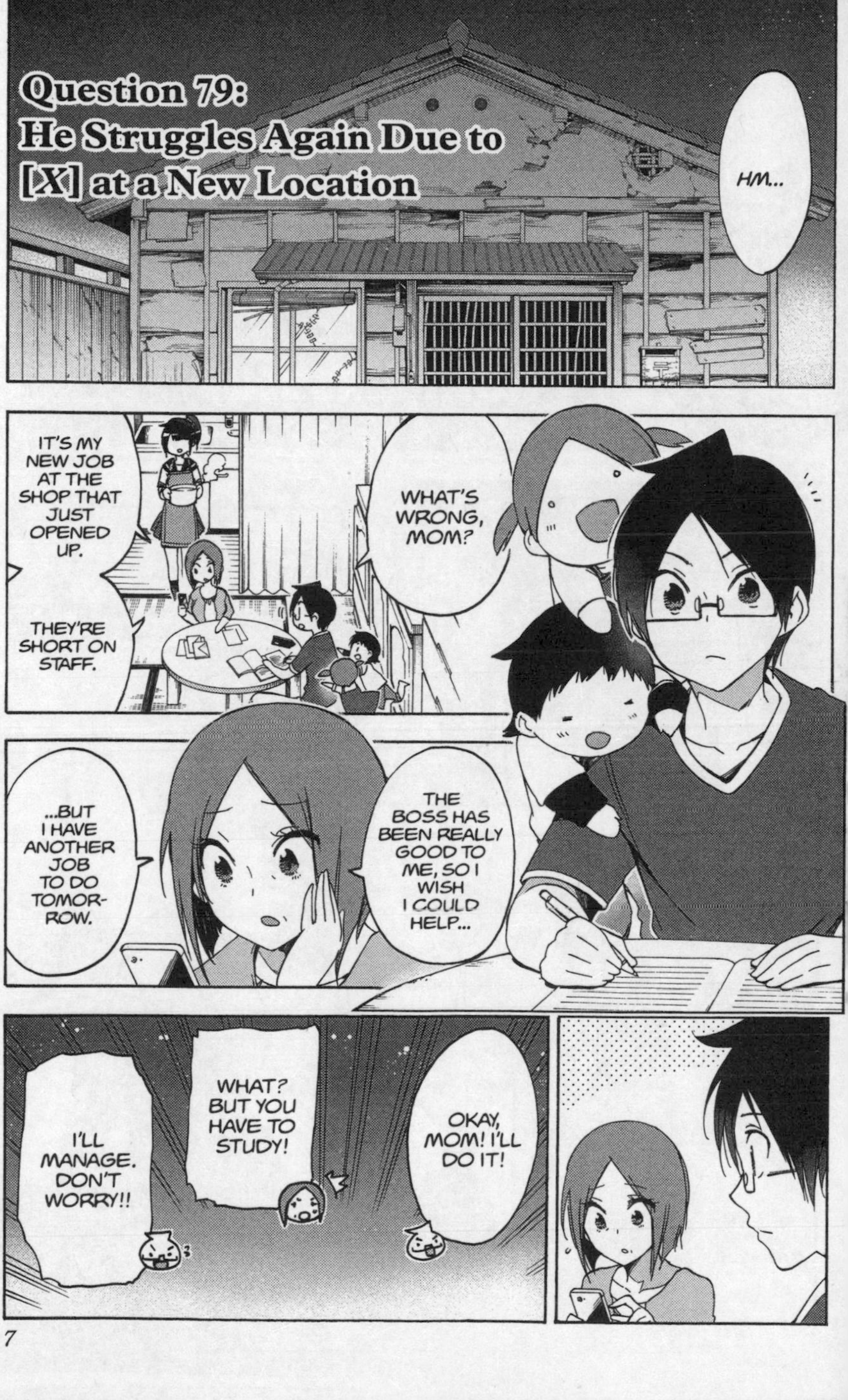
Question 79:
He Struggles Again Due to [X] at a New Location
HM...
WHAT'S WRONG, MOM?
IT'S MY NEW JOB AT THE SHOP THAT JUST OPENED UP.
THEY'RE SHORT ON STAFF.
THE BOSS HAS BEEN REALLY GOOD TO ME, SO I WISH I COULD HELP...
...BUT I HAVE ANOTHER JOB TO DO TOMOR-ROW.
OKAY, MOM! I'LL DO IT!
WHAT? BUT YOU HAVE TO STUDY!
I'LL MANAGE. DON'T WORRY!!

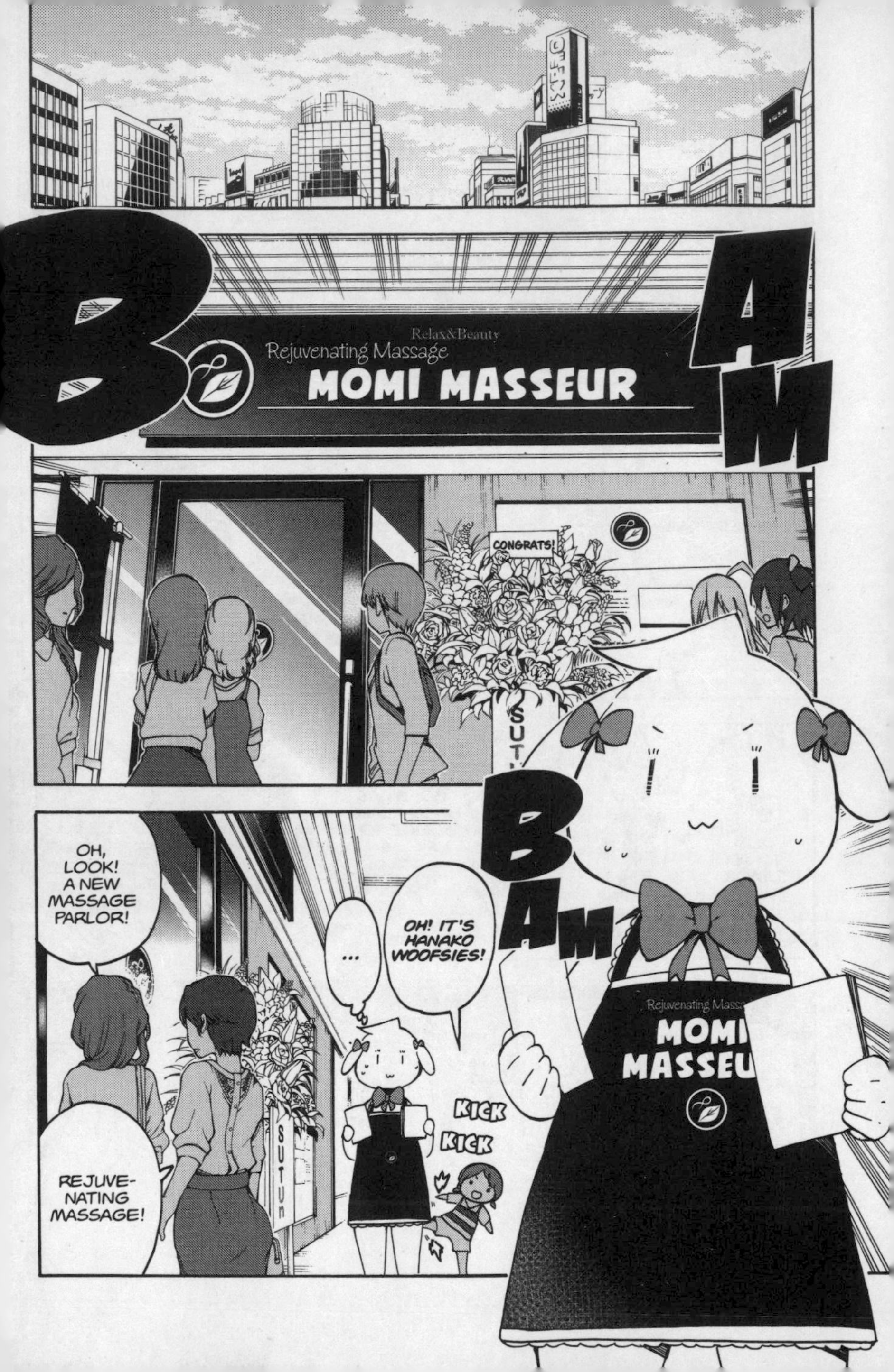
BAM
Relax&Beauty
Rejuvenating Massage
MOMI MASSEUR
CONGRATS!
BAM
OH! IT'S HANAKO WOOFSIES!
...
KICK
KICK
OH, LOOK! A NEW MASSAGE PARLOR!
REJUVENATING MASSAGE!

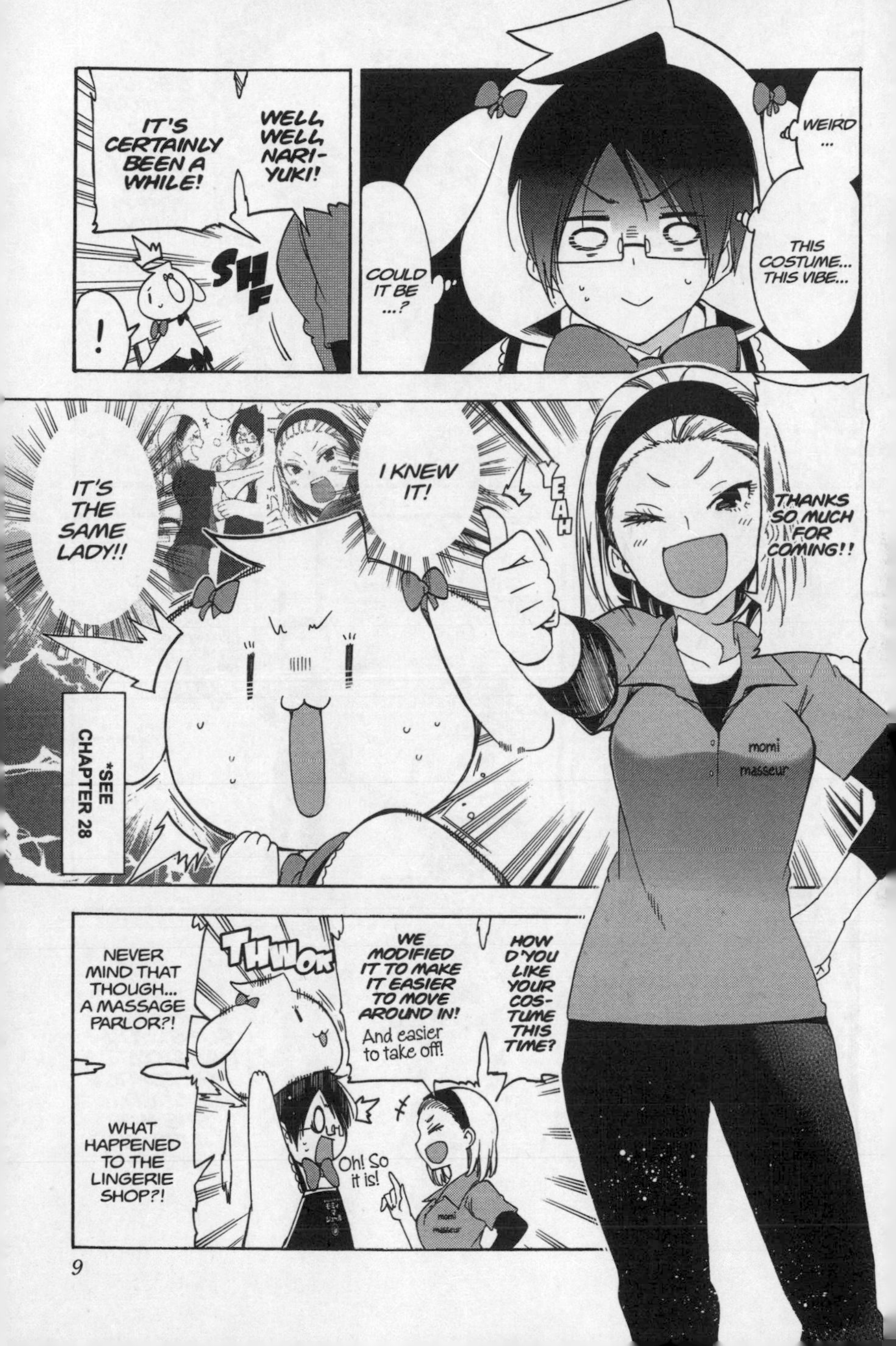

WEIRD ...
THIS COSTUME... THIS VIBE...
COULD IT BE ...?
WELL, WELL, NARI-YUKI!
IT'S CERTAINLY BEEN A WHILE!
SHF
!
THANKS SO MUCH FOR COMING!!
YEAH
I KNEW IT!
IT'S THE SAME LADY!!
*SEE CHAPTER 28
momi masseur
HOW D'YOU LIKE YOUR COS-TUME THIS TIME?
WE MODIFIED IT TO MAKE IT EASIER TO MOVE AROUND IN!
And easier to take off!
THWOK
NEVER MIND THAT THOUGH... A MASSAGE PARLOR?!
WHAT HAPPENED TO THE LINGERIE SHOP?!
Oh! So it is!

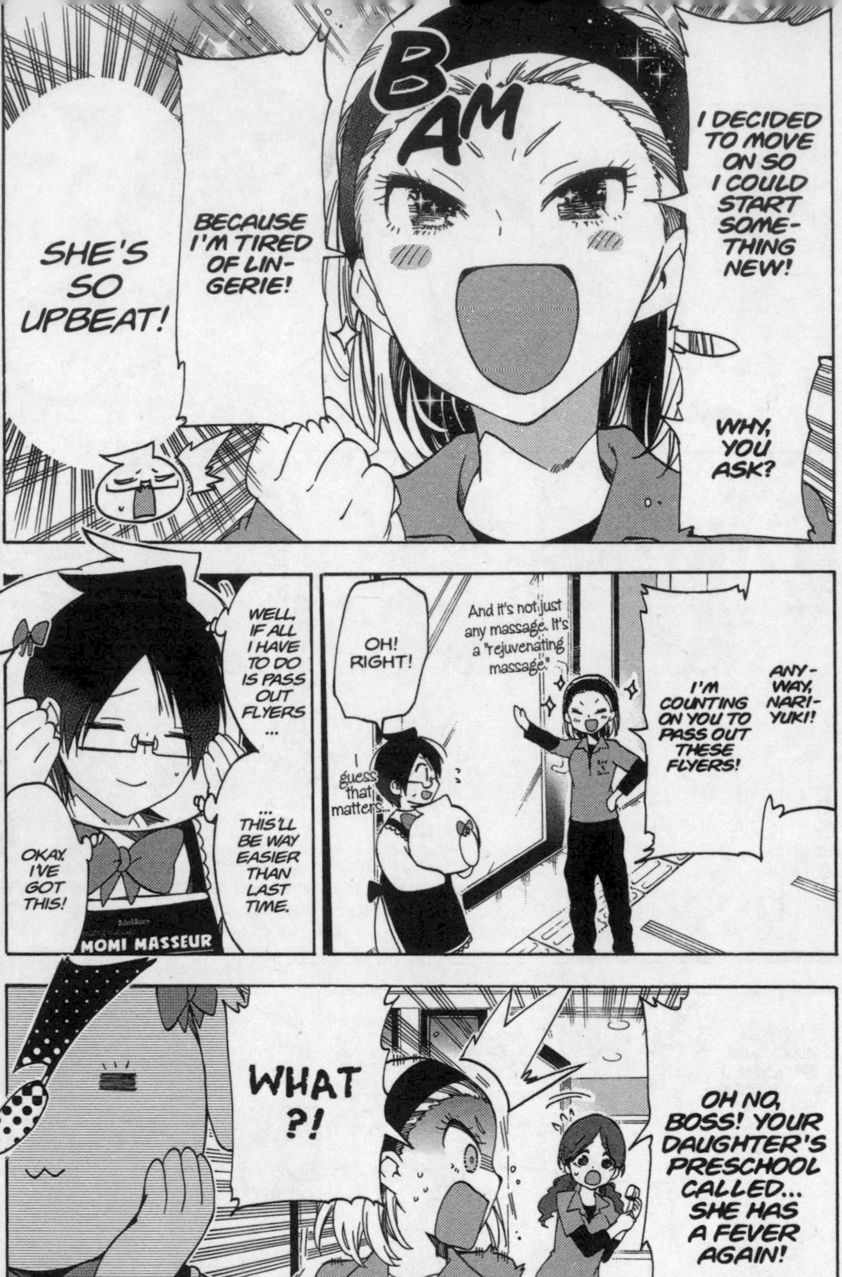
I DECIDED TO MOVE ON SO I COULD START SOMETHING NEW!
WHY, YOU ASK?
BAM
BECAUSE I'M TIRED OF LINGERIE!
SHE'S SO UPBEAT!
ANYWAY, NARIYUKI!
I'M COUNTING ON YOU TO PASS OUT THESE FLYERS!
And it's not just any massage. It's a "rejuvenating massage."
OH! RIGHT!
I guess that matters...
WELL, IF ALL I HAVE TO DO IS PASS OUT FLYERS...
...THIS'LL BE WAY EASIER THAN LAST TIME.
OKAY. I'VE GOT THIS!
MOMI MASSEUR
OH NO, BOSS! YOUR DAUGHTER'S PRESCHOOL CALLED... SHE HAS A FEVER AGAIN!
WHAT?!

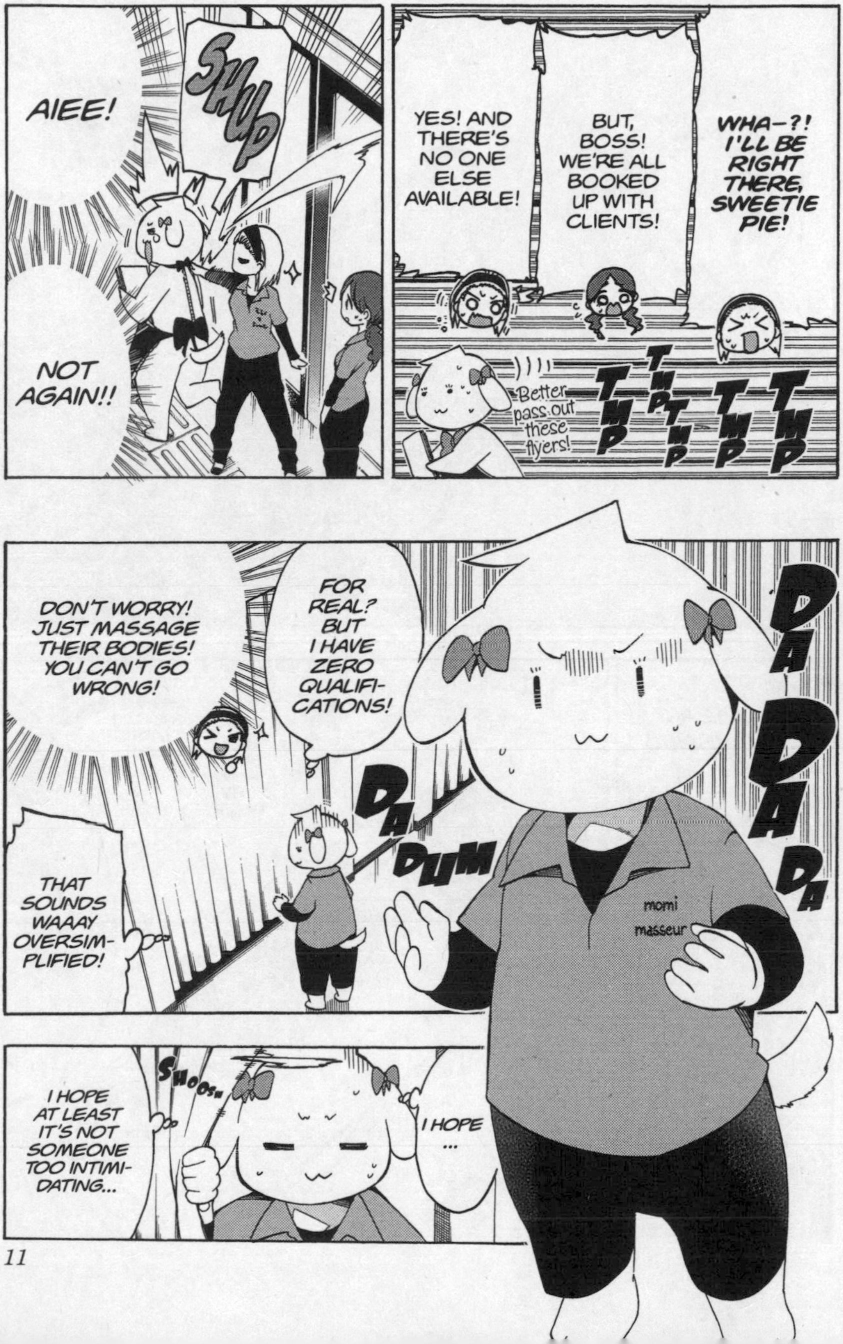
WHA-?! I'LL BE RIGHT THERE, SWEETIE PIE!
BUT, BOSS! WE'RE ALL BOOKED UP WITH CLIENTS!
YES! AND THERE'S NO ONE ELSE AVAILABLE!
TMP TMP TMP TMP TMP
Better pass out these flyers!
SHUP
AIEE!
NOT AGAIN!!
DA DA DA DA
FOR REAL? BUT I HAVE ZERO QUALIFICATIONS!
DON'T WORRY! JUST MASSAGE THEIR BODIES! YOU CAN'T GO WRONG!
DA DUM
THAT SOUNDS WAAAY OVERSIMPLIFIED!
momi masseur
I HOPE ...
SHOOSH
I HOPE AT LEAST IT'S NOT SOMEONE TOO INTIMIDATING...

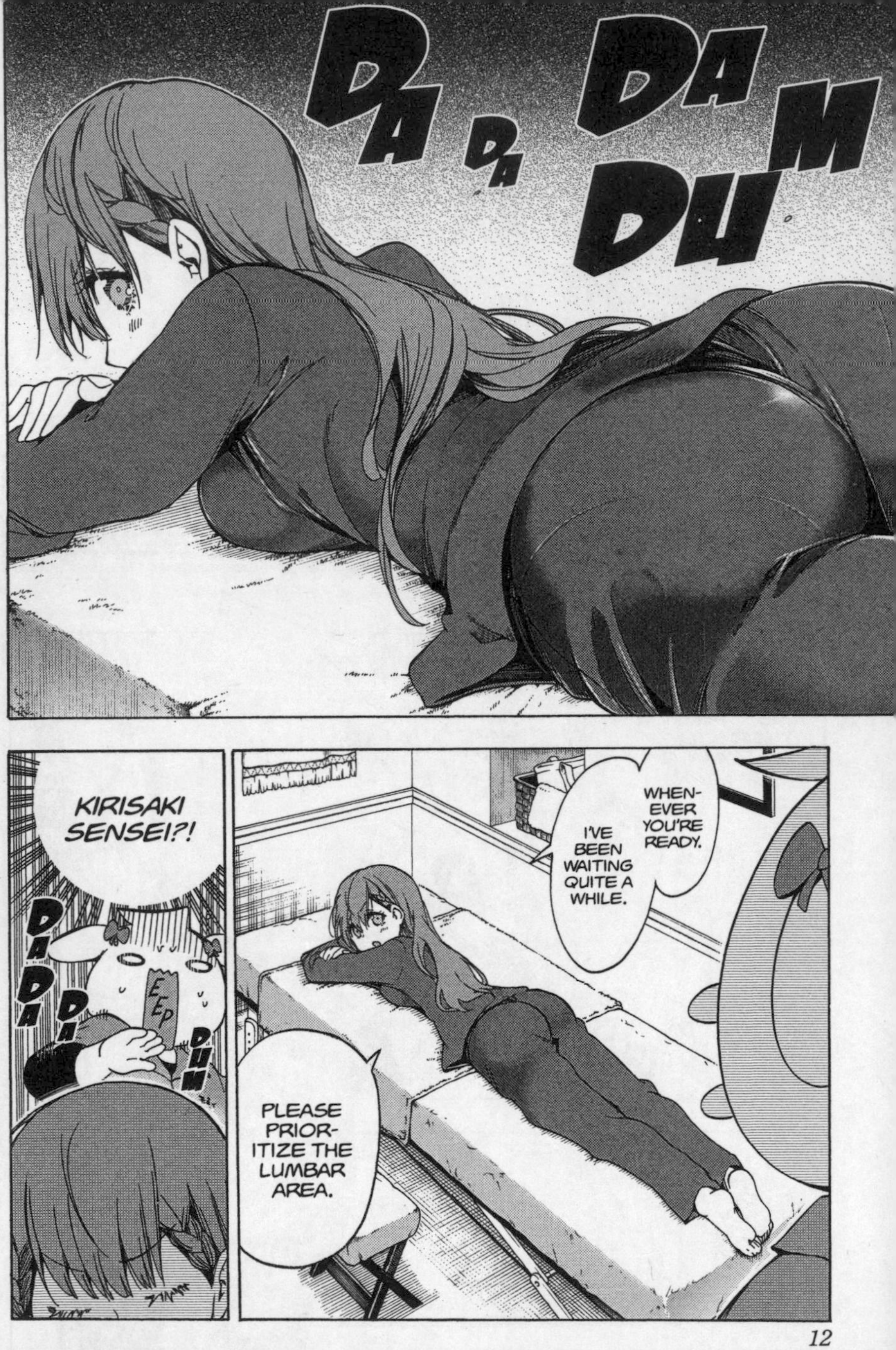
DA DA DAM DUM
WHEN-EVER YOU'RE READY.
I'VE BEEN WAITING QUITE A WHILE.
PLEASE PRIOR-ITIZE THE LUMBAR AREA.
KIRISAKI SENSEI?!
DA DA DA DUM
EEP

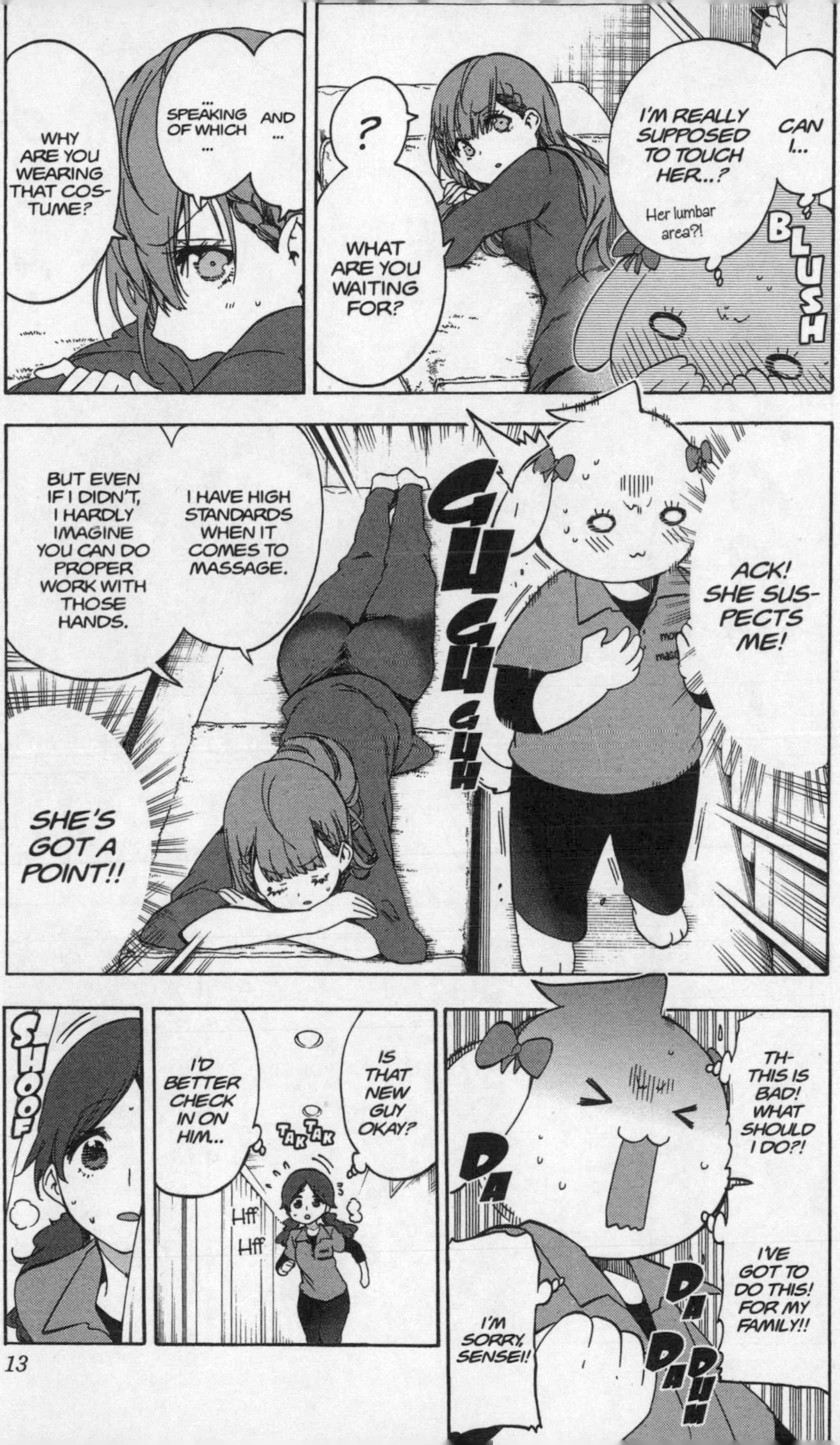
CAN I...
I'M REALLY SUPPOSED TO TOUCH HER...?
Her lumbar area?!
BLUSH
?
WHAT ARE YOU WAITING FOR?
AND ...
... SPEAKING OF WHICH ...
WHY ARE YOU WEARING THAT COSTUME?
ACK! SHE SUSPECTS ME!
GUGUGUGUH
I HAVE HIGH STANDARDS WHEN IT COMES TO MASSAGE.
BUT EVEN IF I DIDN'T, I HARDLY IMAGINE YOU CAN DO PROPER WORK WITH THOSE HANDS.
SHE'S GOT A POINT!!
TH- THIS IS BAD! WHAT SHOULD I DO?!
DA
I'VE GOT TO DO THIS! FOR MY FAMILY!!
I'M SORRY, SENSEI!
DADADADUH
IS THAT NEW GUY OKAY?
TAK TAK
I'D BETTER CHECK IN ON HIM...
Hff
Hff
SHOOF

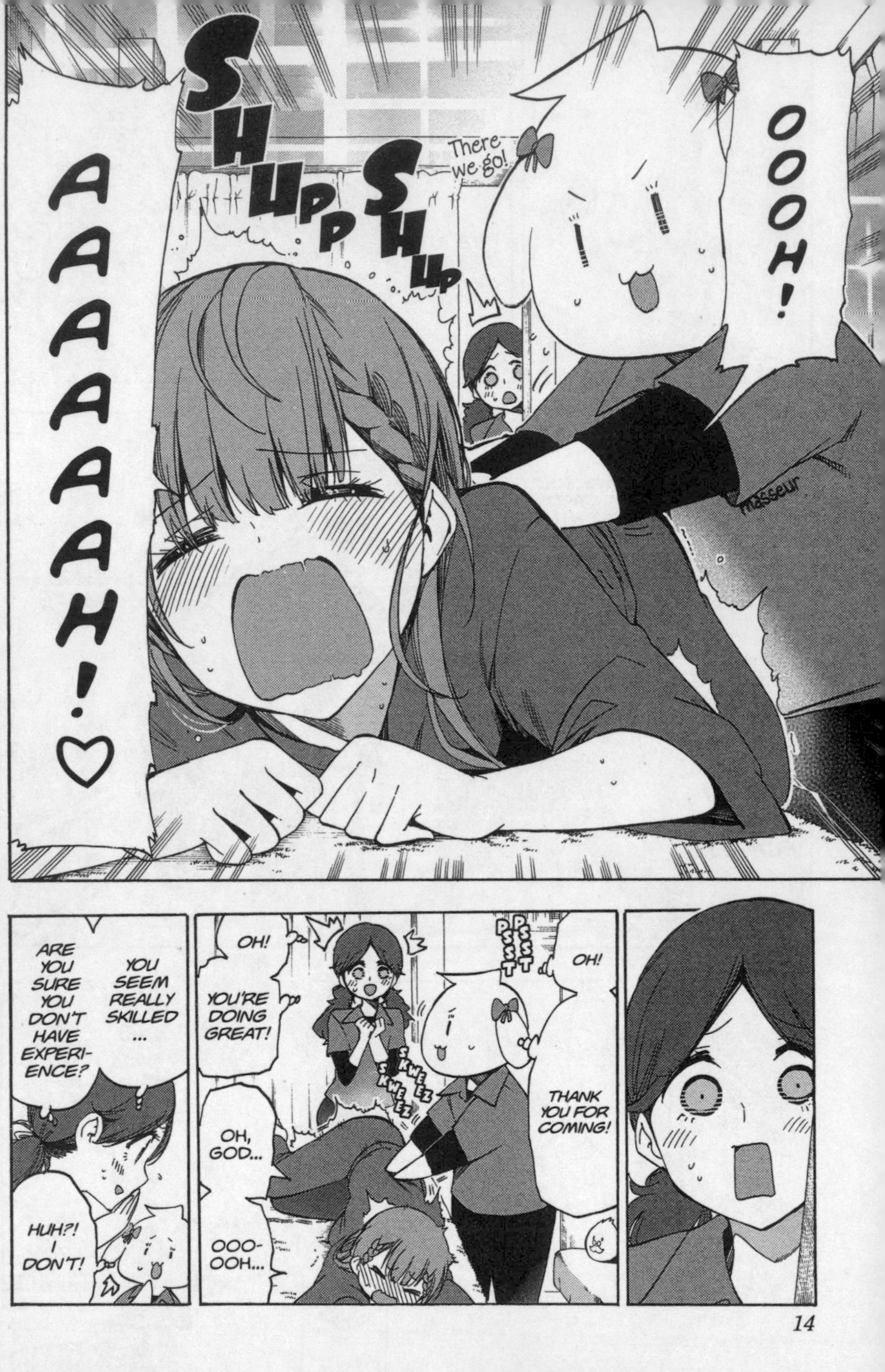
OOOOH!
There we go!
SHUPP SHUP
AAAAAAAH!♡
PSST PSST
OH!
THANK YOU FOR COMING!
OH!
YOU'RE DOING GREAT!
SKWEEZ SKWEEZ
OH, GOD...
OOO-OOH...
YOU SEEM REALLY SKILLED ...
ARE YOU SURE YOU DON'T HAVE EXPERIENCE?
HUH?! I DON'T!

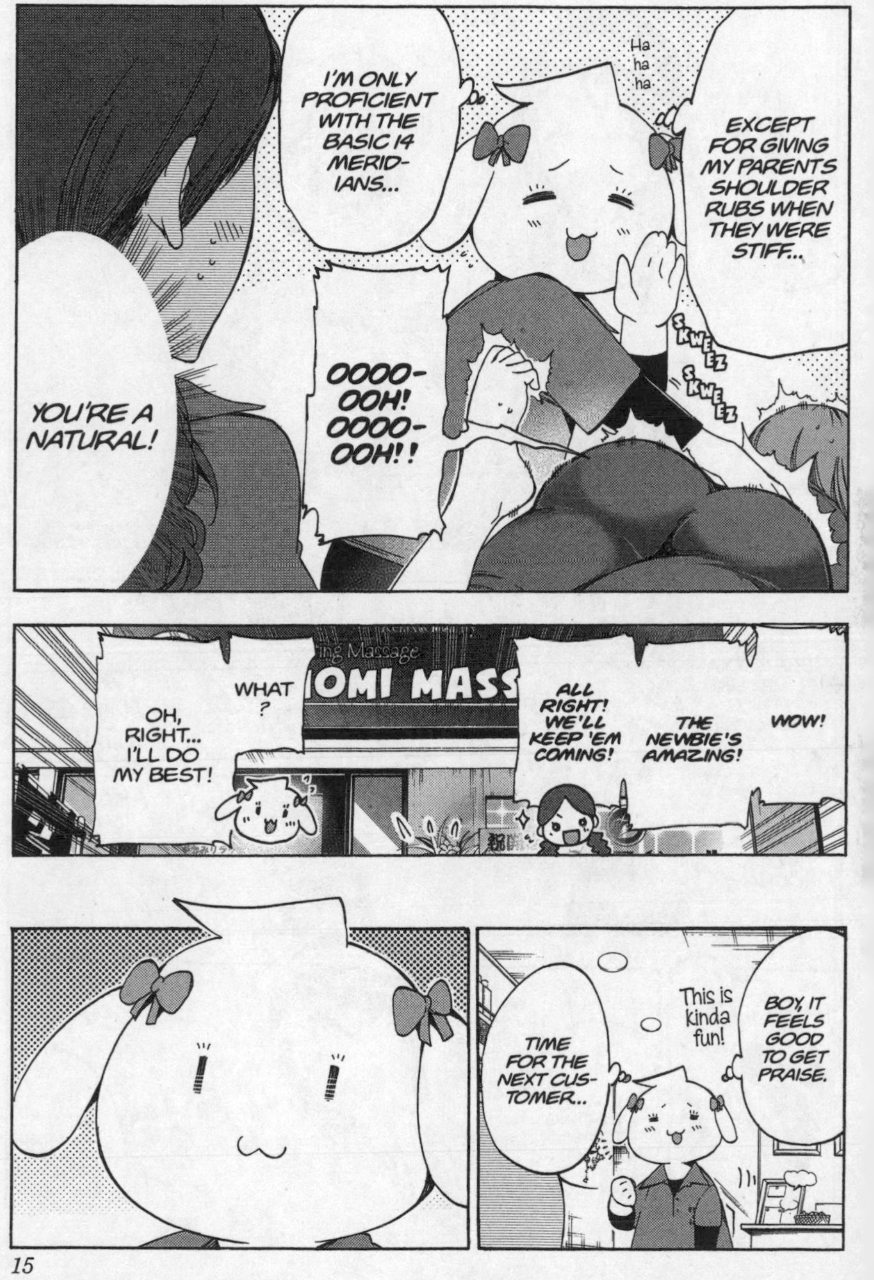
EXCEPT FOR GIVING MY PARENTS SHOULDER RUBS WHEN THEY WERE STIFF...
Ha ha ha
I'M ONLY PROFICIENT WITH THE BASIC 14 MERIDIANS...
SKWEEZ SKWEEZ
OOOO-OOH! OOOO-OOH!!
YOU'RE A NATURAL!
WOW!
THE NEWBIE'S AMAZING!
ALL RIGHT! WE'LL KEEP 'EM COMING!
WHAT?
OH, RIGHT... I'LL DO MY BEST!
BOY, IT FEELS GOOD TO GET PRAISE.
This is kinda fun!
TIME FOR THE NEXT CUSTOMER...

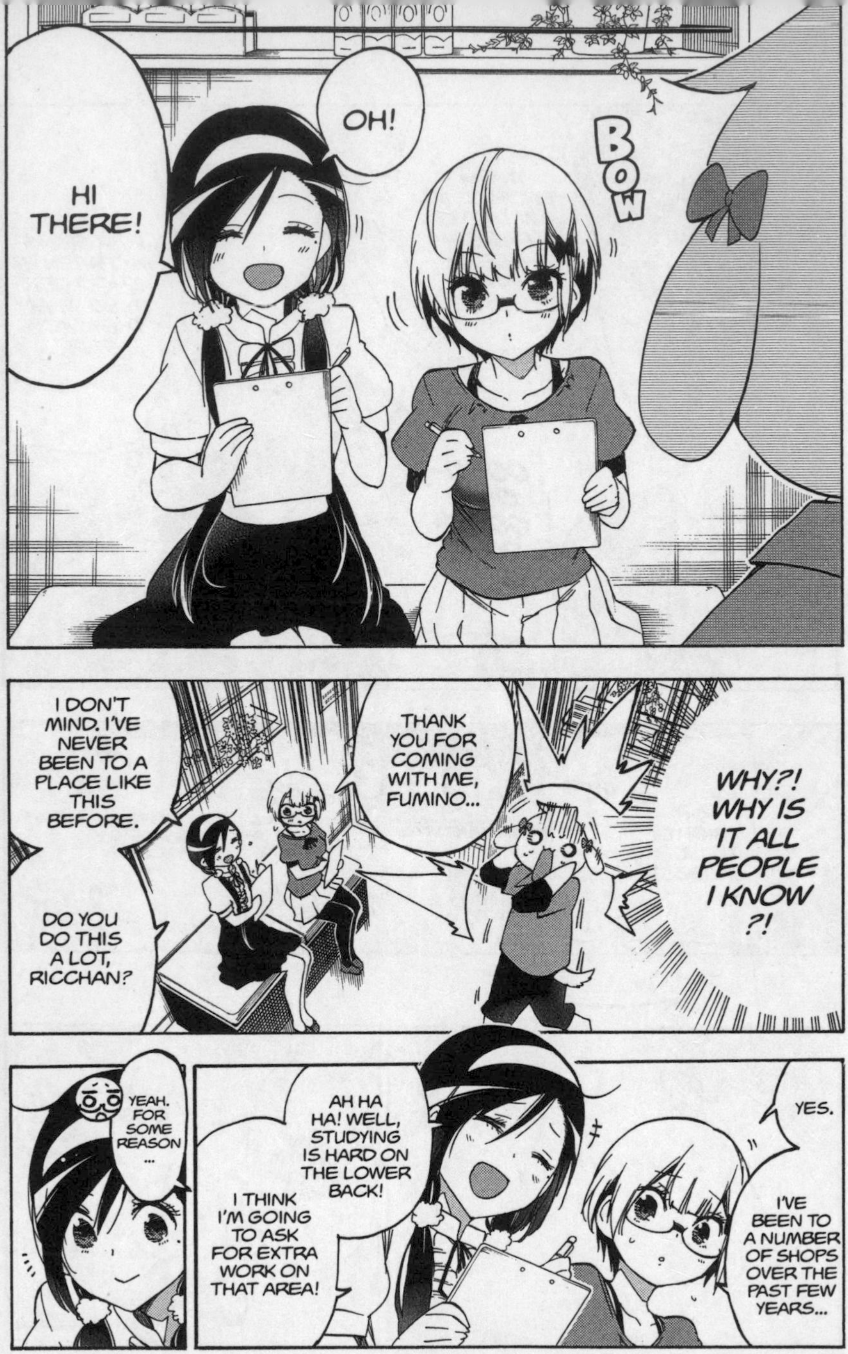
BOW
OH!
HI THERE!
WHY?! WHY IS IT ALL PEOPLE I KNOW ?!
THANK YOU FOR COMING WITH ME, FUMINO...
I DON'T MIND. I'VE NEVER BEEN TO A PLACE LIKE THIS BEFORE.
DO YOU DO THIS A LOT, RICCHAN?
YES.
I'VE BEEN TO A NUMBER OF SHOPS OVER THE PAST FEW YEARS...
AH HA HA! WELL, STUDYING IS HARD ON THE LOWER BACK!
I THINK I'M GOING TO ASK FOR EXTRA WORK ON THAT AREA!
YEAH. FOR SOME REASON ...

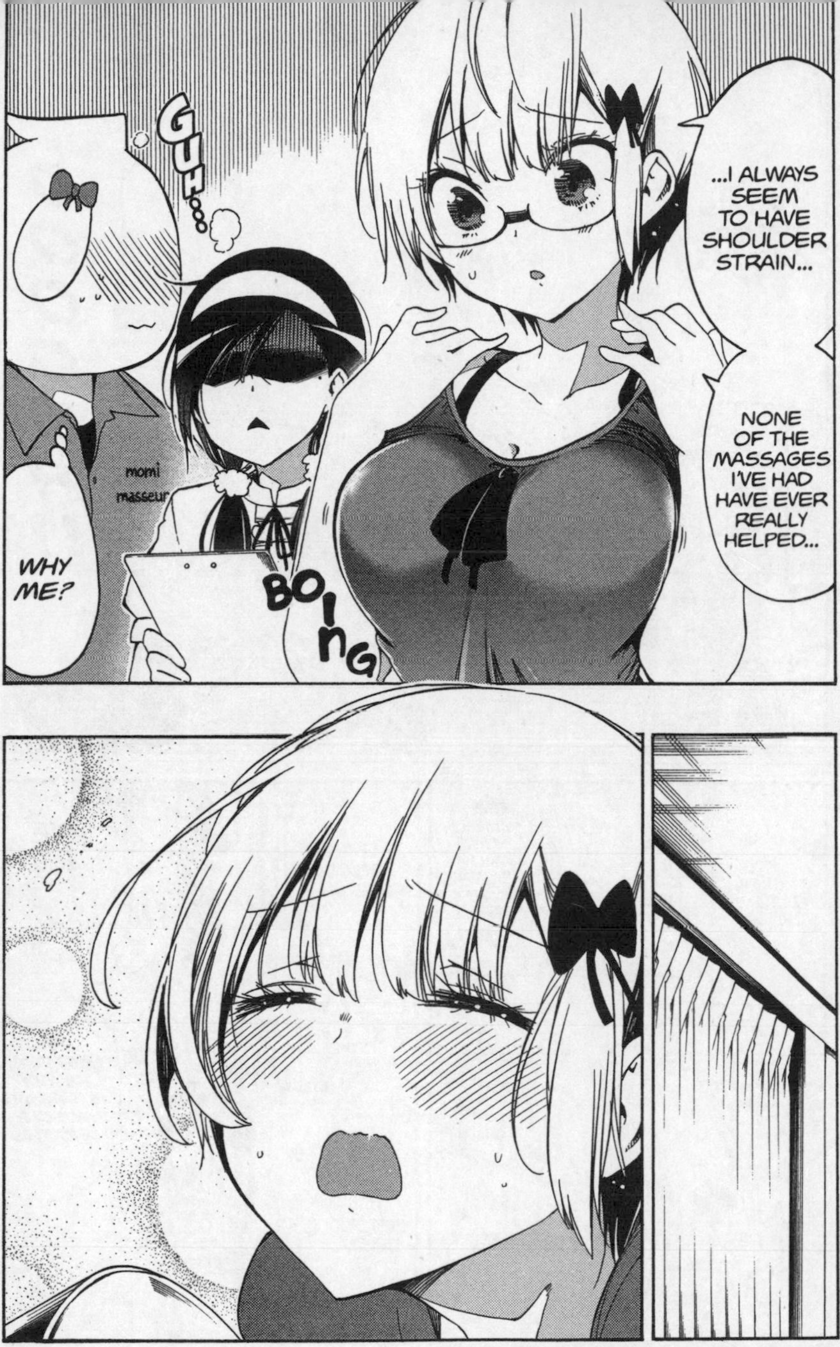
...I ALWAYS SEEM TO HAVE SHOULDER STRAIN...
NONE OF THE MASSAGES I'VE HAD HAVE EVER REALLY HELPED...
GUHooo
BOING
momi masseur
WHY ME?

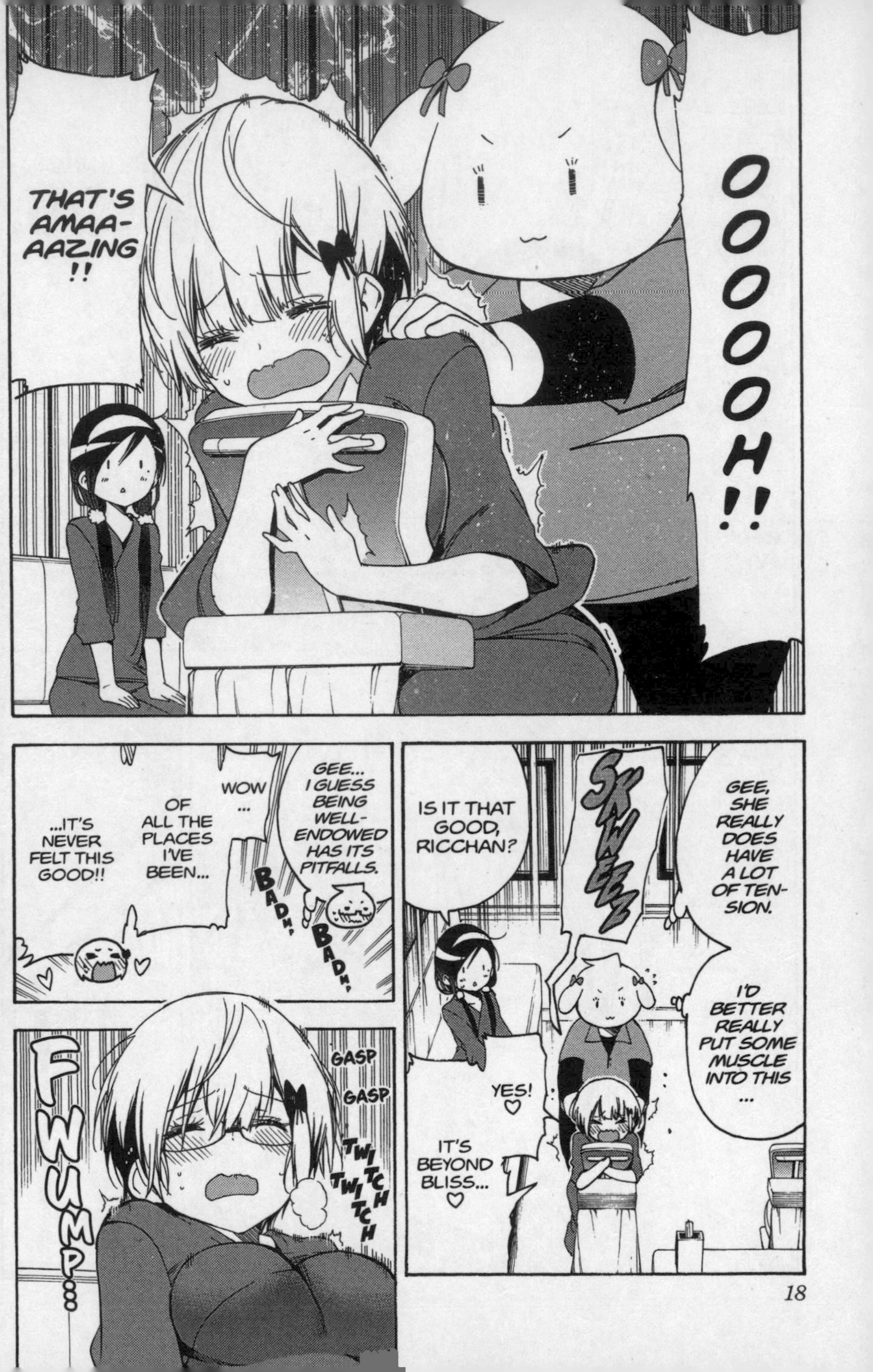
OOOOOOH!!
THAT'S AMAAA-AAZING!!
GEE, SHE REALLY DOES HAVE A LOT OF TEN-SION.
SKWEEZ
IS IT THAT GOOD, RICCHAN?
I'D BETTER REALLY PUT SOME MUSCLE INTO THIS ...
YES! ♥
IT'S BEYOND BLISS... ♥
GEE... I GUESS BEING WELL-ENDOWED HAS ITS PITFALLS.
BADMP
BADMP
WOW ...
OF ALL THE PLACES I'VE BEEN...
...IT'S NEVER FELT THIS GOOD!!
GASP
GASP
TWITCH
TWITCH
FWUMP...

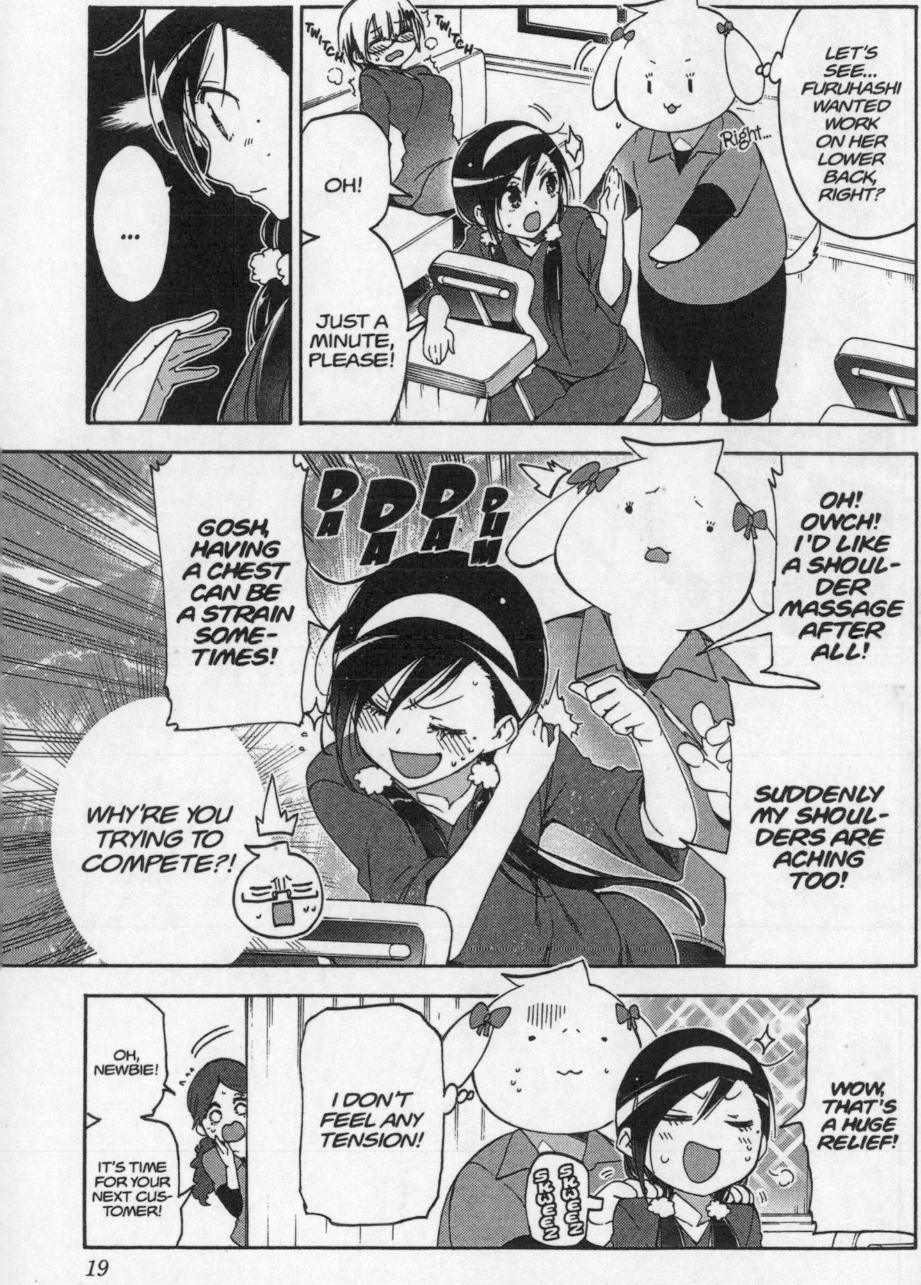
LET'S SEE... FURUHASHI WANTED WORK ON HER LOWER BACK, RIGHT?
Right...
TWITCH TWITCH
OH!
JUST A MINUTE, PLEASE!
...
OH! OWCH! I'D LIKE A SHOULDER-DER MASSAGE AFTER ALL!
DA DA DA DUM
GOSH, HAVING A CHEST CAN BE A STRAIN SOME-TIMES!
SUDDENLY MY SHOUL-DERS ARE ACHING TOO!
WHY'RE YOU TRYING TO COMPETE?!
WOW, THAT'S A HUGE RELIEF!
SKWEEZ SKWEEZ
I DON'T FEEL ANY TENSION!
OH, NEWBIE!
IT'S TIME FOR YOUR NEXT CUS-TOMER!

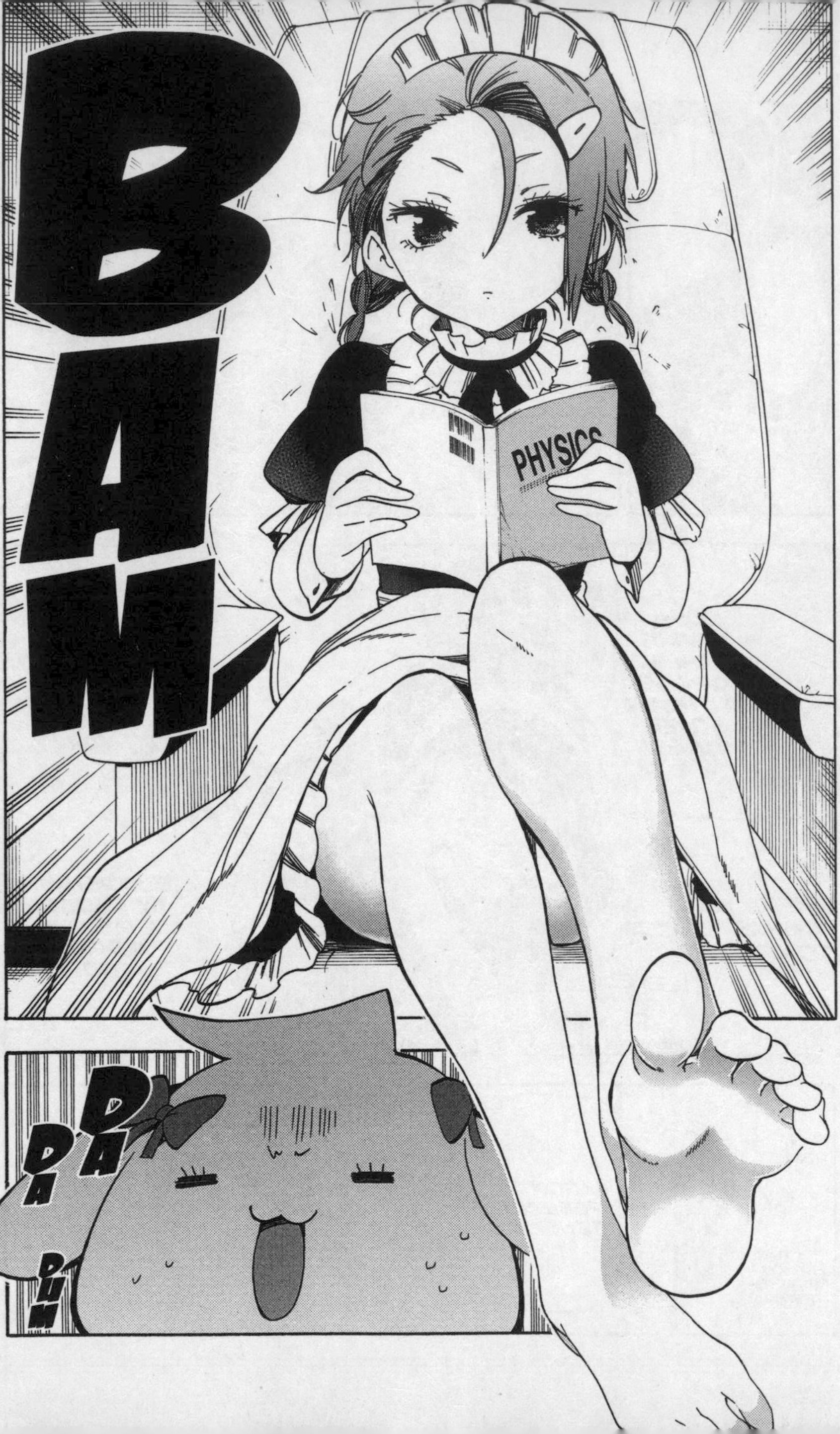
BAM
PHYSICS
DA DA DUM

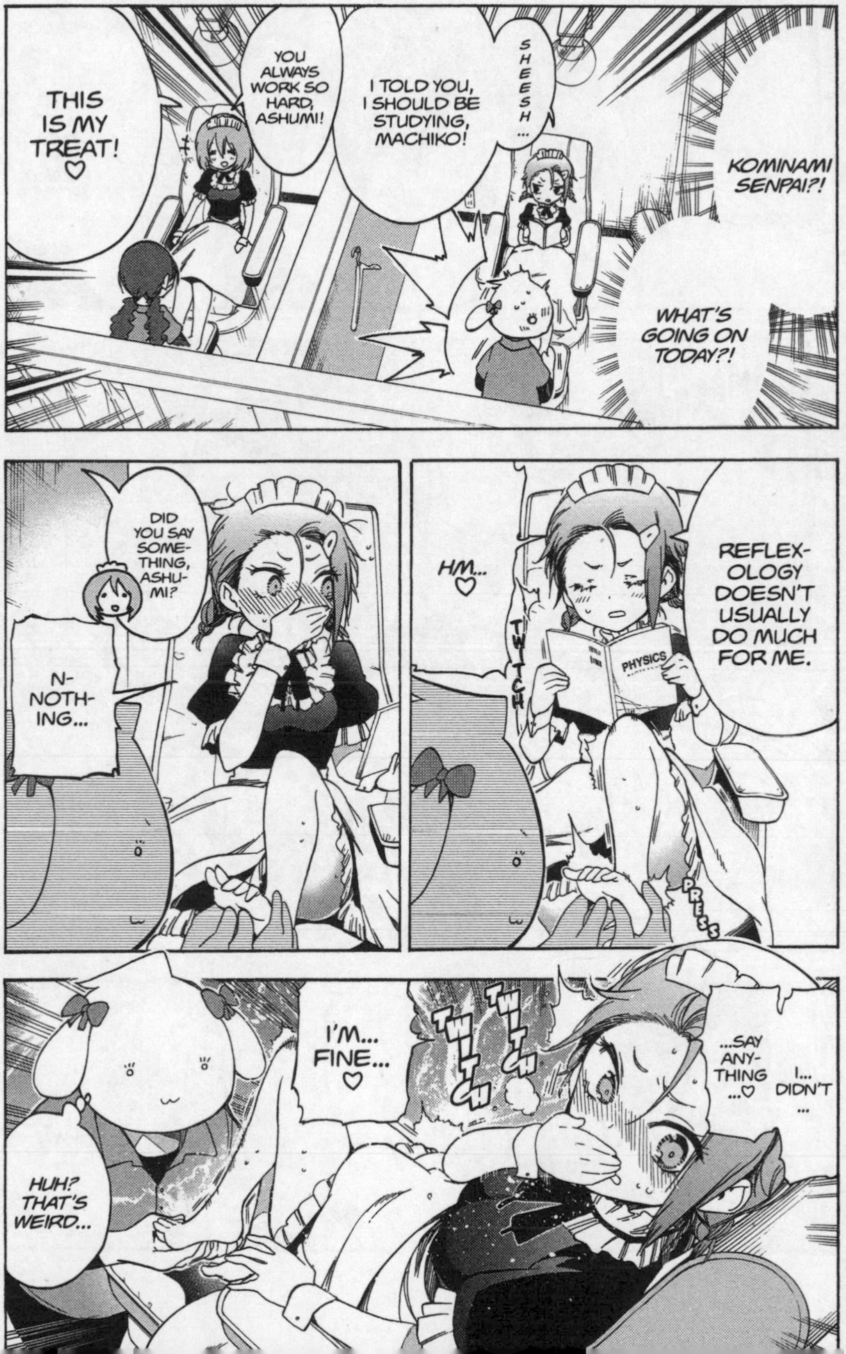
KOMINAMI SENPAI?!
WHAT'S GOING ON TODAY?!
SHEESH...
I TOLD YOU, I SHOULD BE STUDYING, MACHIKO!
YOU ALWAYS WORK SO HARD, ASHUMI!
THIS IS MY TREAT! ♡
REFLEX-OLOGY DOESN'T USUALLY DO MUCH FOR ME.
HM... ♡
TWITCH
PHYSICS
PRESS
DID YOU SAY SOME-THING, ASHU-MI?
N-NOTH-ING...
I... DIDN'T ...
...SAY ANY-THING ...♡
TWITCH
TWITCH
I'M... FINE... ♡
HUH? THAT'S WEIRD...

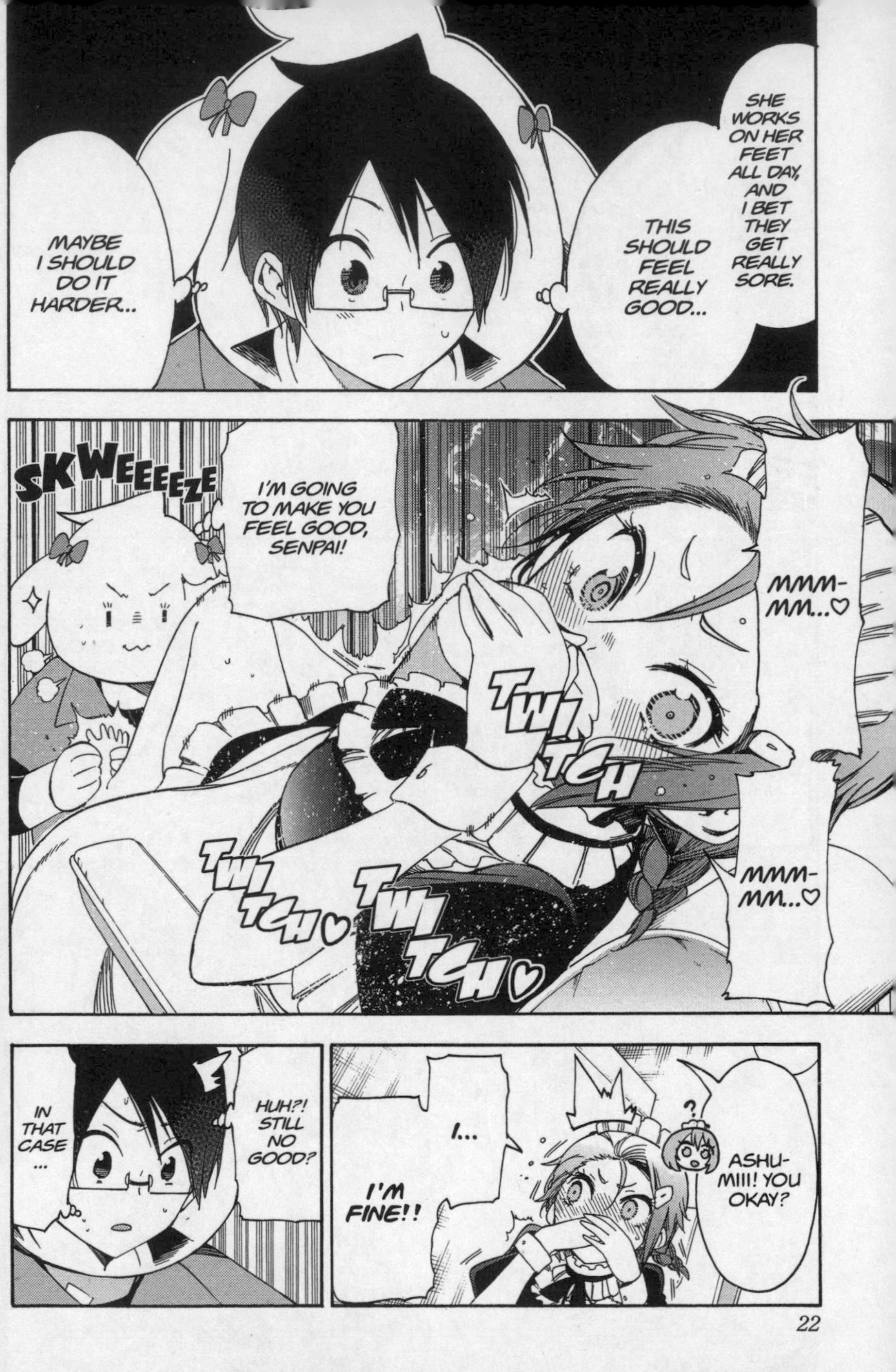
SHE WORKS ON HER FEET ALL DAY, AND I BET THEY GET REALLY SORE.
THIS SHOULD FEEL REALLY GOOD...
MAYBE I SHOULD DO IT HARDER...
MMM-MM...♡
I'M GOING TO MAKE YOU FEEL GOOD, SENPAI!
SKWEEEEEZE
TWITCH
MMM-MM...♡
TWITCH♡
TWITCH♡
ASHU-MIII! YOU OKAY?
?
I...
I'M FINE!!
HUH?! STILL NO GOOD?
IN THAT CASE ...

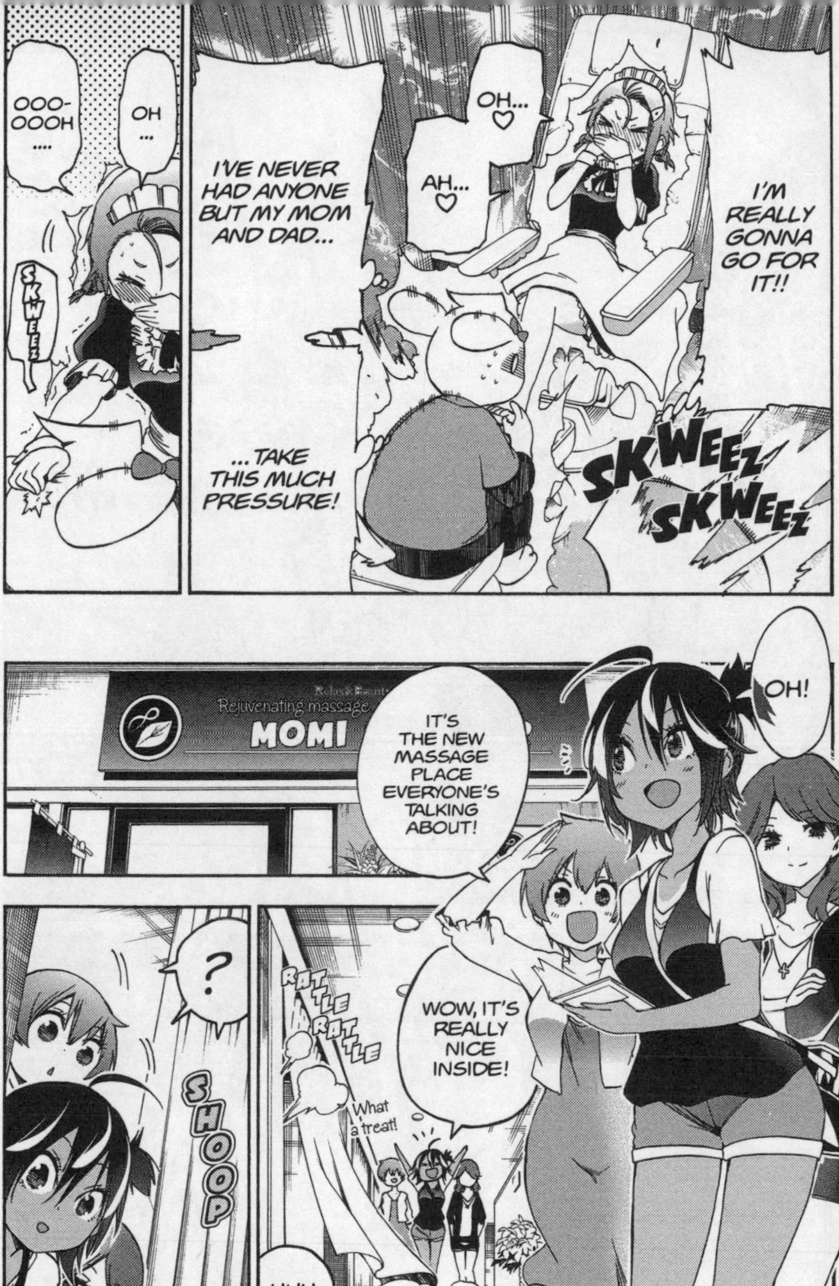
I'M REALLY GONNA GO FOR IT!!
OH...
AH...
I'VE NEVER HAD ANYONE BUT MY MOM AND DAD...
...TAKE THIS MUCH PRESSURE!
SKWEEZ SKWEEZ
OH...
OOO-OOOH...
SKWEEZ
OH!
IT'S THE NEW MASSAGE PLACE EVERYONE'S TALKING ABOUT!
Rejuvenating massage
MOMI
WOW, IT'S REALLY NICE INSIDE!
What a treat!
RATTLE RATTLE
SHOOP
HUH?!
?

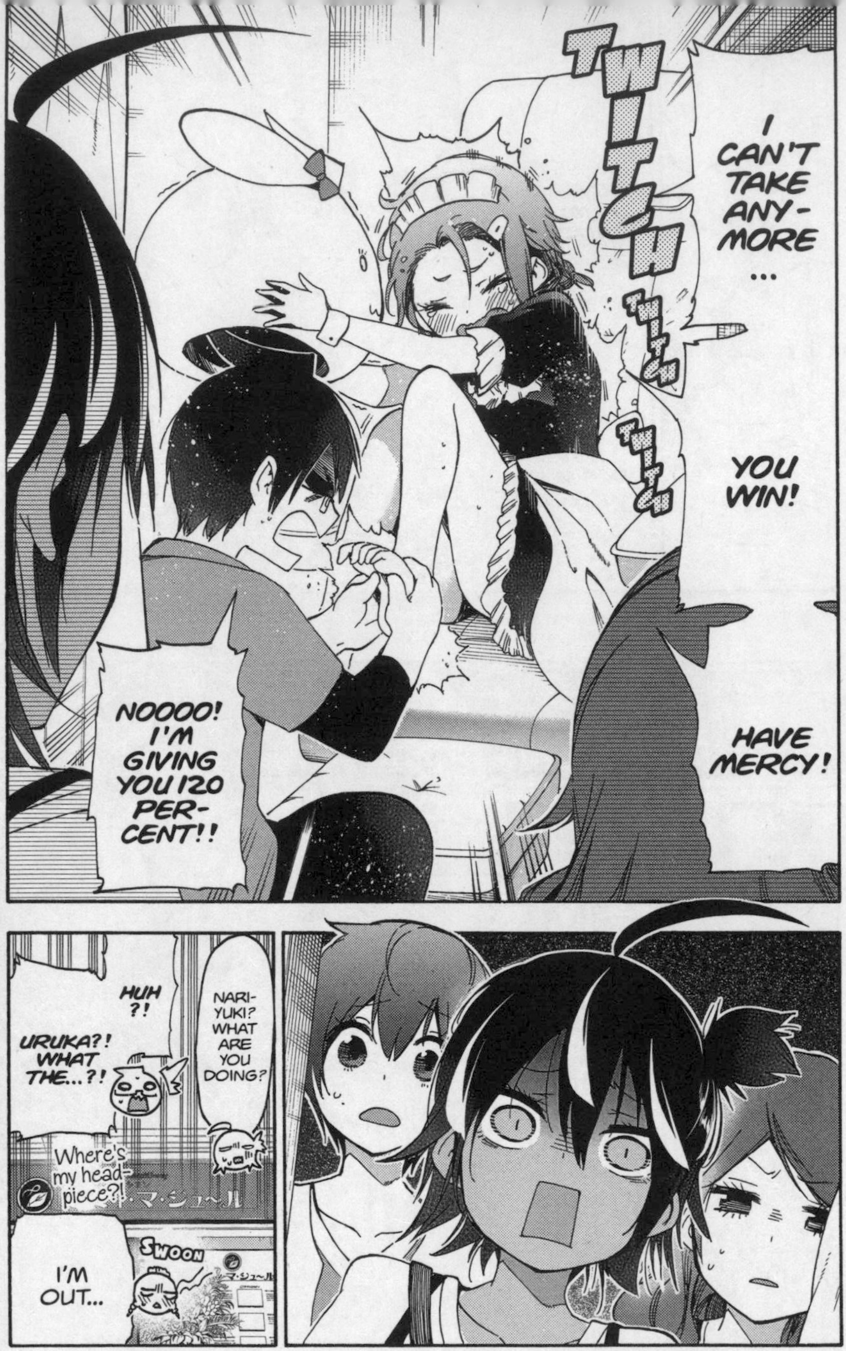
TWITCH
I CAN'T TAKE ANY-MORE ...
TWITCH TWITCH
YOU WIN!
HAVE MERCY!
NOOOO! I'M GIVING YOU 120 PER-CENT!!
NARI-YUKI? WHAT ARE YOU DOING?
HUH ?!
URUKA?! WHAT THE...?!
Where's my head-piece?!
SWOON
I'M OUT...

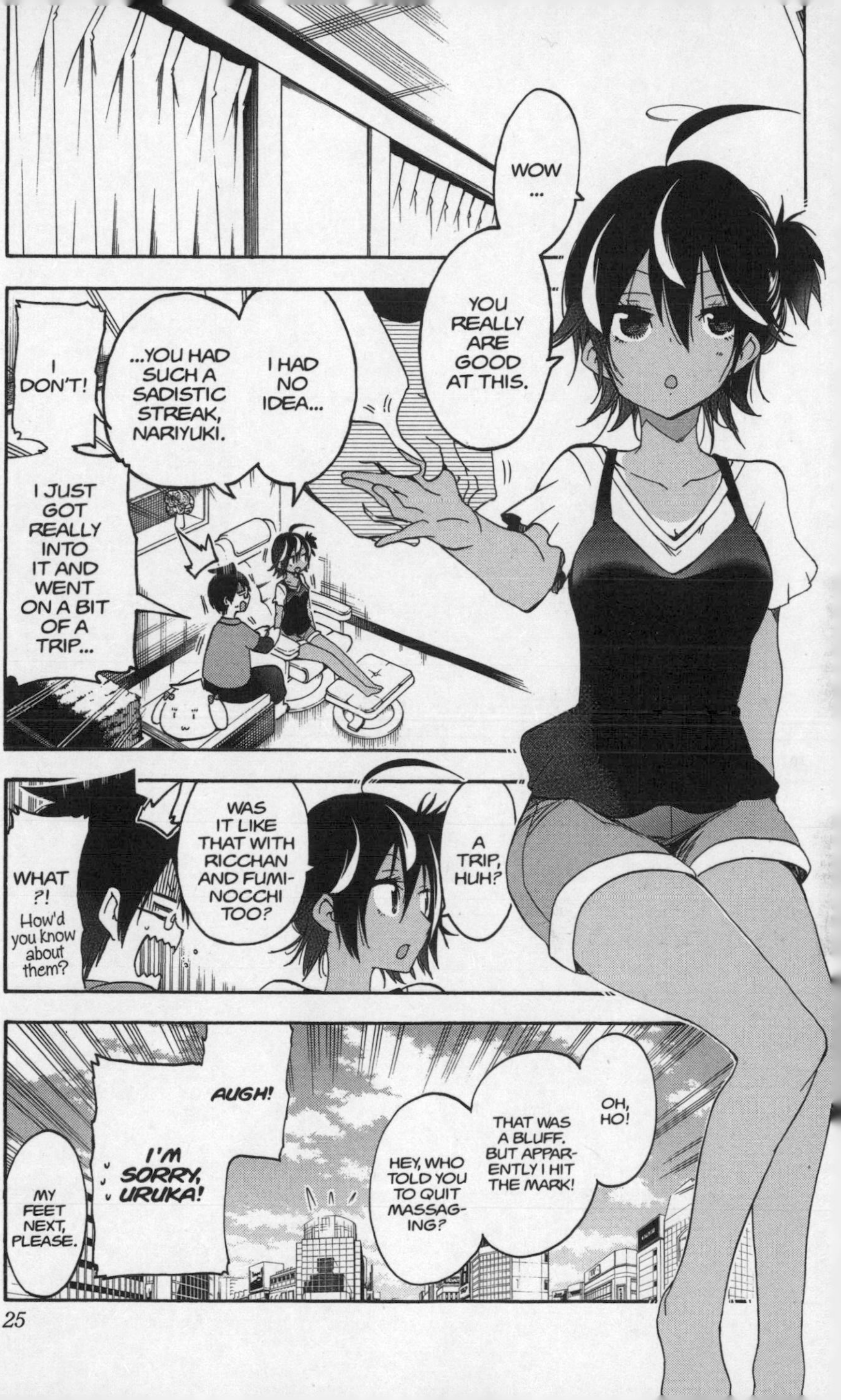
WOW ...
YOU REALLY ARE GOOD AT THIS.
I HAD NO IDEA...
...YOU HAD SUCH A SADISTIC STREAK, NARIYUKI.
I DON'T!
I JUST GOT REALLY INTO IT AND WENT ON A BIT OF A TRIP...
A TRIP, HUH?
WAS IT LIKE THAT WITH RICCHAN AND FUMI-NOCCHI TOO?
WHAT?!
How'd you know about them?
OH, HO!
THAT WAS A BLUFF. BUT APPARENTLY I HIT THE MARK!
HEY, WHO TOLD YOU TO QUIT MASSAGING?
AUGH!
I'M SORRY, URUKA!
MY FEET NEXT, PLEASE.

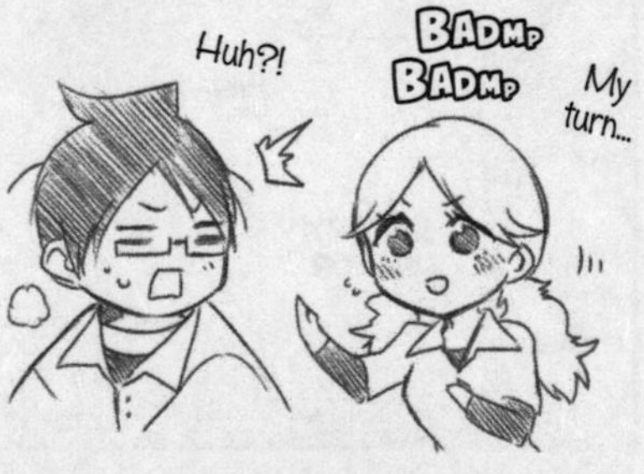
BADMP
BADMP
My turn...
Huh?!

Question 80: At Steam's Edge, a Disastrous [X] Increases the Predecessor's Distress

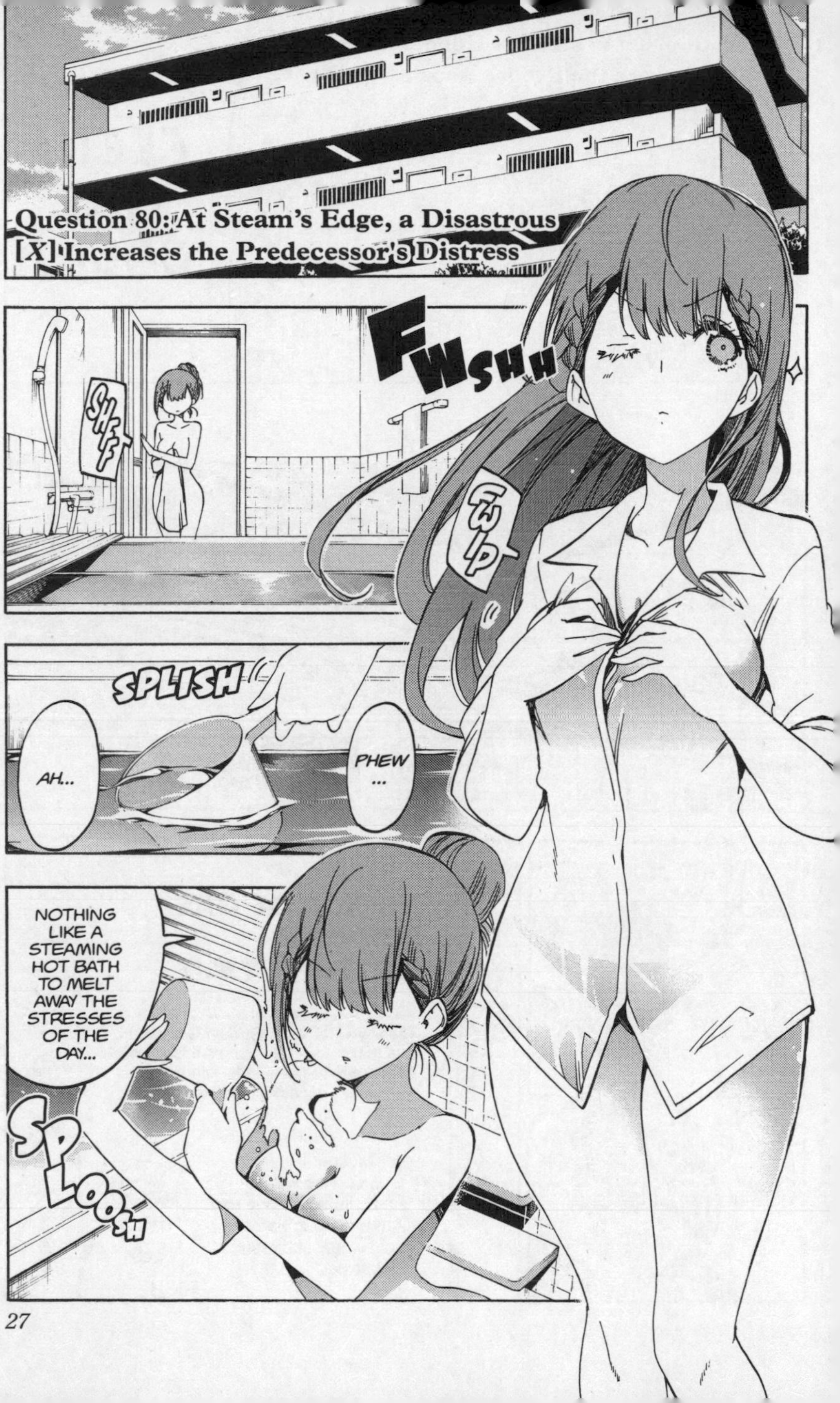

FWSHH
FWIP
SHFF
SPLISH
PHEW...
AH...
NOTHING LIKE A STEAMING HOT BATH TO MELT AWAY THE STRESSES OF THE DAY...
SPLOOSH

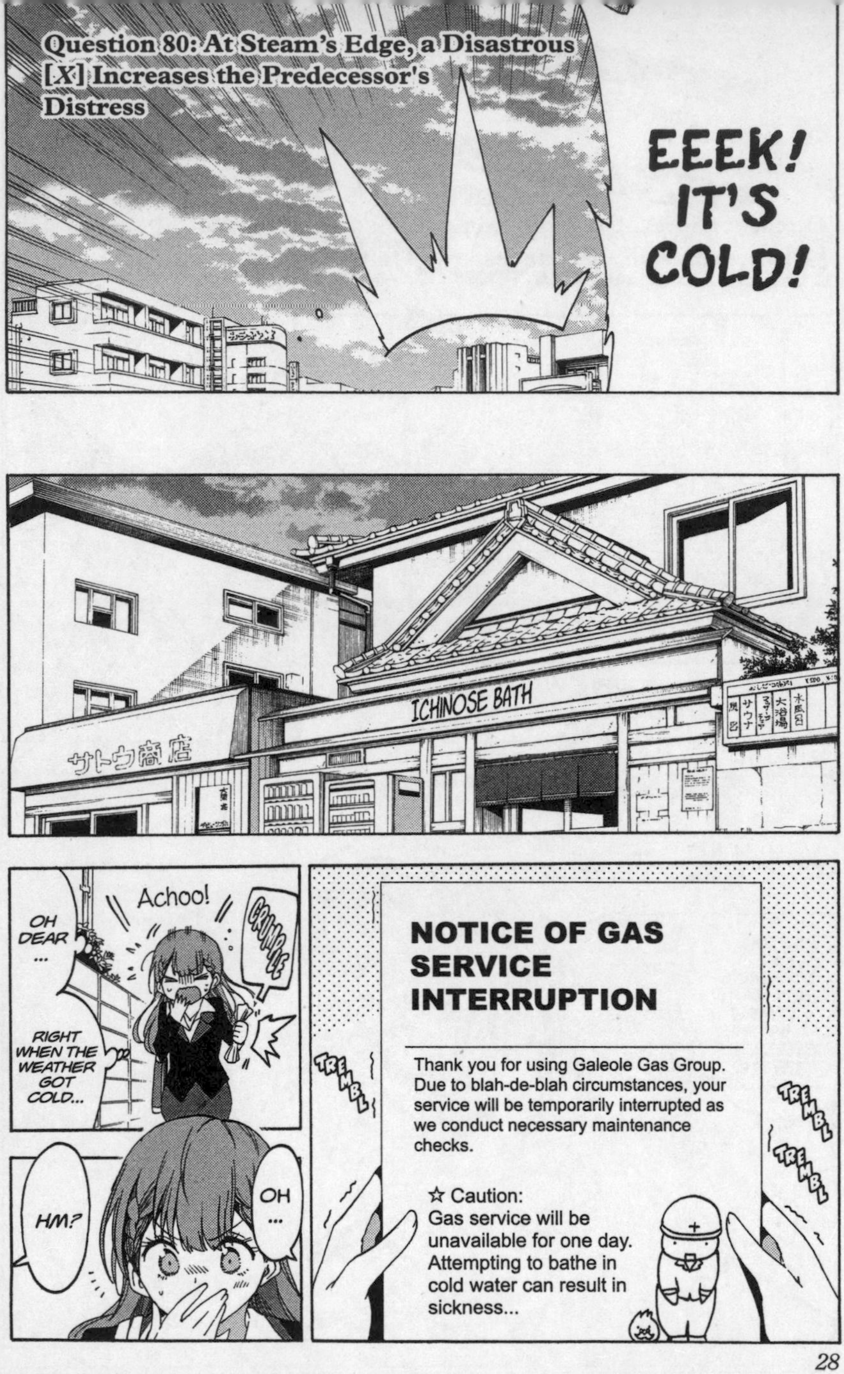
EEEK! IT'S COLD!
Question 80: At Steam's Edge, a Disastrous [X] Increases the Predecessor's Distress
ICHINOSE BATH
サトウ商店
TREMBL
TREMBL
TREMBL
NOTICE OF GAS SERVICE INTERRUPTION
Thank you for using Galeole Gas Group. Due to blah-de-blah circumstances, your service will be temporarily interrupted as we conduct necessary maintenance checks.
☆ Caution:
Gas service will be unavailable for one day. Attempting to bathe in cold water can result in sickness...
CRUMPLE
Achoo!
OH DEAR...
RIGHT WHEN THE WEATHER GOT COLD...
OH...
HM?

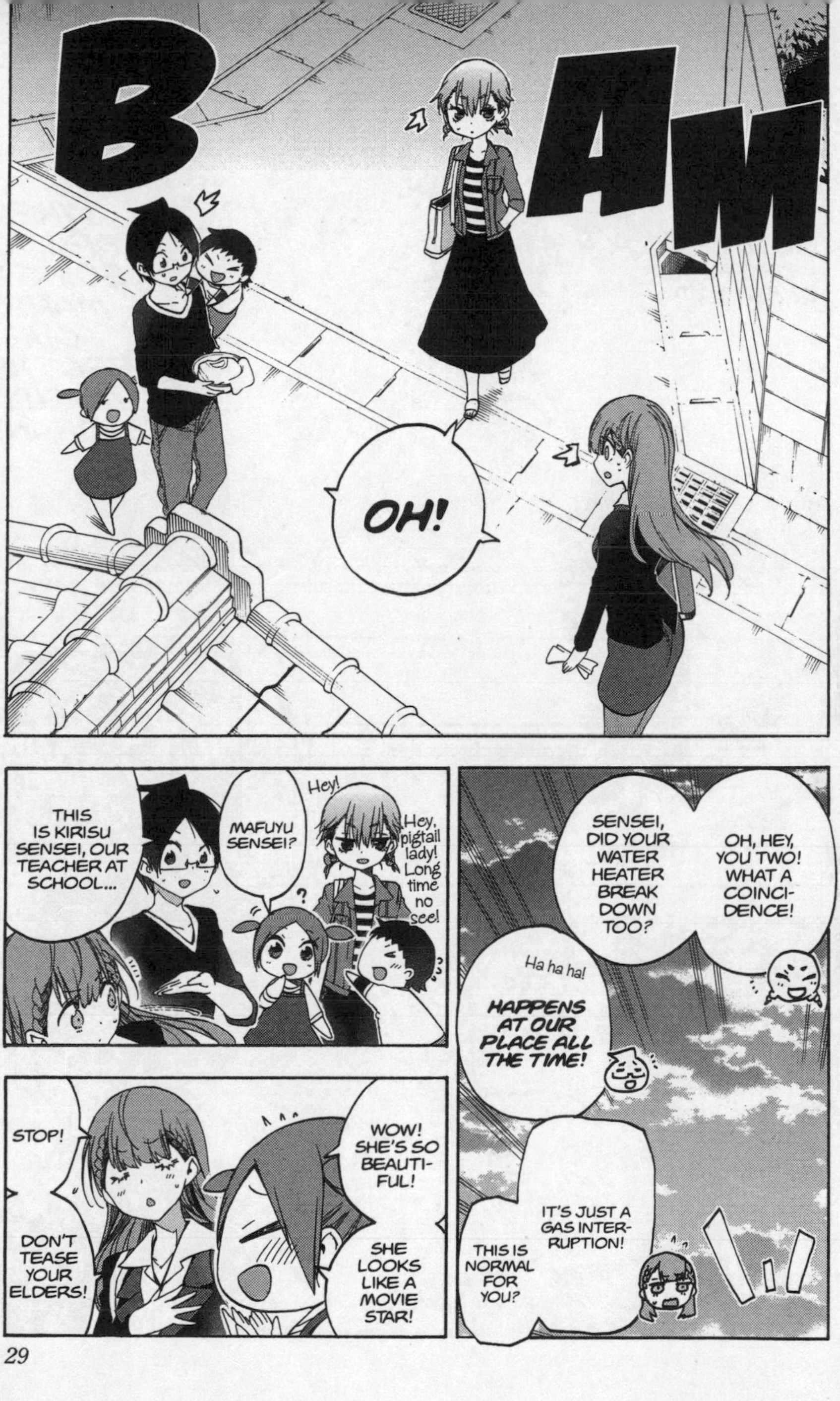
BAM
OH!
OH, HEY, YOU TWO! WHAT A COINCIDENCE!
SENSEI, DID YOUR WATER HEATER BREAK DOWN TOO?
Ha ha ha!
HAPPENS AT OUR PLACE ALL THE TIME!
IT'S JUST A GAS INTERRUPTION!
THIS IS NORMAL FOR YOU?
Hey, pigtail lady! Long time no see!
Hey!
MAFUYU SENSEI?
THIS IS KIRISU SENSEI, OUR TEACHER AT SCHOOL...
WOW! SHE'S SO BEAUTIFUL!
SHE LOOKS LIKE A MOVIE STAR!
STOP!
DON'T TEASE YOUR ELDERS!

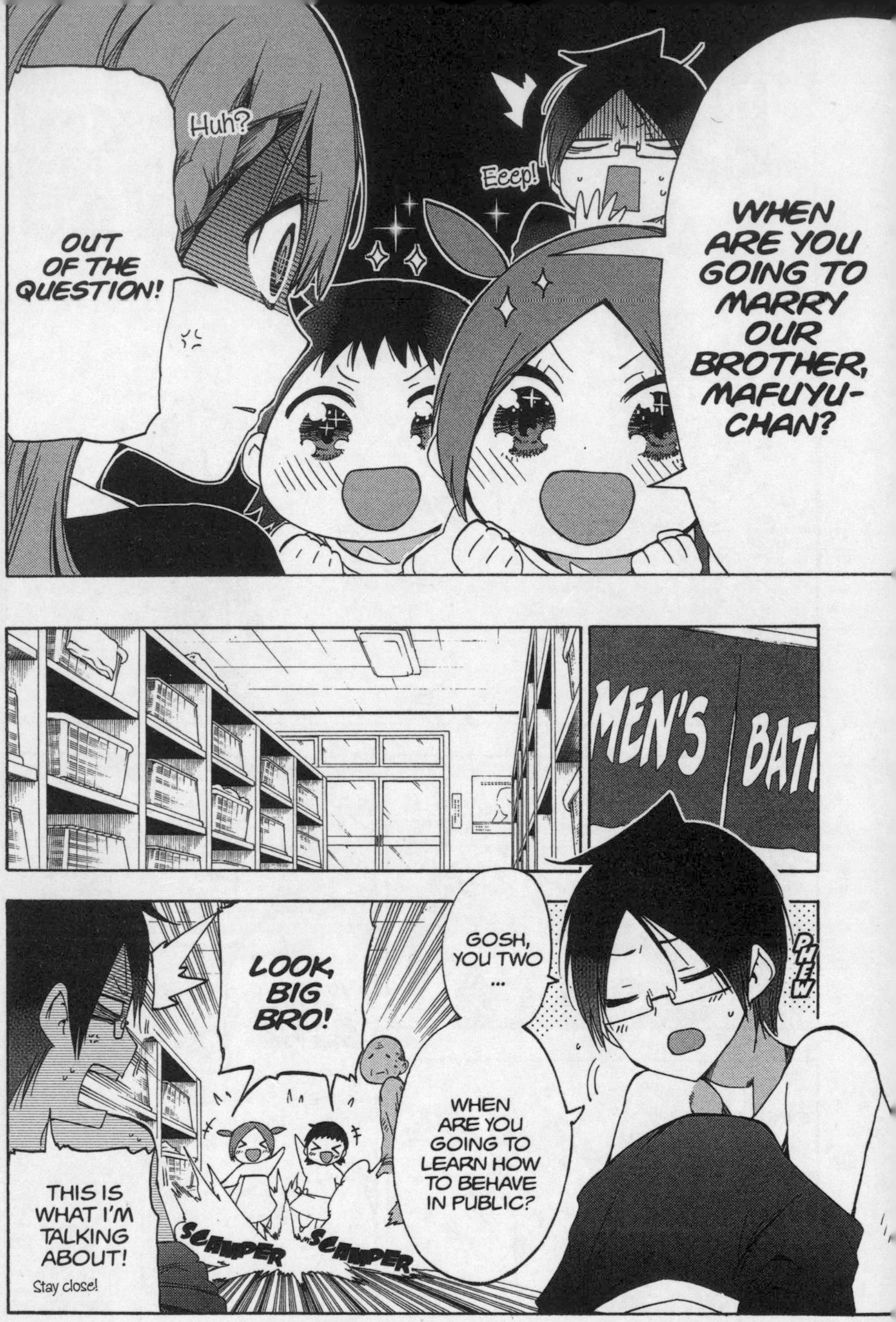

WHEN ARE YOU GOING TO MARRY OUR BROTHER, MAFUYU-CHAN?
Eeep!
Huh?
OUT OF THE QUESTION!
MEN'S BAT
PHEW
GOSH, YOU TWO ...
WHEN ARE YOU GOING TO LEARN HOW TO BEHAVE IN PUBLIC?
LOOK, BIG BRO!
SCAMPER SCAMPER
THIS IS WHAT I'M TALKING ABOUT!
Stay close!

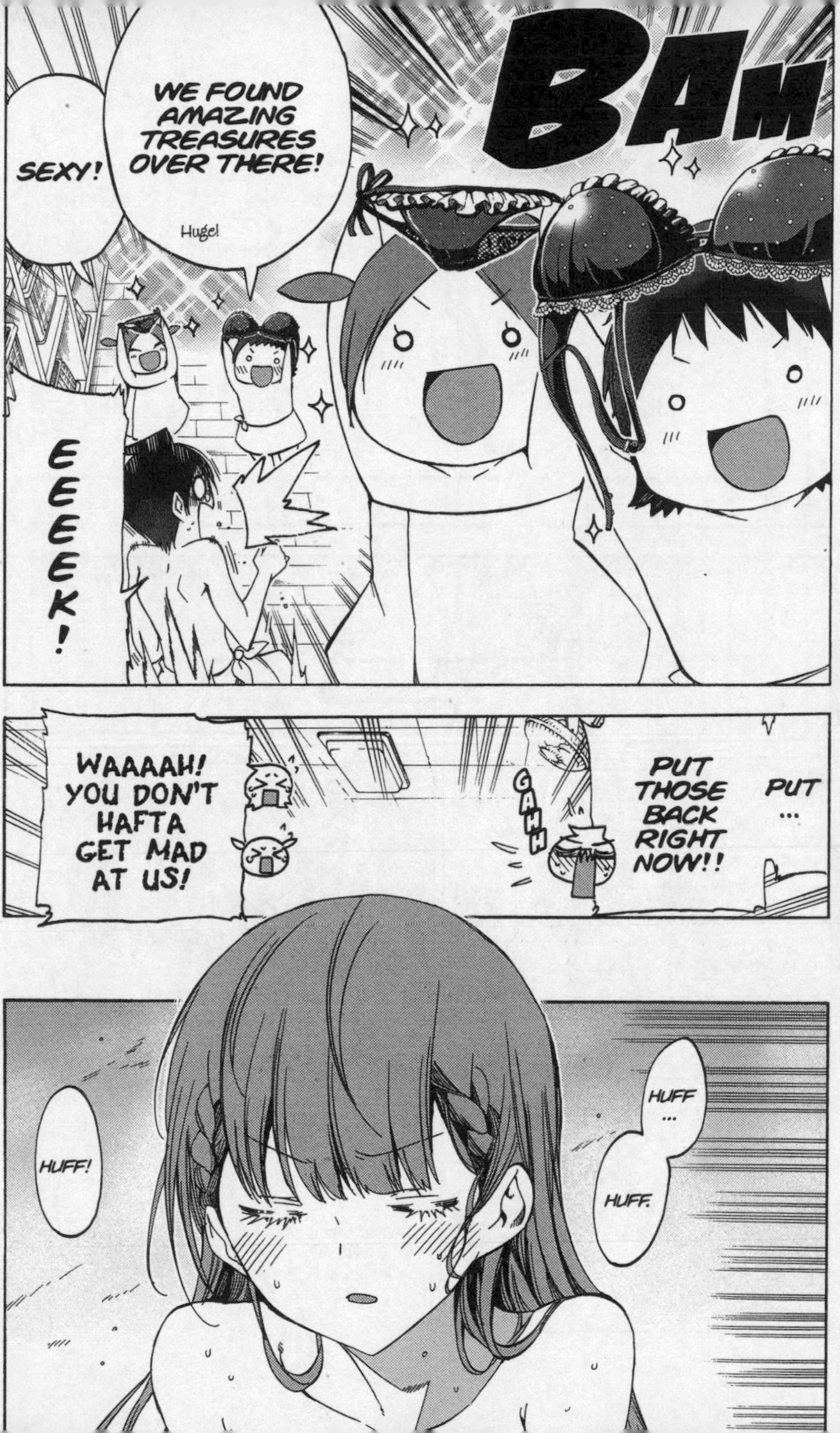
BAM
WE FOUND AMAZING TREASURES OVER THERE!
SEXY!
Huge!
EEEEEK!
PUT ...
PUT THOSE BACK RIGHT NOW!!
GAHH
WAAAAH! YOU DON'T HAFTA GET MAD AT US!
HUFF ...
HUFF.
HUFF!

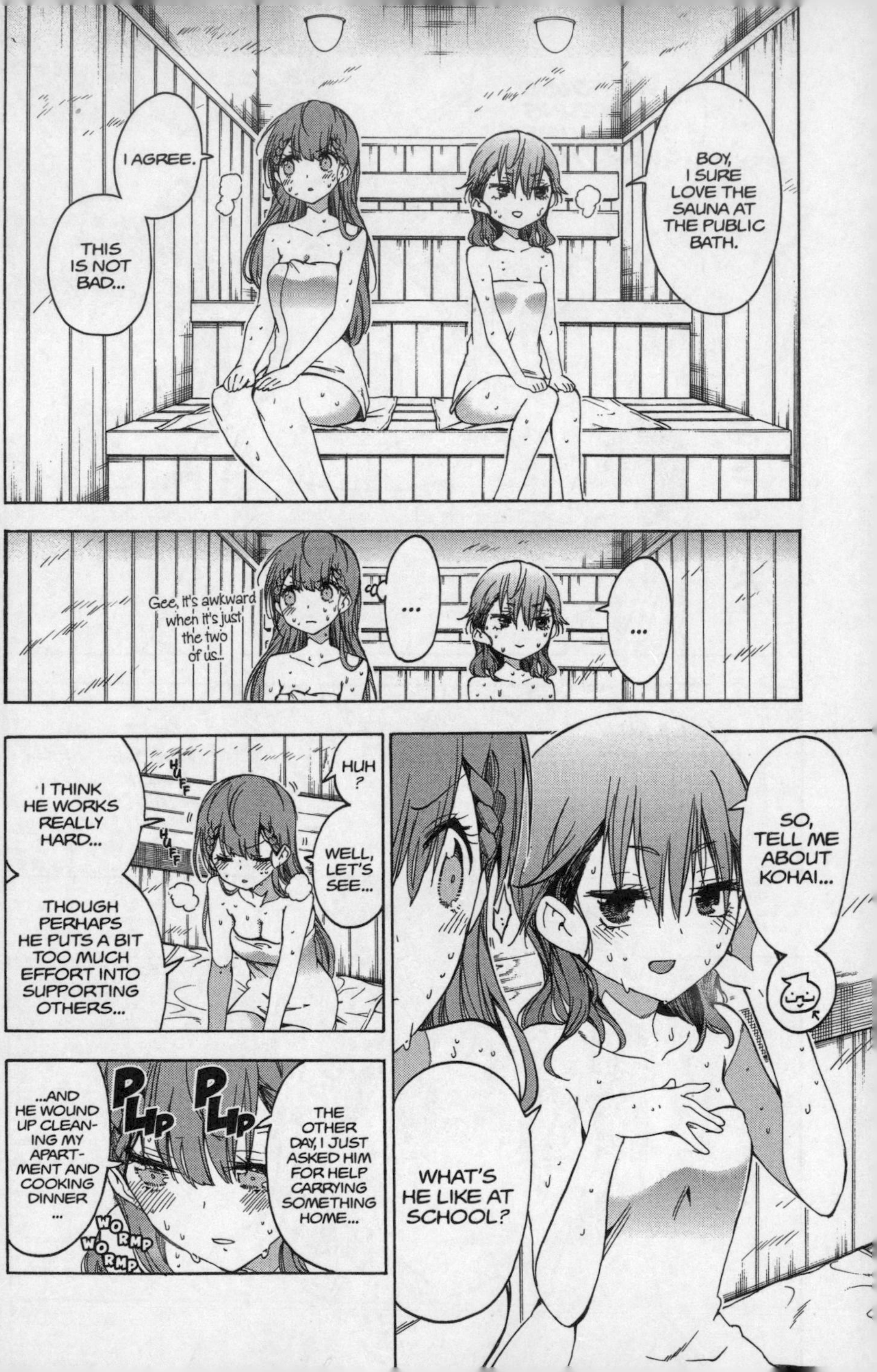
BOY, I SURE LOVE THE SAUNA AT THE PUBLIC BATH.
I AGREE.
THIS IS NOT BAD...
...
...
Gee, it's awkward when it's just the two of us..
SO, TELL ME ABOUT KOHAI...
WHAT'S HE LIKE AT SCHOOL?
HUH?
WELL, LET'S SEE...
HUFF
HUFF
I THINK HE WORKS REALLY HARD...
THOUGH PERHAPS HE PUTS A BIT TOO MUCH EFFORT INTO SUPPORTING OTHERS...
THE OTHER DAY, I JUST ASKED HIM FOR HELP CARRYING SOMETHING HOME...
PLIP
PLIP
...AND HE WOUND UP CLEANING MY APARTMENT AND COOKING DINNER ...
WORMP
WORMP

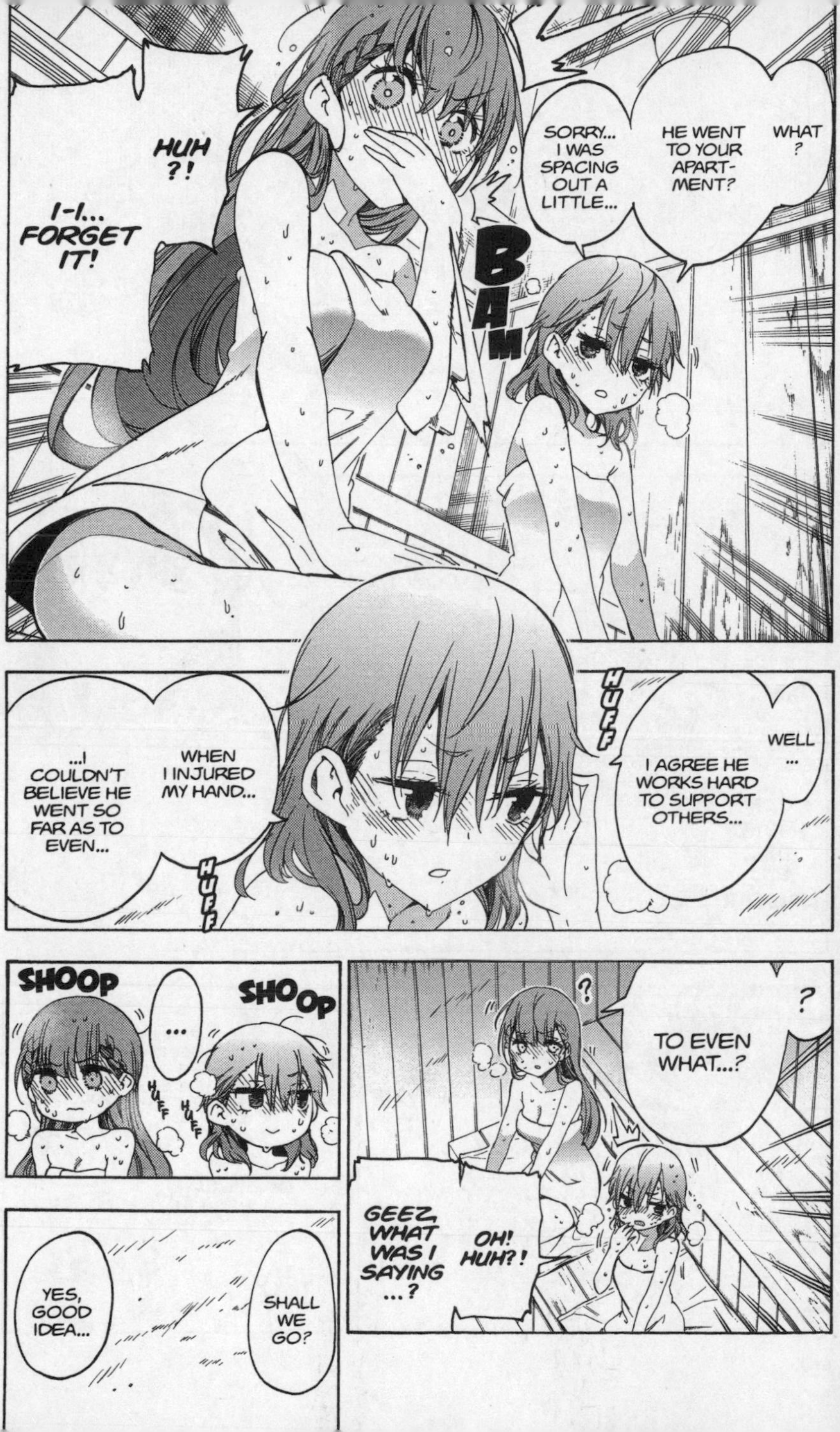
WHAT?
HE WENT TO YOUR APARTMENT?
SORRY... I WAS SPACING OUT A LITTLE...
BAM
HUH?!
I-I... FORGET IT!
HUFF
WELL...
I AGREE HE WORKS HARD TO SUPPORT OTHERS...
WHEN I INJURED MY HAND...
...I COULDN'T BELIEVE HE WENT SO FAR AS TO EVEN...
HUFF
?
TO EVEN WHAT...?
?
OH! HUH?!
GEEZ, WHAT WAS I SAYING...?
SHOOP
...
SHOOP
HUFF
HUFF
SHALL WE GO?
YES, GOOD IDEA...

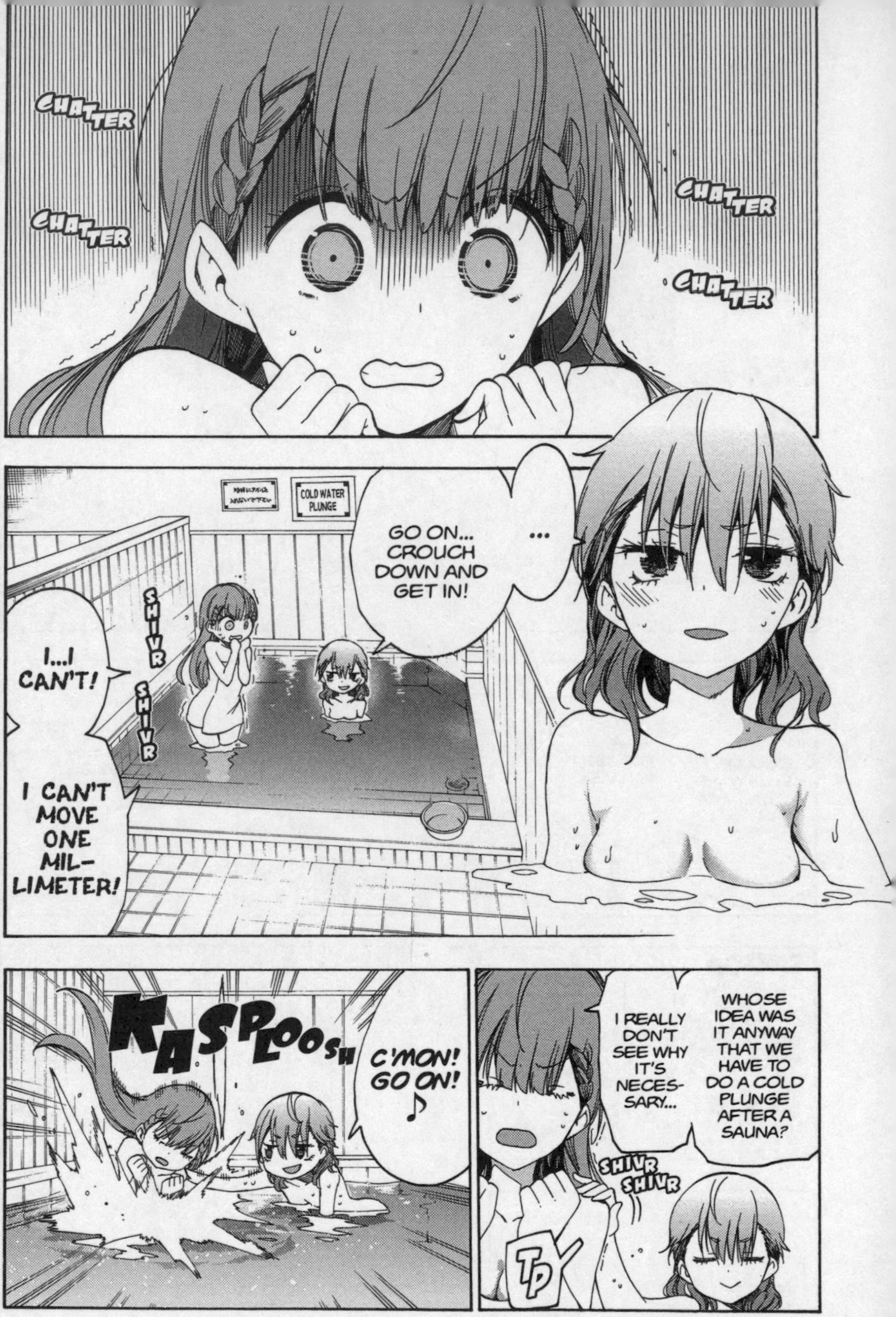
CHATTER
CHATTER
CHATTER
CHATTER
...
GO ON... CROUCH DOWN AND GET IN!
COLD WATER PLUNGE
SHIVR SHIVR
I...I CAN'T!
I CAN'T MOVE ONE MIL-LIMETER!
WHOSE IDEA WAS IT ANYWAY THAT WE HAVE TO DO A COLD PLUNGE AFTER A SAUNA?
I REALLY DON'T SEE WHY IT'S NECES-SARY...
SHIVR SHIVR
TP
C'MON! GO ON! ♪
KASPLOOSH

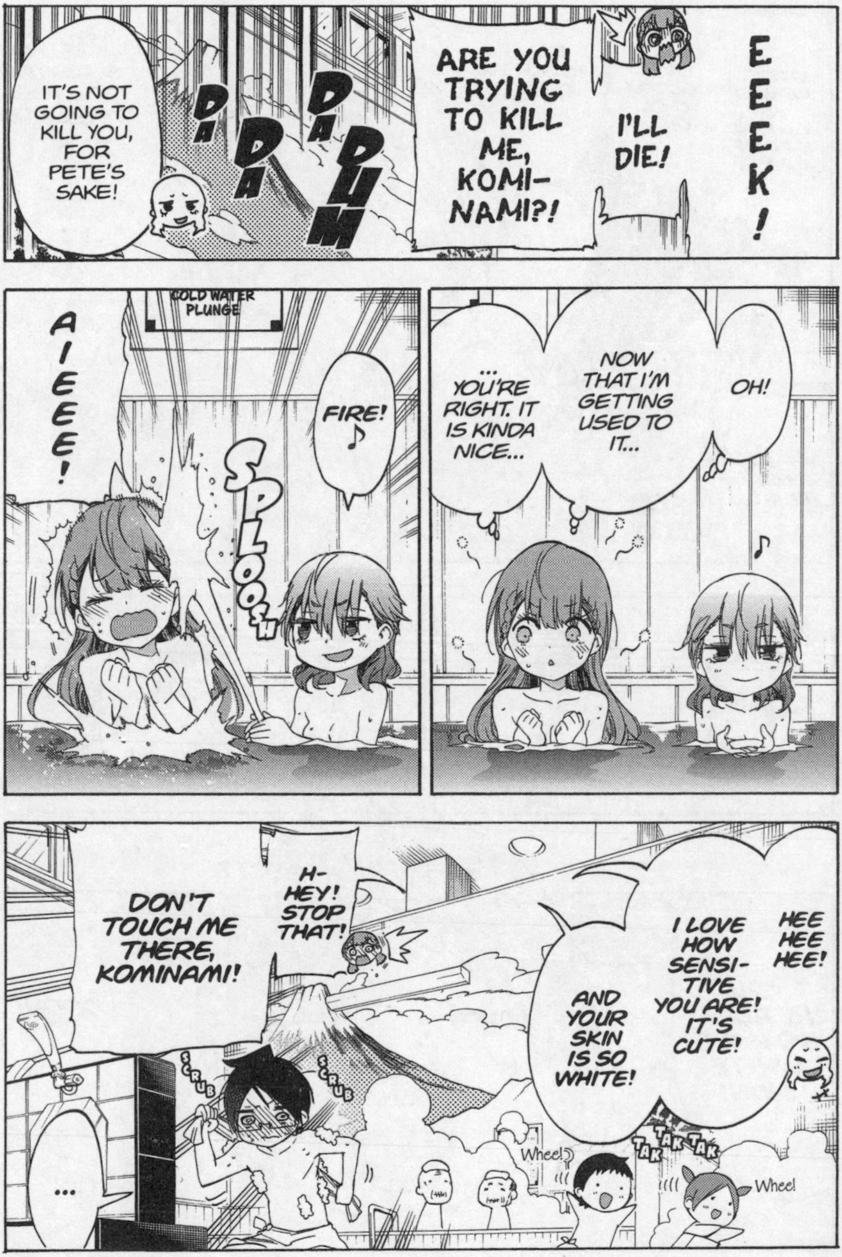
EEEK!
I'LL DIE!
ARE YOU TRYING TO KILL ME, KOMI-NAMI?!
DA DA DA DUM
IT'S NOT GOING TO KILL YOU, FOR PETE'S SAKE!
OH!
NOW THAT I'M GETTING USED TO IT...
...YOU'RE RIGHT. IT IS KINDA NICE...
COLD WATER PLUNGE
FIRE! ♪
SPLOOSH
AIEEEE!
HEE HEE HEE!
I LOVE HOW SENSI-TIVE YOU ARE! IT'S CUTE!
AND YOUR SKIN IS SO WHITE!
H-HEY! STOP THAT!
DON'T TOUCH ME THERE, KOMINAMI!
TAK TAK TAK TAK
Whee!
Whee!
SCRUB SCRUB
...

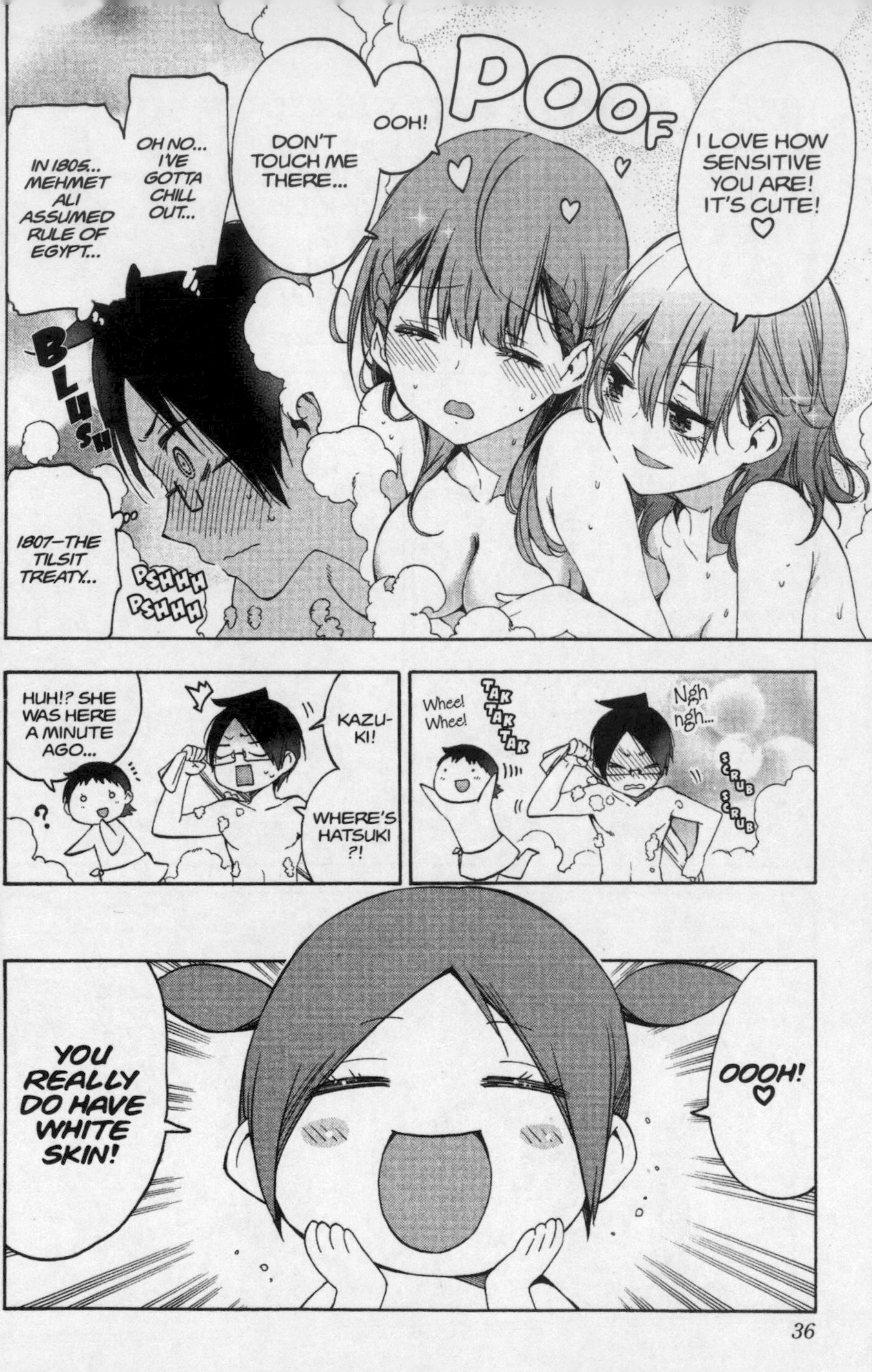
I LOVE HOW SENSITIVE YOU ARE! IT'S CUTE! ♡
POOF
OOH!
DON'T TOUCH ME THERE...
OH NO... I'VE GOTTA CHILL OUT...
IN 1805... MEHMET ALI ASSUMED RULE OF EGYPT...
BLUSH
1807—THE TILSIT TREATY...
PSHHH PSHHH
Ngh ngh...
TAK TAK TAK
Whee! Whee!
SCRUB SCRUB
KAZU-KI!
WHERE'S HATSUKI?!
HUH!? SHE WAS HERE A MINUTE AGO...
OOOH! ♡
YOU REALLY DO HAVE WHITE SKIN!

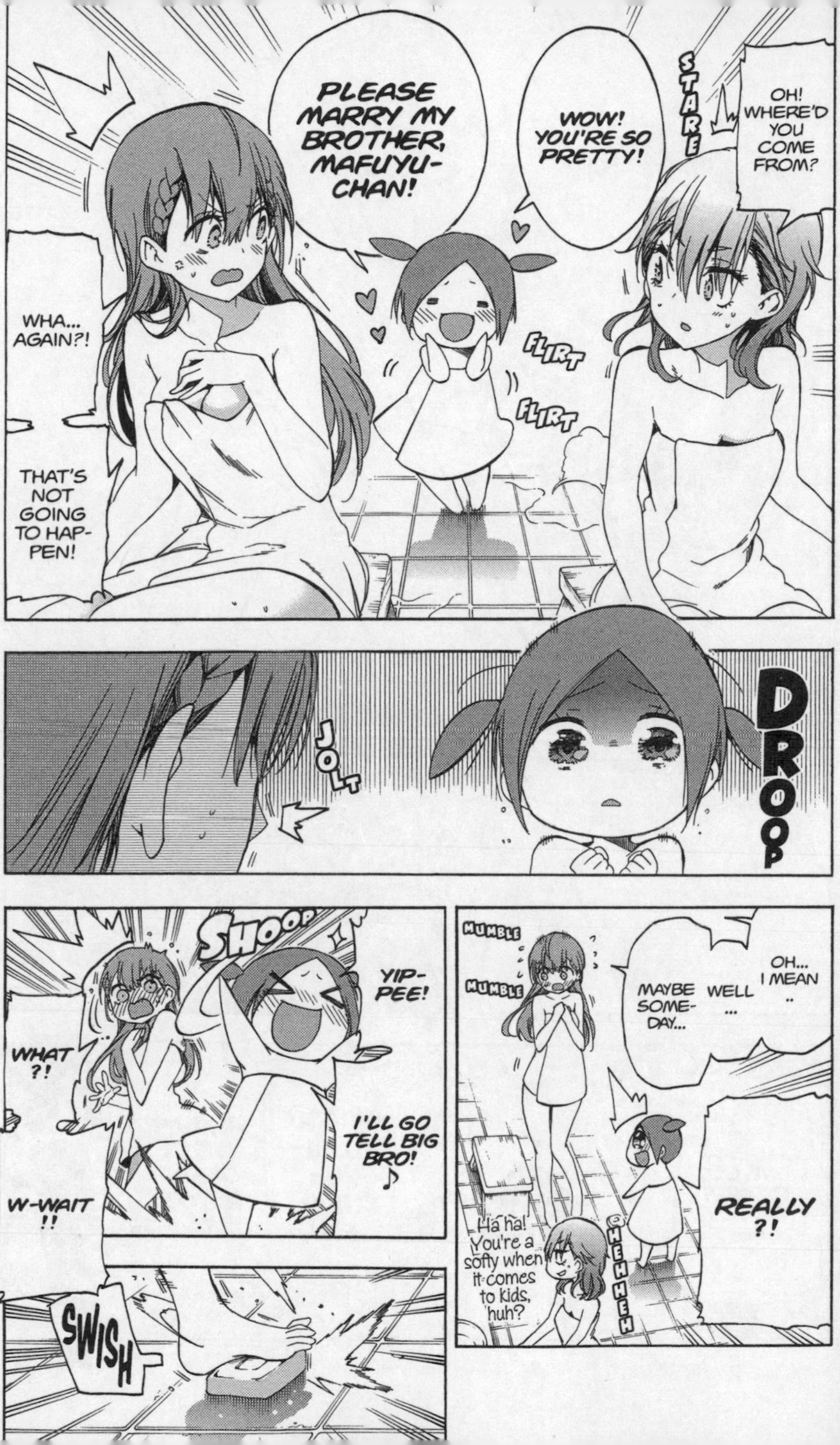
OH! WHERE'D YOU COME FROM?
STARE
WOW! YOU'RE SO PRETTY!
PLEASE MARRY MY BROTHER, MAFUYU-CHAN!
FLIRT
FLIRT
WHA... AGAIN?!
THAT'S NOT GOING TO HAP-PEN!
DROOP
JOLT
OH... I MEAN ..
WELL ...
MAYBE SOME-DAY...
MUMBLE
MUMBLE
REALLY ?!
HEH HEH
Ha ha! You're a softy when it comes to kids, huh?
SHOOP
YIP-PEE!
WHAT ?!
I'LL GO TELL BIG BRO! ♪
W-WAIT !!
SWISH

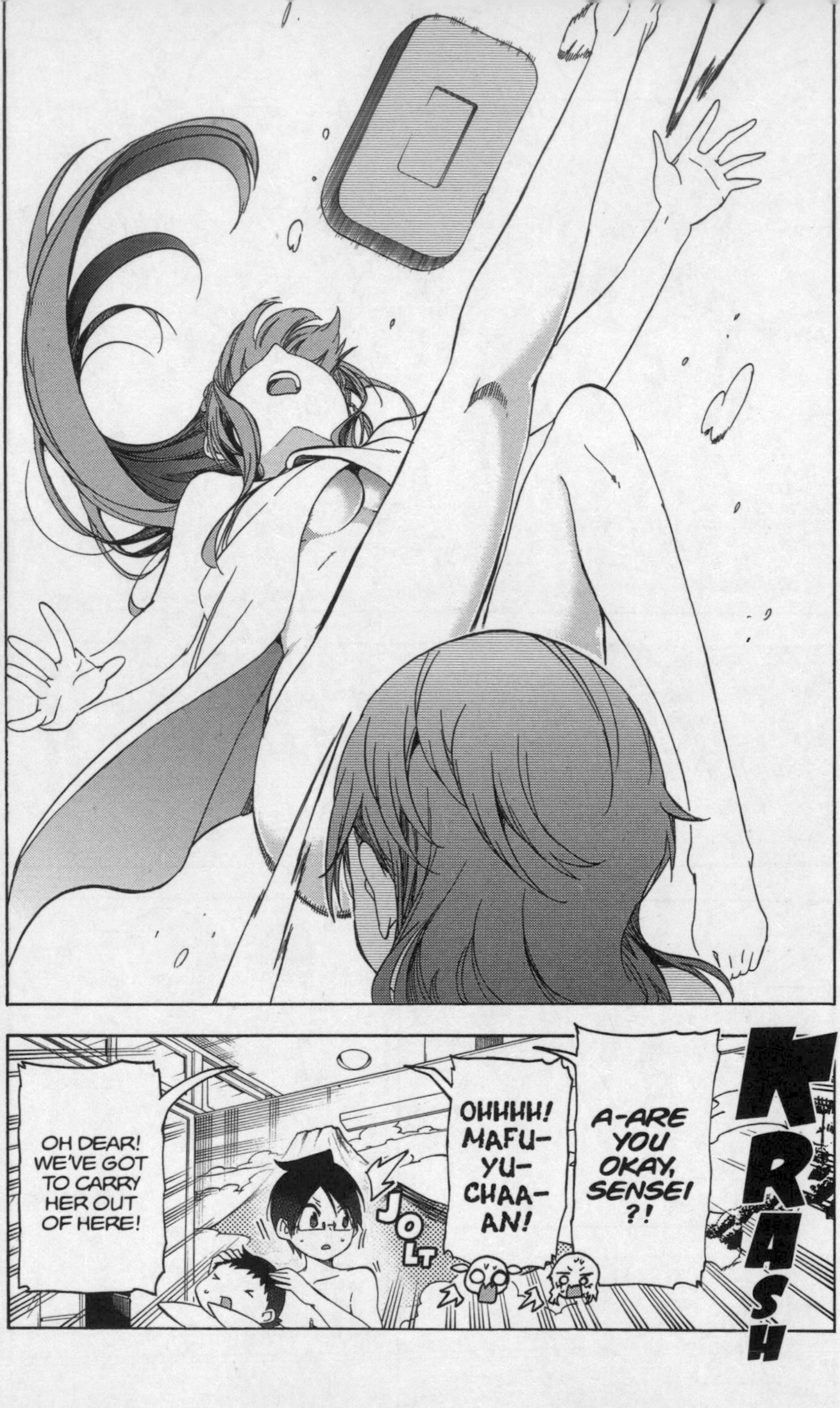
KRASH
A-ARE YOU OKAY, SENSEI?!
OHHHH! MAFU-YU-CHAAAN!
JOLT
OH DEAR! WE'VE GOT TO CARRY HER OUT OF HERE!

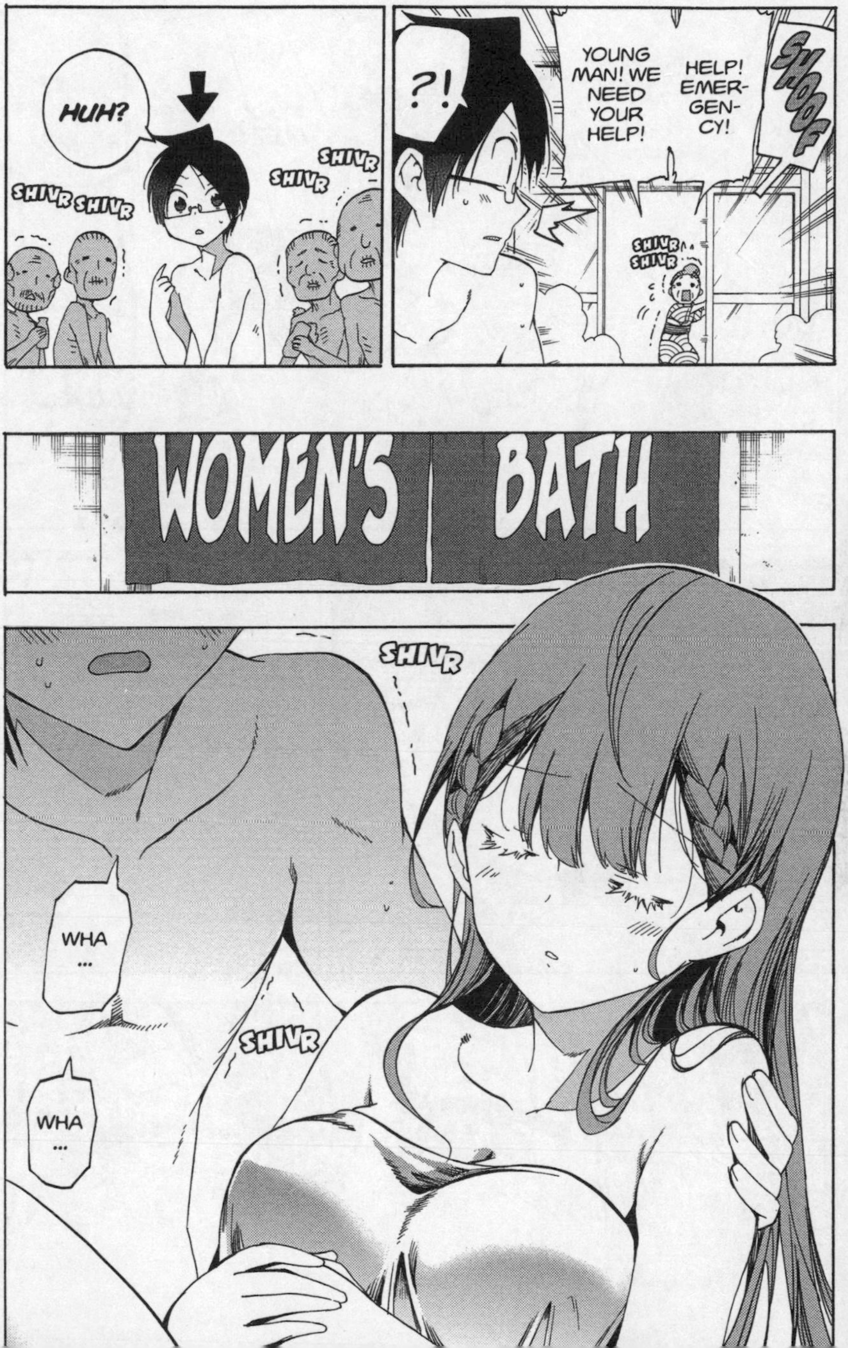
SHOOF
HELP! EMERGENCY!
YOUNG MAN! WE NEED YOUR HELP!
?!
SHIVR SHIVR
SHIVR
SHIVR
HUH?
SHIVR SHIVR
WOMEN'S BATH
SHIVR
WHA...
SHIVR
WHA...

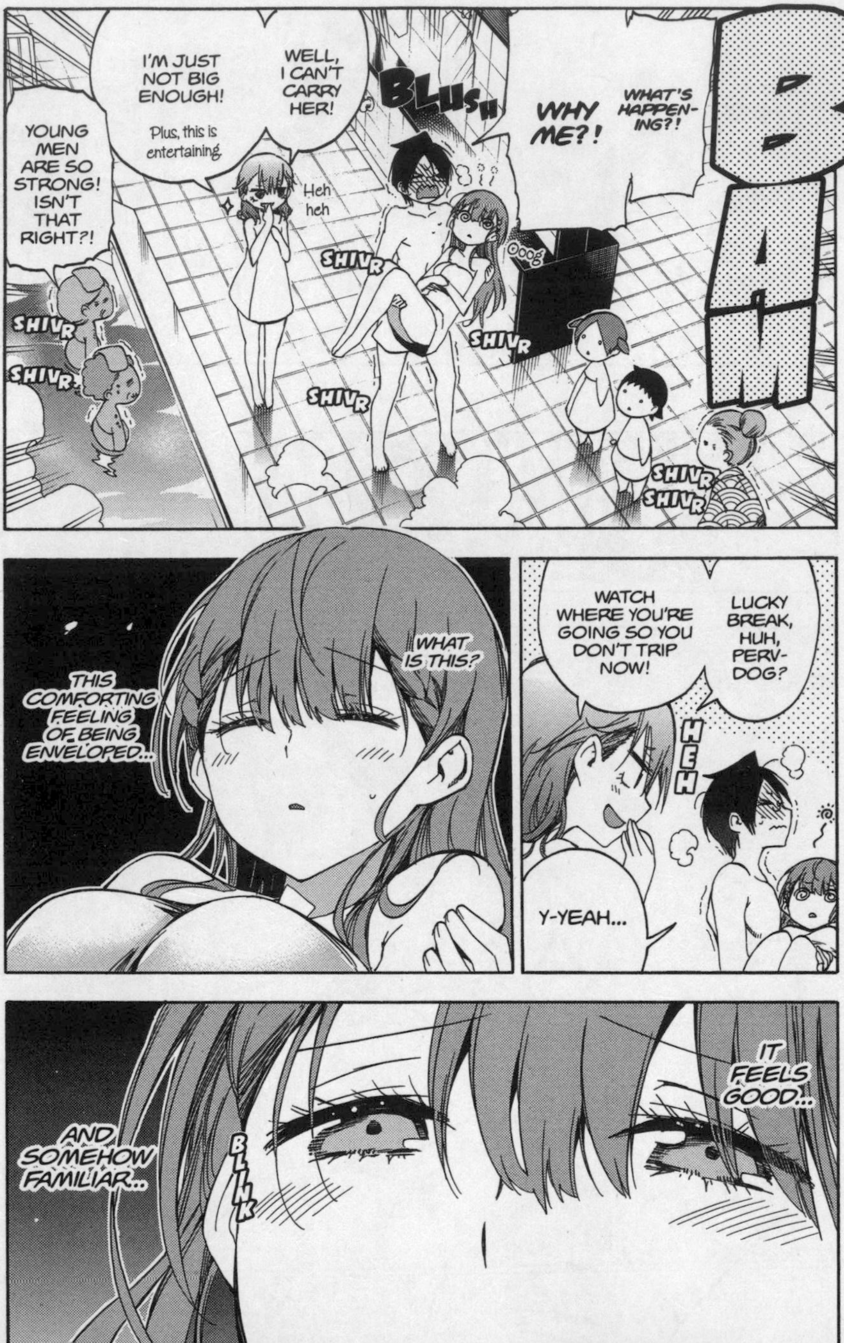
BAM
WHAT'S HAPPENING?!
WHY ME?!
BLUSH
WELL, I CAN'T CARRY HER!
I'M JUST NOT BIG ENOUGH!
Plus, this is entertaining.
Heh heh
Ooog
YOUNG MEN ARE SO STRONG! ISN'T THAT RIGHT?!
SHIVR
SHIVR
SHIVR
SHIVR
SHIVR
SHIVR
SHIVR
LUCKY BREAK, HUH, PERV-DOG?
WATCH WHERE YOU'RE GOING SO YOU DON'T TRIP NOW!
HEH
Y-YEAH...
WHAT IS THIS?
THIS COMFORTING FEELING OF BEING ENVELOPED...
IT FEELS GOOD...
BLINK
AND SOMEHOW FAMILIAR...

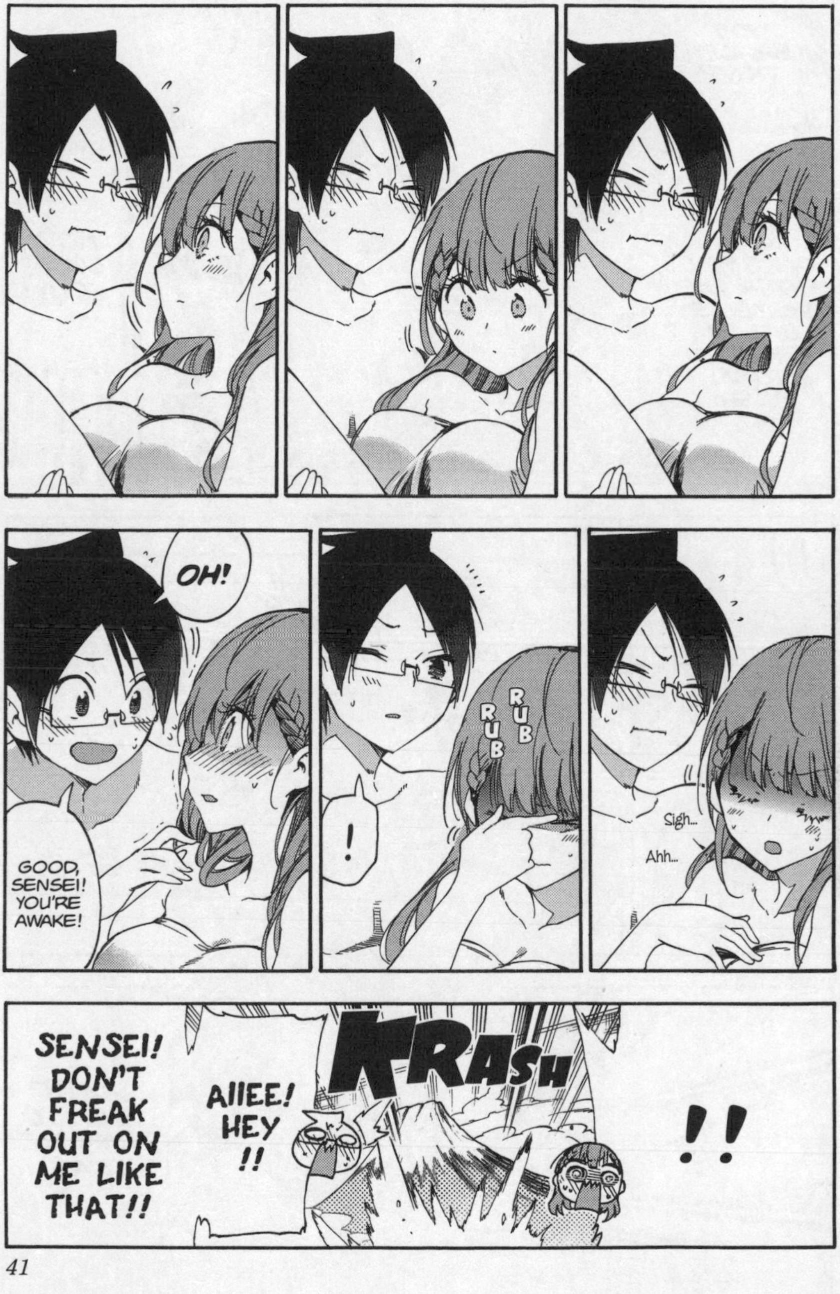
Sigh...
Ahh...
RUB RUB
!
OH!
GOOD, SENSEI! YOU'RE AWAKE!
!!
KRASH
AIIEE! HEY !!
SENSEI! DON'T FREAK OUT ON ME LIKE THAT!!

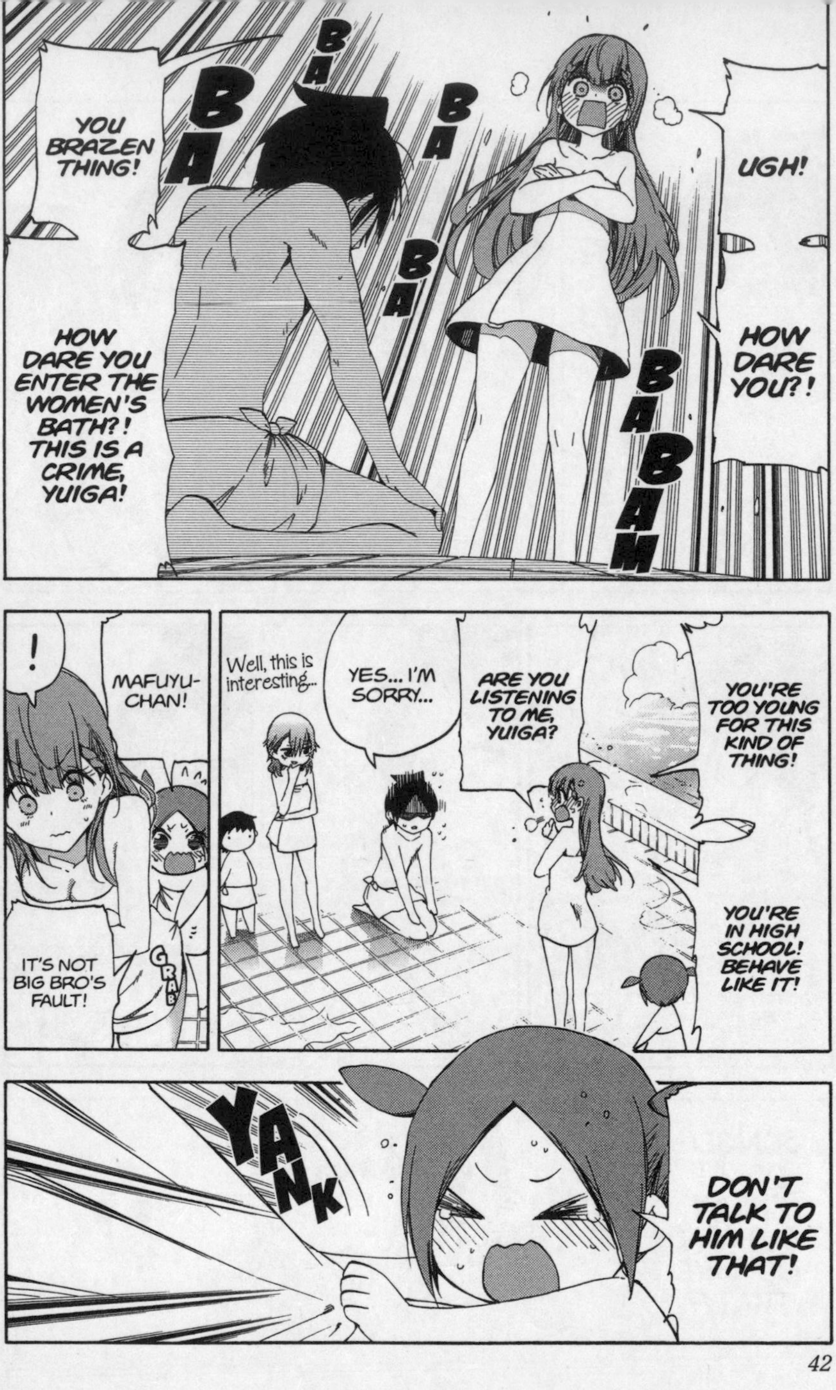
UGH!
HOW DARE YOU?!
BA BA BA BA BA BAM
YOU BRAZEN THING!
HOW DARE YOU ENTER THE WOMEN'S BATH?! THIS IS A CRIME, YUIGA!
YOU'RE TOO YOUNG FOR THIS KIND OF THING!
ARE YOU LISTENING TO ME, YUIGA?
YES... I'M SORRY...
Well, this is interesting...
YOU'RE IN HIGH SCHOOL! BEHAVE LIKE IT!
!
MAFUYU-CHAN!
GRAB
IT'S NOT BIG BRO'S FAULT!
DON'T TALK TO HIM LIKE THAT!
YANK

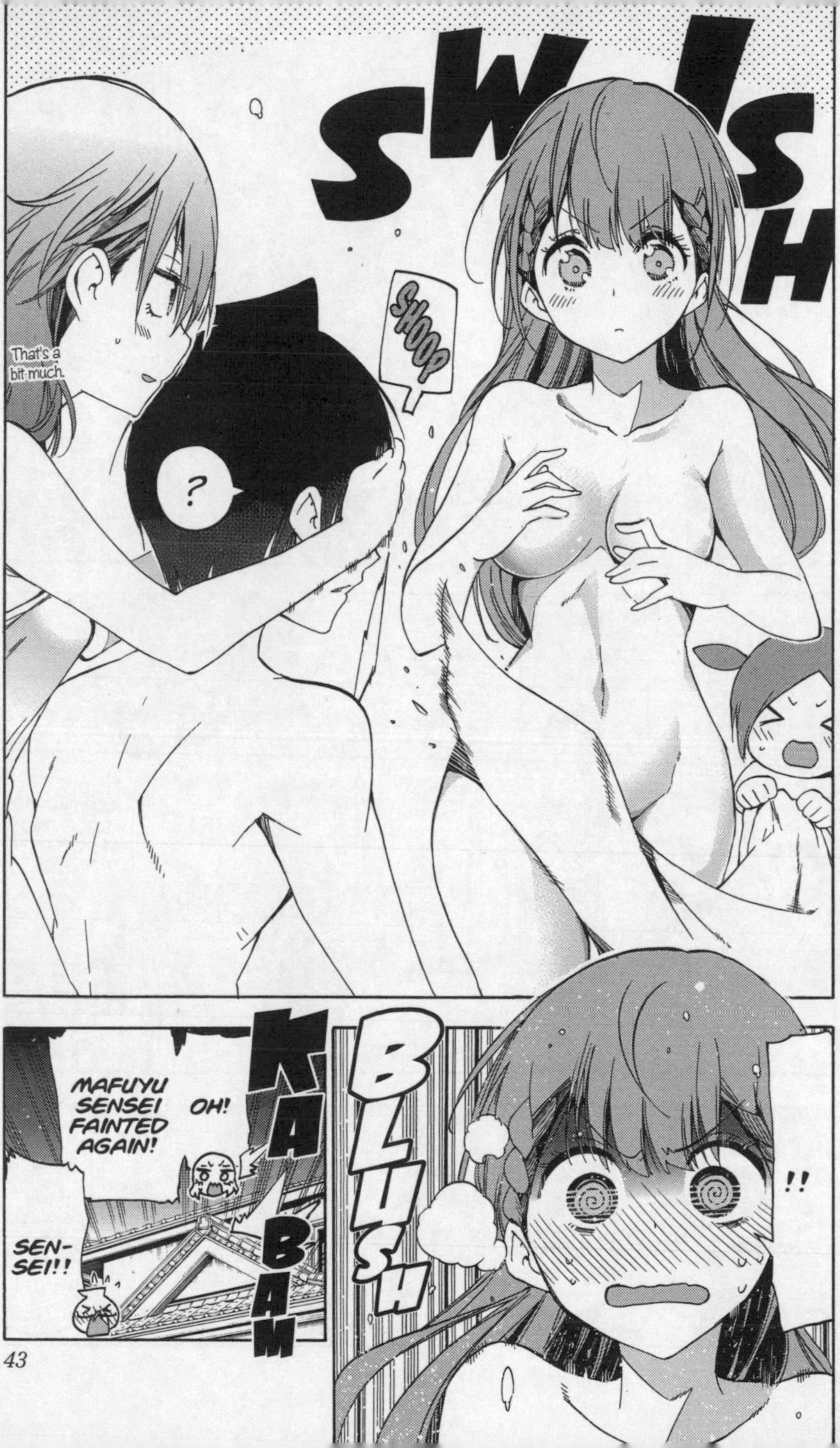
SWISH
SHOOP
?
That's a bit much.
BLUSH
!!
KABAM
OH!
MAFUYU SENSEI FAINTED AGAIN!
SEN-SEI!!

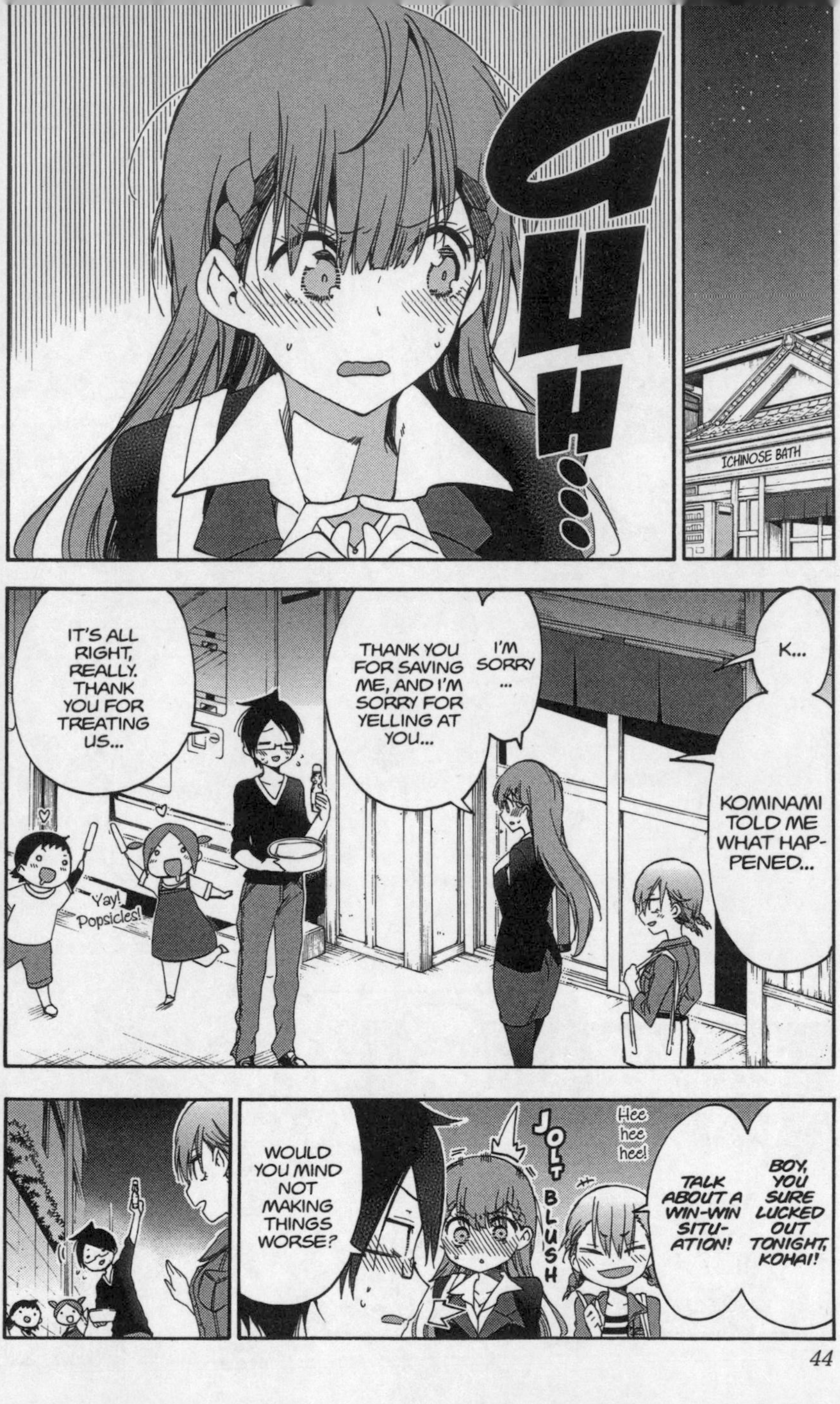

ICHINOSE BATH
GUH...
K...
KOMINAMI TOLD ME WHAT HAPPENED...
I'M SORRY ...
THANK YOU FOR SAVING ME, AND I'M SORRY FOR YELLING AT YOU...
IT'S ALL RIGHT, REALLY. THANK YOU FOR TREATING US...
Yay! Popsicles!
BOY, YOU SURE LUCKED OUT TONIGHT, KOHAI!
TALK ABOUT A WIN-WIN SITUATION!
Hee hee hee!
JOLT
BLUSH
WOULD YOU MIND NOT MAKING THINGS WORSE?

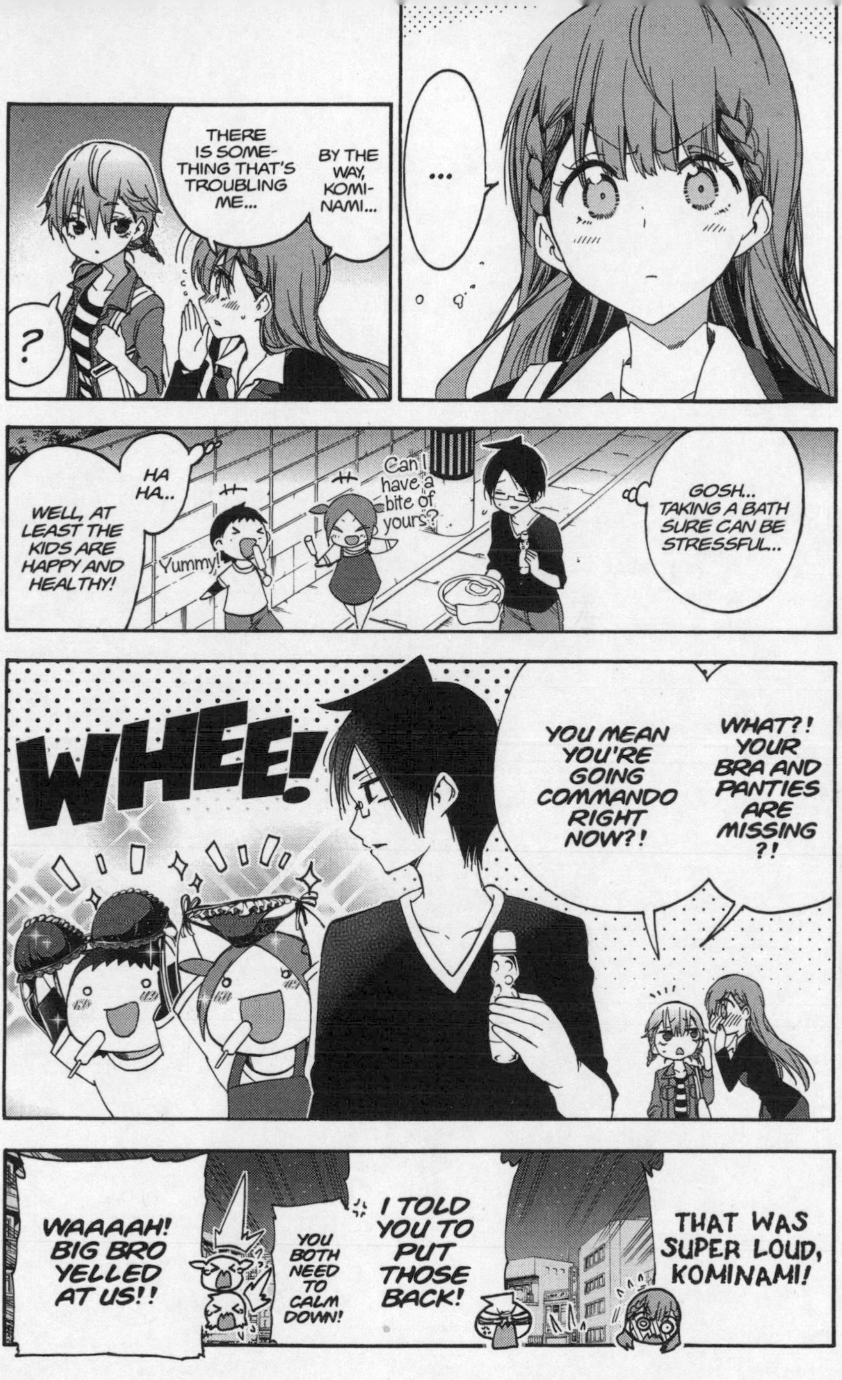
...
BY THE WAY, KOMINAMI...
THERE IS SOMETHING THAT'S TROUBLING ME...
?
GOSH... TAKING A BATH SURE CAN BE STRESSFUL...
Can I have a bite of yours?
Yummy!
HA HA..
WELL, AT LEAST THE KIDS ARE HAPPY AND HEALTHY!
WHAT?! YOUR BRA AND PANTIES ARE MISSING?!
YOU MEAN YOU'RE GOING COMMANDO RIGHT NOW?!
WHEE!
THAT WAS SUPER LOUD, KOMINAMI!
I TOLD YOU TO PUT THOSE BACK!
YOU BOTH NEED TO CALM DOWN!
WAAAAH! BIG BRO YELLED AT US!!

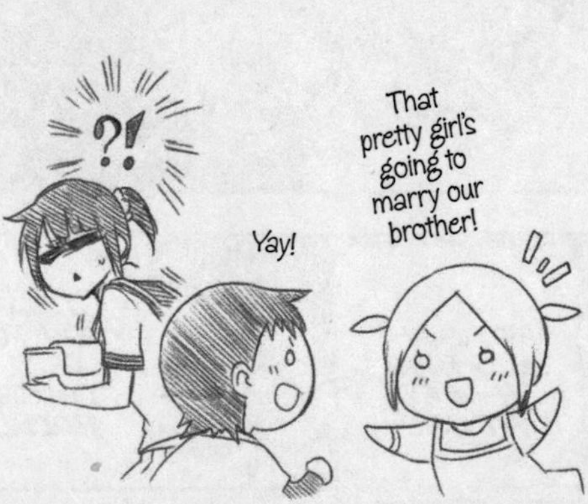
That pretty girl's going to marry our brother!
Yay!
?!

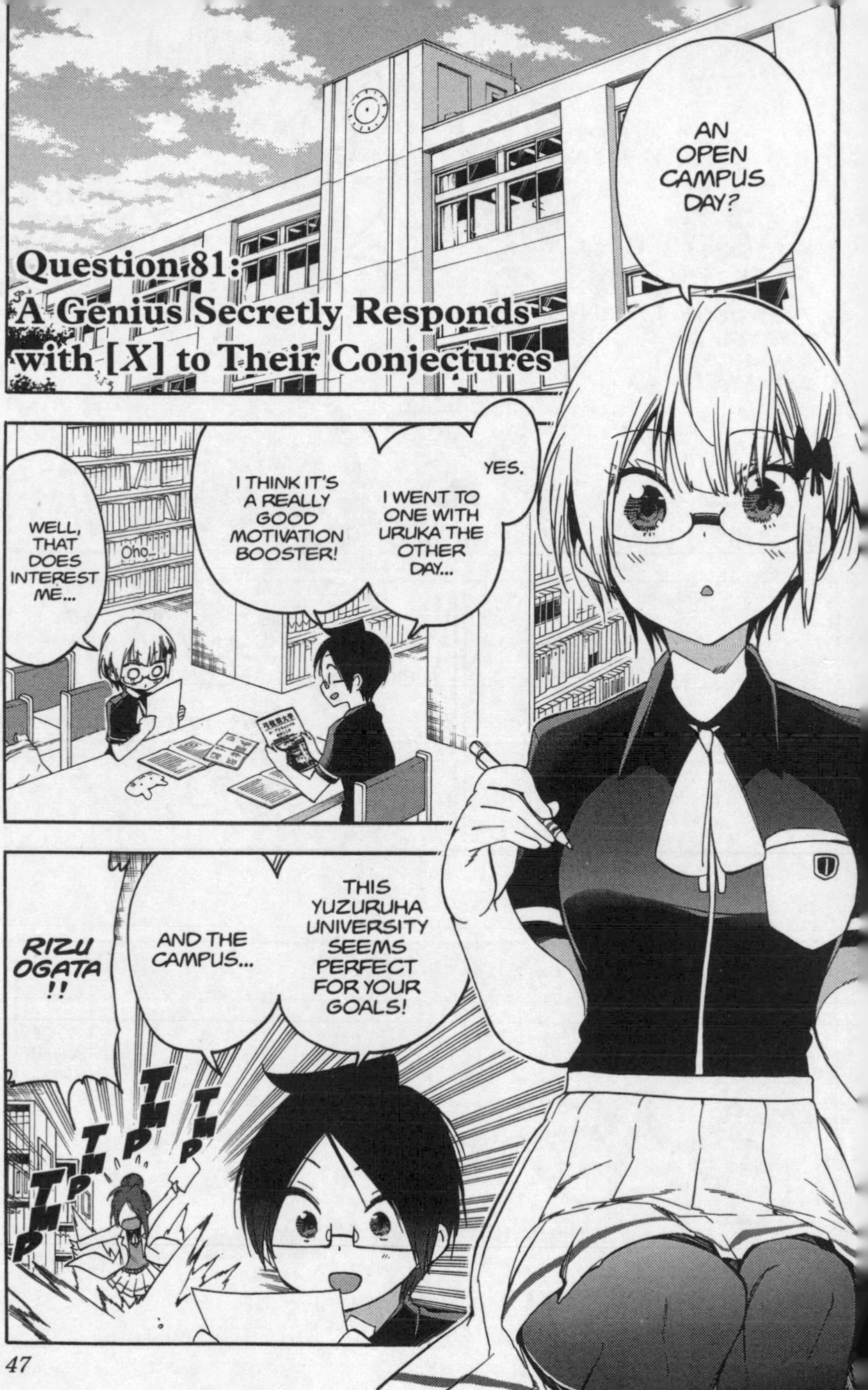
Question 81:
A Genius Secretly Responds with [X] to Their Conjectures
AN OPEN CAMPUS DAY?
YES.
I WENT TO ONE WITH URUKA THE OTHER DAY...
I THINK IT'S A REALLY GOOD MOTIVATION BOOSTER!
WELL, THAT DOES INTEREST ME...
Oho...
THIS YUZURUHA UNIVERSITY SEEMS PERFECT FOR YOUR GOALS!
AND THE CAMPUS...
RIZU OGATA!!
THMP THMP THMP THMP THMP

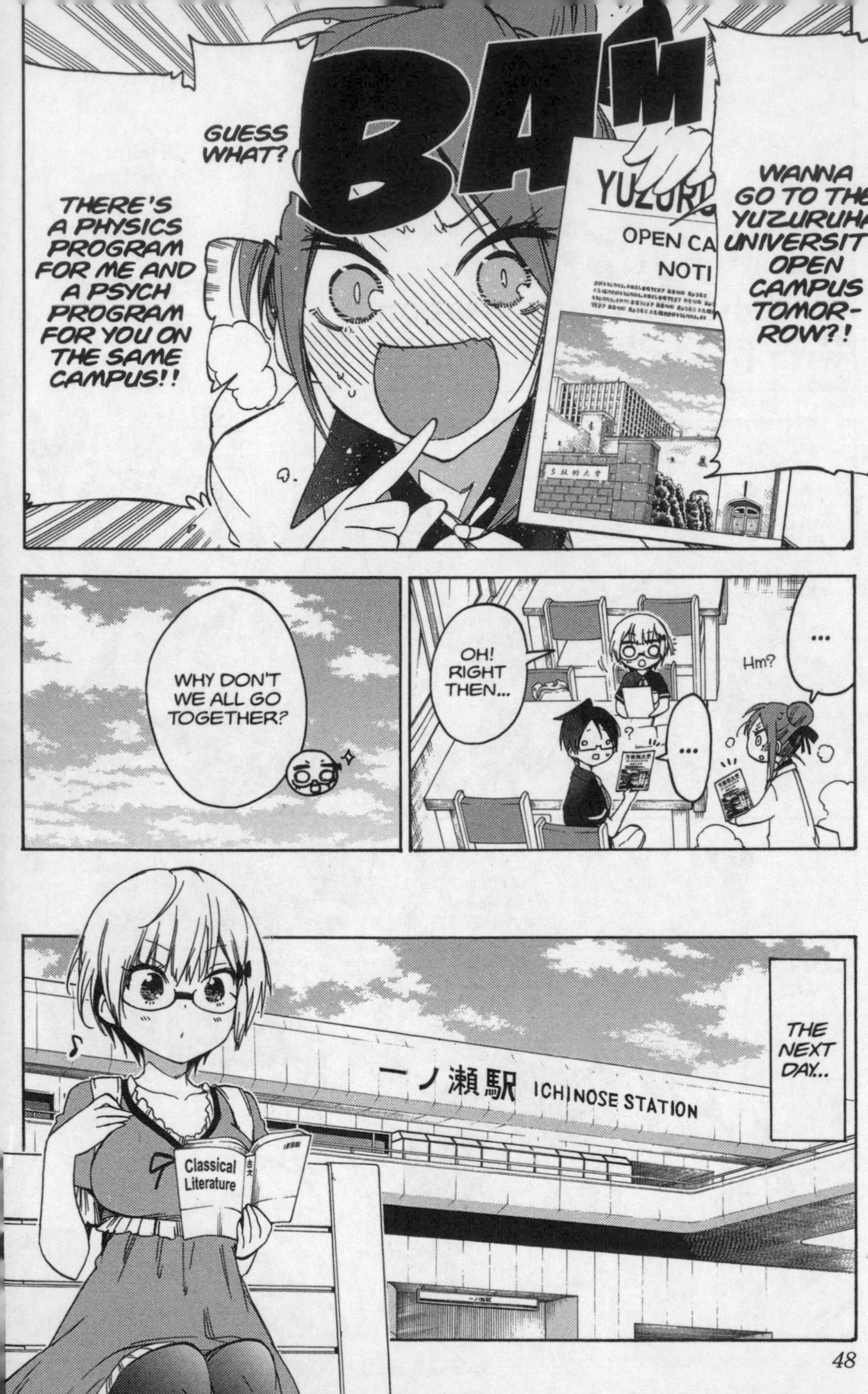
WANNA GO TO THE YUZURUHA UNIVERSITY OPEN CAMPUS TOMOR-ROW?!
BAM
YUZURI
OPEN CA
NOTI
GUESS WHAT?
THERE'S A PHYSICS PROGRAM FOR ME AND A PSYCH PROGRAM FOR YOU ON THE SAME CAMPUS!!
...
Hm?
OH! RIGHT THEN...
...
WHY DON'T WE ALL GO TOGETHER?
THE NEXT DAY...
一ノ瀬駅 ICHINOSE STATION
Classical Literature

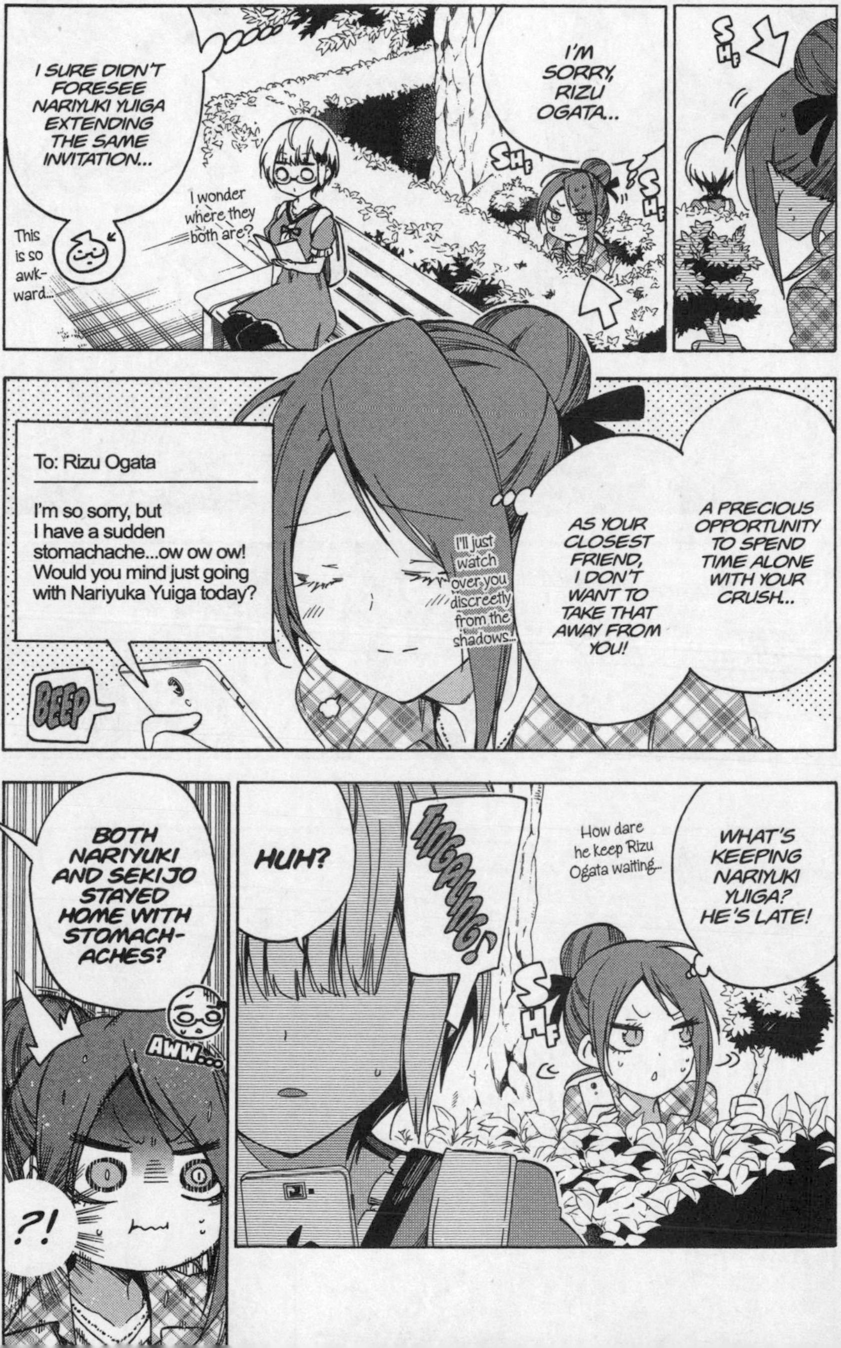
SHF
I'M SORRY, RIZU OGATA...
SHF
SHF
I SURE DIDN'T FORESEE NARIYUKI YUIGA EXTENDING THE SAME INVITATION...
I wonder where they both are?
This is so awk-ward...
A PRECIOUS OPPORTUNITY TO SPEND TIME ALONE WITH YOUR CRUSH...
AS YOUR CLOSEST FRIEND, I DON'T WANT TO TAKE THAT AWAY FROM YOU!
I'll just watch over you discreetly from the shadows...
To: Rizu Ogata
I'm so sorry, but I have a sudden stomachache...ow ow ow! Would you mind just going with Nariyuka Yuiga today?
BEEP
WHAT'S KEEPING NARIYUKI YUIGA? HE'S LATE!
How dare he keep Rizu Ogata waiting...
SHF
TINGALING!
HUH?
BOTH NARIYUKI AND SEKIJO STAYED HOME WITH STOMACH-ACHES?
AWW...
?!

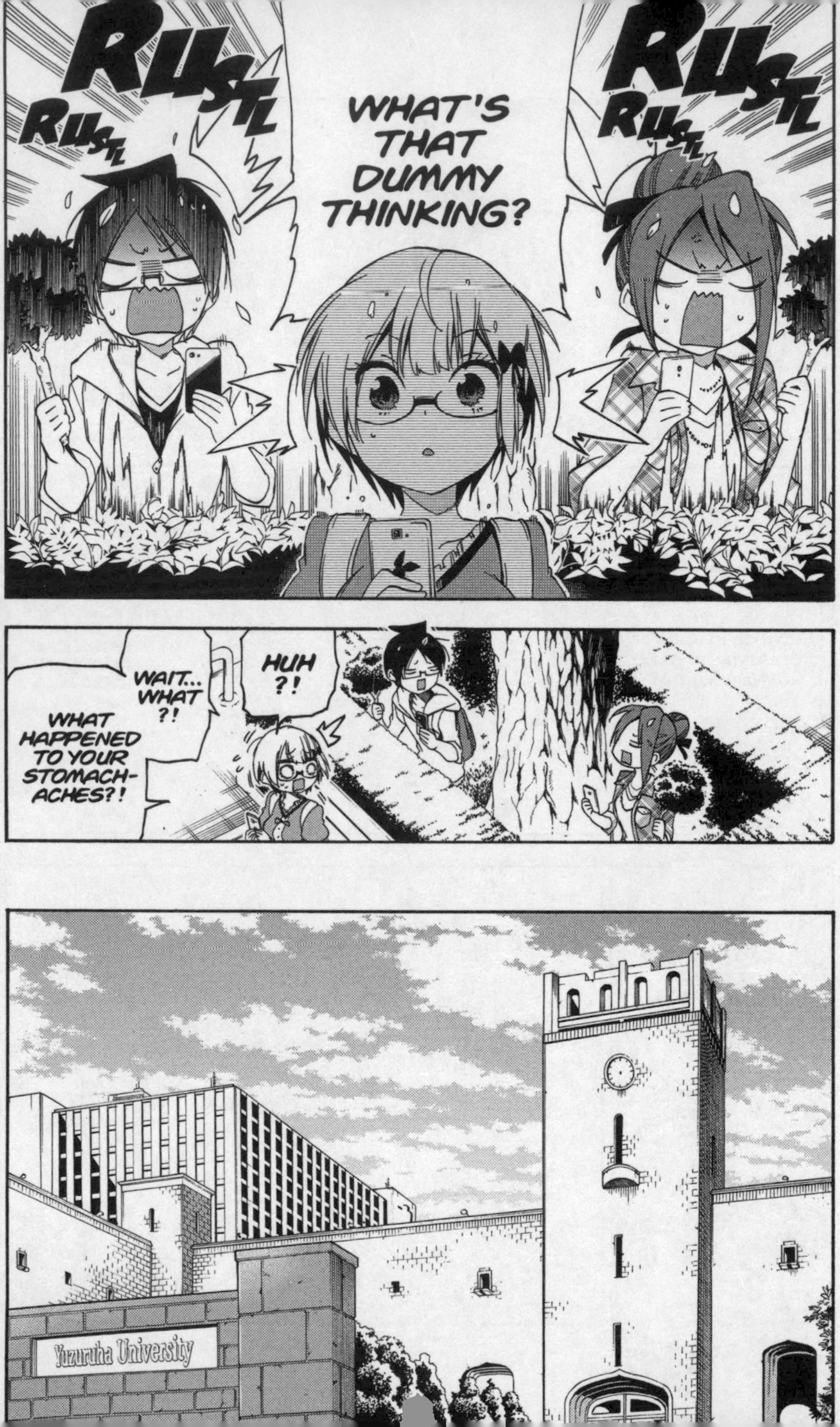
RUSTL RUSTL
WHAT'S THAT DUMMY THINKING?
RUSTL RUSTL
HUH?!
WAIT... WHAT?!
WHAT HAPPENED TO YOUR STOMACH-ACHES?!
Yuzuruha University

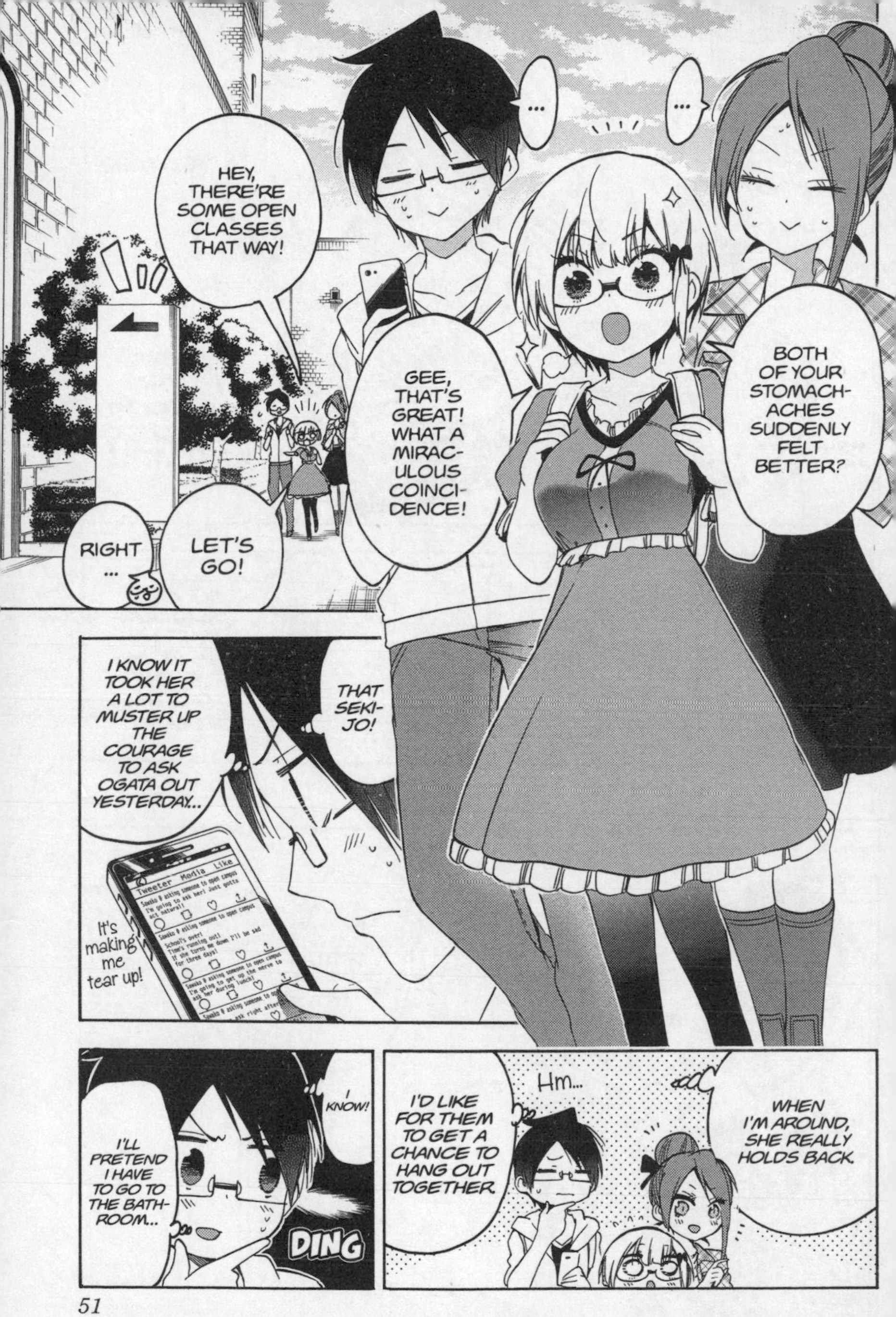
...
...
BOTH OF YOUR STOMACHACHES SUDDENLY FELT BETTER?
GEE, THAT'S GREAT! WHAT A MIRACULOUS COINCIDENCE!
HEY, THERE'RE SOME OPEN CLASSES THAT WAY!
LET'S GO!
RIGHT ...
THAT SEKI-JO!
I KNOW IT TOOK HER A LOT TO MUSTER UP THE COURAGE TO ASK OGATA OUT YESTERDAY...
Tweeter Media Like
Sawako @ asking someone to open campus
I'm going to ask her! Just gotta act natural!
Sawako @ asking someone to open campus
School's over! Time's running out! If she turns me down I'll be sad for three days!
Sawako @ asking someone to open campus
I'm going to get up the nerve to ask her during lunch!
It's making me tear up!
WHEN I'M AROUND, SHE REALLY HOLDS BACK.
Hm...
I'D LIKE FOR THEM TO GET A CHANCE TO HANG OUT TOGETHER.
I KNOW!
I'LL PRETEND I HAVE TO GO TO THE BATHROOM...
DING

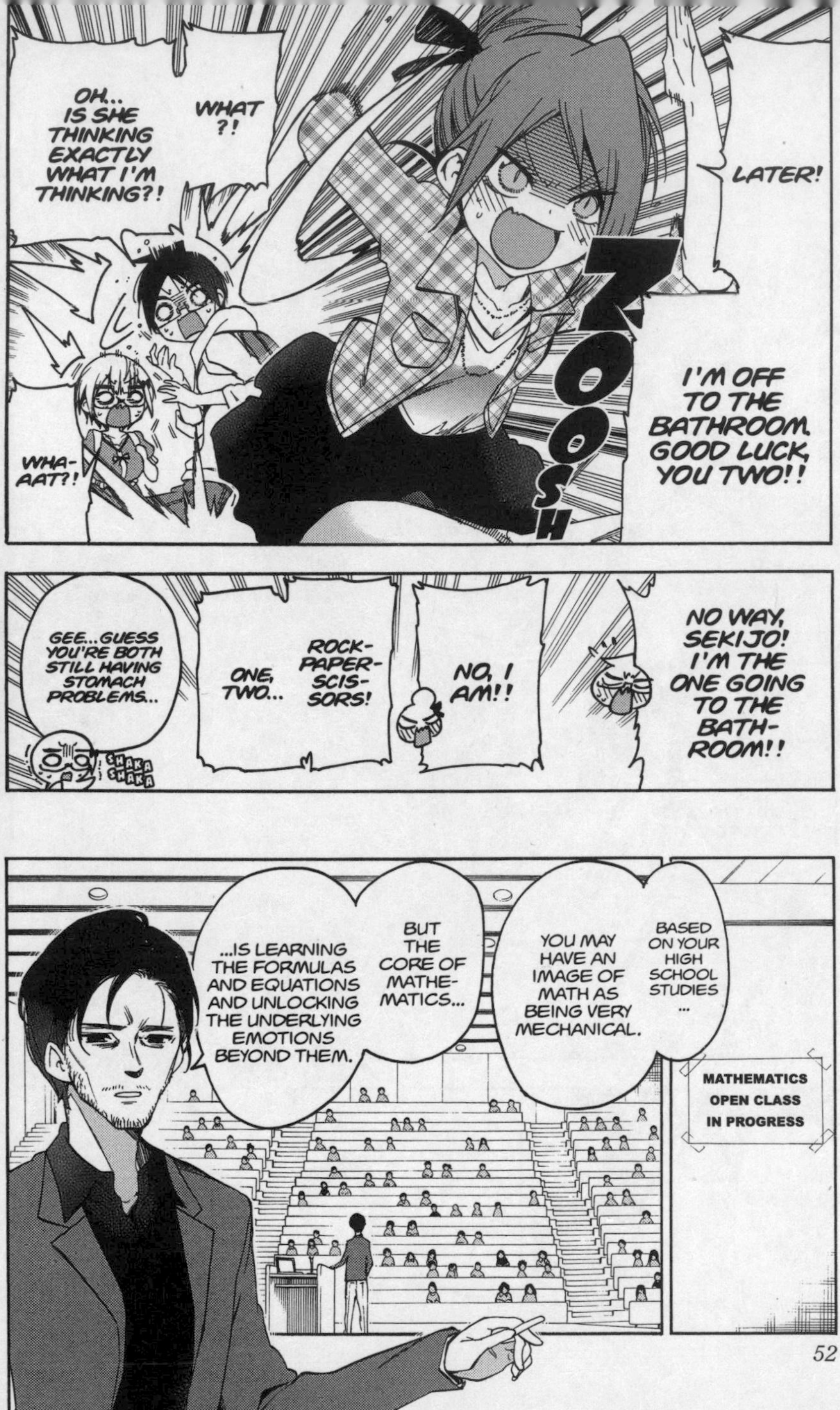
LATER!
I'M OFF TO THE BATHROOM. GOOD LUCK, YOU TWO!!
ZOOOSH
WHAT?!
OH... IS SHE THINKING EXACTLY WHAT I'M THINKING?!
WHA-AAT?!
NO WAY, SEKIJO! I'M THE ONE GOING TO THE BATHROOM!!
NO, I AM!!
ROCK-PAPER-SCISSORS!
ONE, TWO...
GEE...GUESS YOU'RE BOTH STILL HAVING STOMACH PROBLEMS...
SHAKA SHAKA
MATHEMATICS OPEN CLASS IN PROGRESS
BASED ON YOUR HIGH SCHOOL STUDIES...
YOU MAY HAVE AN IMAGE OF MATH AS BEING VERY MECHANICAL.
BUT THE CORE OF MATHEMATICS...
...IS LEARNING THE FORMULAS AND EQUATIONS AND UNLOCKING THE UNDERLYING EMOTIONS BEYOND THEM.

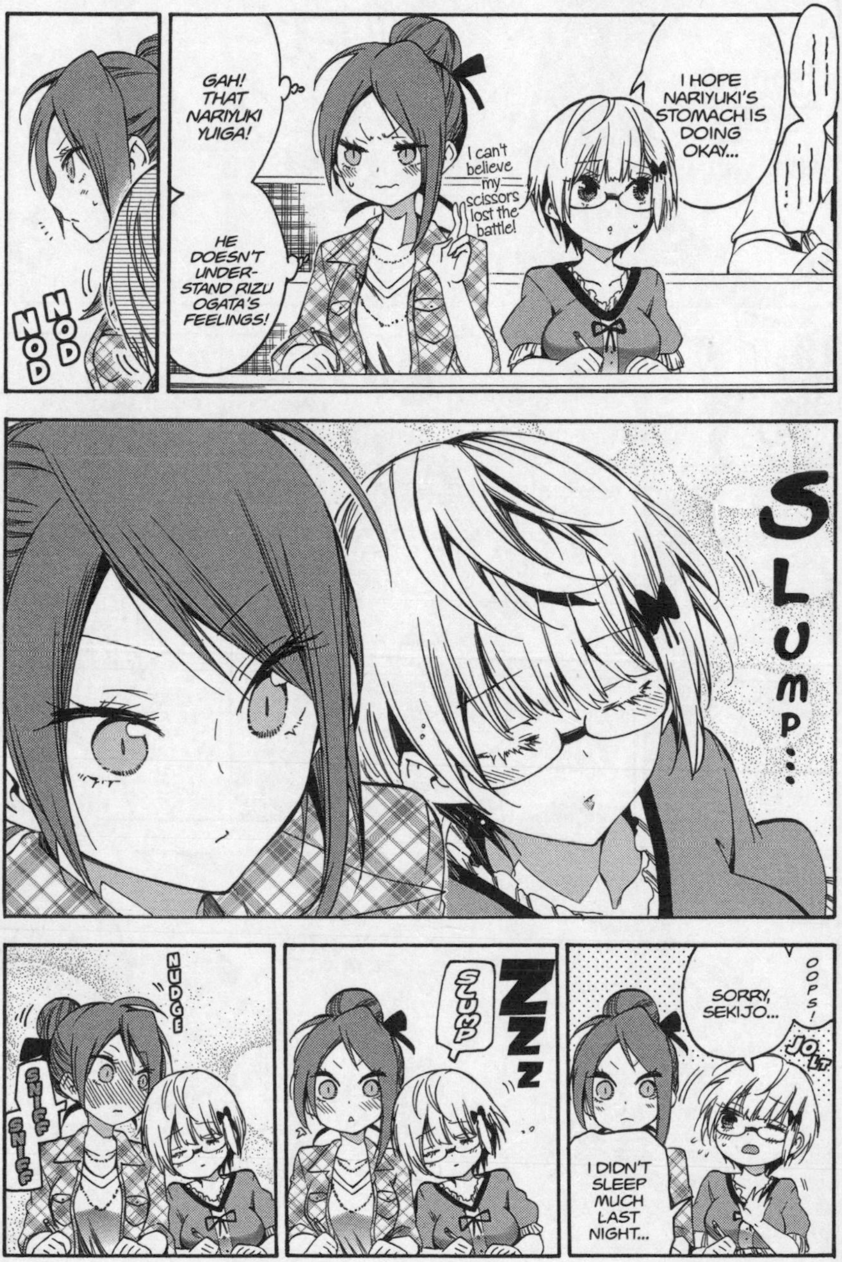
I HOPE NARIYUKI'S STOMACH IS DOING OKAY...
GAH! THAT NARIYUKI YUIGA!
I can't believe my scissors lost the battle!
HE DOESN'T UNDER-STAND RIZU OGATA'S FEELINGS!
NOD NOD
SLUMP...
OOPS!
SORRY, SEKIJO...
JOLT
I DIDN'T SLEEP MUCH LAST NIGHT...
ZZZ
SLUMP
NUDGE
SNIFF SNIFF

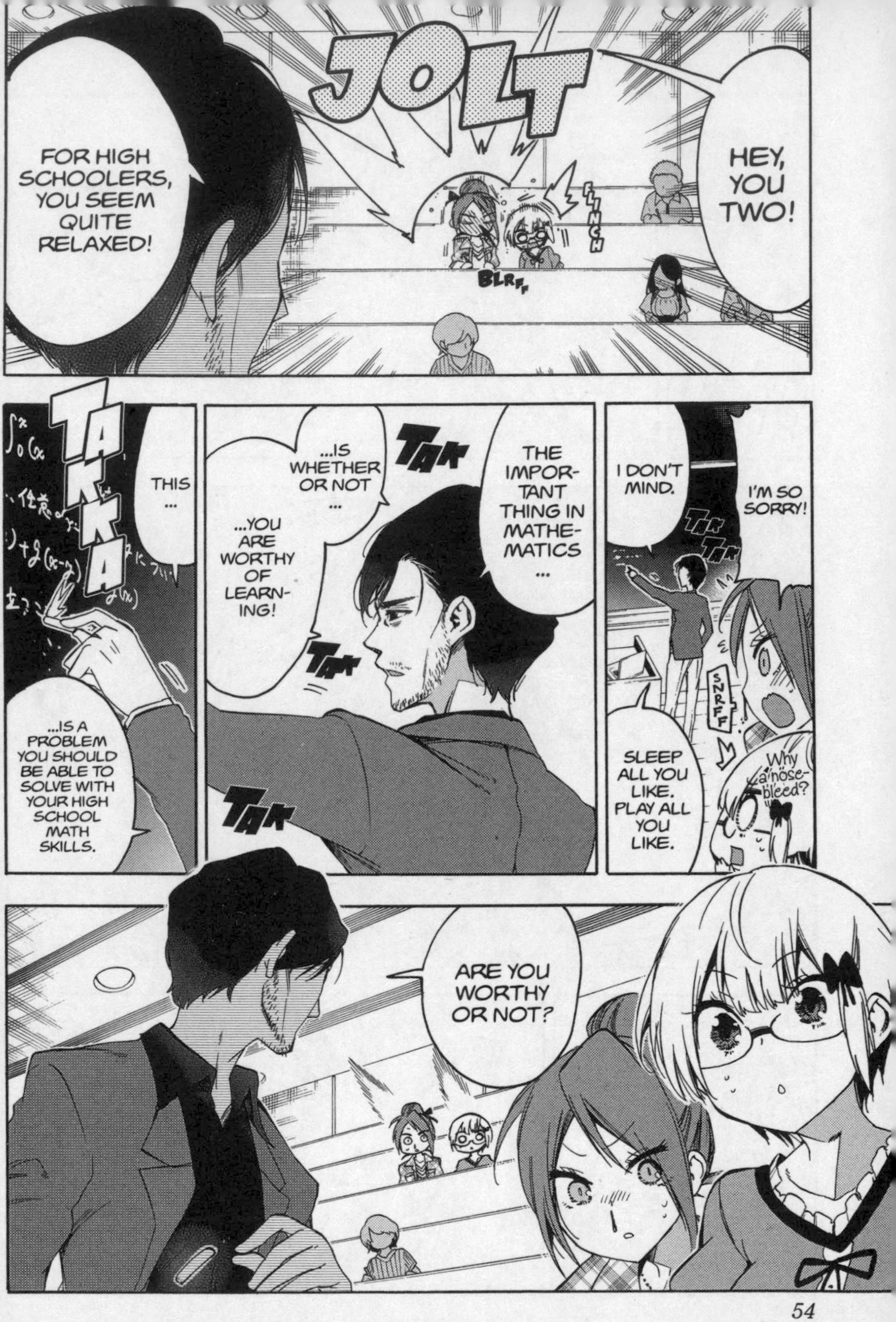

HEY, YOU TWO!
JOLT
FLINCH
BLRFF
FOR HIGH SCHOOLERS, YOU SEEM QUITE RELAXED!
I'M SO SORRY!
I DON'T MIND.
TAK TAK
SNRFF
Why a nose-bleed?
SLEEP ALL YOU LIKE. PLAY ALL YOU LIKE.
THE IMPORTANT THING IN MATHEMATICS ...
...IS WHETHER OR NOT ...
TAK
...YOU ARE WORTHY OF LEARNING!
TAK
TAK
TAKKA
THIS ...
...IS A PROBLEM YOU SHOULD BE ABLE TO SOLVE WITH YOUR HIGH SCHOOL MATH SKILLS.
ARE YOU WORTHY OR NOT?

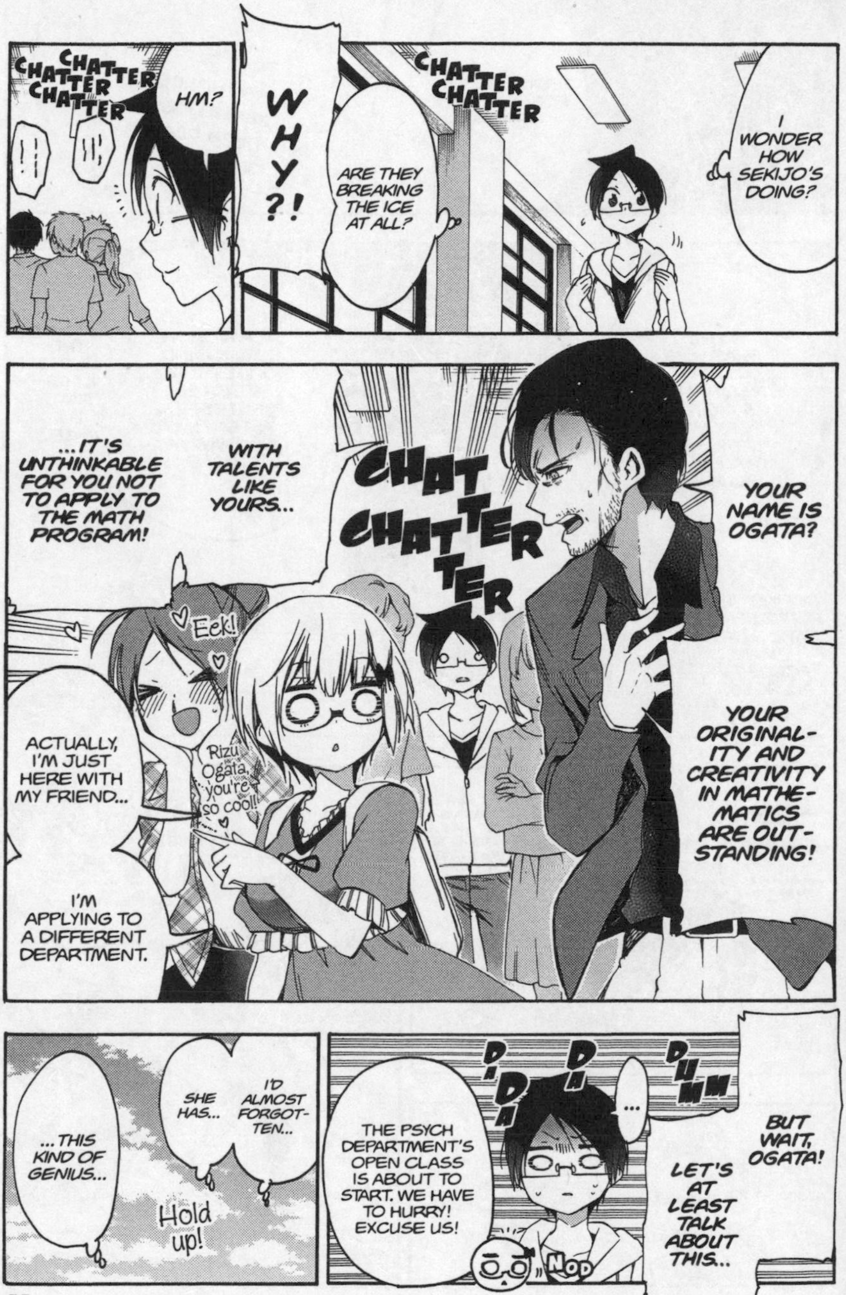
I WONDER HOW SEKIJO'S DOING?
CHATTER CHATTER
ARE THEY BREAKING THE ICE AT ALL?
WHY?!
HM?
CHATTER CHATTER CHATTER
!!
YOUR NAME IS OGATA?
YOUR ORIGINALITY AND CREATIVITY IN MATHEMATICS ARE OUTSTANDING!
CHAT CHATTER
WITH TALENTS LIKE YOURS...
...IT'S UNTHINKABLE FOR YOU NOT TO APPLY TO THE MATH PROGRAM!
Eek!
Rizu Ogata, you're so cool!
ACTUALLY, I'M JUST HERE WITH MY FRIEND...
I'M APPLYING TO A DIFFERENT DEPARTMENT.
BUT WAIT, OGATA!
LET'S AT LEAST TALK ABOUT THIS...
DUHN
DA DA DA
...
THE PSYCH DEPARTMENT'S OPEN CLASS IS ABOUT TO START. WE HAVE TO HURRY! EXCUSE US!
NOD
I'D ALMOST FORGOTTEN...
SHE HAS...
...THIS KIND OF GENIUS...
Hold up!

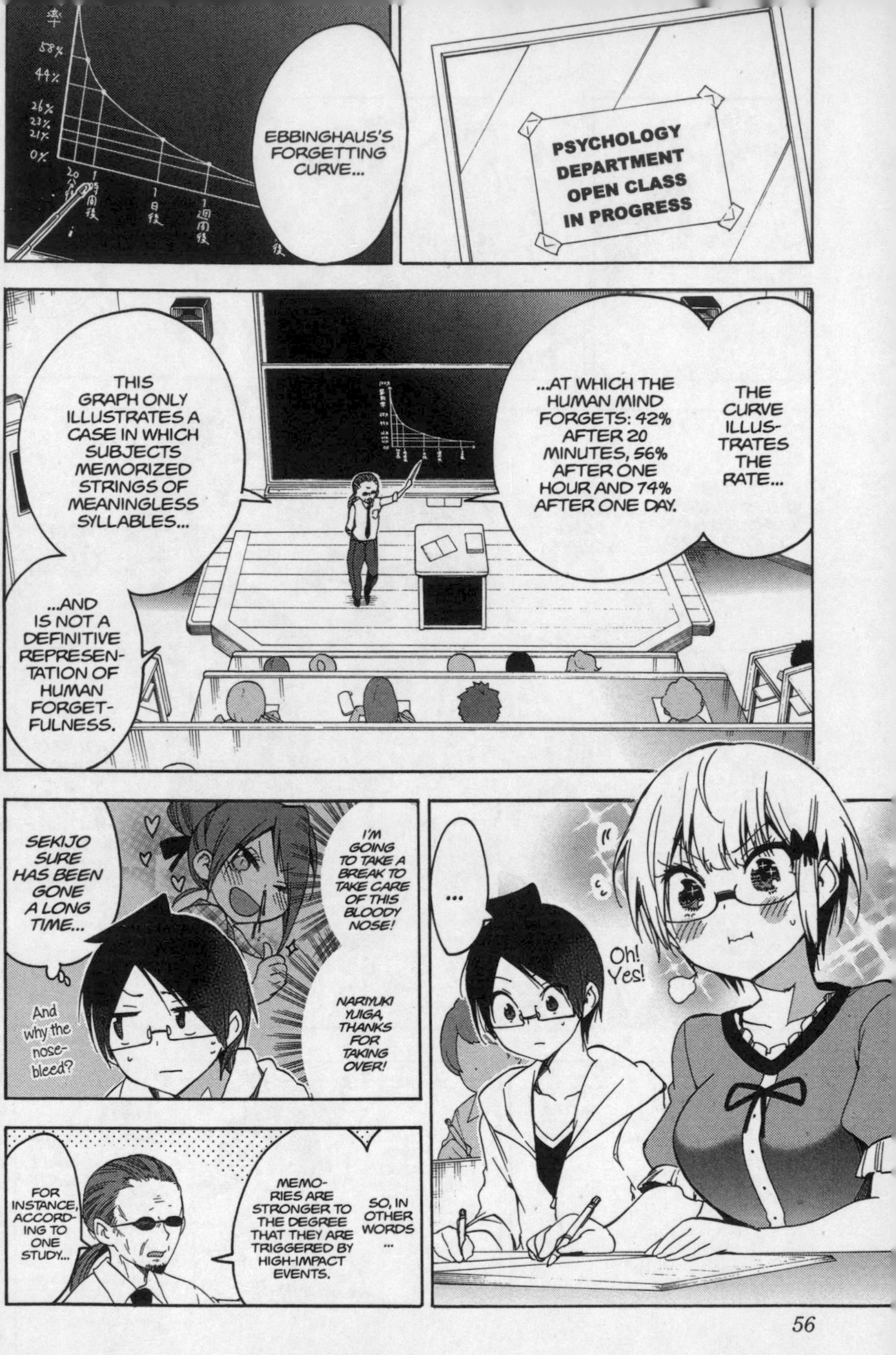
PSYCHOLOGY DEPARTMENT OPEN CLASS IN PROGRESS
EBBINGHAUS'S FORGETTING CURVE...
58%
44%
26%
23%
21%
0%
THE CURVE ILLUSTRATES THE RATE...
...AT WHICH THE HUMAN MIND FORGETS: 42% AFTER 20 MINUTES, 56% AFTER ONE HOUR AND 74% AFTER ONE DAY.
THIS GRAPH ONLY ILLUSTRATES A CASE IN WHICH SUBJECTS MEMORIZED STRINGS OF MEANINGLESS SYLLABLES...
...AND IS NOT A DEFINITIVE REPRESENTATION OF HUMAN FORGETFULNESS.
...
Oh! Yes!
I'M GOING TO TAKE A BREAK TO TAKE CARE OF THIS BLOODY NOSE!
SEKIJO SURE HAS BEEN GONE A LONG TIME...
NARIYUKI YUIGA, THANKS FOR TAKING OVER!
And why the nose-bleed?
SO, IN OTHER WORDS...
MEMORIES ARE STRONGER TO THE DEGREE THAT THEY ARE TRIGGERED BY HIGH-IMPACT EVENTS.
FOR INSTANCE, ACCORDING TO ONE STUDY...

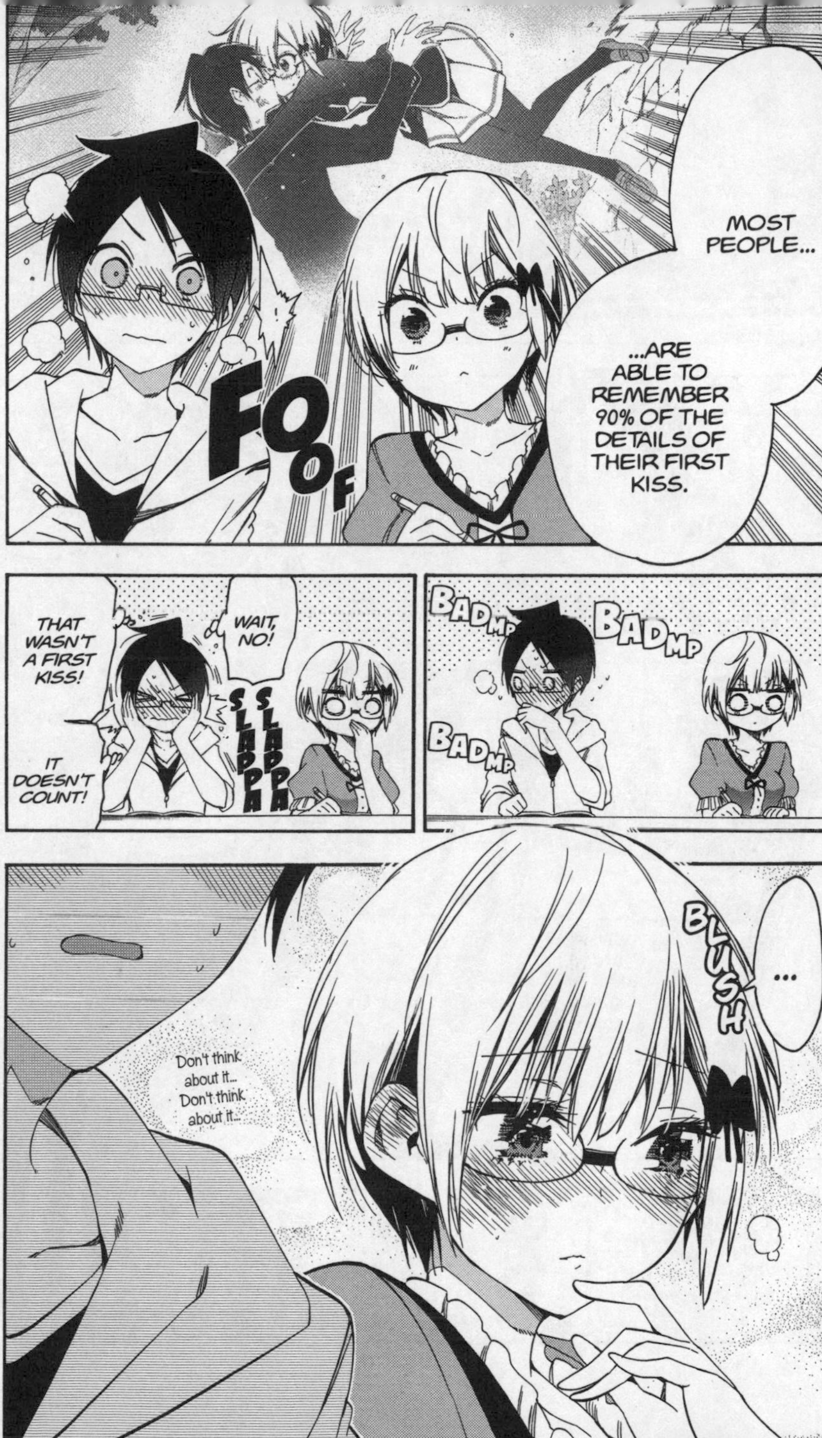
MOST PEOPLE...
...ARE ABLE TO REMEMBER 90% OF THE DETAILS OF THEIR FIRST KISS.
FOOOF
BADMP
BADMP
BADMP
WAIT, NO!
THAT WASN'T A FIRST KISS!
IT DOESN'T COUNT!
SLAPPA
SLAPPA
BLUSH
...
Don't think about it... Don't think about it...

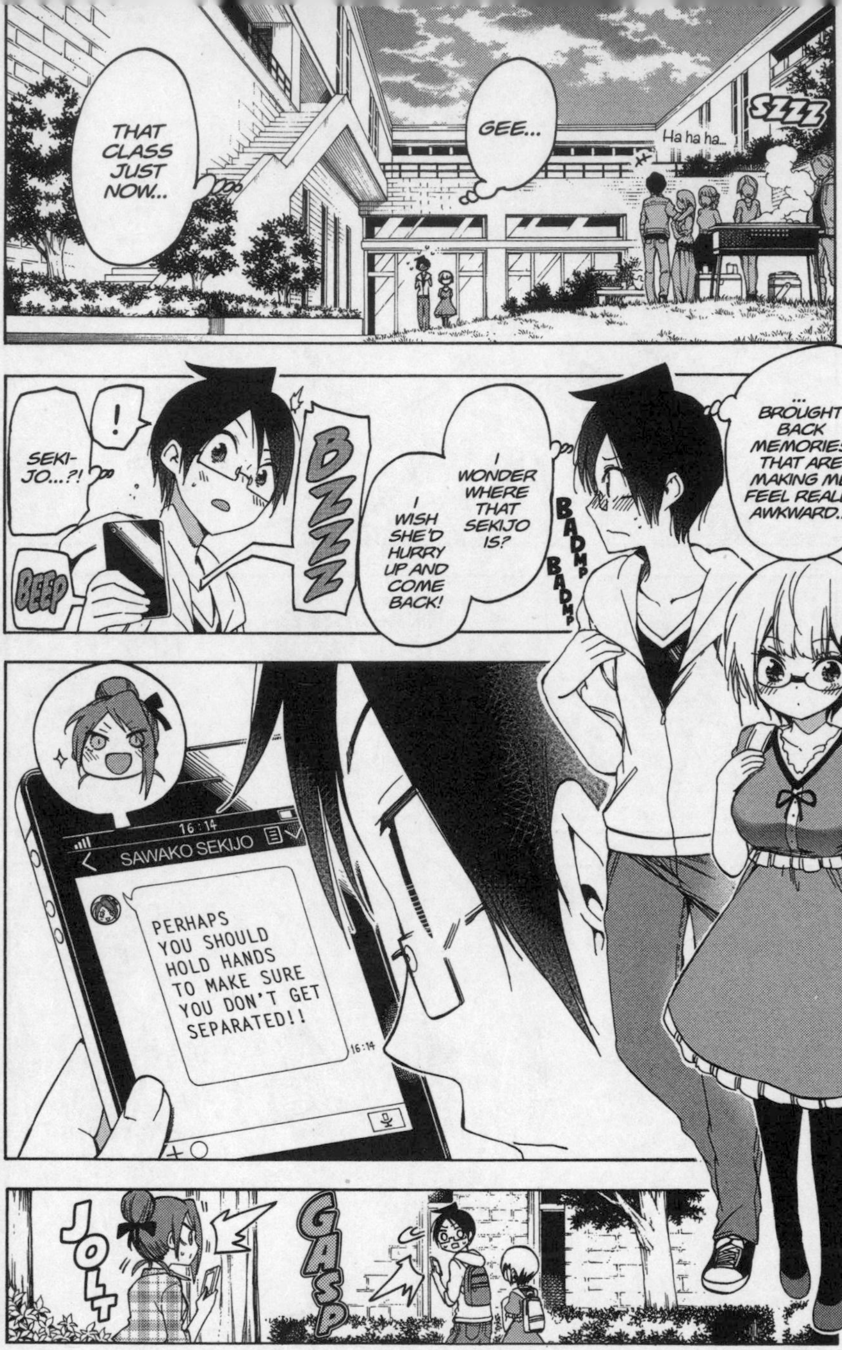
SZZZ
Ha ha ha...
GEE...
THAT CLASS JUST NOW...
...BROUGHT BACK MEMORIES THAT ARE MAKING ME FEEL REALLY AWKWARD...
BADMP BADMP
I WONDER WHERE THAT SEKIJO IS?
I WISH SHE'D HURRY UP AND COME BACK!
BZZZ
!
SEKI-JO...?!
BEEP
16:14
SAWAKO SEKIJO
PERHAPS YOU SHOULD HOLD HANDS TO MAKE SURE YOU DON'T GET SEPARATED!!
16:14
GASP
JOLT

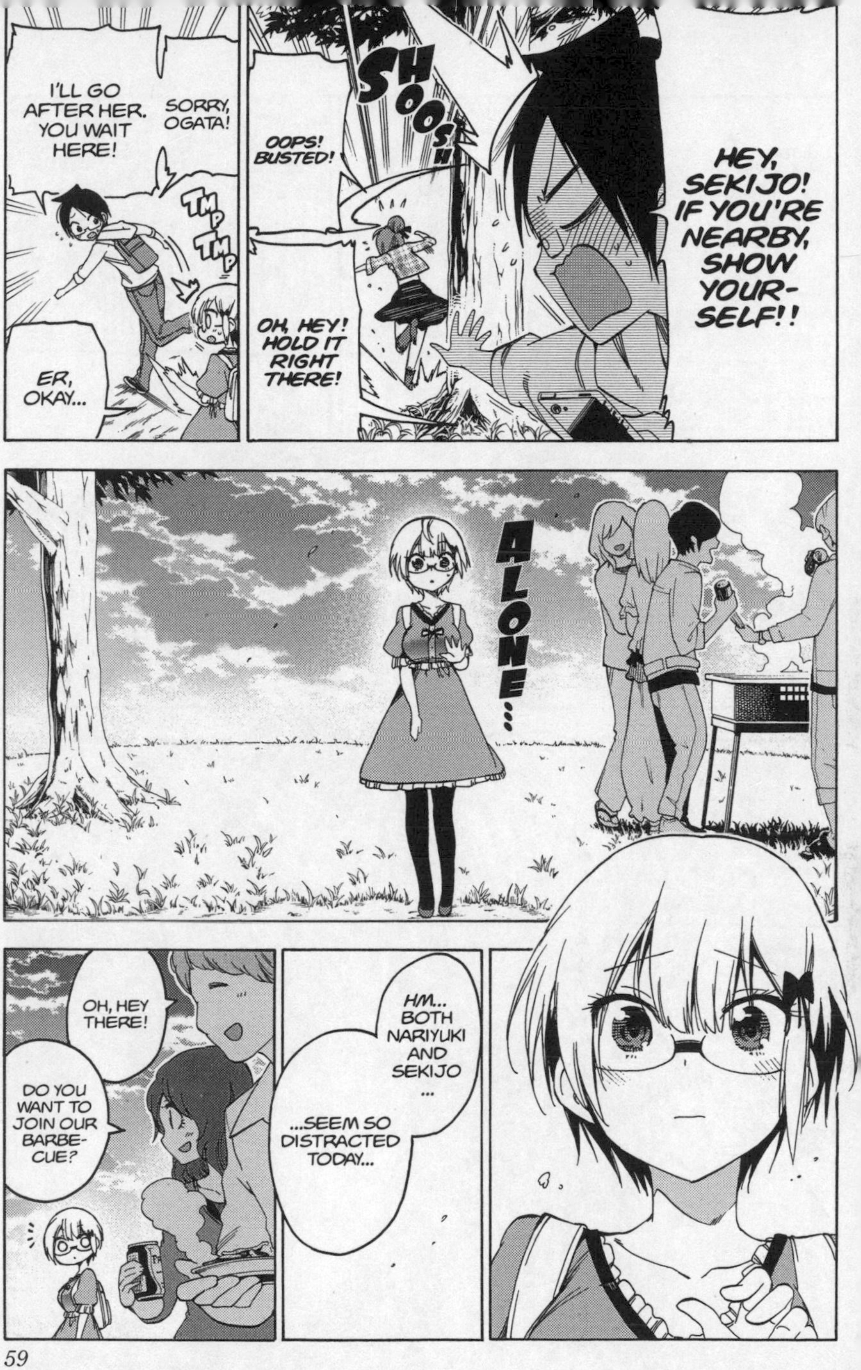
HEY, SEKIJO! IF YOU'RE NEARBY, SHOW YOUR-SELF!!
SHOOSH
OOPS! BUSTED!
OH, HEY! HOLD IT RIGHT THERE!
SORRY, OGATA!
I'LL GO AFTER HER. YOU WAIT HERE!
TMP TMP
ER, OKAY...
ALONE...
HM... BOTH NARIYUKI AND SEKIJO ...
...SEEM SO DISTRACTED TODAY...
OH, HEY THERE!
DO YOU WANT TO JOIN OUR BARBE-CUE?

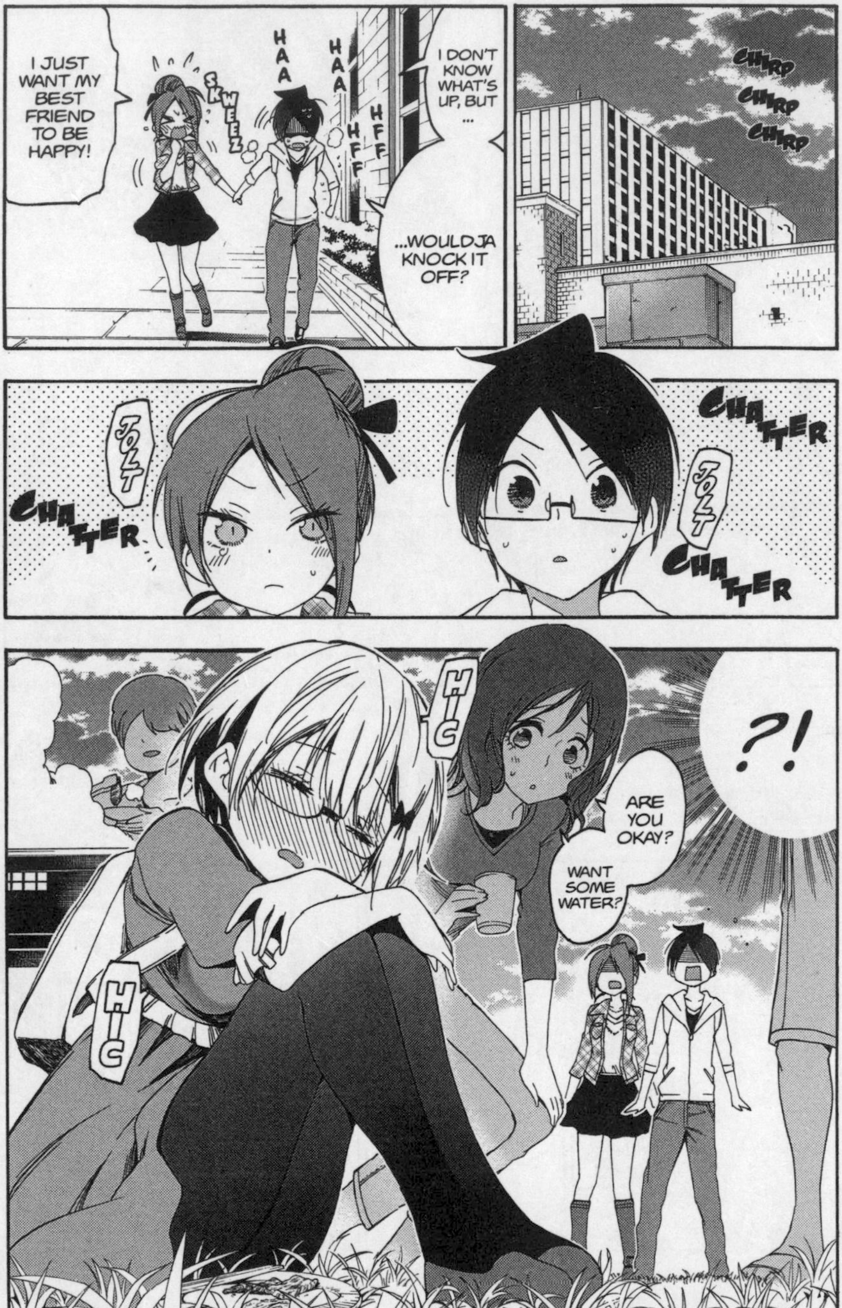
CHIRP
CHIRP
CHIRP
I DON'T KNOW WHAT'S UP, BUT ...
...WOULDJA KNOCK IT OFF?
HAA HAA
HFF HFF
SKWEEZ
I JUST WANT MY BEST FRIEND TO BE HAPPY!
CHATTER
JOLT
CHATTER
JOLT
CHATTER
?!
ARE YOU OKAY?
WANT SOME WATER?
HIC
HIC

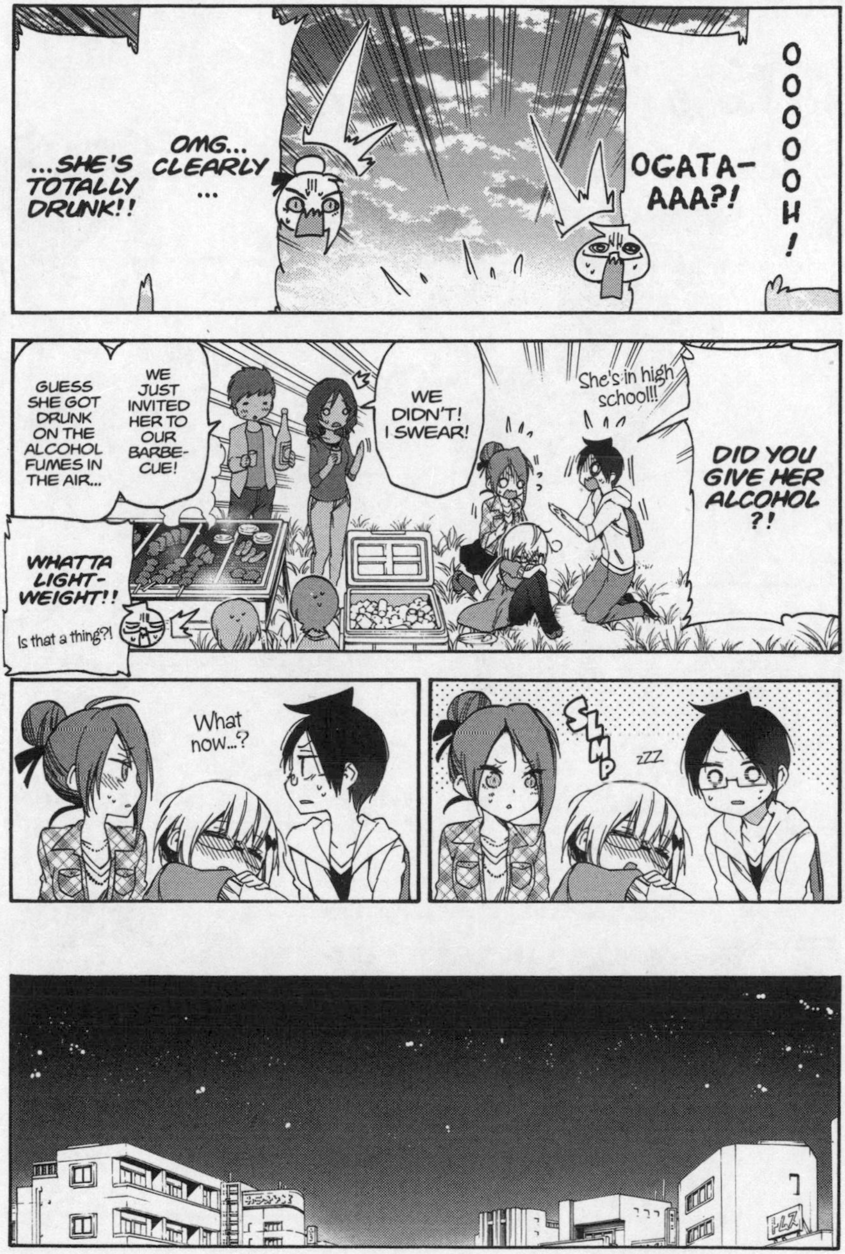
OOOOOH!
OGATA-AAA?!
OMG... CLEARLY ...
...SHE'S TOTALLY DRUNK!!
DID YOU GIVE HER ALCOHOL?!
She's in high school!!!
WE DIDN'T! I SWEAR!
WE JUST INVITED HER TO OUR BARBE-CUE!
GUESS SHE GOT DRUNK ON THE ALCOHOL FUMES IN THE AIR...
WHATTA LIGHT-WEIGHT!!
Is that a thing?!
SLMP
ZZZ
What now...?

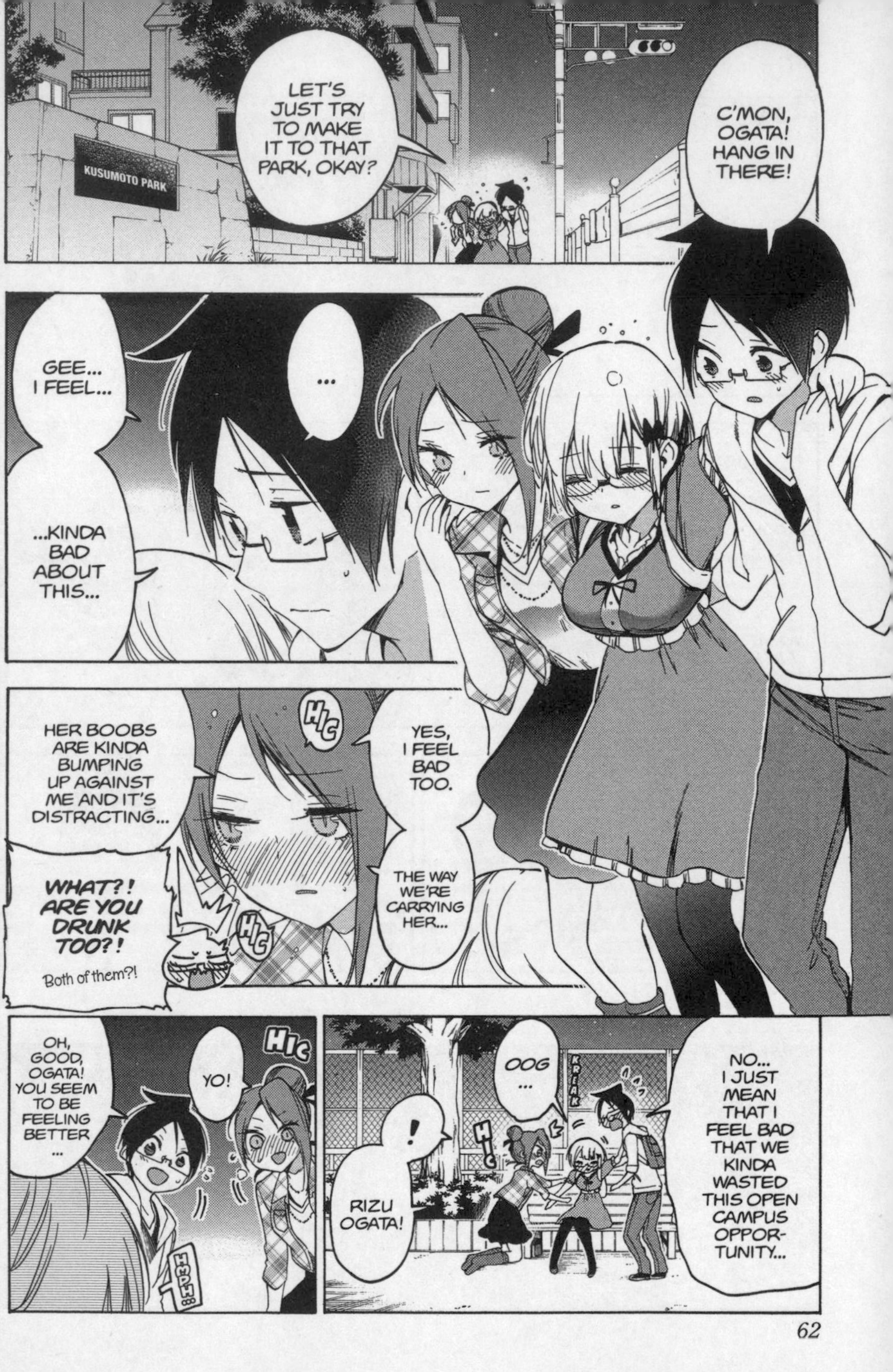
C'MON, OGATA! HANG IN THERE!
LET'S JUST TRY TO MAKE IT TO THAT PARK, OKAY?
KUSUMOTO PARK
...
GEE... I FEEL...
...KINDA BAD ABOUT THIS...
HIC
YES, I FEEL BAD TOO.
THE WAY WE'RE CARRYING HER...
HER BOOBS ARE KINDA BUMPING UP AGAINST ME AND IT'S DISTRACTING...
HIC
WHAT?! ARE YOU DRUNK TOO?!
Both of them?!
NO... I JUST MEAN THAT I FEEL BAD THAT WE KINDA WASTED THIS OPEN CAMPUS OPPOR-TUNITY...
KRIAK
OOG...
HIC
!
RIZU OGATA!
HIC
YO!
OH, GOOD, OGATA! YOU SEEM TO BE FEELING BETTER...
HMPH!!

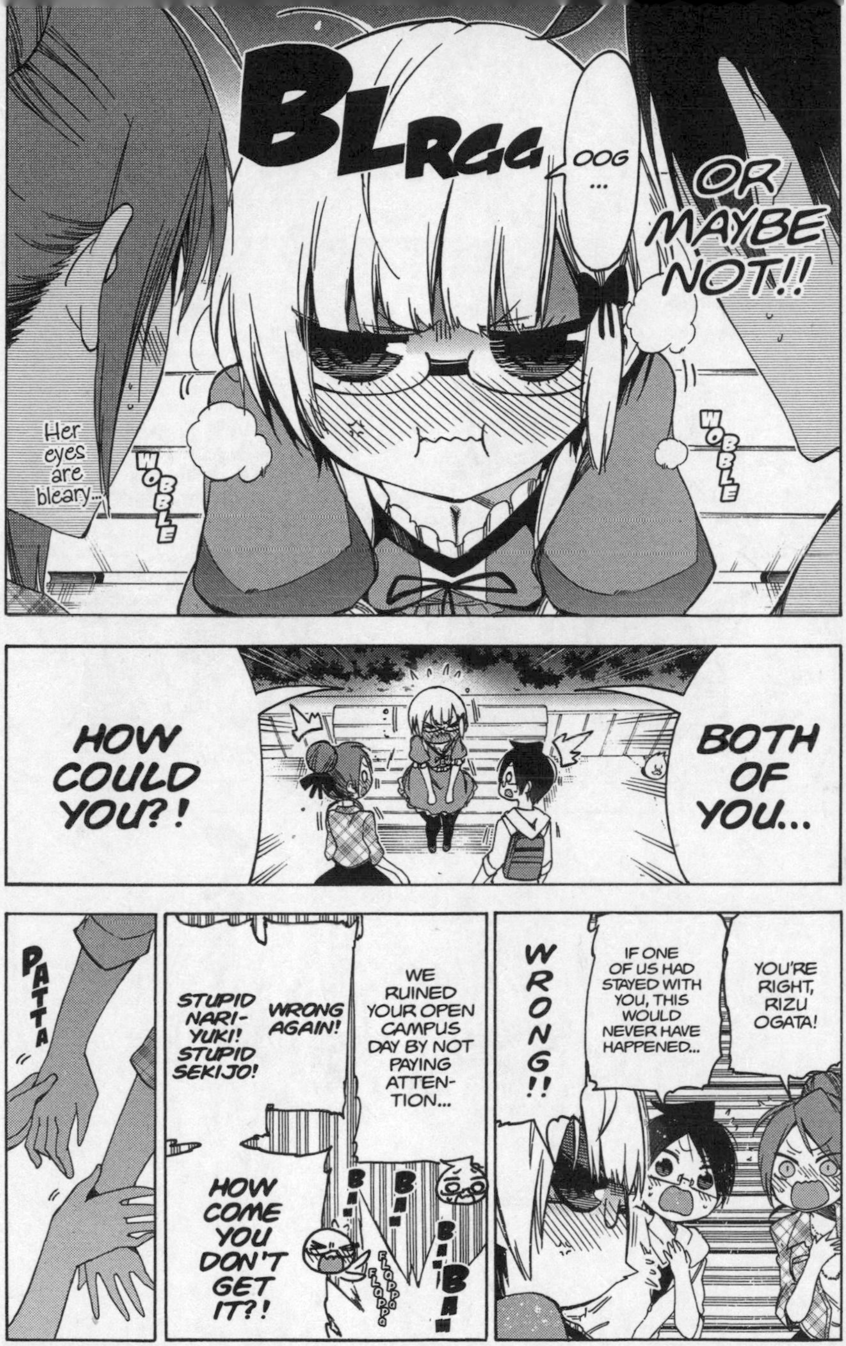
OR MAYBE NOT!!
OOG ...
BLRGG
WOBBLE
Her eyes are bleary...
WOBBLE
BOTH OF YOU...
HOW COULD YOU?!
YOU'RE RIGHT, RIZU OGATA!
IF ONE OF US HAD STAYED WITH YOU, THIS WOULD NEVER HAVE HAPPENED...
WRONG!!
WE RUINED YOUR OPEN CAMPUS DAY BY NOT PAYING ATTEN-TION...
WRONG AGAIN!
STUPID NARI-YUKI! STUPID SEKIJO!
BA BA
BA BA
BA
FLAPPA FLAPPA
HOW COME YOU DON'T GET IT?!
PATTA

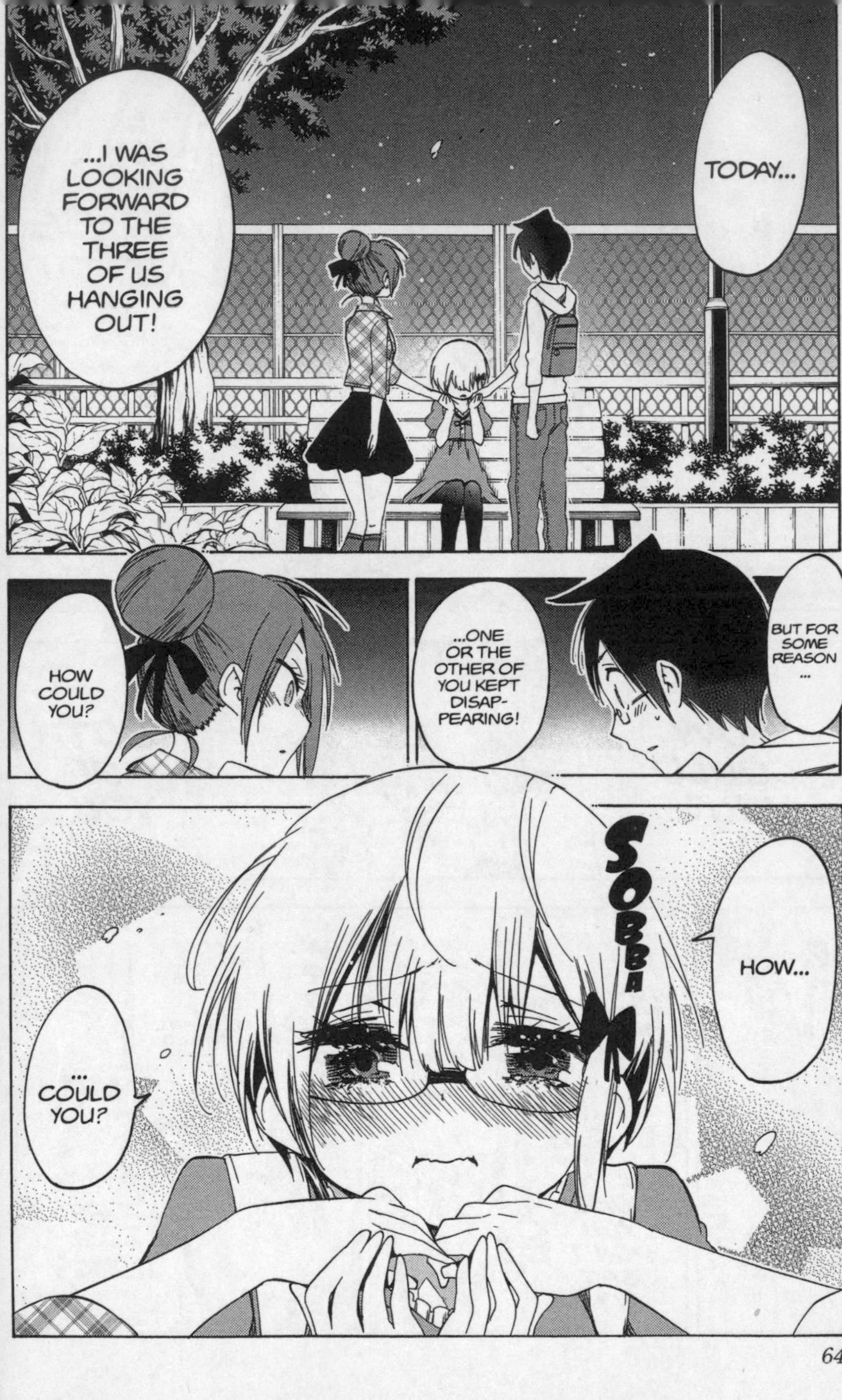
TODAY...
...I WAS LOOKING FORWARD TO THE THREE OF US HANGING OUT!
BUT FOR SOME REASON ...
...ONE OR THE OTHER OF YOU KEPT DISAP-PEARING!
HOW COULD YOU?
SOBBA
HOW...
... COULD YOU?

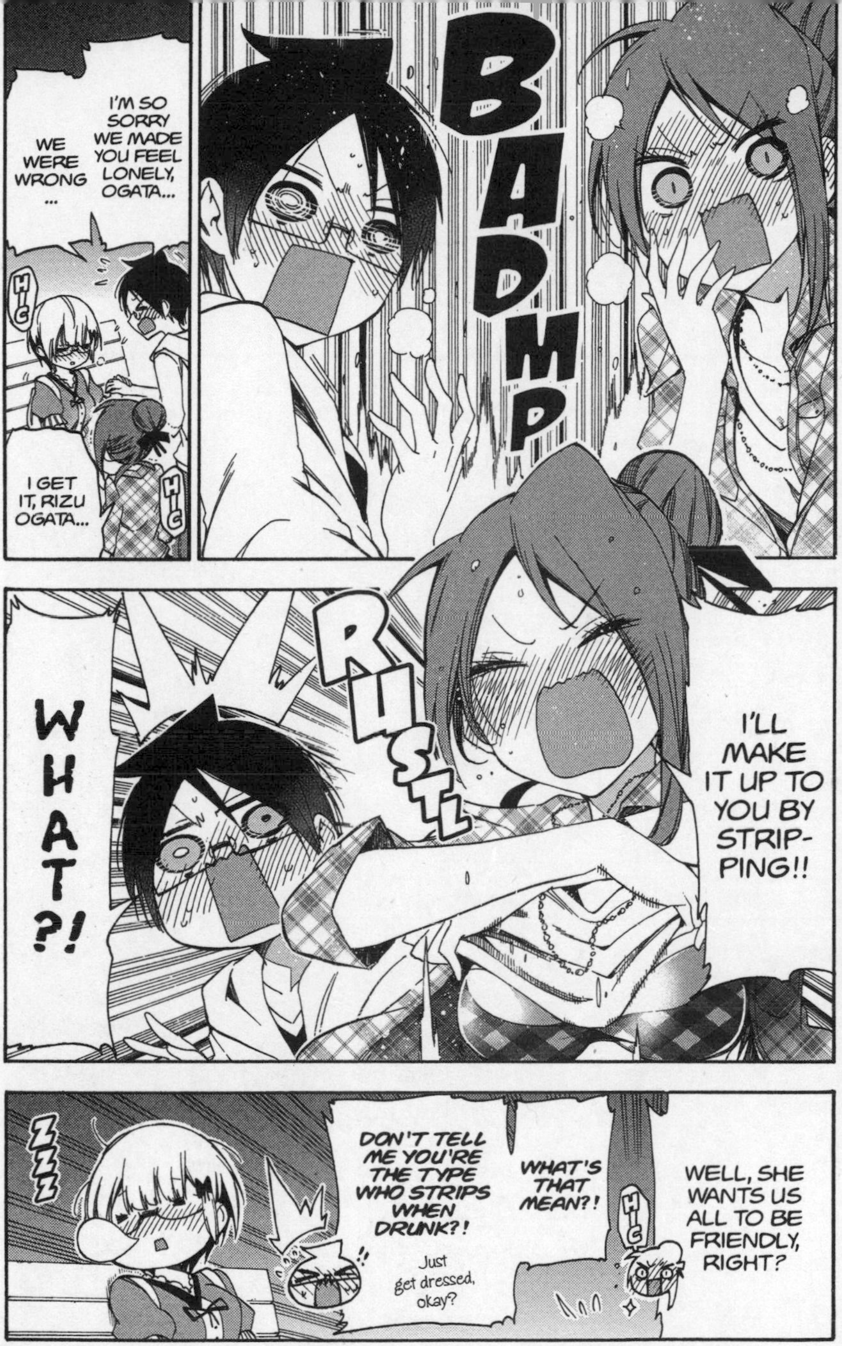
BADUMP
I'M SO SORRY WE MADE YOU FEEL LONELY, OGATA...
WE WERE WRONG ...
HIC
HIC
I GET IT, RIZU OGATA...
I'LL MAKE IT UP TO YOU BY STRIP-PING!!
RUSTL
WHAT?!
WELL, SHE WANTS US ALL TO BE FRIENDLY, RIGHT?
HIC
WHAT'S THAT MEAN?!
DON'T TELL ME YOU'RE THE TYPE WHO STRIPS WHEN DRUNK?!
Just get dressed, okay?
ZZZ

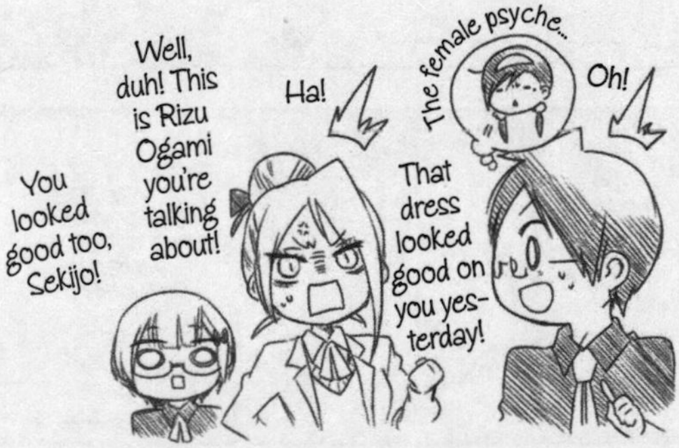
Oh!
The female psyche...
That dress looked good on you yes-terday!
Ha!
Well, duh! This is Rizu Ogami you're talking about!
You looked good too, Sekijo!

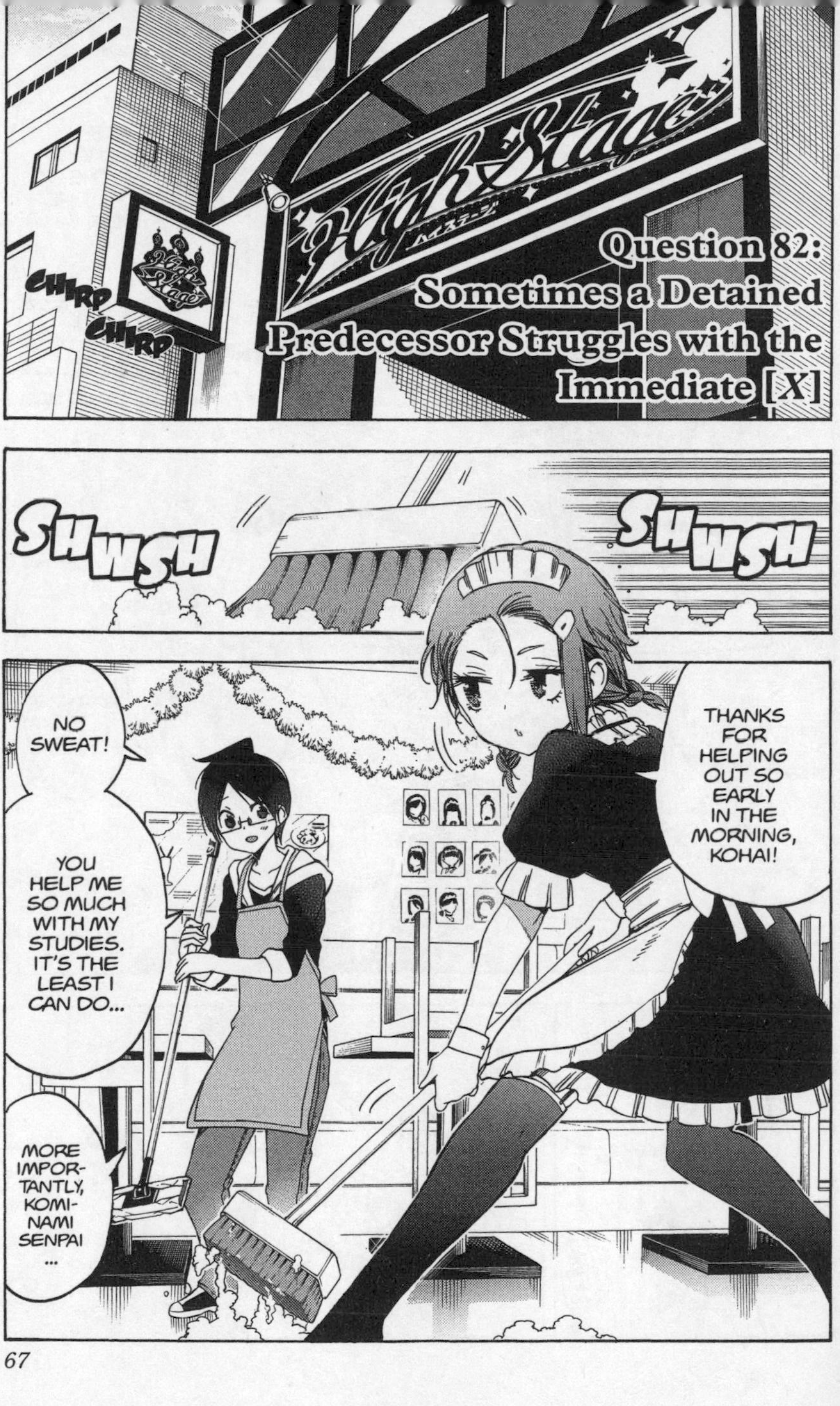
High Stage
CHIRP CHIRP
Question 82: Sometimes a Detained Predecessor Struggles with the Immediate [X]
SHWSH
SHWSH
THANKS FOR HELPING OUT SO EARLY IN THE MORNING, KOHAI!
NO SWEAT!
YOU HELP ME SO MUCH WITH MY STUDIES. IT'S THE LEAST I CAN DO...
MORE IMPORTANTLY, KOMINAMI SENPAI...

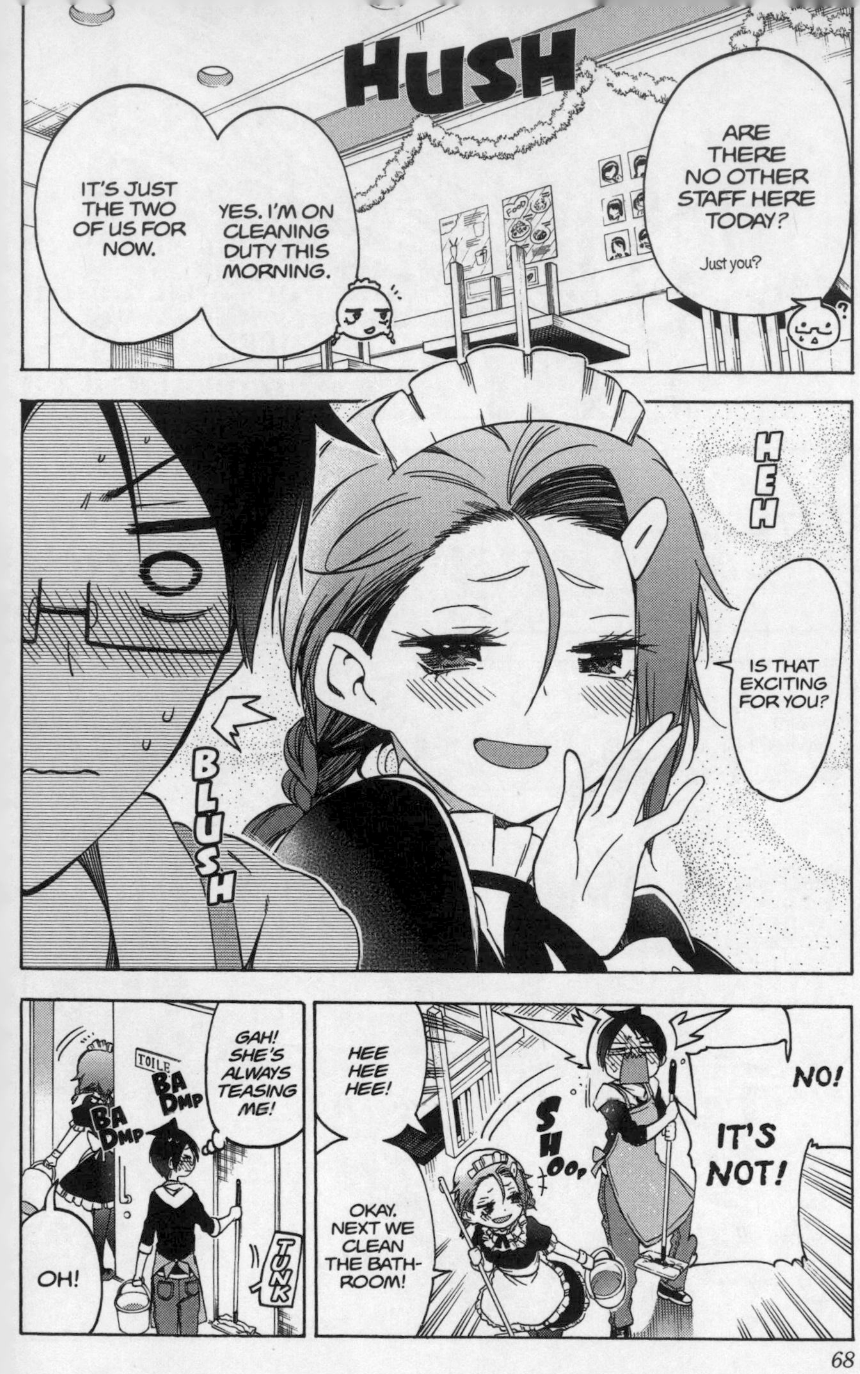
HUSH
ARE THERE NO OTHER STAFF HERE TODAY?
Just you?
YES. I'M ON CLEANING DUTY THIS MORNING.
IT'S JUST THE TWO OF US FOR NOW.
HEH
IS THAT EXCITING FOR YOU?
BLUSH
NO!
IT'S NOT!
SHOOP
HEE HEE HEE!
OKAY. NEXT WE CLEAN THE BATH-ROOM!
GAH! SHE'S ALWAYS TEASING ME!
TOILE
BA DMP
BA DMP
TUNK
OH!

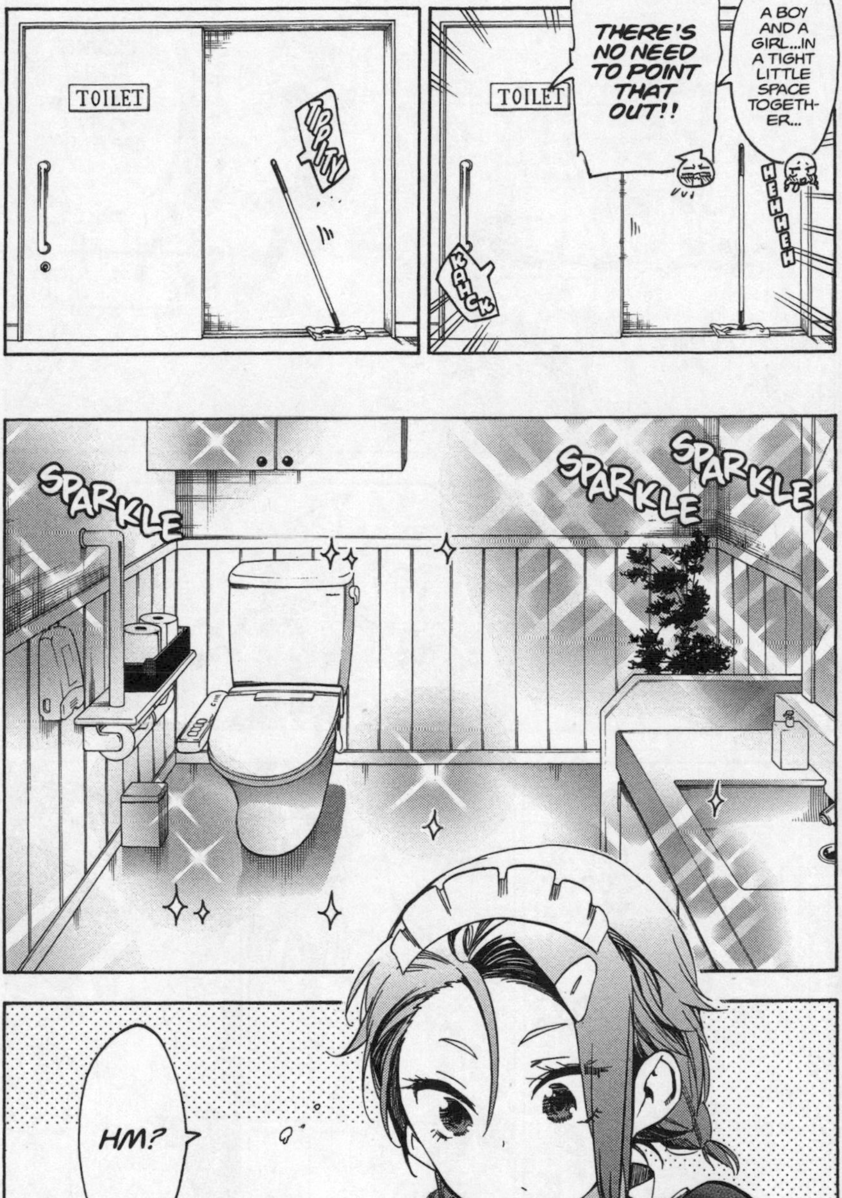
A BOY AND A GIRL...IN A TIGHT LITTLE SPACE TOGETHER...
HEHHEH
THERE'S NO NEED TO POINT THAT OUT!!
TOILET
KAHCK
TOILET
TIPPITY
SPARKLE
SPARKLE
SPARKLE
HM?

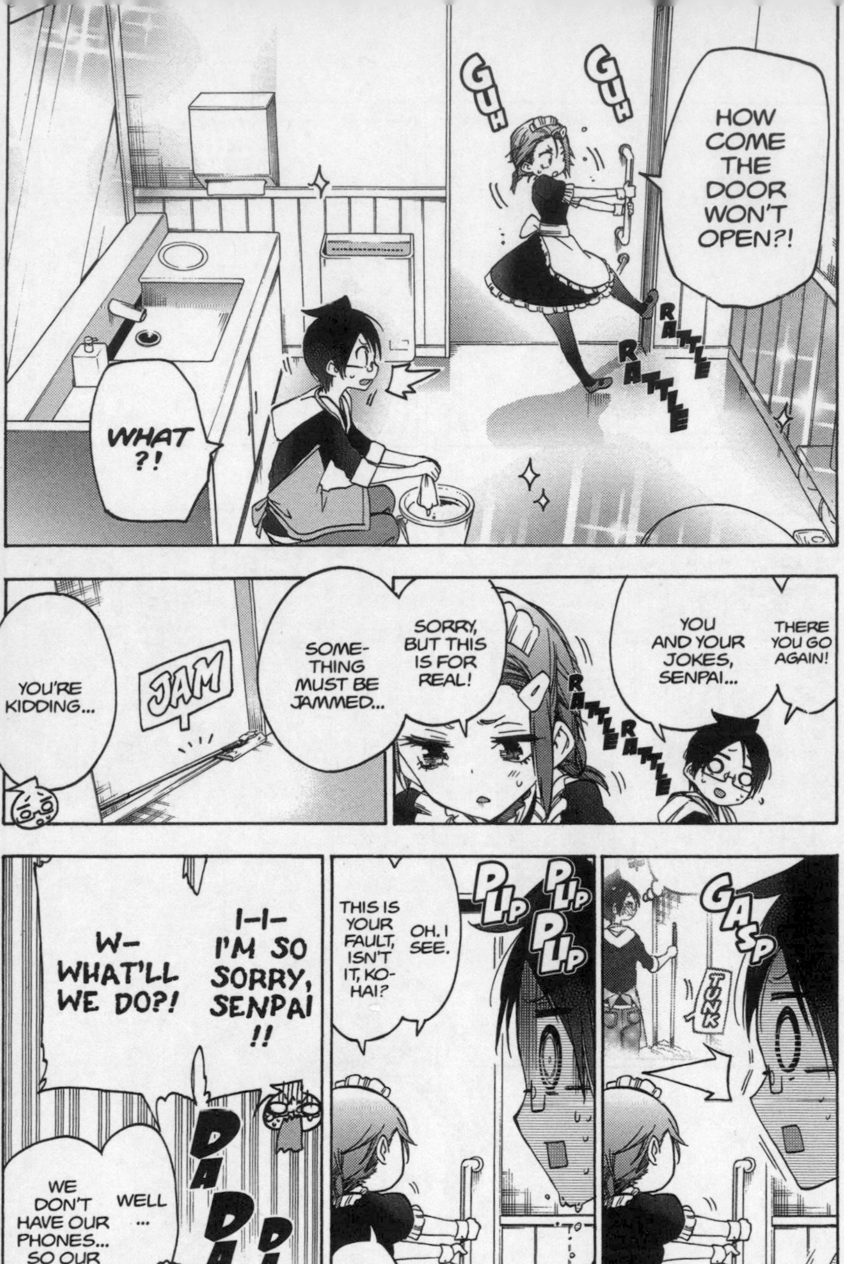
GUH
GUH
HOW COME THE DOOR WON'T OPEN?!
RATTLE
RATTLE
WHAT?!
THERE YOU GO AGAIN!
YOU AND YOUR JOKES, SENPAI...
RATTLE
RATTLE
SORRY, BUT THIS IS FOR REAL!
SOME-THING MUST BE JAMMED...
JAM
YOU'RE KIDDING...
GASP
TUNK
GUH
GUH
PLUP
PLUP
PLUP
OH. I SEE.
THIS IS YOUR FAULT, ISN'T IT, KO-HAI?
GOTCHA.
GUH
GUH
I-I-I'M SO SORRY, SENPAI!!
W-WHAT'LL WE DO?!
DA
DA
DA
DUM
WELL...
WE DON'T HAVE OUR PHONES... SO OUR ONLY OPTION IS...

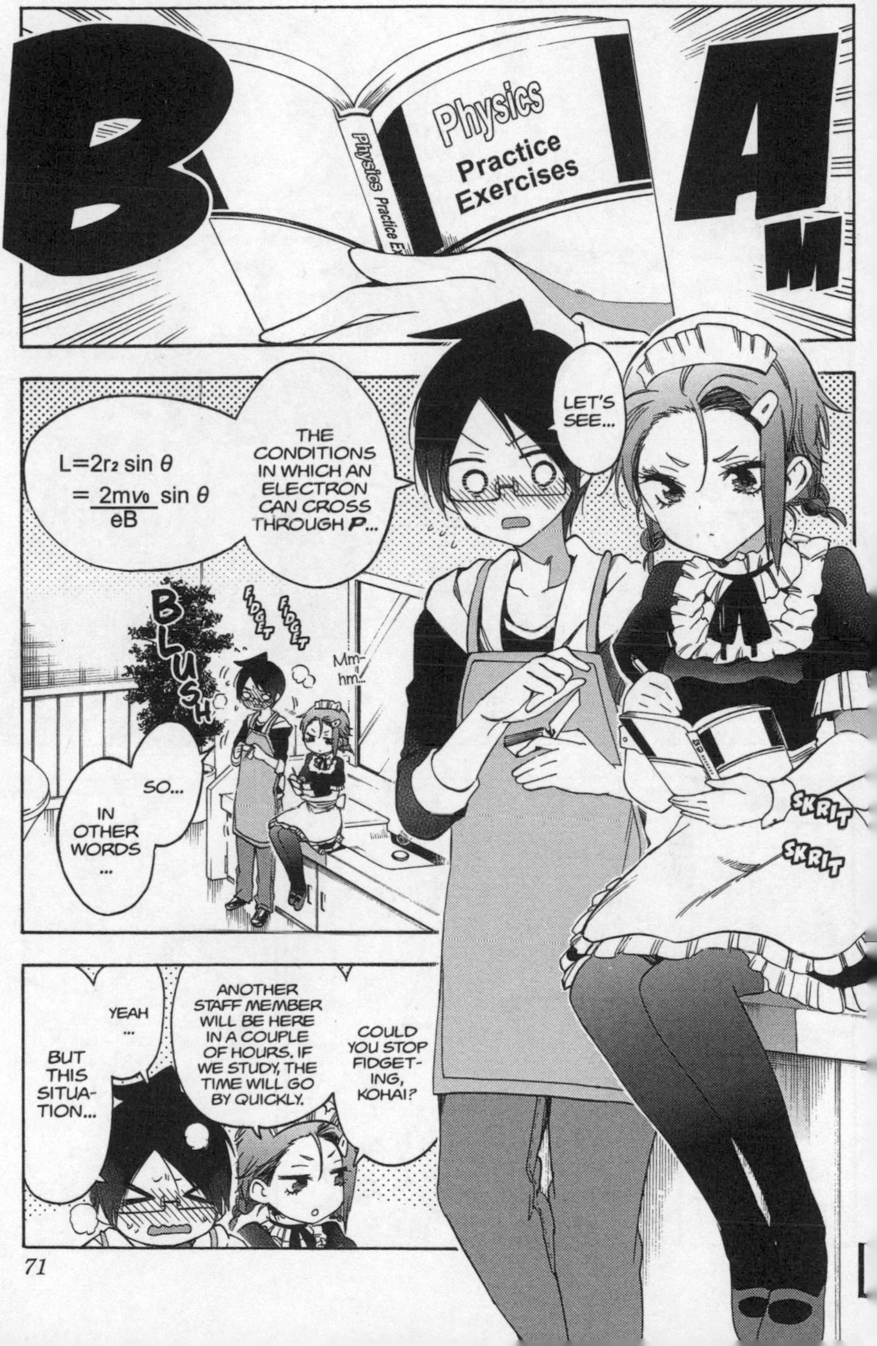
BAM
Physics
Physics Practice Exercises
Physics Practice Ex
LET'S SEE...
SKRIT
SKRIT
THE CONDITIONS IN WHICH AN ELECTRON CAN CROSS THROUGH P...
$L=2r_2 \sin\theta = \dfrac{2mv_0}{eB}\sin\theta$
BLUSH
FIDGET
FIDGET
Mm-hm...
SO...
IN OTHER WORDS...
COULD YOU STOP FIDGET-ING, KOHAI?
ANOTHER STAFF MEMBER WILL BE HERE IN A COUPLE OF HOURS. IF WE STUDY, THE TIME WILL GO BY QUICKLY.
YEAH...
BUT THIS SITUA-TION...

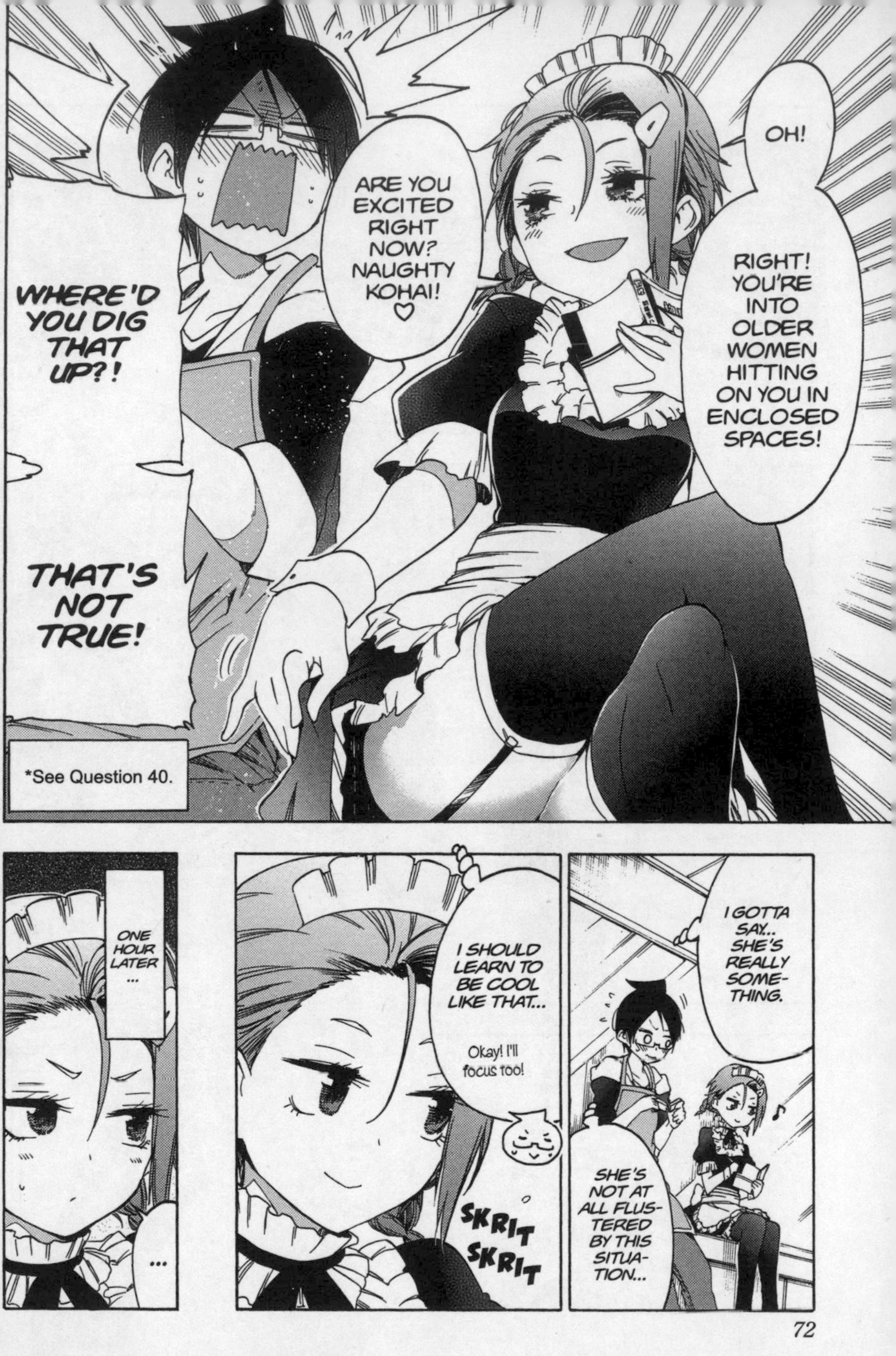
OH!
RIGHT! YOU'RE INTO OLDER WOMEN HITTING ON YOU IN ENCLOSED SPACES!
ARE YOU EXCITED RIGHT NOW? NAUGHTY KOHAI! ♡
WHERE'D YOU DIG THAT UP?!
THAT'S NOT TRUE!
*See Question 40.
I GOTTA SAY... SHE'S REALLY SOME-THING.
SHE'S NOT AT ALL FLUS-TERED BY THIS SITUA-TION...
I SHOULD LEARN TO BE COOL LIKE THAT...
Okay! I'll focus too!
SKRIT SKRIT
ONE HOUR LATER ...
...

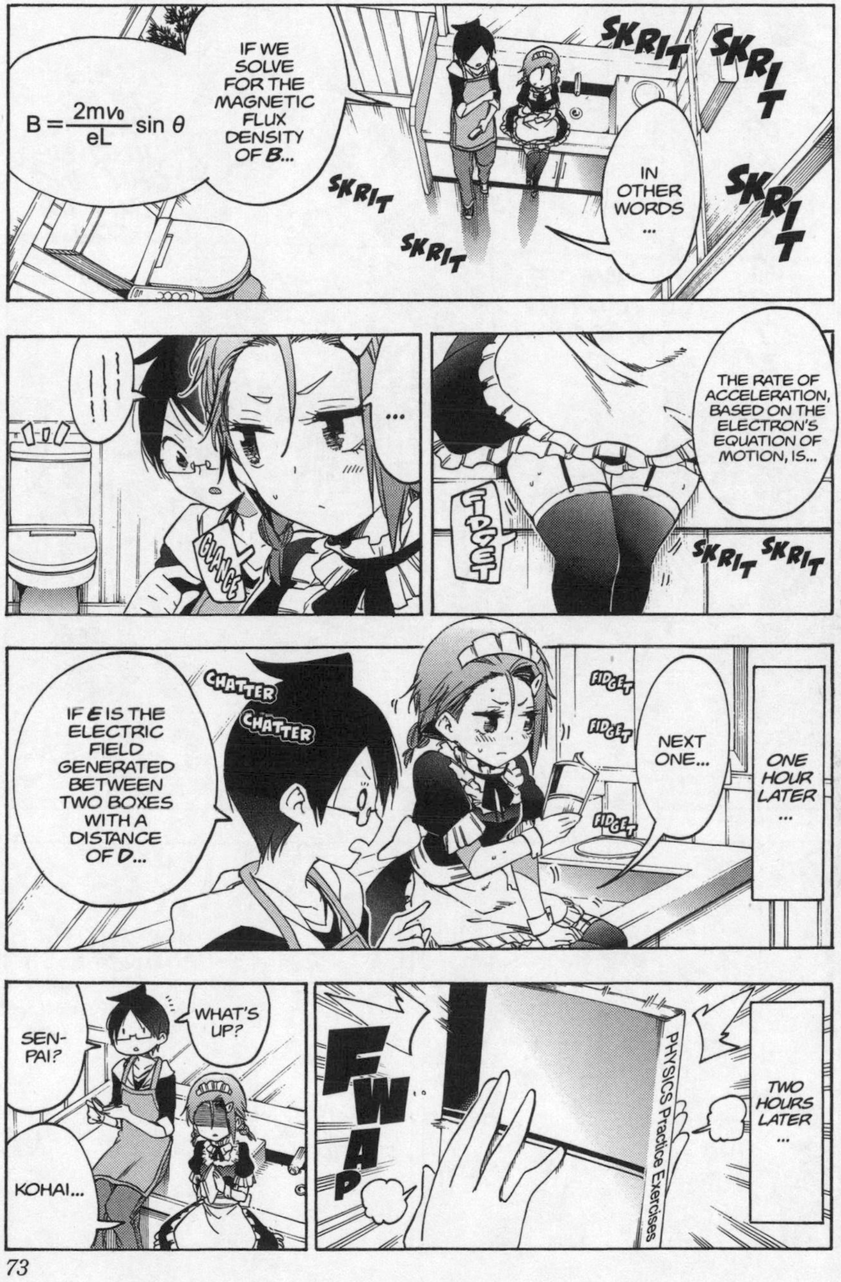
SKRIT SKRIT
IN OTHER WORDS ...
SKRIT SKRIT
SKRIT
SKRIT
IF WE SOLVE FOR THE MAGNETIC FLUX DENSITY OF B...
$B = \frac{2mv_0}{eL} \sin\theta$
THE RATE OF ACCELERATION, BASED ON THE ELECTRON'S EQUATION OF MOTION, IS...
SKRIT SKRIT
FIDGET
...
!!!
GLANCE
ONE HOUR LATER ...
NEXT ONE...
FIDGET
FIDGET
FIDGET
CHATTER
CHATTER
IF E IS THE ELECTRIC FIELD GENERATED BETWEEN TWO BOXES WITH A DISTANCE OF D...
TWO HOURS LATER ...
PHYSICS Practice Exercises
FWAP
WHAT'S UP?
SEN-PAI?
KOHAI...

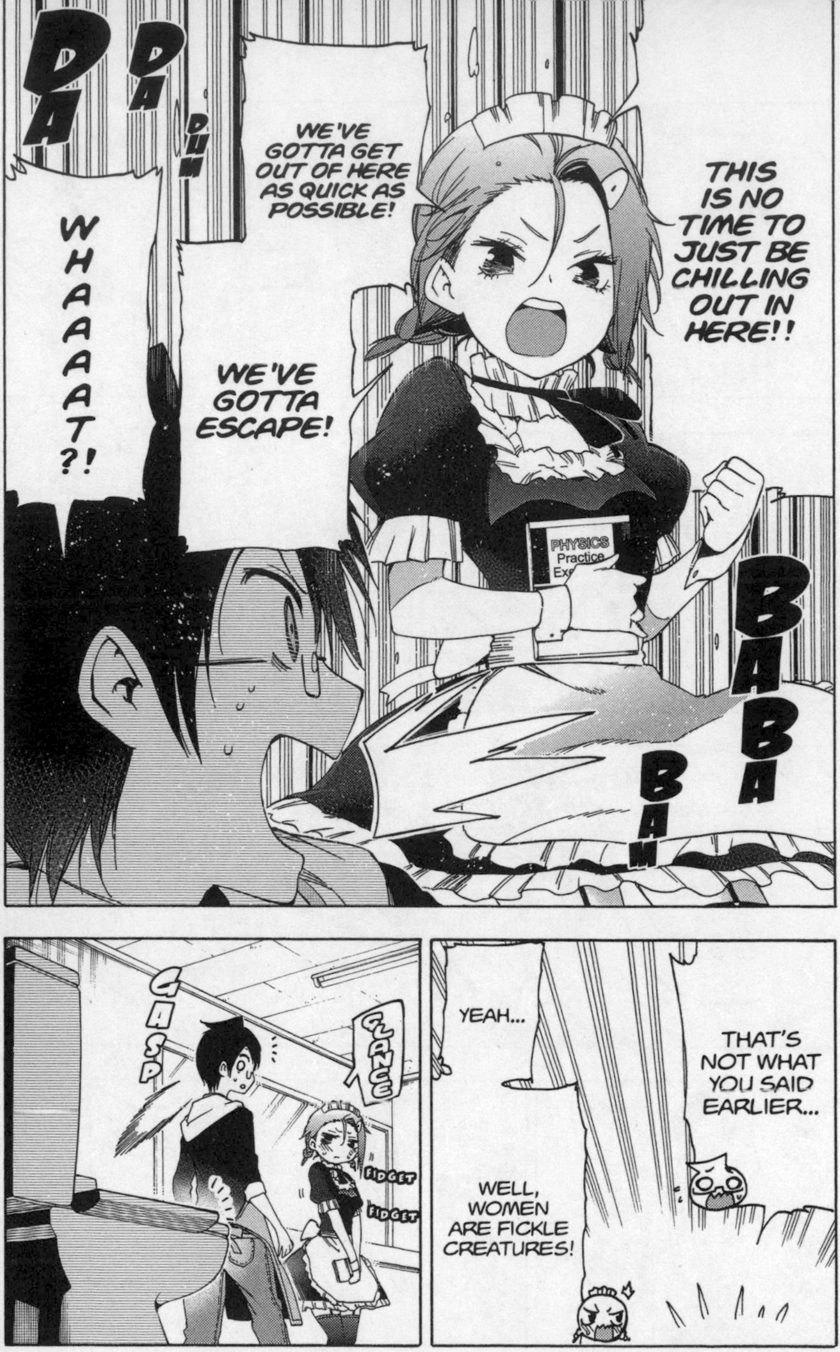
DA
DA
DUM
THIS IS NO TIME TO JUST BE CHILLING OUT IN HERE!!
WE'VE GOTTA GET OUT OF HERE AS QUICK AS POSSIBLE!
WE'VE GOTTA ESCAPE!
WHAAAAAT?!
PHYSICS Practice
BABA
BAM
THAT'S NOT WHAT YOU SAID EARLIER...
YEAH...
WELL, WOMEN ARE FICKLE CREATURES!
GLANCE
GASP
FIDGET
FIDGET

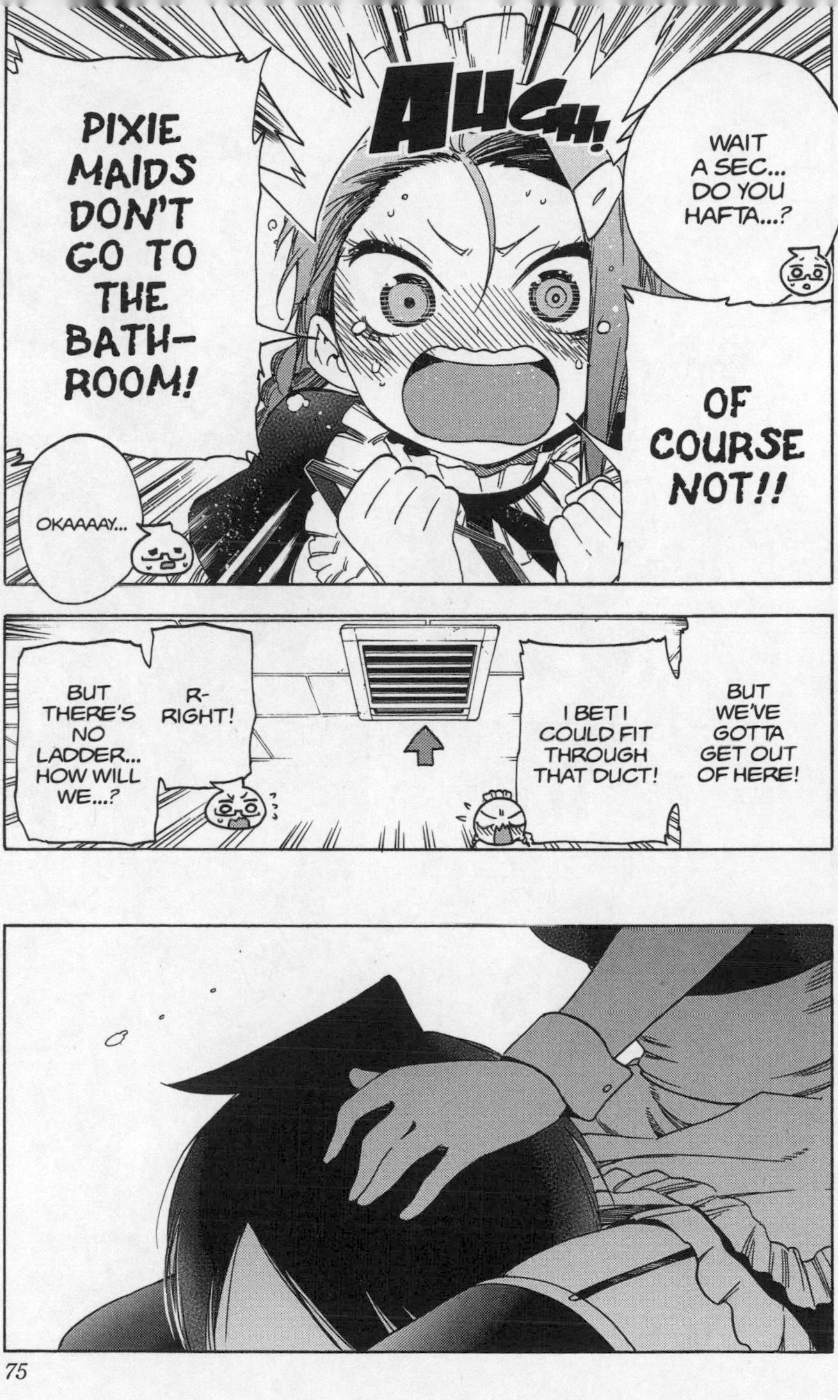
WAIT A SEC... DO YOU HAFTA...?
AUGH!
OF COURSE NOT!!
PIXIE MAIDS DON'T GO TO THE BATH-ROOM!
OKAAAAY...
BUT WE'VE GOTTA GET OUT OF HERE!
I BET I COULD FIT THROUGH THAT DUCT!
R-RIGHT!
BUT THERE'S NO LADDER... HOW WILL WE...?

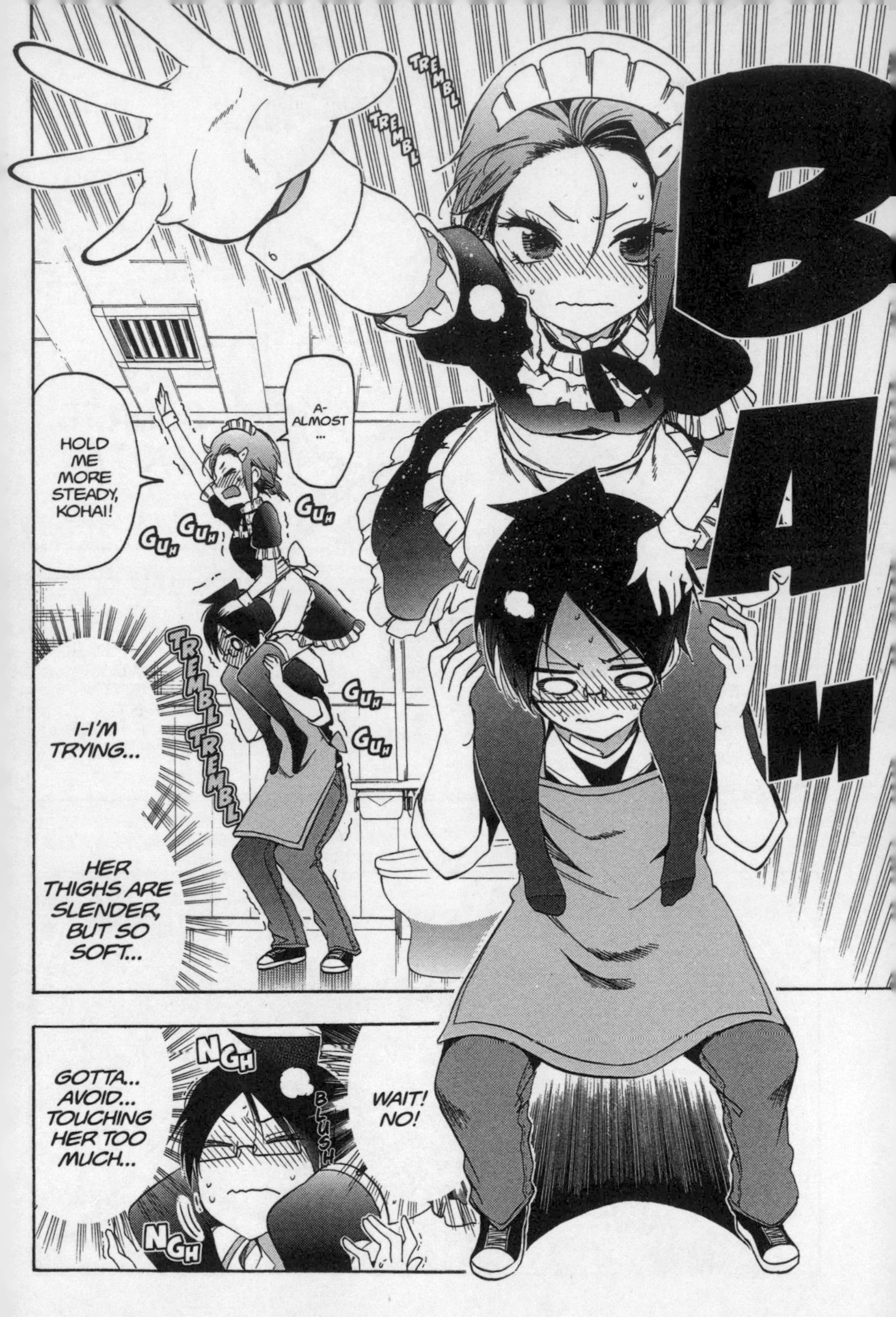
TREMBL
TREMBL
BAM
A-ALMOST...
HOLD ME MORE STEADY, KOHAI!
GUH
GUH
GUH
GUH
GUH
TREMBL TREMBL TREMBL
I-I'M TRYING...
HER THIGHS ARE SLENDER, BUT SO SOFT...
NGH
BLUSH
WAIT! NO!
GOTTA... AVOID... TOUCHING HER TOO MUCH...
NGH

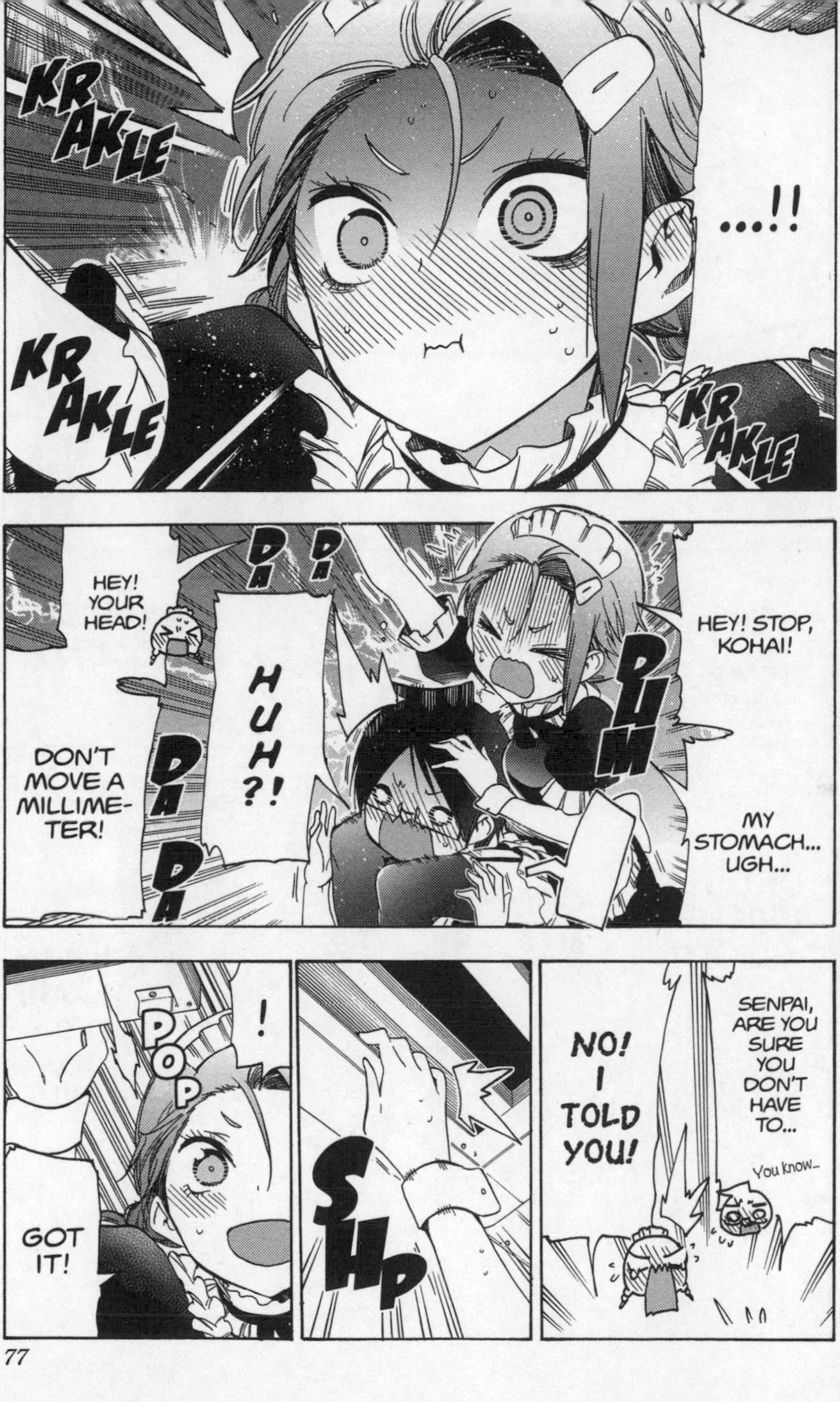
...!!
KRAKLE
KRAKLE
KRAKLE
HEY! STOP, KOHAI!
DUM
MY STOMACH... UGH...
HUH?!
DA DA
HEY! YOUR HEAD!
DON'T MOVE A MILLIMETER!
DA DA
SENPAI, ARE YOU SURE YOU DON'T HAVE TO...
You know...
NO! I TOLD YOU!
SHP
!
POP POP
GOT IT!

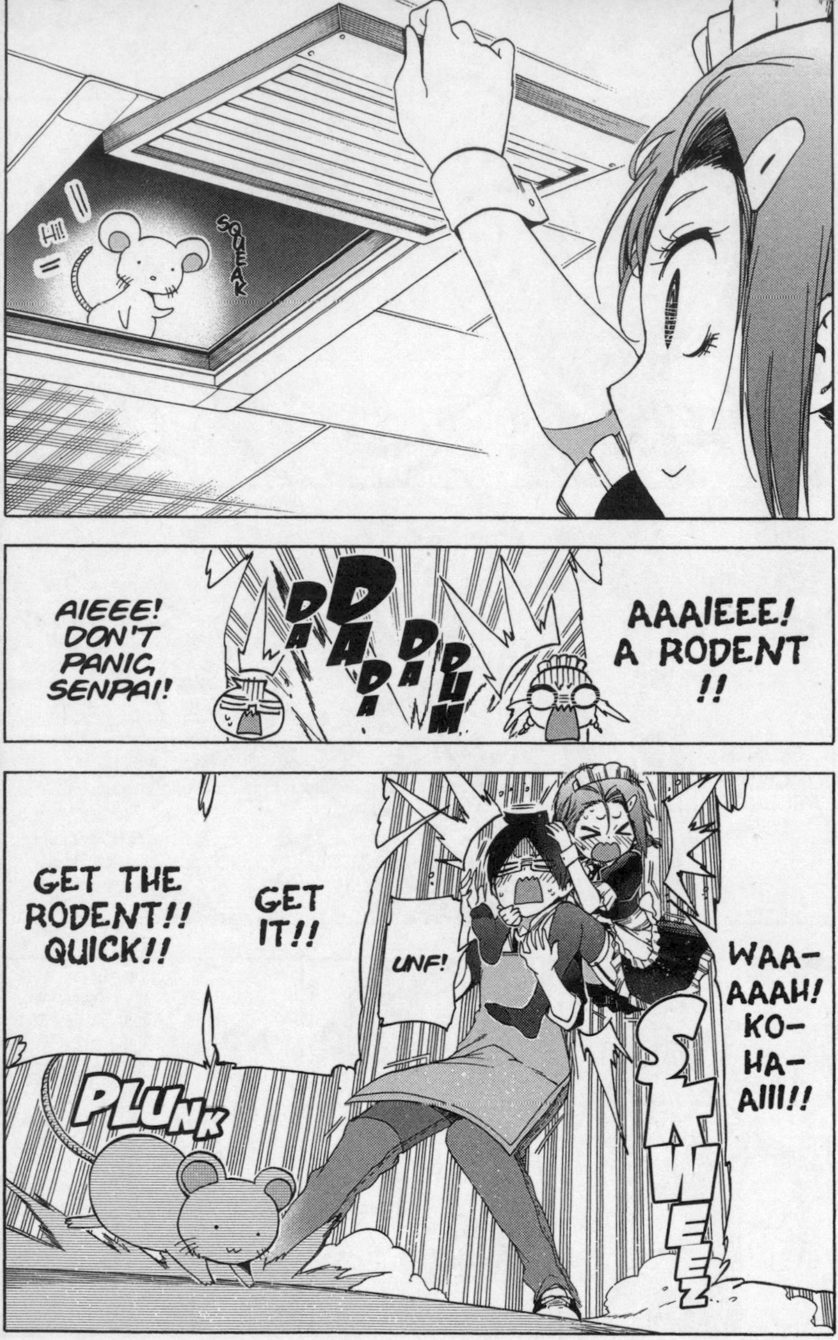
SQUEAK
HI!
AAAIEEE! A RODENT !!
DADADADADUM
AIEEE! DON'T PANIC, SENPAI!
WAA-AAAH! KO-HA-AIII!!
UNF!
GET IT!!
GET THE RODENT!! QUICK!!
PLUNK

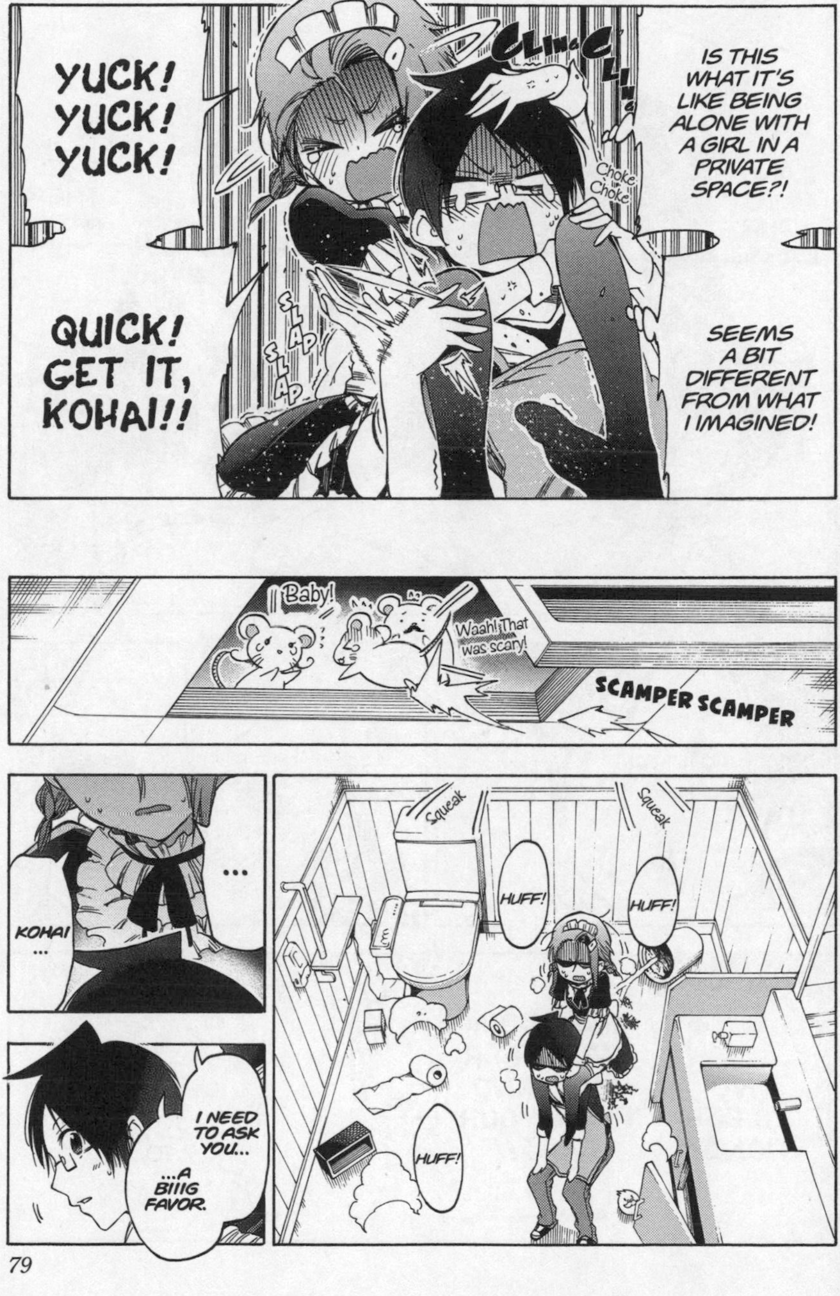
IS THIS WHAT IT'S LIKE BEING ALONE WITH A GIRL IN A PRIVATE SPACE?!
CLING CLING
YUCK! YUCK! YUCK!
Choke Choke
SEEMS A BIT DIFFERENT FROM WHAT I IMAGINED!
SLAP SLAP
QUICK! GET IT, KOHAI!!
Waah! That was scary!
Baby!
SCAMPER SCAMPER
Squeak
Squeak
HUFF!
HUFF!
HUFF!
...
KOHAI ...
I NEED TO ASK YOU...
...A BIIIG FAVOR.

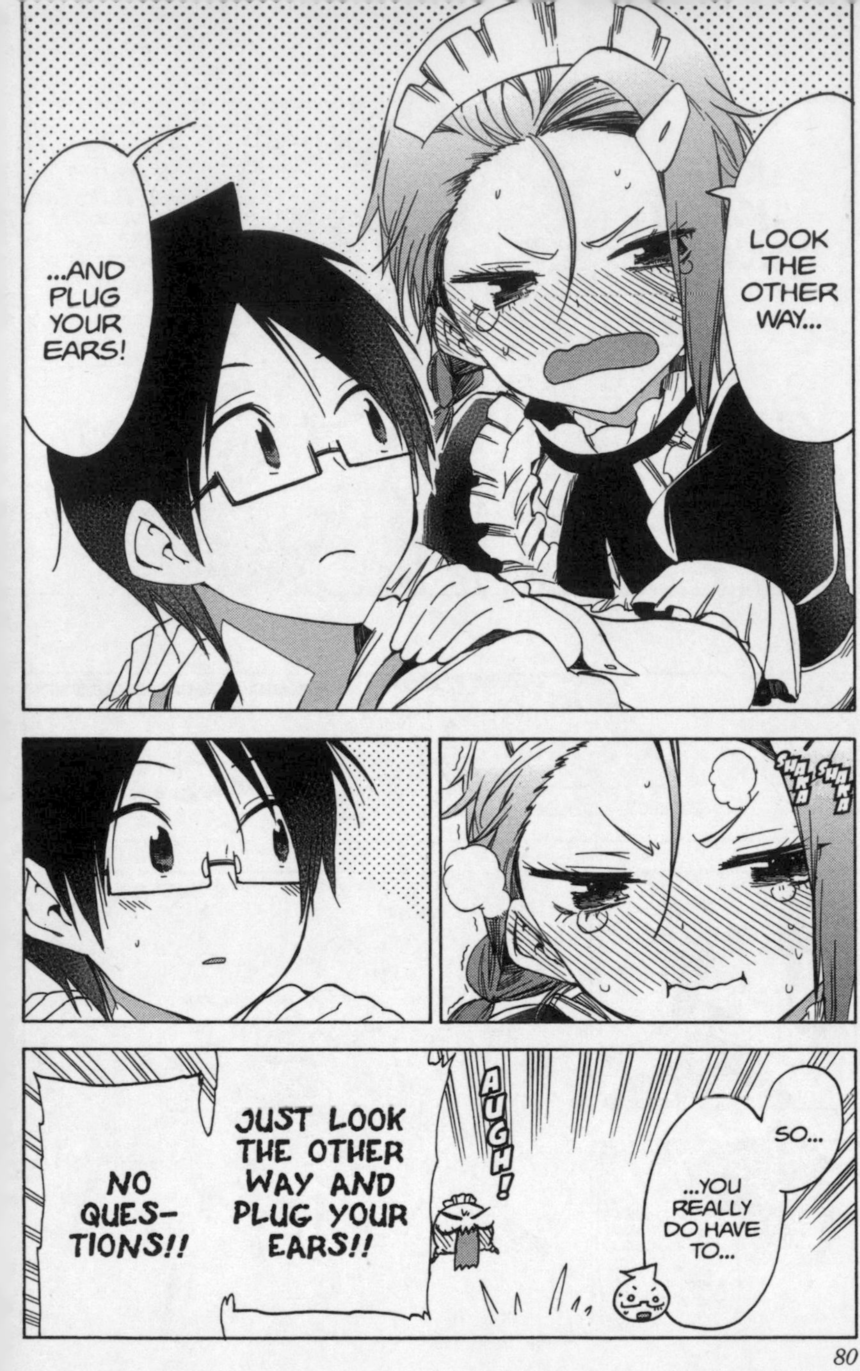
LOOK THE OTHER WAY...
...AND PLUG YOUR EARS!
SHAKA
SHAKA
SO...
...YOU REALLY DO HAVE TO...
AUGH!
JUST LOOK THE OTHER WAY AND PLUG YOUR EARS!!
NO QUES-TIONS!!

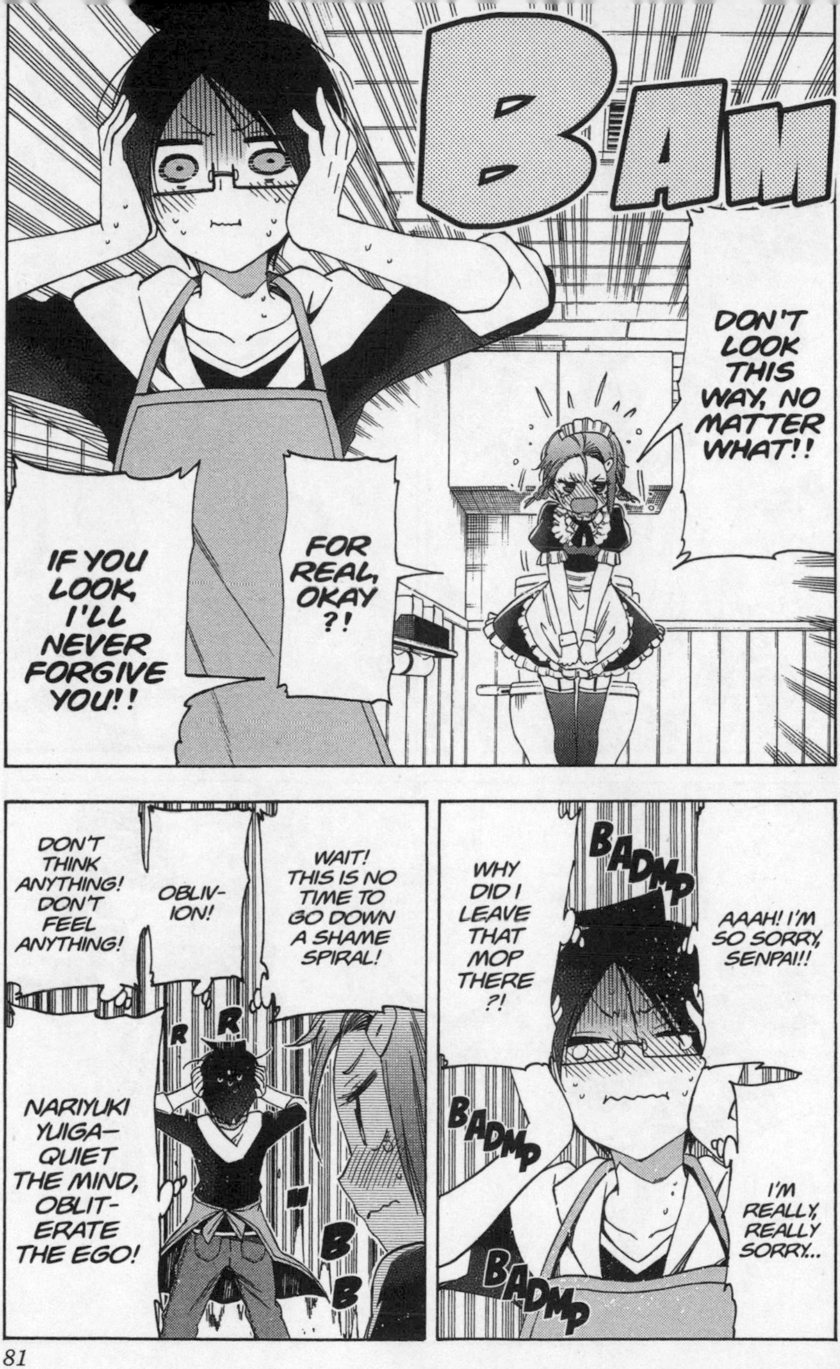

BAM
DON'T LOOK THIS WAY, NO MATTER WHAT!!
FOR REAL, OKAY?!
IF YOU LOOK, I'LL NEVER FORGIVE YOU!!
BADMP
AAAH! I'M SO SORRY, SENPAI!!
WHY DID I LEAVE THAT MOP THERE?!
BADMP
I'M REALLY, REALLY SORRY...
BADMP
WAIT! THIS IS NO TIME TO GO DOWN A SHAME SPIRAL!
OBLIV-ION!
DON'T THINK ANYTHING! DON'T FEEL ANYTHING!
R R
NARIYUKI YUIGA—QUIET THE MIND, OBLIT-ERATE THE EGO!
B B

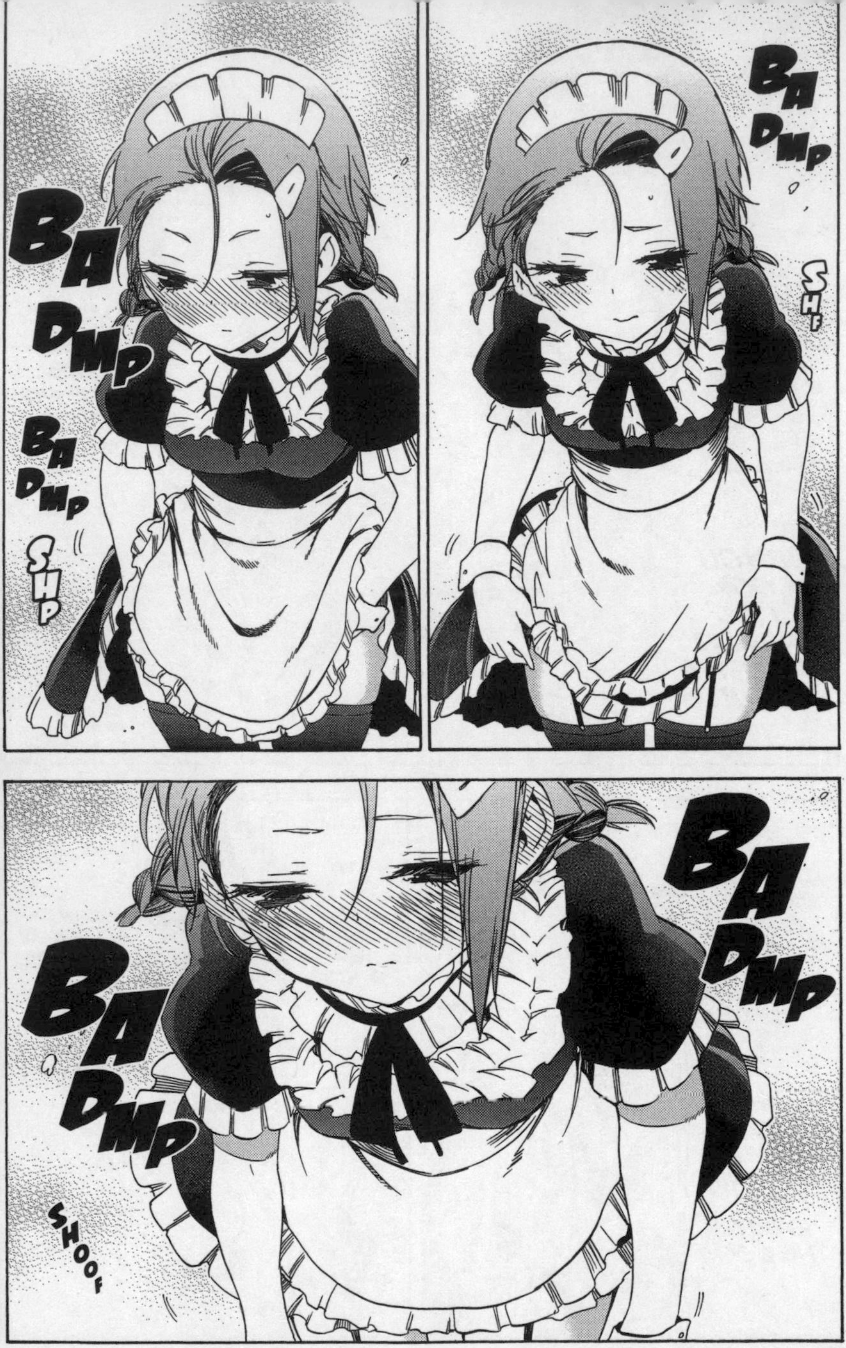
BADMP
SHF
BADMP
BADMP
SHP
BADMP
BADMP
SHOOF

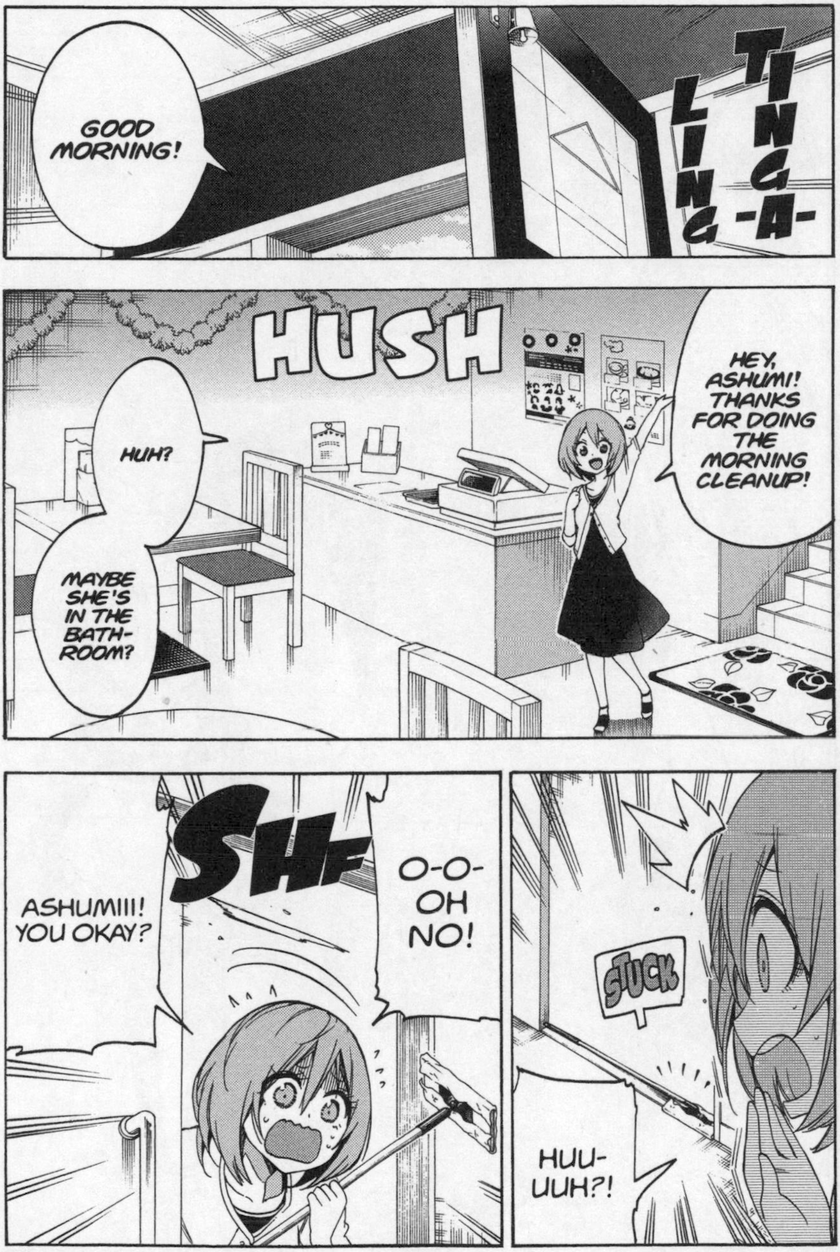
TING-A-LING
GOOD MORNING!
HEY, ASHUMI! THANKS FOR DOING THE MORNING CLEANUP!
HUSH
HUH?
MAYBE SHE'S IN THE BATH-ROOM?
STUCK
HUU-UUH?!
SHF
O-O-OH NO!
ASHUMIII! YOU OKAY?

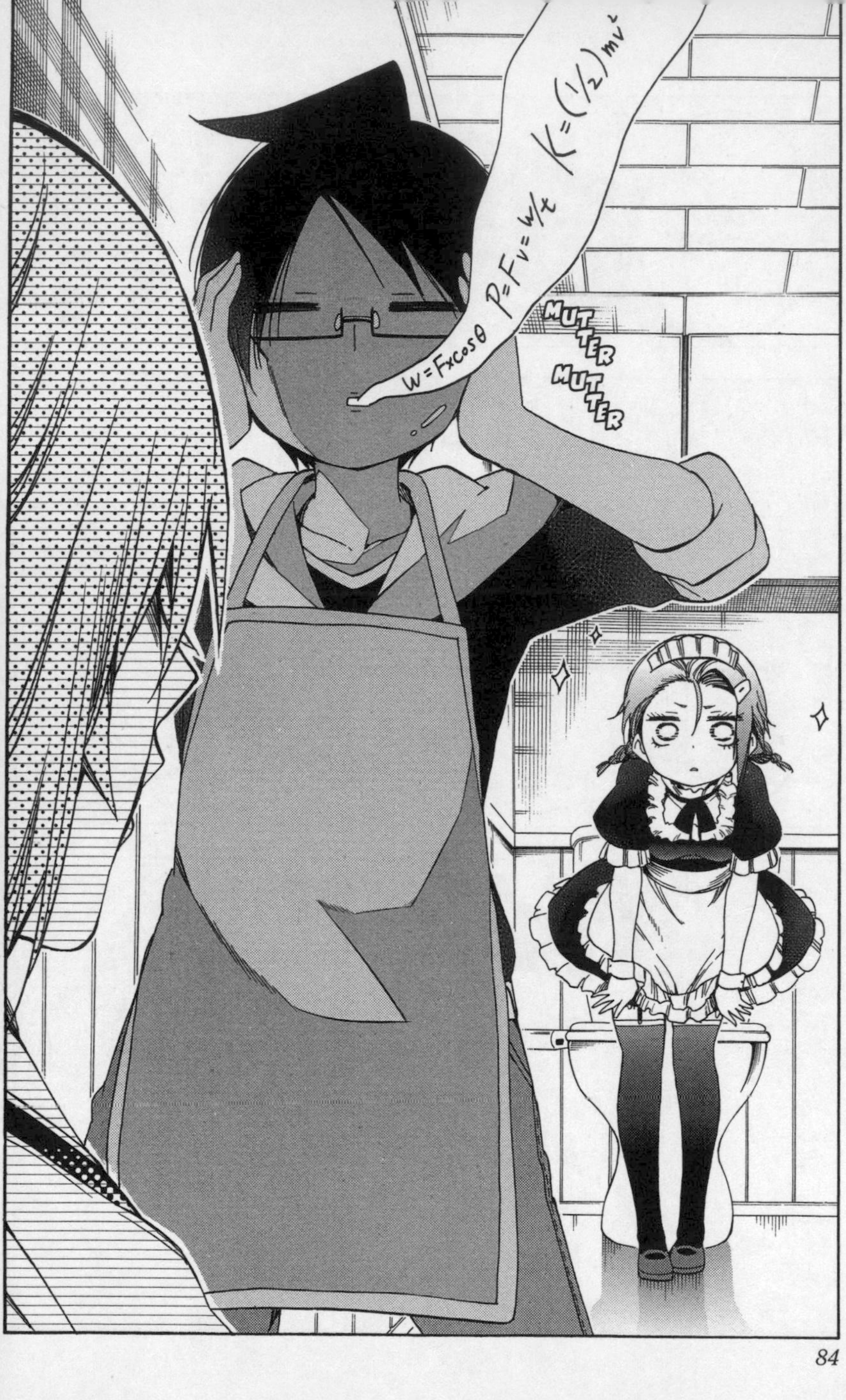
$W=Fx\cos\theta$ $P=Fv=W/t$ $K=(1/2)mv^2$
MUTTER MUTTER

O-OH! MACHIKO! WE'RE SAVED!!
OH!
GASP
THANK GOODNESS!
I WAS WORRIED!
TREMBL
TREMBL
TREMBL
WHAT... WERE YOU DOING?
ASHUMI... WE'RE NOT THAT KIND OF ESTABLISHMENT... YOU KNOW THAT, RIGHT?
THAT KIND?
WHAT?! NO!!
THAT'S NOT WHAT WE...
AUGH! GET OUT OF HERE! BOTH OF YOU!!

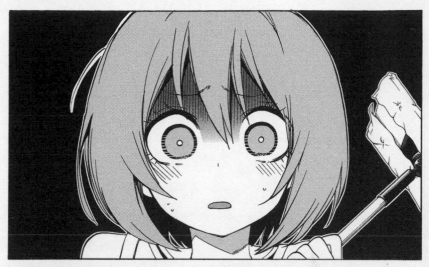

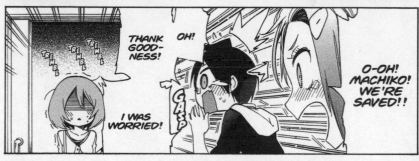

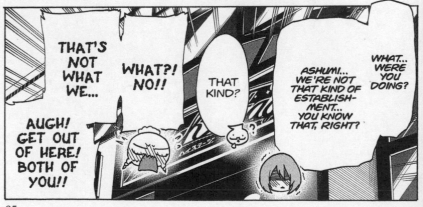

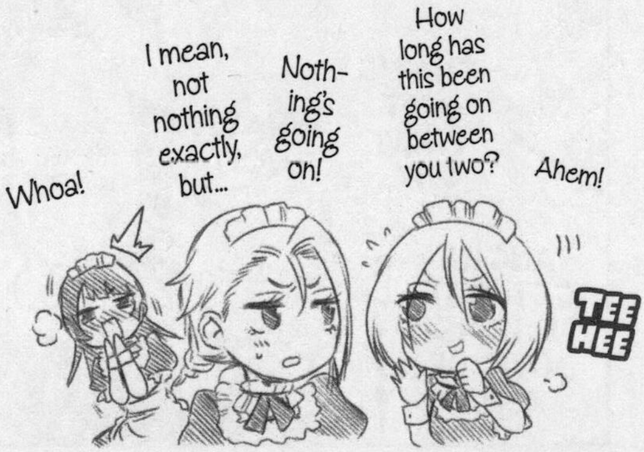
How long has this been going on between you two?
Ahem!
TEE HEE
Noth-ing's going on!
I mean, not nothing exactly, but...
Whoa!

Question 83: An [X]'s Joke Makes a Genius Dance

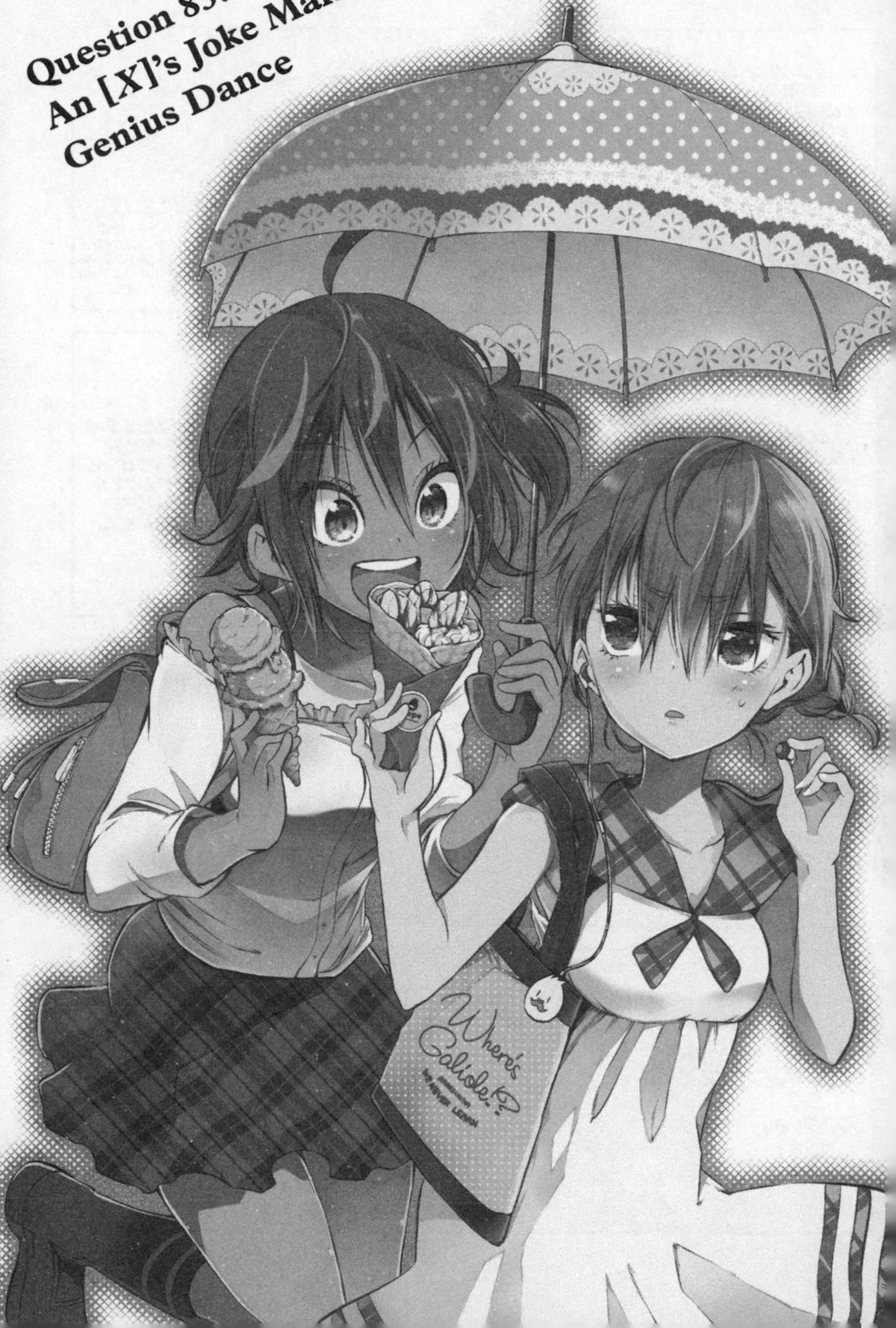
Where's Galiole!?
WE NEVER LEARN

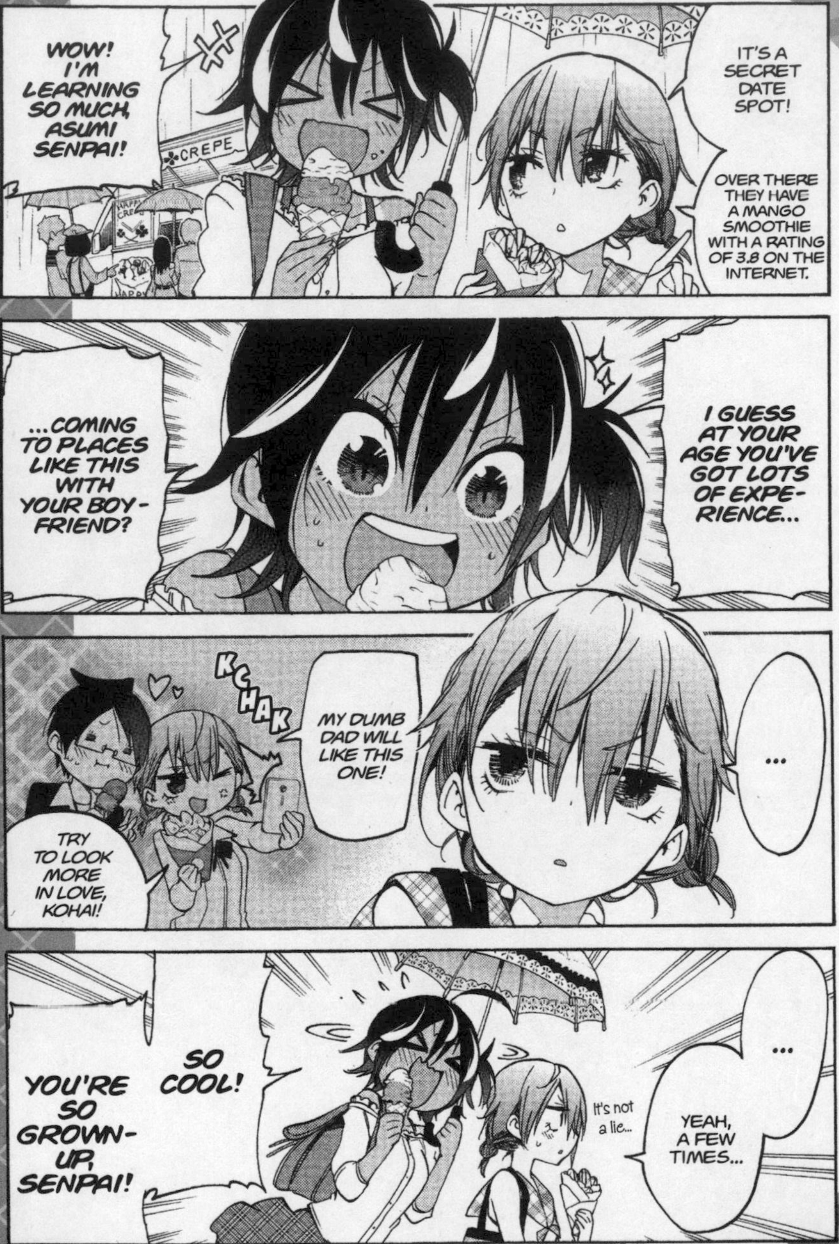
IT'S A SECRET DATE SPOT!
OVER THERE THEY HAVE A MANGO SMOOTHIE WITH A RATING OF 3.8 ON THE INTERNET.
CREPE
WOW! I'M LEARNING SO MUCH, ASUMI SENPAI!
I GUESS AT YOUR AGE YOU'VE GOT LOTS OF EXPE-RIENCE...
...COMING TO PLACES LIKE THIS WITH YOUR BOY-FRIEND?
...
MY DUMB DAD WILL LIKE THIS ONE!
KCHAK
TRY TO LOOK MORE IN LOVE, KOHAI!
... YEAH, A FEW TIMES...
It's not a lie...
SO COOL!
YOU'RE SO GROWN-UP, SENPAI!

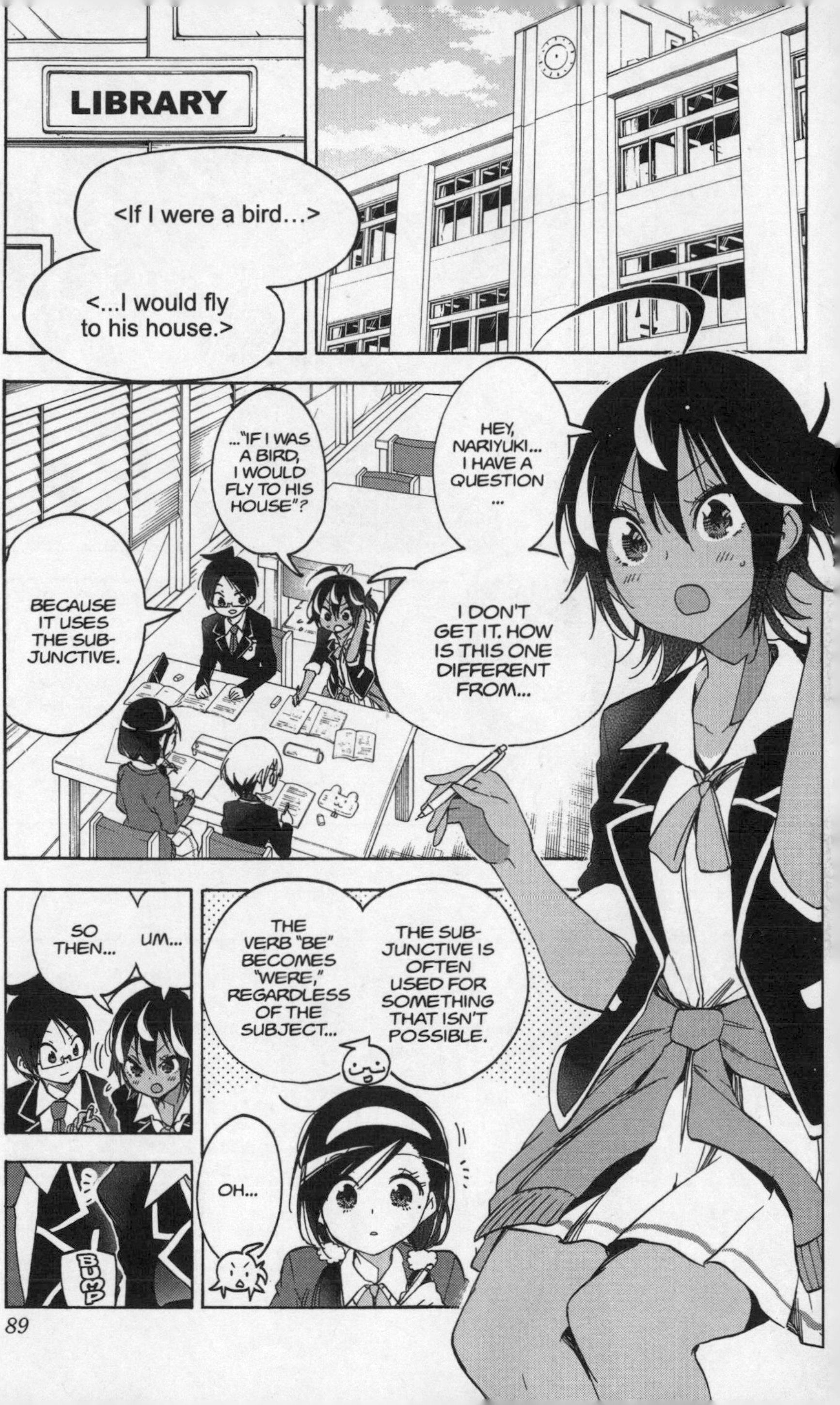
LIBRARY
<If I were a bird…>
<...I would fly to his house.>
HEY, NARIYUKI... I HAVE A QUESTION ...
I DON'T GET IT. HOW IS THIS ONE DIFFERENT FROM...
..."IF I WAS A BIRD, I WOULD FLY TO HIS HOUSE"?
BECAUSE IT USES THE SUB-JUNCTIVE.
THE SUB-JUNCTIVE IS OFTEN USED FOR SOMETHING THAT ISN'T POSSIBLE.
THE VERB "BE" BECOMES "WERE," REGARDLESS OF THE SUBJECT...
UM...
SO THEN...
OH...
BUMP

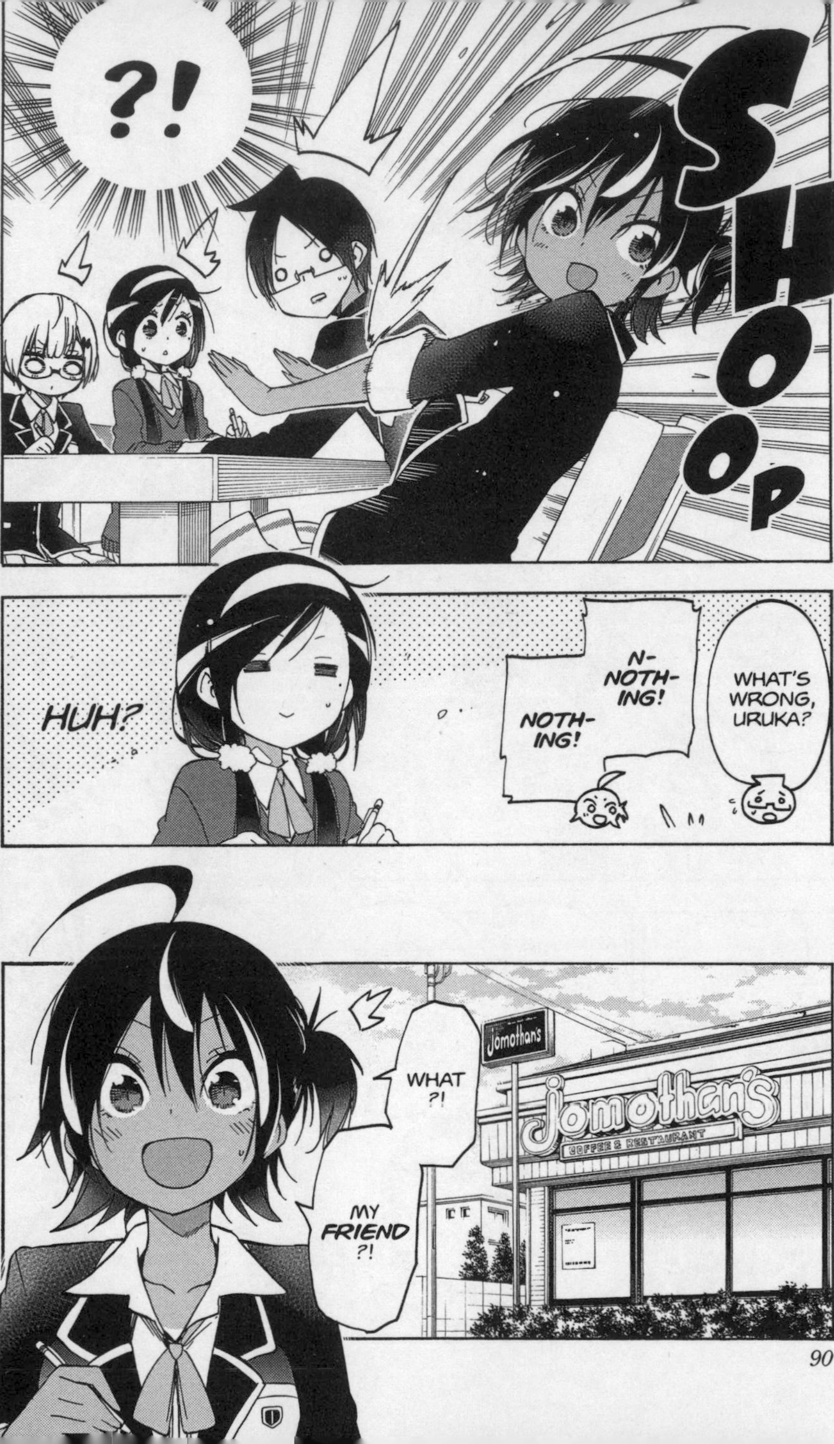
SHOOOP
?!
WHAT'S WRONG, URUKA?
N-NOTHING!
NOTHING!
HUH?
jomothan's
jomothan's
COFFEE & RESTAURANT
WHAT ?!
MY FRIEND ?!

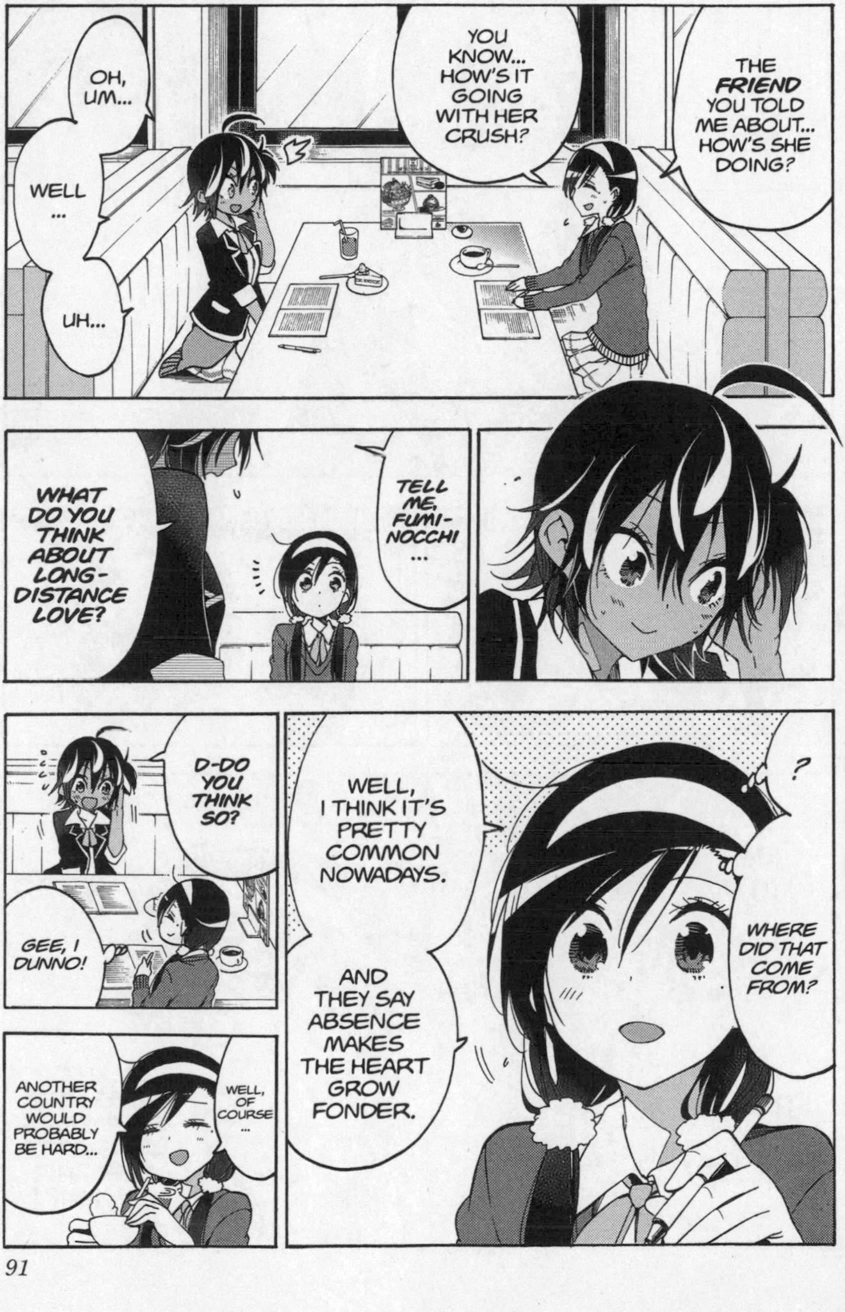
THE FRIEND YOU TOLD ME ABOUT... HOW'S SHE DOING?
YOU KNOW... HOW'S IT GOING WITH HER CRUSH?
OH, UM...
WELL ...
UH...
TELL ME, FUMI-NOCCHI ...
WHAT DO YOU THINK ABOUT LONG-DISTANCE LOVE?
?
WHERE DID THAT COME FROM?
WELL, I THINK IT'S PRETTY COMMON NOWADAYS.
AND THEY SAY ABSENCE MAKES THE HEART GROW FONDER.
D-DO YOU THINK SO?
GEE, I DUNNO!
WELL, OF COURSE ...
ANOTHER COUNTRY WOULD PROBABLY BE HARD...

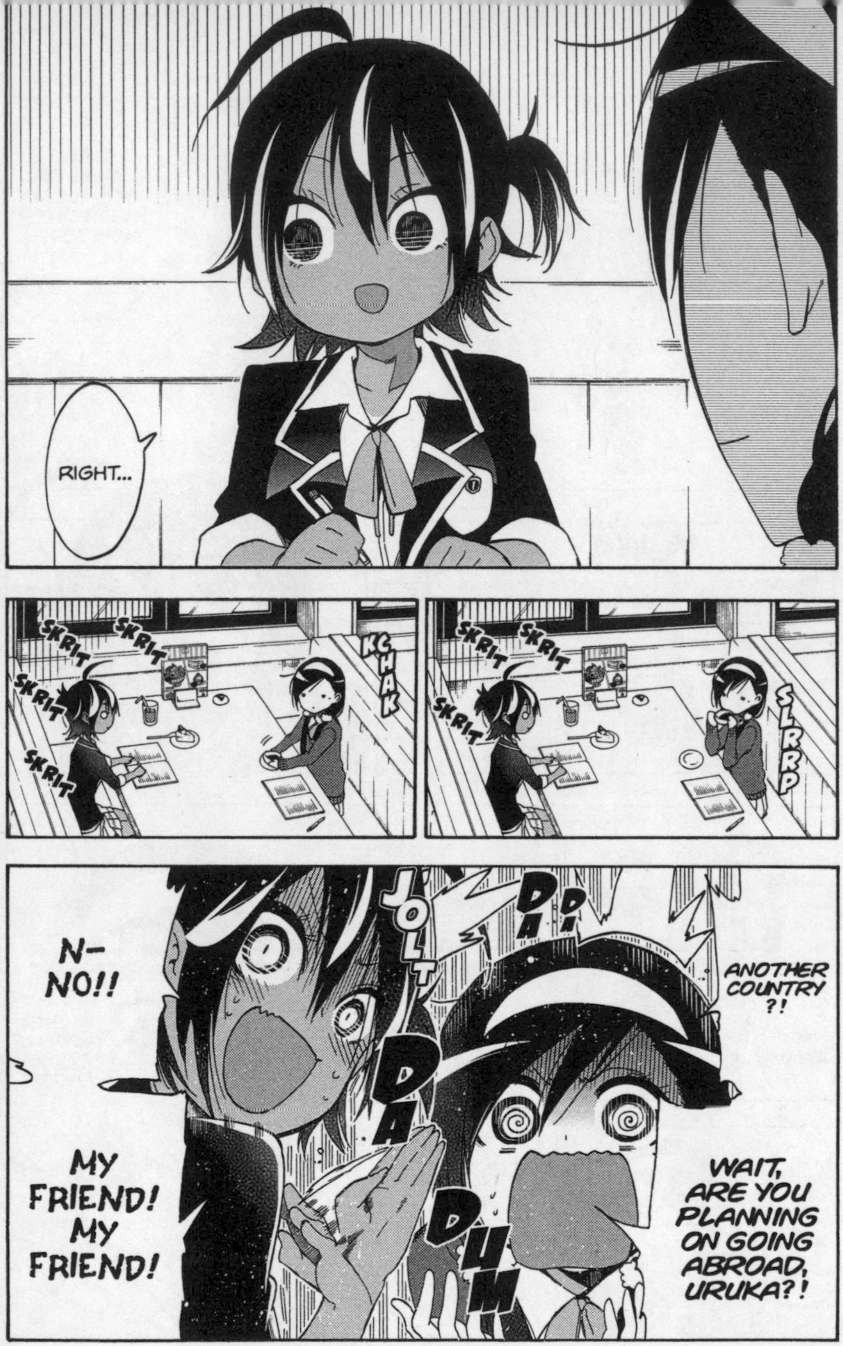
RIGHT...
SKRIT
SKRIT
SKRIT
SLRRP
KCHAK
SKRIT
SKRIT
SKRIT
SKRIT
ANOTHER COUNTRY ?!
DA DI
WAIT, ARE YOU PLANNING ON GOING ABROAD, URUKA?!
JOLT
DA DA DUM
N-NO!!
MY FRIEND! MY FRIEND!

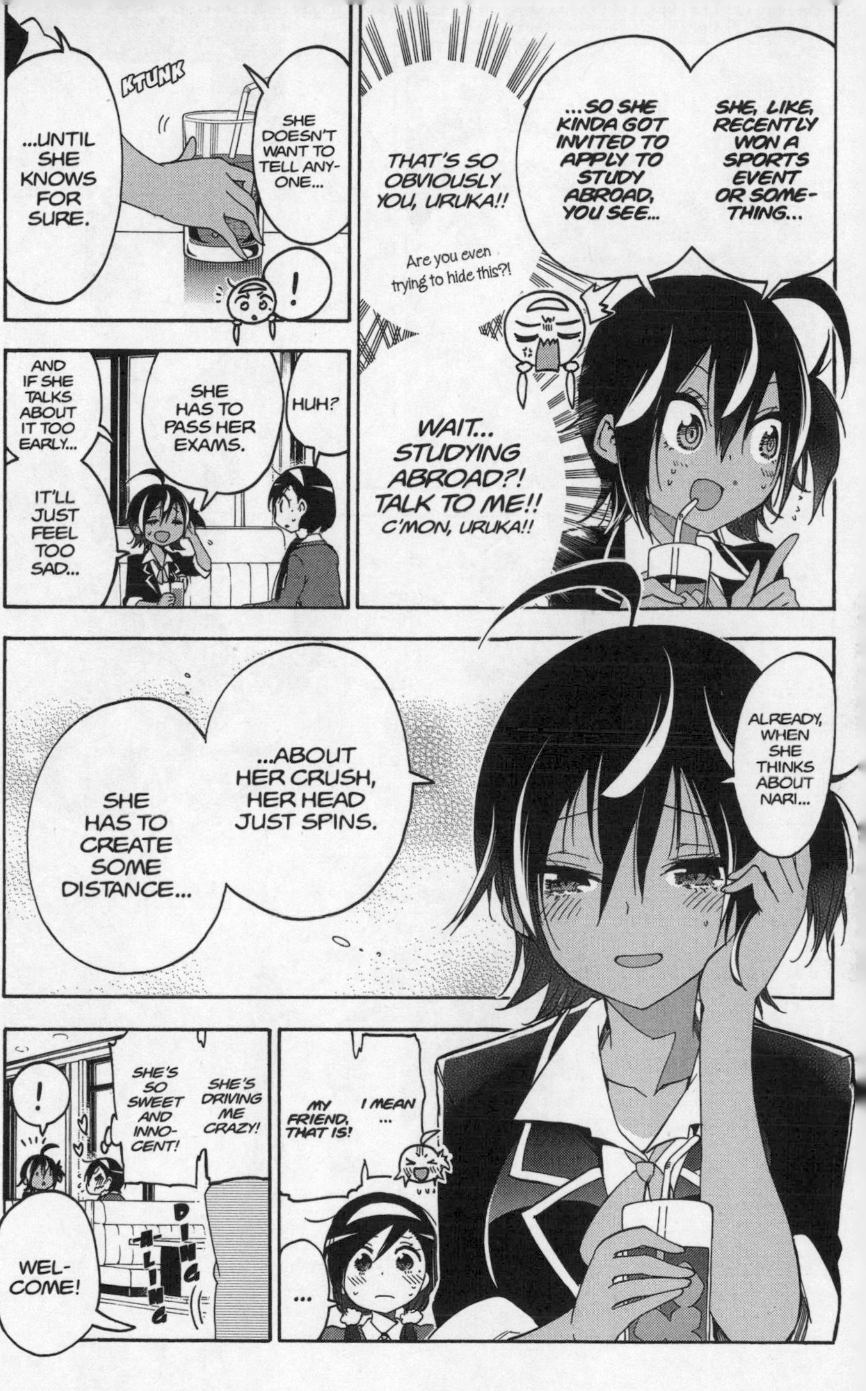
SHE, LIKE, RECENTLY WON A SPORTS EVENT OR SOMETHING...
...SO SHE KINDA GOT INVITED TO APPLY TO STUDY ABROAD, YOU SEE...
THAT'S SO OBVIOUSLY YOU, URUKA!!
Are you even trying to hide this?!
WAIT... STUDYING ABROAD?! TALK TO ME!! C'MON, URUKA!!
KTUNK
SHE DOESN'T WANT TO TELL ANYONE...
...UNTIL SHE KNOWS FOR SURE.
!
HUH?
SHE HAS TO PASS HER EXAMS.
AND IF SHE TALKS ABOUT IT TOO EARLY...
IT'LL JUST FEEL TOO SAD...
ALREADY, WHEN SHE THINKS ABOUT NARI...
...ABOUT HER CRUSH, HER HEAD JUST SPINS.
SHE HAS TO CREATE SOME DISTANCE...
I MEAN...
MY FRIEND, THAT IS!
...
SHE'S DRIVING ME CRAZY!
SHE'S SO SWEET AND INNOCENT!
!
DING-A-LING
WELCOME!

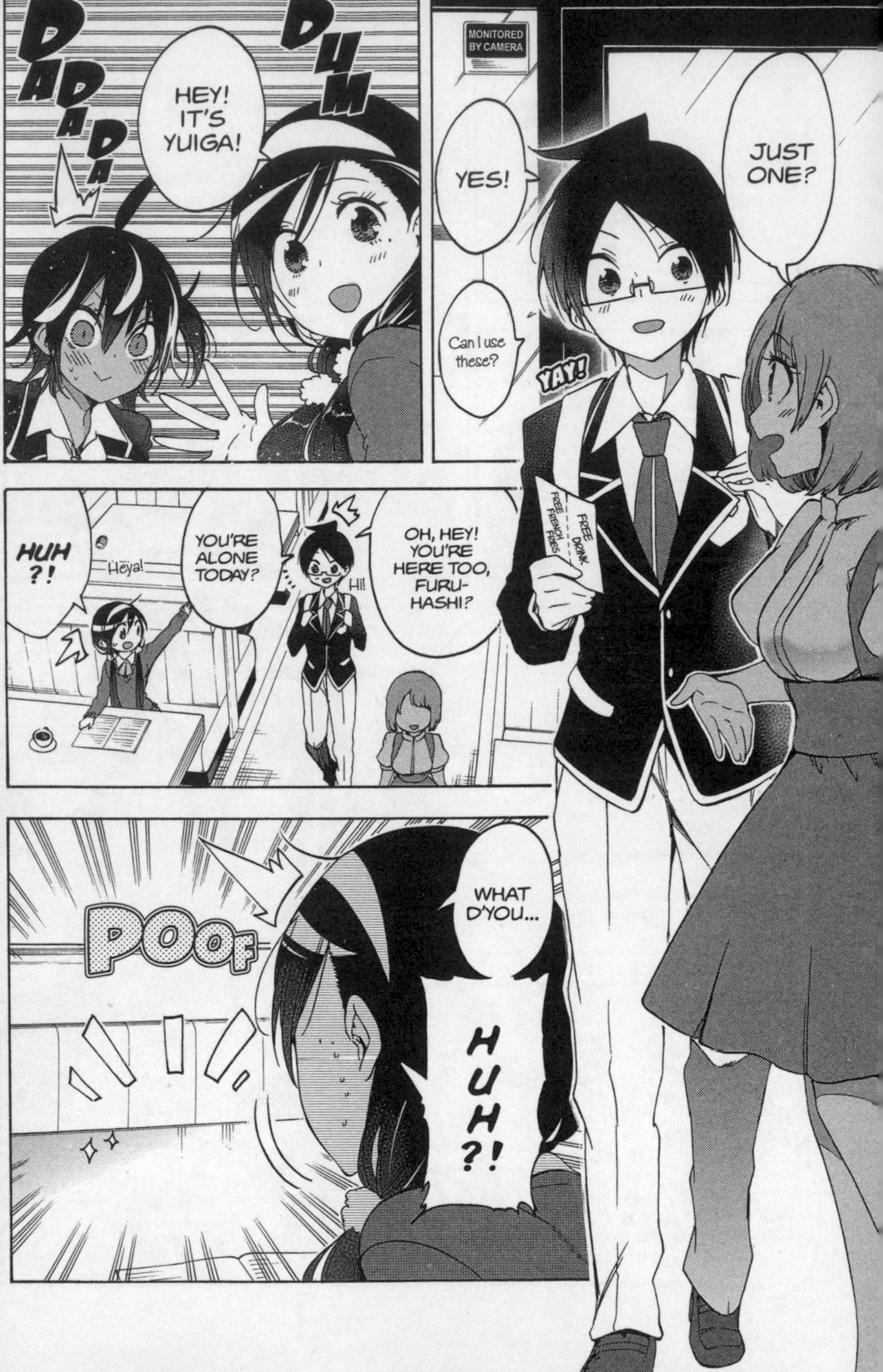
MONITORED BY CAMERA
JUST ONE?
YES!
Can I use these?
YAY!
FREE DRINK
FREE FRENCH FRIES
DUM
DADADADA
HEY! IT'S YUIGA!
OH, HEY! YOU'RE HERE TOO, FURUHASHI?
Hi!
YOU'RE ALONE TODAY?
Heya!
HUH?!
WHAT D'YOU...
POOF
HUH?!

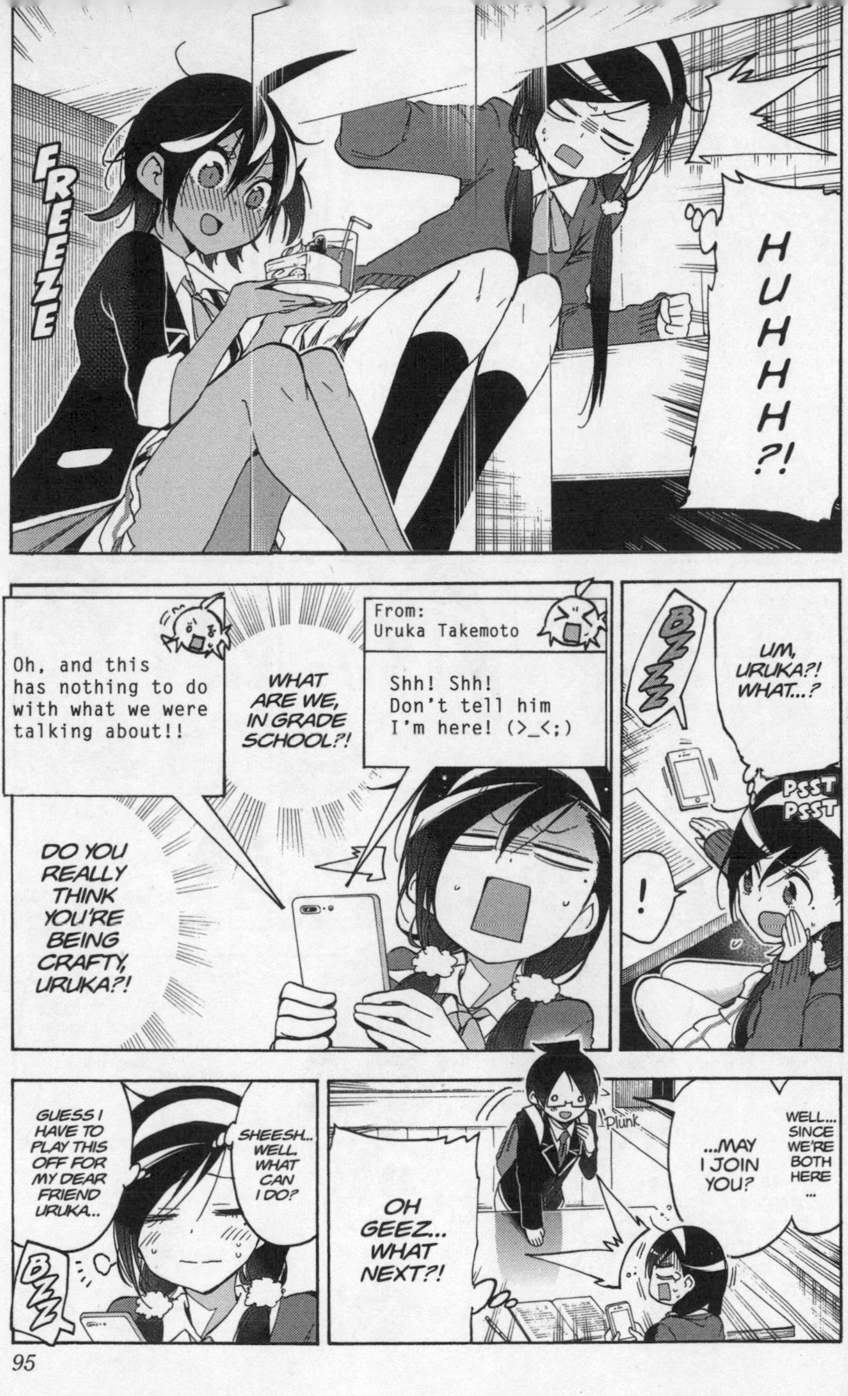
HUHHHH?!
FREEZE
BZZ
UM, URUKA?! WHAT...?
PSST PSST
!
From: Uruka Takemoto
Shh! Shh! Don't tell him I'm here! (>_<;)
WHAT ARE WE, IN GRADE SCHOOL?!
Oh, and this has nothing to do with what we were talking about!!
DO YOU REALLY THINK YOU'RE BEING CRAFTY, URUKA?!
Plunk
WELL... SINCE WE'RE BOTH HERE...
...MAY I JOIN YOU?
OH GEEZ... WHAT NEXT?!
SHEESH... WELL. WHAT CAN I DO?
GUESS I HAVE TO PLAY THIS OFF FOR MY DEAR FRIEND URUKA...
BZZ

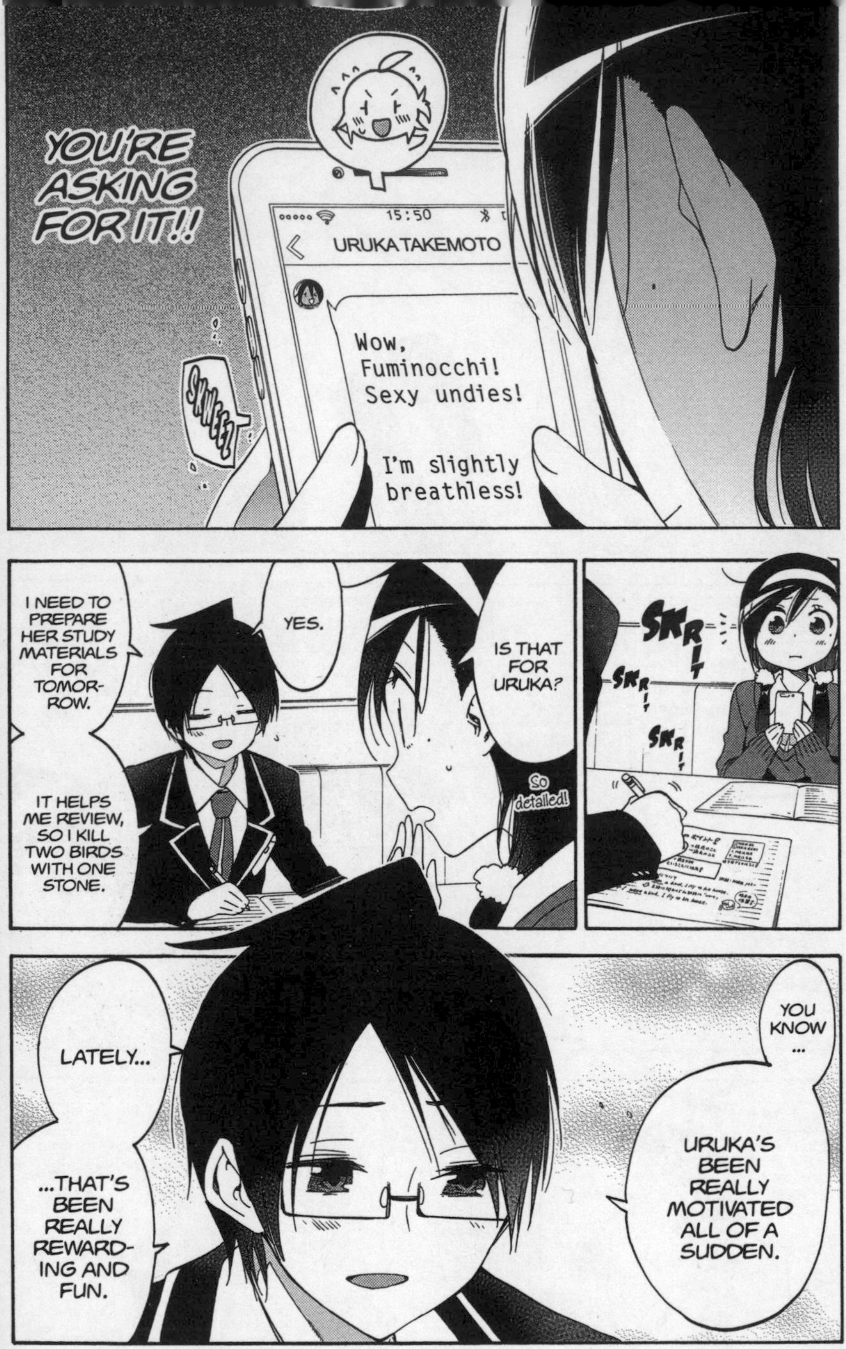
15:50
URUKA TAKEMOTO
Wow, Fuminocchi! Sexy undies!
I'm slightly breathless!
YOU'RE ASKING FOR IT!!
SKWEEZ
SKRIT
SKRIT
SKRIT
IS THAT FOR URUKA?
So detailed!
YES.
I NEED TO PREPARE HER STUDY MATERIALS FOR TOMORROW.
IT HELPS ME REVIEW, SO I KILL TWO BIRDS WITH ONE STONE.
YOU KNOW...
URUKA'S BEEN REALLY MOTIVATED ALL OF A SUDDEN.
LATELY...
...THAT'S BEEN REALLY REWARDING AND FUN.

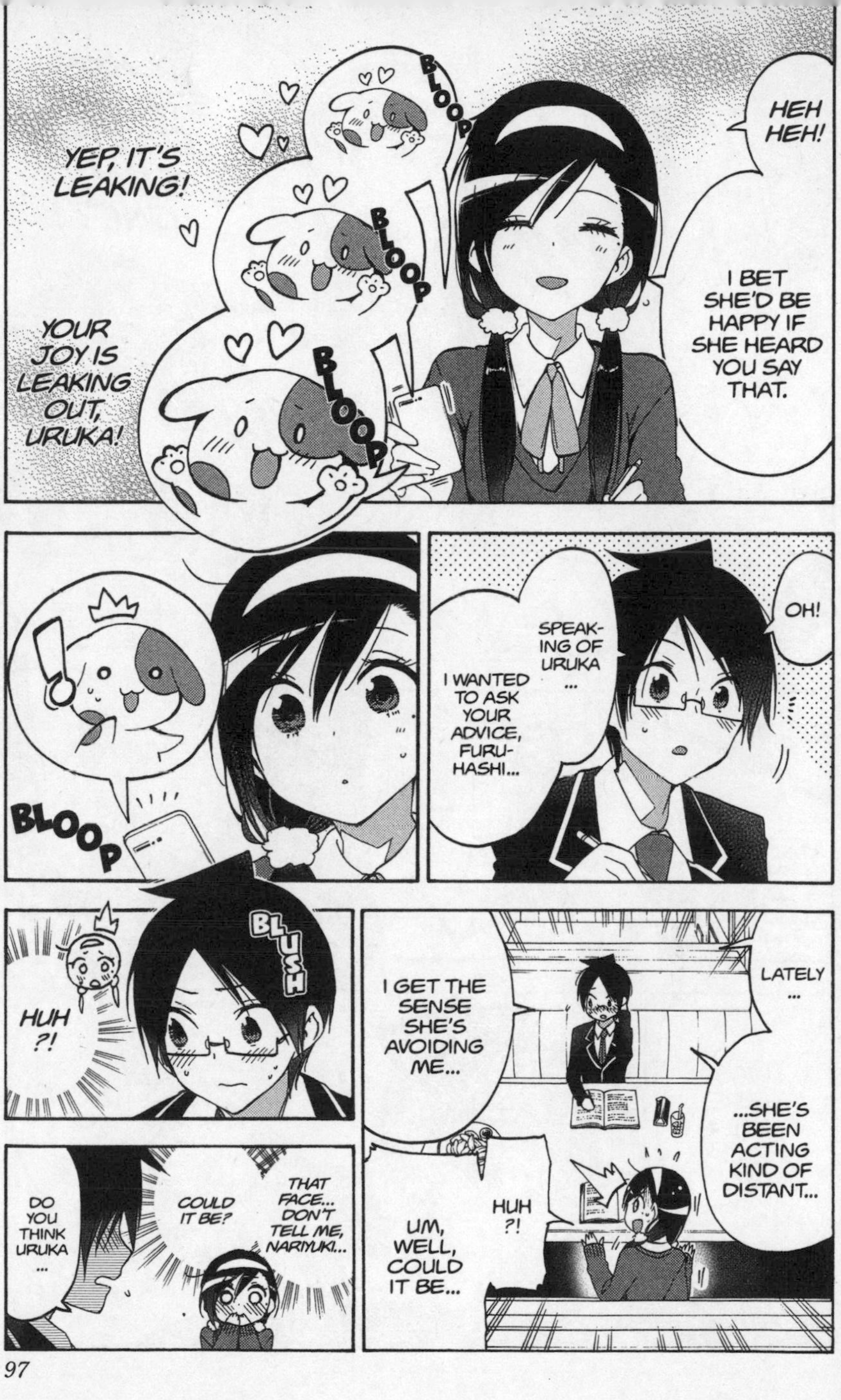
HEH HEH!
BLOOP
YEP, IT'S LEAKING!
I BET SHE'D BE HAPPY IF SHE HEARD YOU SAY THAT.
BLOOP
BLOOP
YOUR JOY IS LEAKING OUT, URUKA!
OH!
SPEAK-ING OF URUKA ...
I WANTED TO ASK YOUR ADVICE, FURU-HASHI...
BLOOP
LATELY ...
...SHE'S BEEN ACTING KIND OF DISTANT...
I GET THE SENSE SHE'S AVOIDING ME...
HUH ?!
UM, WELL, COULD IT BE...
BLUSH
HUH ?!
THAT FACE... DON'T TELL ME, NARIYUKI...
COULD IT BE?
DO YOU THINK URUKA ...

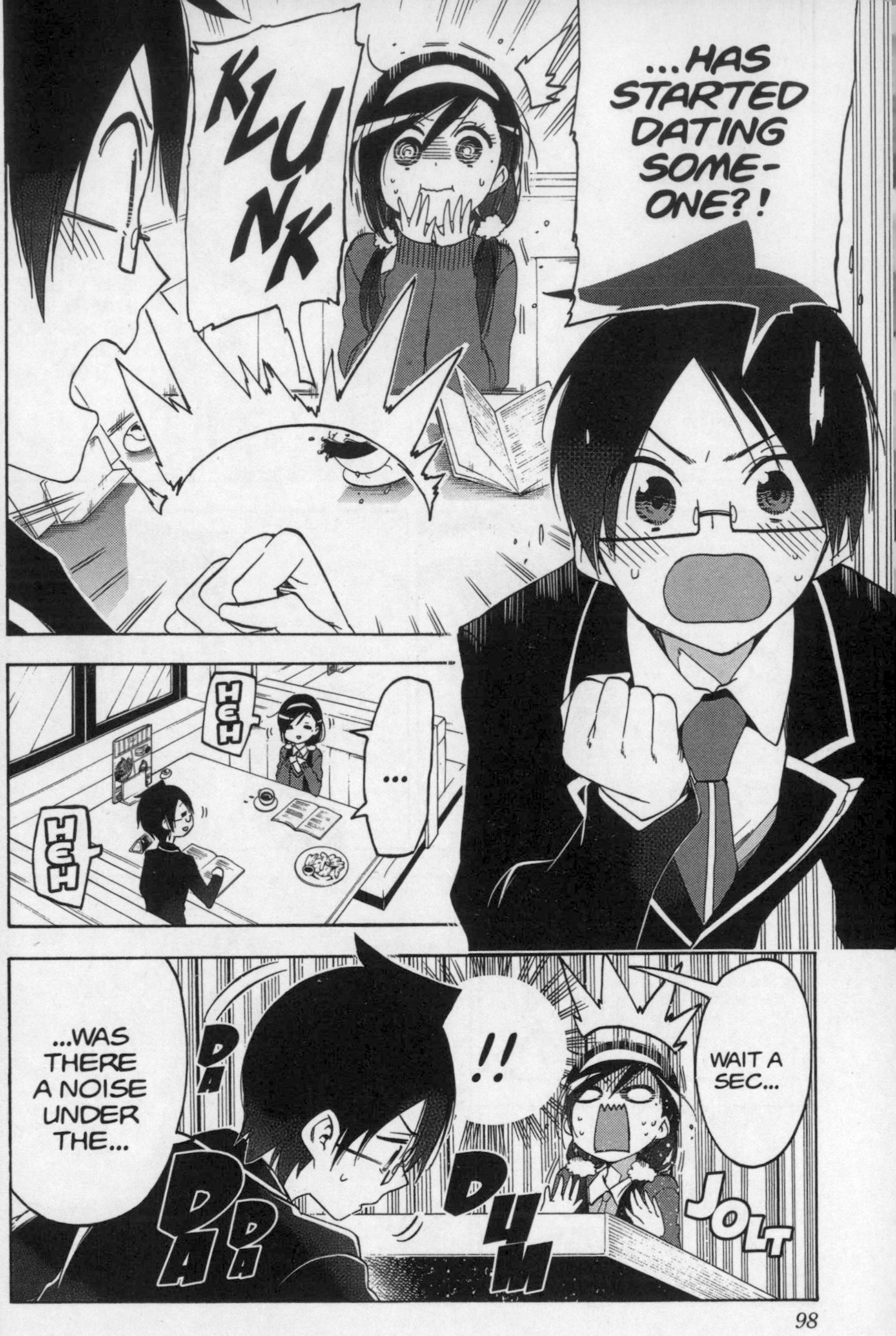
...HAS STARTED DATING SOME-ONE?!
KLUNK
...
HEH
HEH
WAIT A SEC...
JOLT
!!
DUM
DA DA DA
...WAS THERE A NOISE UNDER THE...

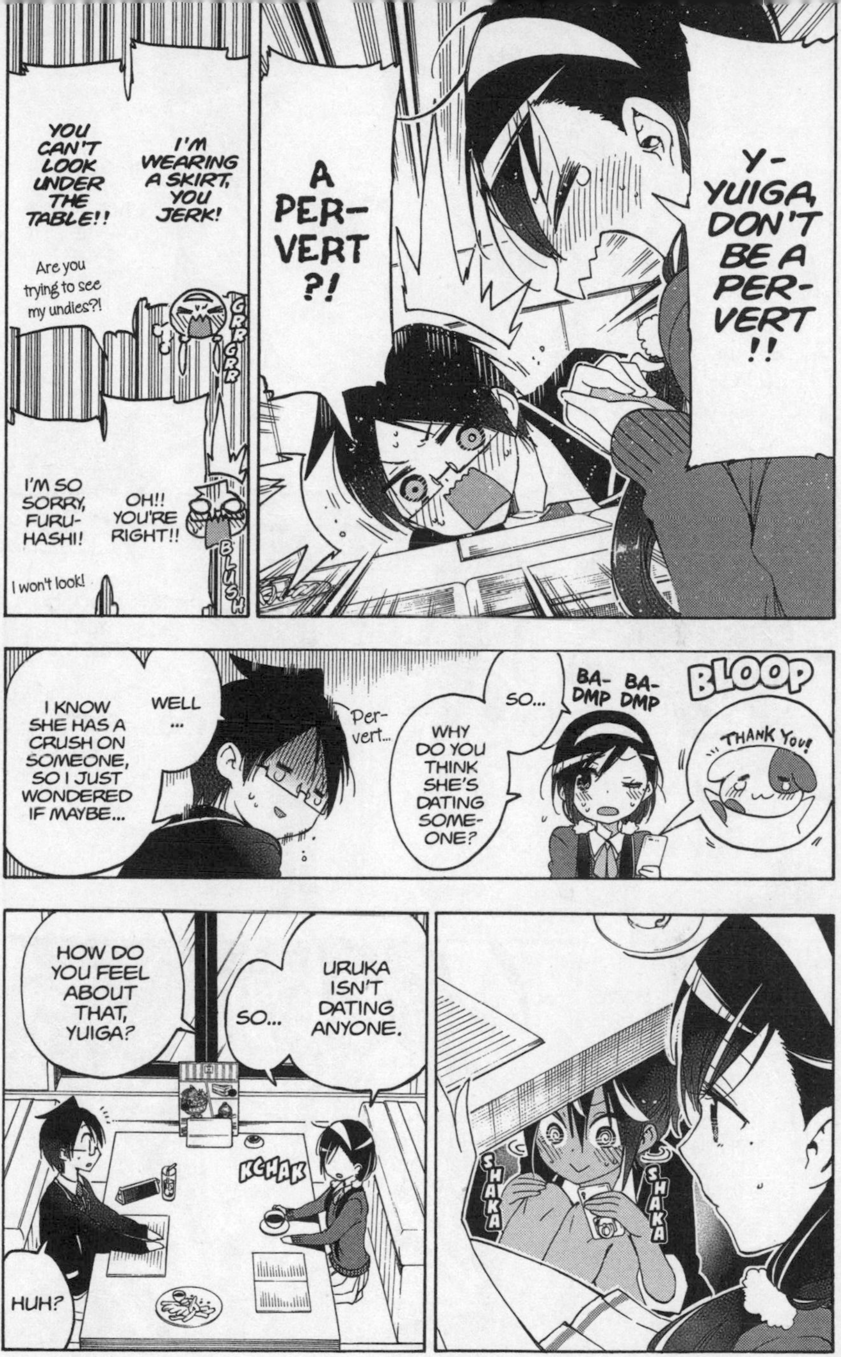
Y-YUIGA, DON'T BE A PERVERT!!
A PERVERT?!
I'M WEARING A SKIRT, YOU JERK!
YOU CAN'T LOOK UNDER THE TABLE!!
Are you trying to see my undies?!
GRR GRR GRR
OH!! YOU'RE RIGHT!!
I'M SO SORRY, FURUHASHI!
I won't look!
BLUSH
BLOOP
THANK YOU!
BA-DMP BA-DMP
SO...
WHY DO YOU THINK SHE'S DATING SOMEONE?
Per-vert...
WELL...
I KNOW SHE HAS A CRUSH ON SOMEONE, SO I JUST WONDERED IF MAYBE...
SHAKA
SHAKA
URUKA ISN'T DATING ANYONE.
SO...
HOW DO YOU FEEL ABOUT THAT, YUIGA?
KCHAK
HUH?

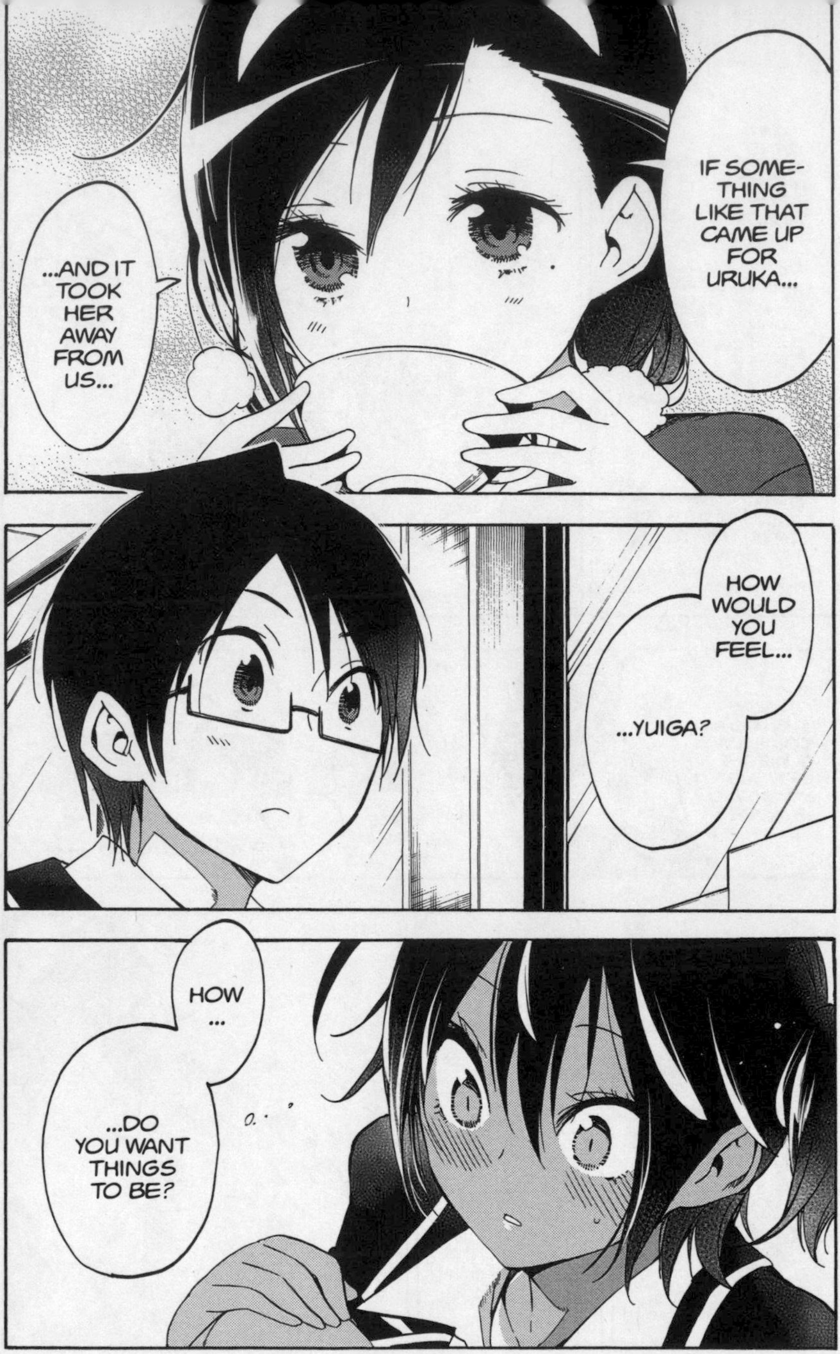
IF SOME-THING LIKE THAT CAME UP FOR URUKA...
...AND IT TOOK HER AWAY FROM US...
HOW WOULD YOU FEEL...
...YUIGA?
HOW ...
...DO YOU WANT THINGS TO BE?

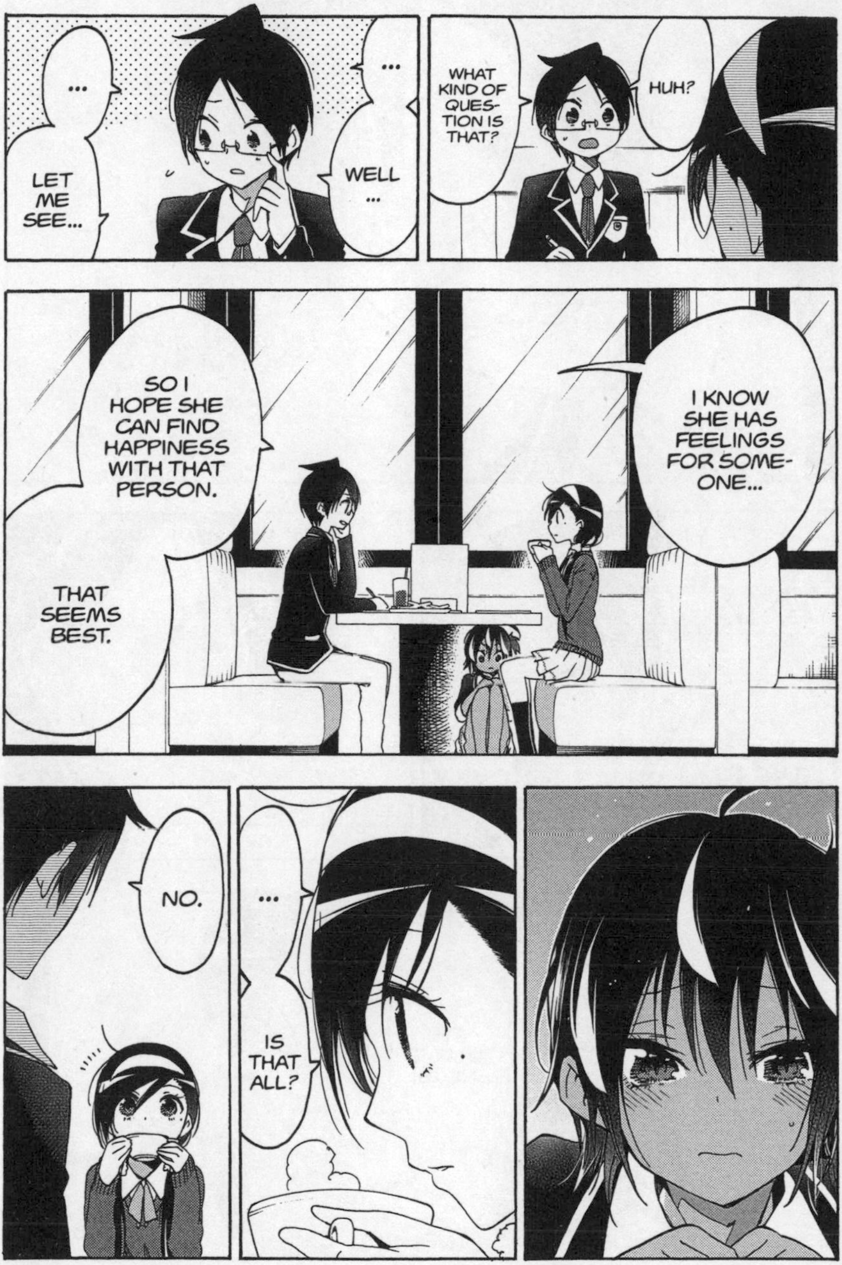
HUH?
WHAT KIND OF QUES-TION IS THAT?
... WELL ...
... LET ME SEE...
I KNOW SHE HAS FEELINGS FOR SOME-ONE...
SO I HOPE SHE CAN FIND HAPPINESS WITH THAT PERSON.
THAT SEEMS BEST.
... IS THAT ALL?
NO.

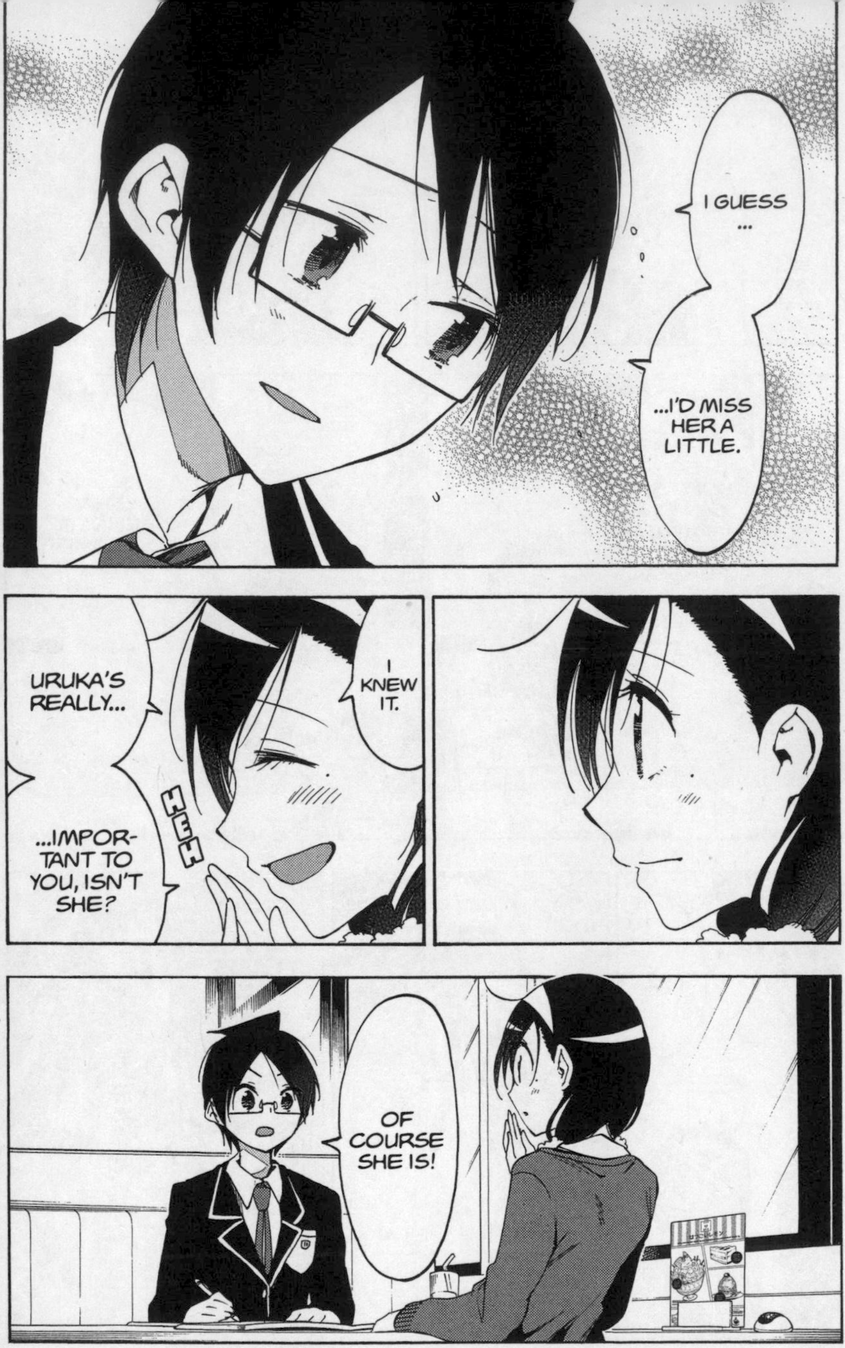
I GUESS ...
...I'D MISS HER A LITTLE.
I KNEW IT.
URUKA'S REALLY...
HEH HEH
...IMPOR-TANT TO YOU, ISN'T SHE?
OF COURSE SHE IS!

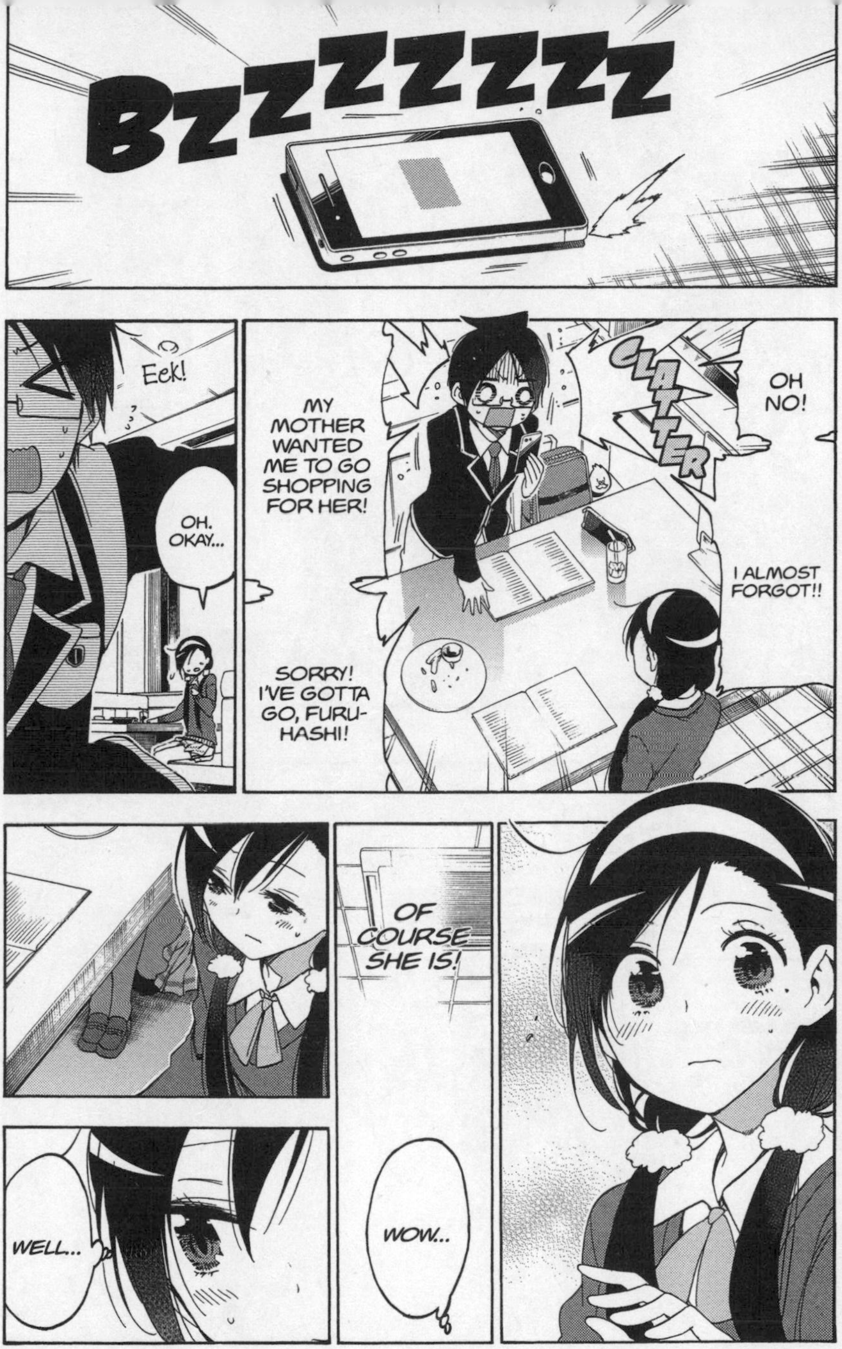
BZZZZZZZ
OH NO!
CLATTER
I ALMOST FORGOT!!
MY MOTHER WANTED ME TO GO SHOPPING FOR HER!
SORRY! I'VE GOTTA GO, FURU-HASHI!
Eek!
OH. OKAY...
OF COURSE SHE IS!
WOW...
WELL...

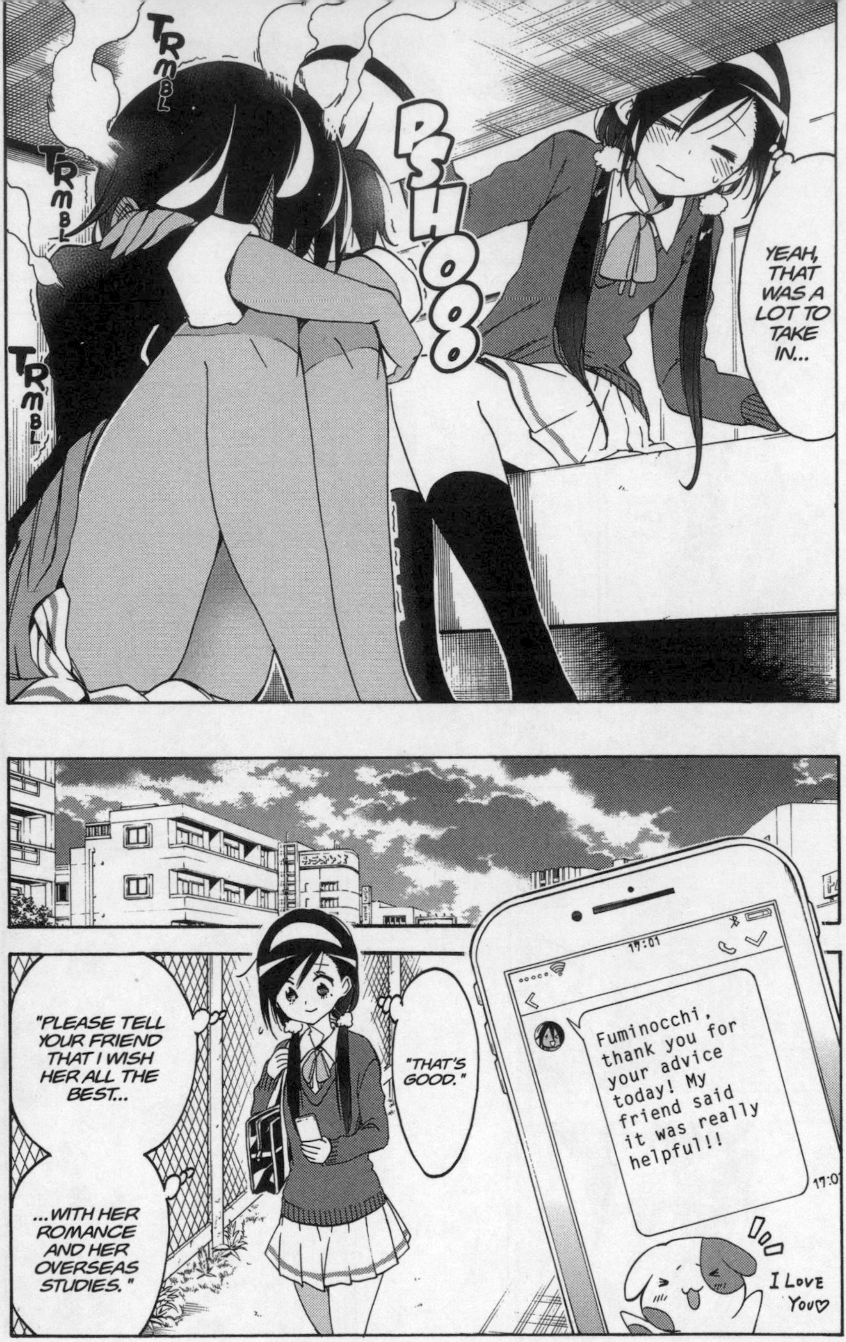
YEAH, THAT WAS A LOT TO TAKE IN...
PSHOOO
TRMBL
TRMBL
TRMBL
Fuminocchi, thank you for your advice today! My friend said it was really helpful!!
17:01
17:01
I LOVE YOU♡
"THAT'S GOOD."
"PLEASE TELL YOUR FRIEND THAT I WISH HER ALL THE BEST...
...WITH HER ROMANCE AND HER OVERSEAS STUDIES."

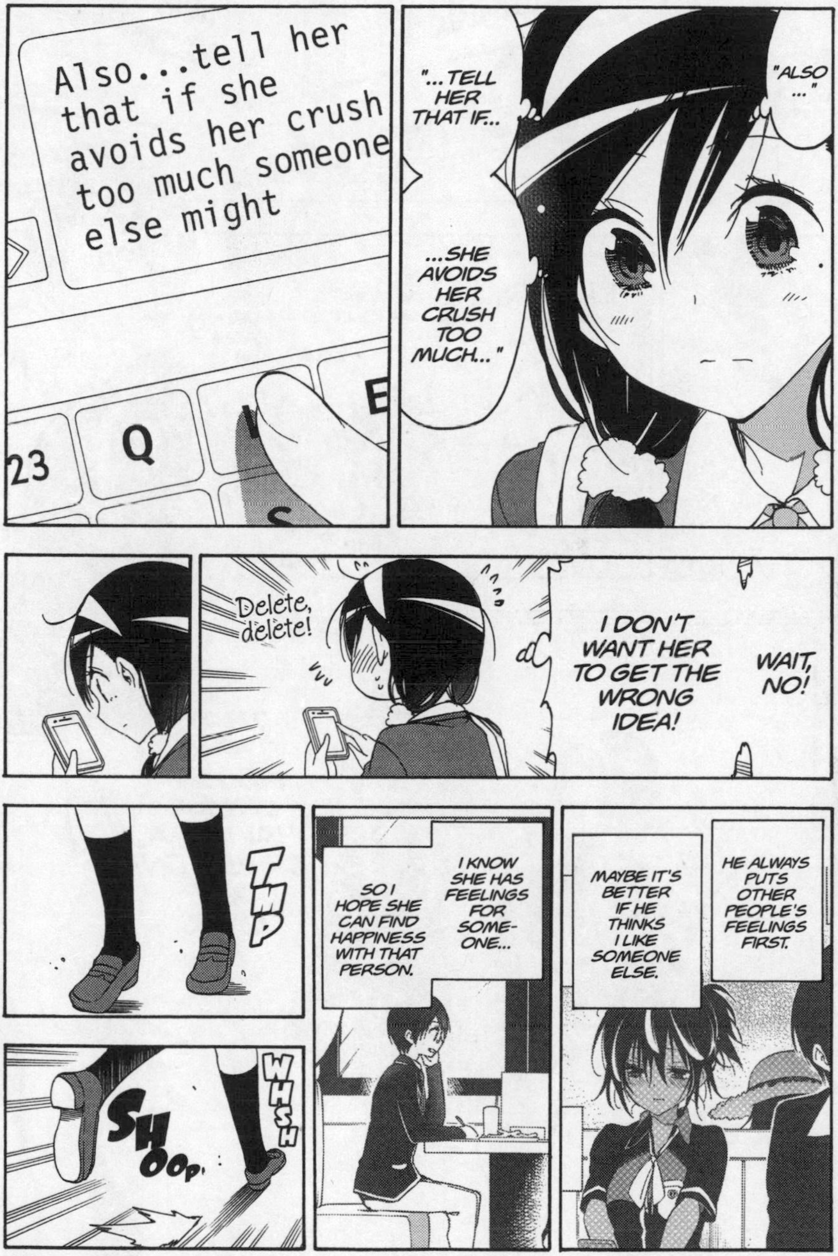
"ALSO ..."
"...TELL HER THAT IF...
...SHE AVOIDS HER CRUSH TOO MUCH..."
Also...tell her that if she avoids her crush too much someone else might
WAIT, NO!
I DON'T WANT HER TO GET THE WRONG IDEA!
Delete, delete!
HE ALWAYS PUTS OTHER PEOPLE'S FEELINGS FIRST.
MAYBE IT'S BETTER IF HE THINKS I LIKE SOMEONE ELSE.
I KNOW SHE HAS FEELINGS FOR SOME-ONE...
SO I HOPE SHE CAN FIND HAPPINESS WITH THAT PERSON.
TMP
WHSH
SHOOP

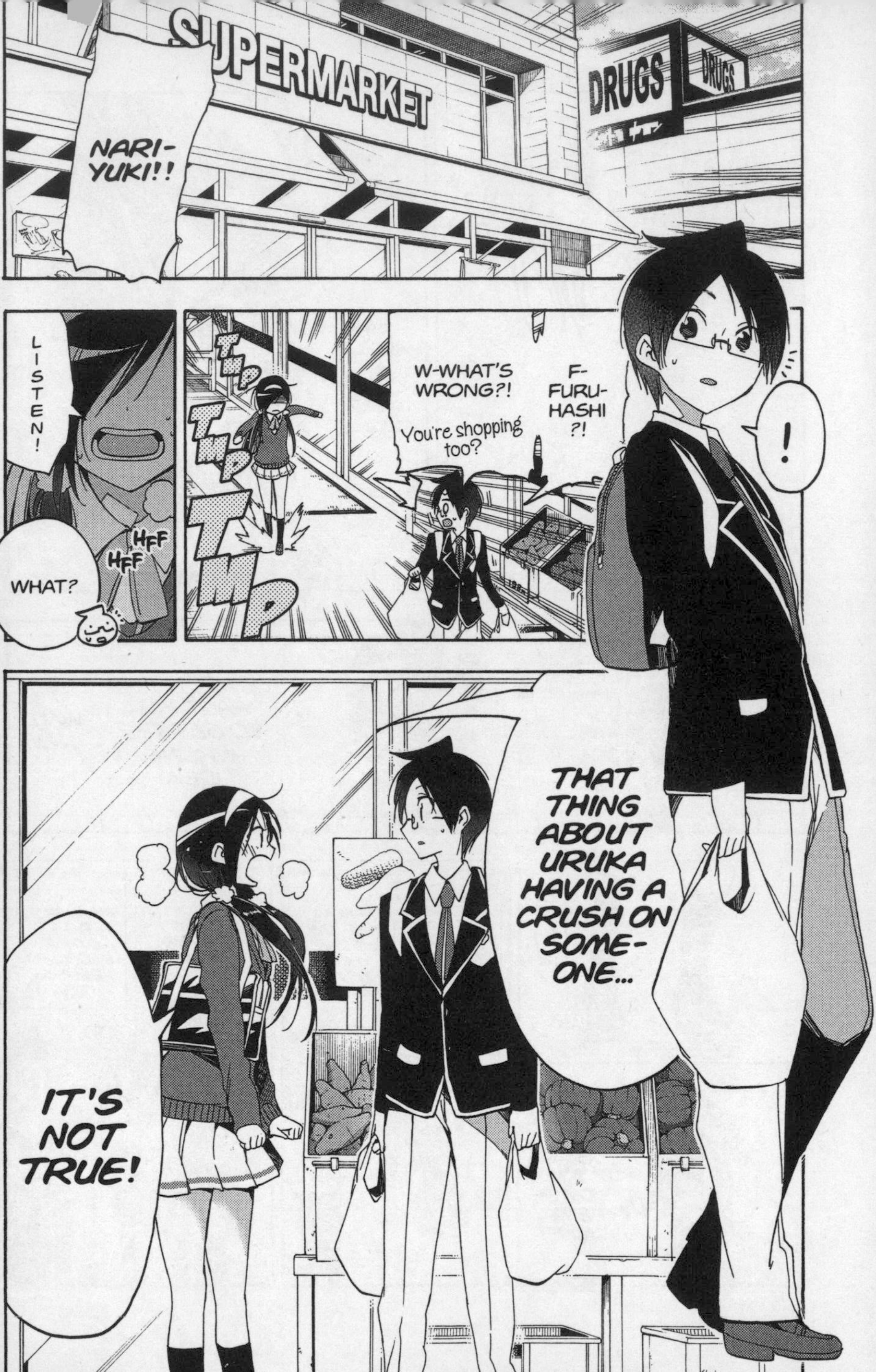
SUPERMARKET
DRUGS
DRUGS
NARI-YUKI!!
!
F-FURU-HASHI?!
W-WHAT'S WRONG?!
You're shopping too?
TMP TMP TMP
LISTEN!
HFF HFF
WHAT?
THAT THING ABOUT URUKA HAVING A CRUSH ON SOME-ONE...
IT'S NOT TRUE!

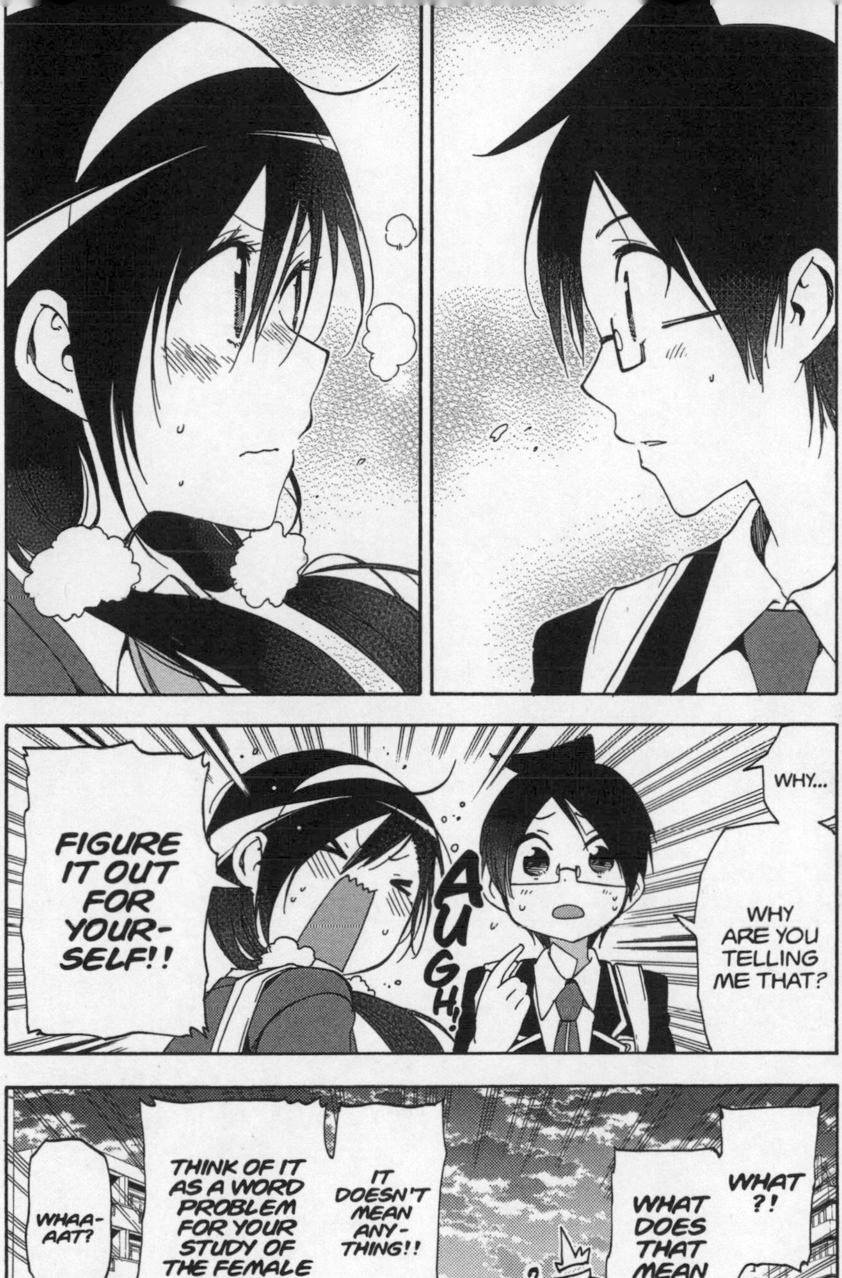
WHY...
WHY ARE YOU TELLING ME THAT?
AUGH!
FIGURE IT OUT FOR YOURSELF!!
WHAT?!
WHAT DOES THAT MEAN?!
IT DOESN'T MEAN ANYTHING!!
THINK OF IT AS A WORD PROBLEM FOR YOUR STUDY OF THE FEMALE PSYCHE!
WHAA-AAT?

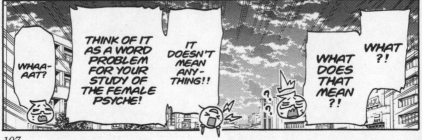

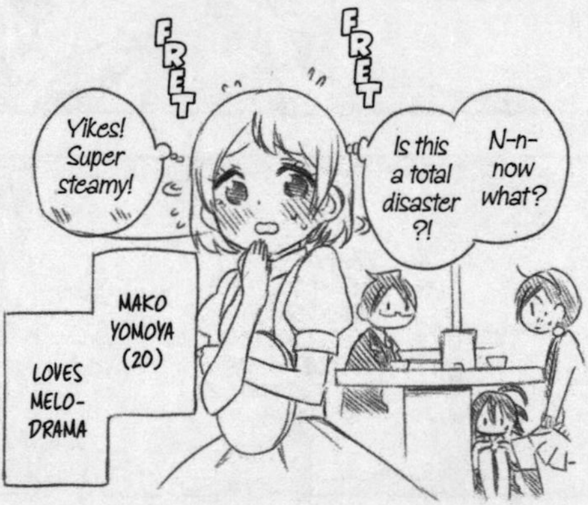
N-n-now what?
Is this a total disaster?!
FRET
FRET
Yikes! Super steamy!
MAKO YOMOYA (20)
LOVES MELO-DRAMA

Question 84: A Certain Book Alludes to a Predecessor's [X]

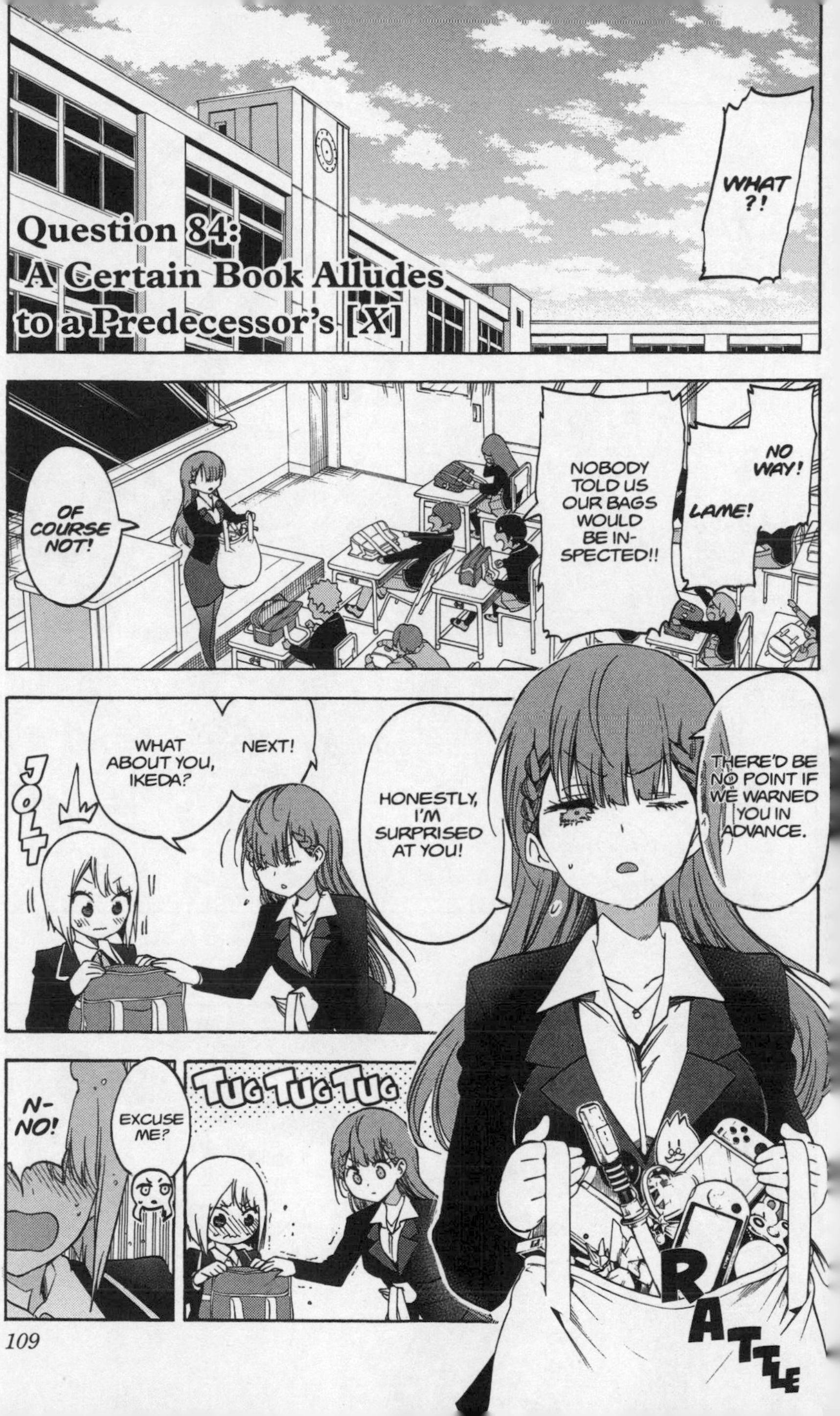
WHAT?!
NO WAY!
LAME!
NOBODY TOLD US OUR BAGS WOULD BE IN-SPECTED!!
OF COURSE NOT!
THERE'D BE NO POINT IF WE WARNED YOU IN ADVANCE.
RATTLE
HONESTLY, I'M SURPRISED AT YOU!
NEXT!
WHAT ABOUT YOU, IKEDA?
JOLT
TUG TUG TUG
EXCUSE ME?
N-NO!

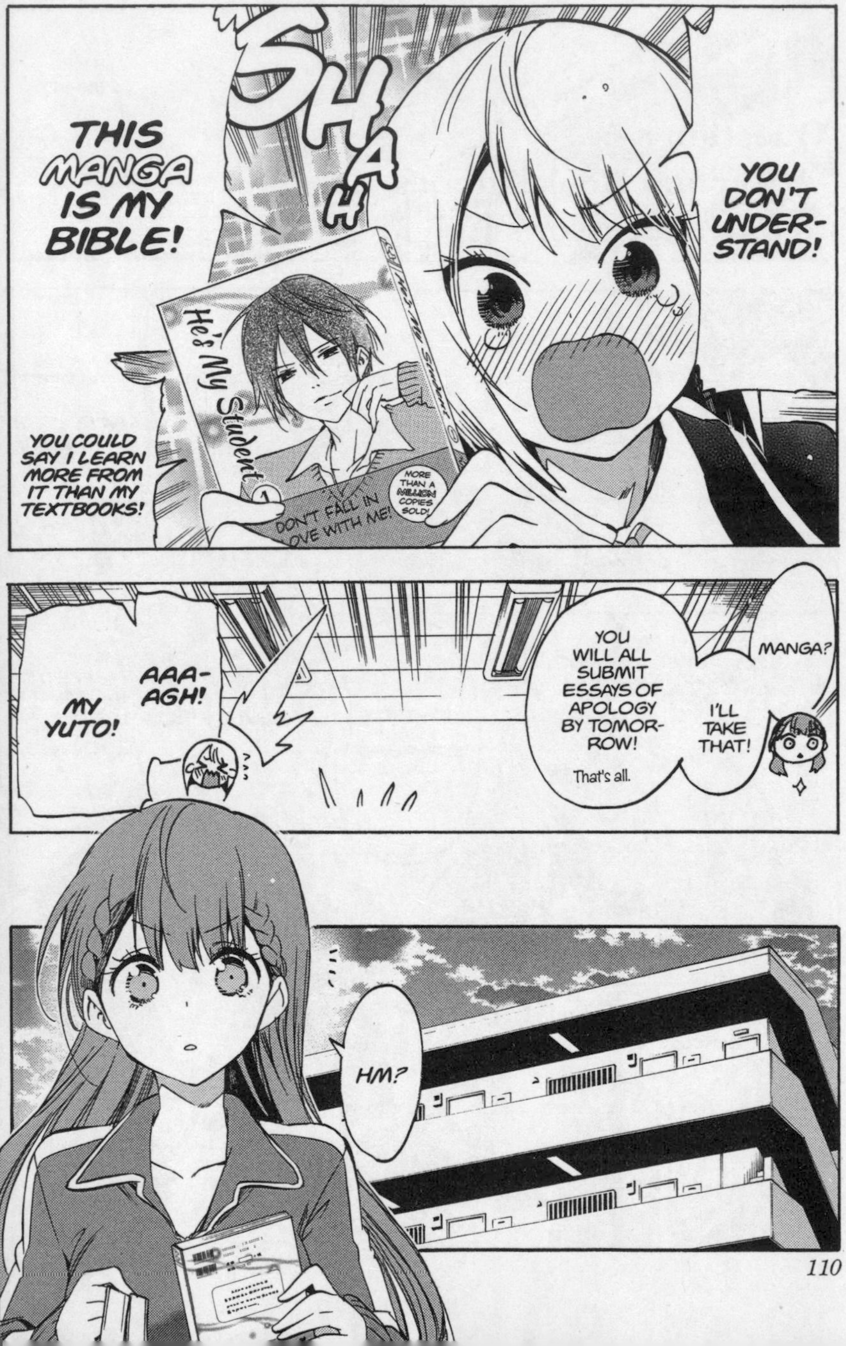
SHAH
YOU DON'T UNDER-STAND!
THIS MANGA IS MY BIBLE!
He's My Student
MORE THAN A MILLION COPIES SOLD!
DON'T FALL IN OVE WITH ME!
YOU COULD SAY I LEARN MORE FROM IT THAN MY TEXTBOOKS!
MANGA?
I'LL TAKE THAT!
YOU WILL ALL SUBMIT ESSAYS OF APOLOGY BY TOMOR-ROW!
That's all.
AAA-AGH!
MY YUTO!
HM?

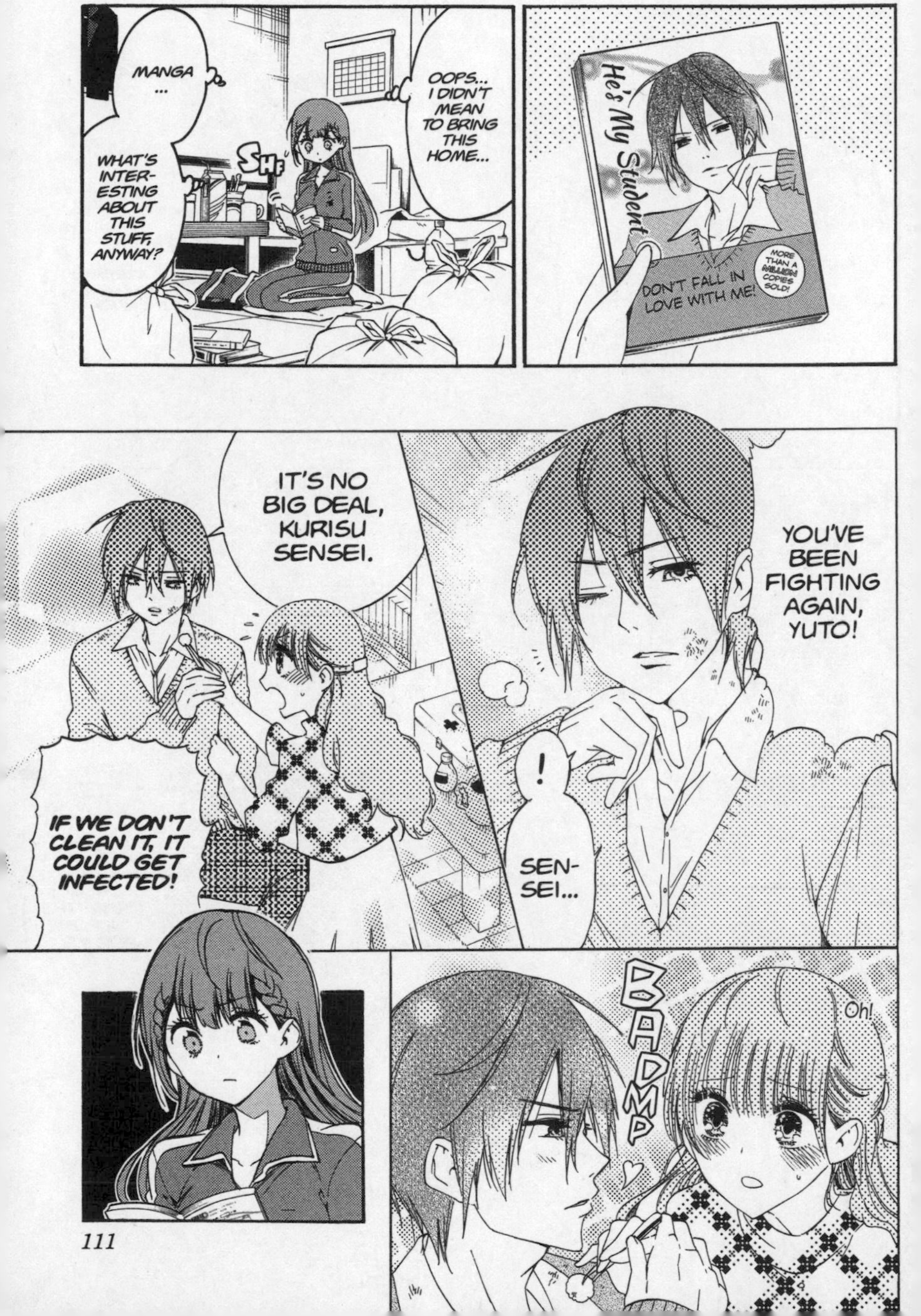
He's My Student
DON'T FALL IN LOVE WITH ME!
MORE THAN A MILLION COPIES SOLD!
OOPS... I DIDN'T MEAN TO BRING THIS HOME...
SHF
MANGA ...
WHAT'S INTERESTING ABOUT THIS STUFF, ANYWAY?
YOU'VE BEEN FIGHTING AGAIN, YUTO!
!
SEN-SEI...
IT'S NO BIG DEAL, KURISU SENSEI.
IF WE DON'T CLEAN IT, IT COULD GET INFECTED!
Oh!
BADMP

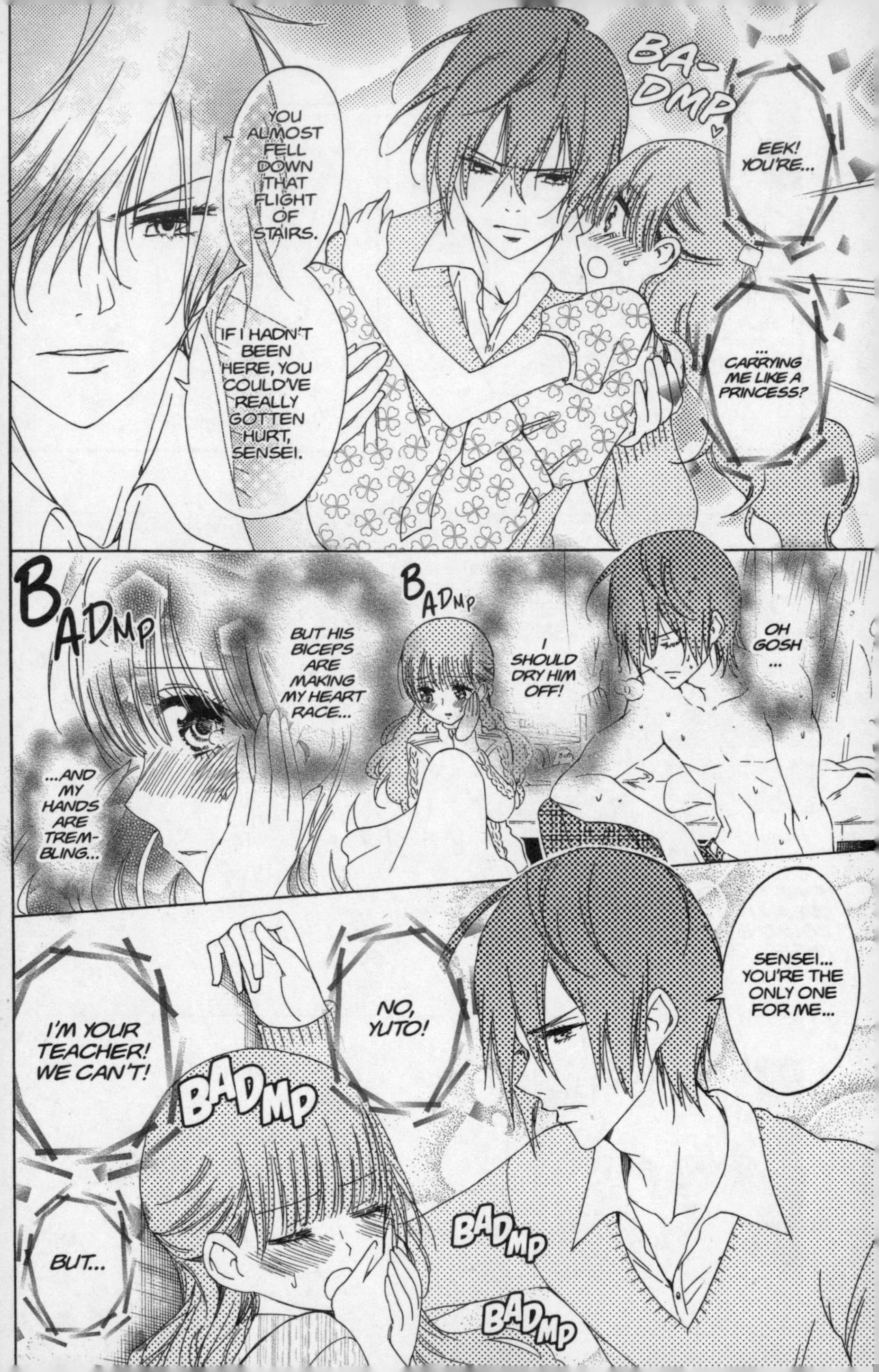
BA-DMP
EEK! YOU'RE...
...CARRYING ME LIKE A PRINCESS?
YOU ALMOST FELL DOWN THAT FLIGHT OF STAIRS.
IF I HADN'T BEEN HERE, YOU COULD'VE REALLY GOTTEN HURT, SENSEI.
OH GOSH...
I SHOULD DRY HIM OFF!
BADMP
BUT HIS BICEPS ARE MAKING MY HEART RACE...
BADMP
...AND MY HANDS ARE TREMBLING...
SENSEI... YOU'RE THE ONLY ONE FOR ME...
NO, YUTO!
I'M YOUR TEACHER! WE CAN'T!
BADMP
BUT...
BADMP
BADMP

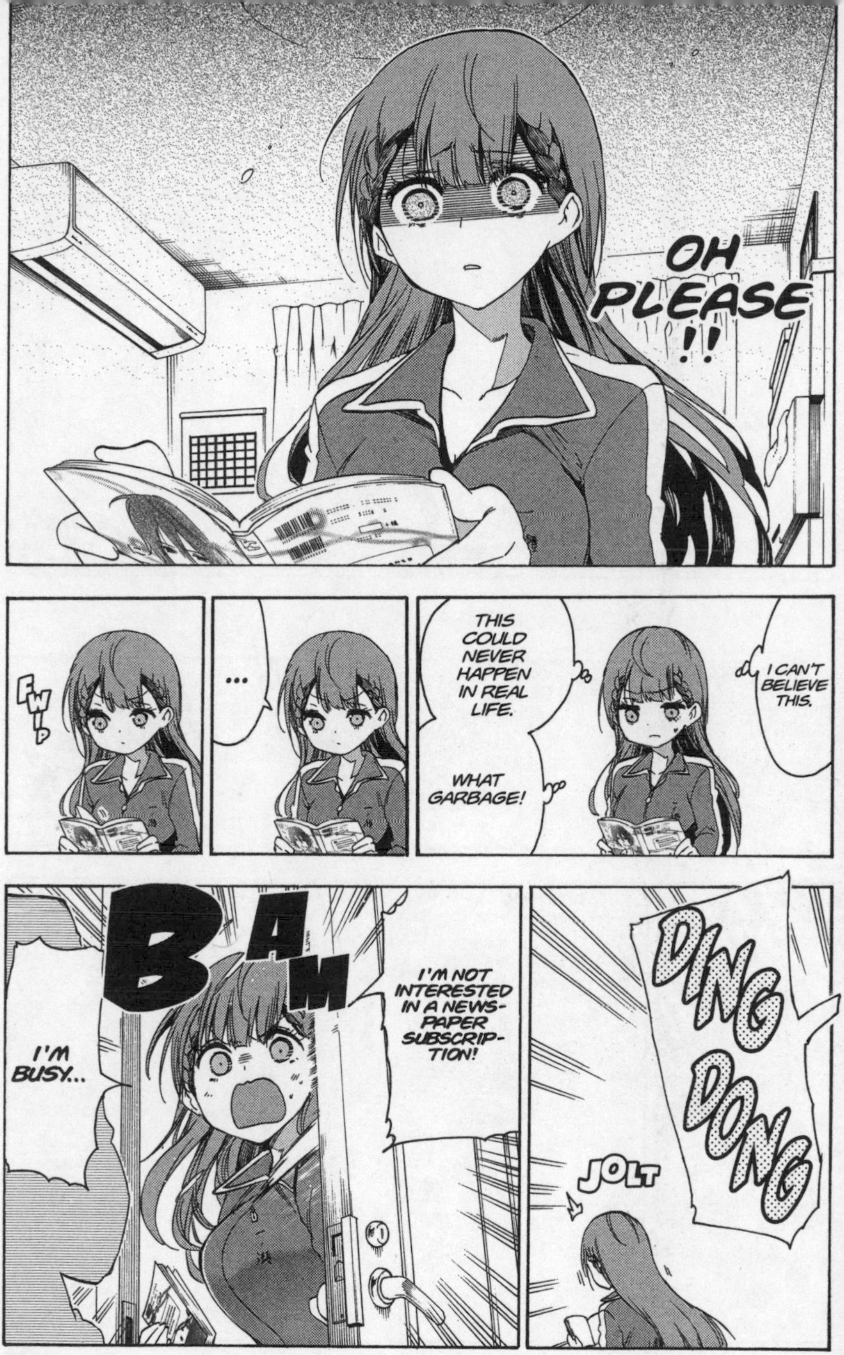
OH PLEASE!!
I CAN'T BELIEVE THIS.
THIS COULD NEVER HAPPEN IN REAL LIFE.
WHAT GARBAGE!
...
FWIP
DING DONG
JOLT
BAM
I'M NOT INTERESTED IN A NEWS-PAPER SUBSCRIP-TION!
I'M BUSY...

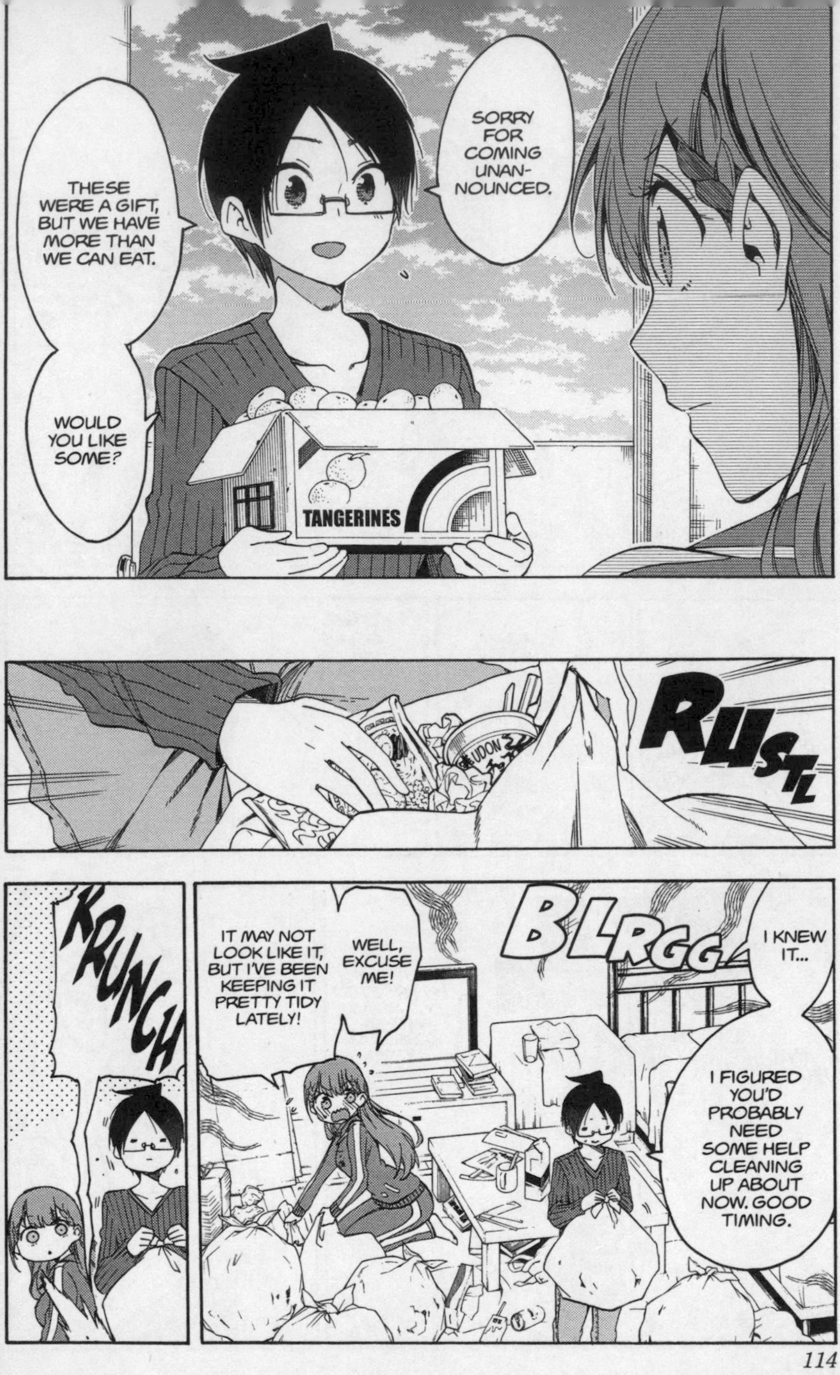
SORRY FOR COMING UNANNOUNCED.
THESE WERE A GIFT, BUT WE HAVE MORE THAN WE CAN EAT.
WOULD YOU LIKE SOME?
TANGERINES
RUSTL
UDON
BLRGG
I KNEW IT...
I FIGURED YOU'D PROBABLY NEED SOME HELP CLEANING UP ABOUT NOW. GOOD TIMING.
WELL, EXCUSE ME!
IT MAY NOT LOOK LIKE IT, BUT I'VE BEEN KEEPING IT PRETTY TIDY LATELY!
KRUNCH

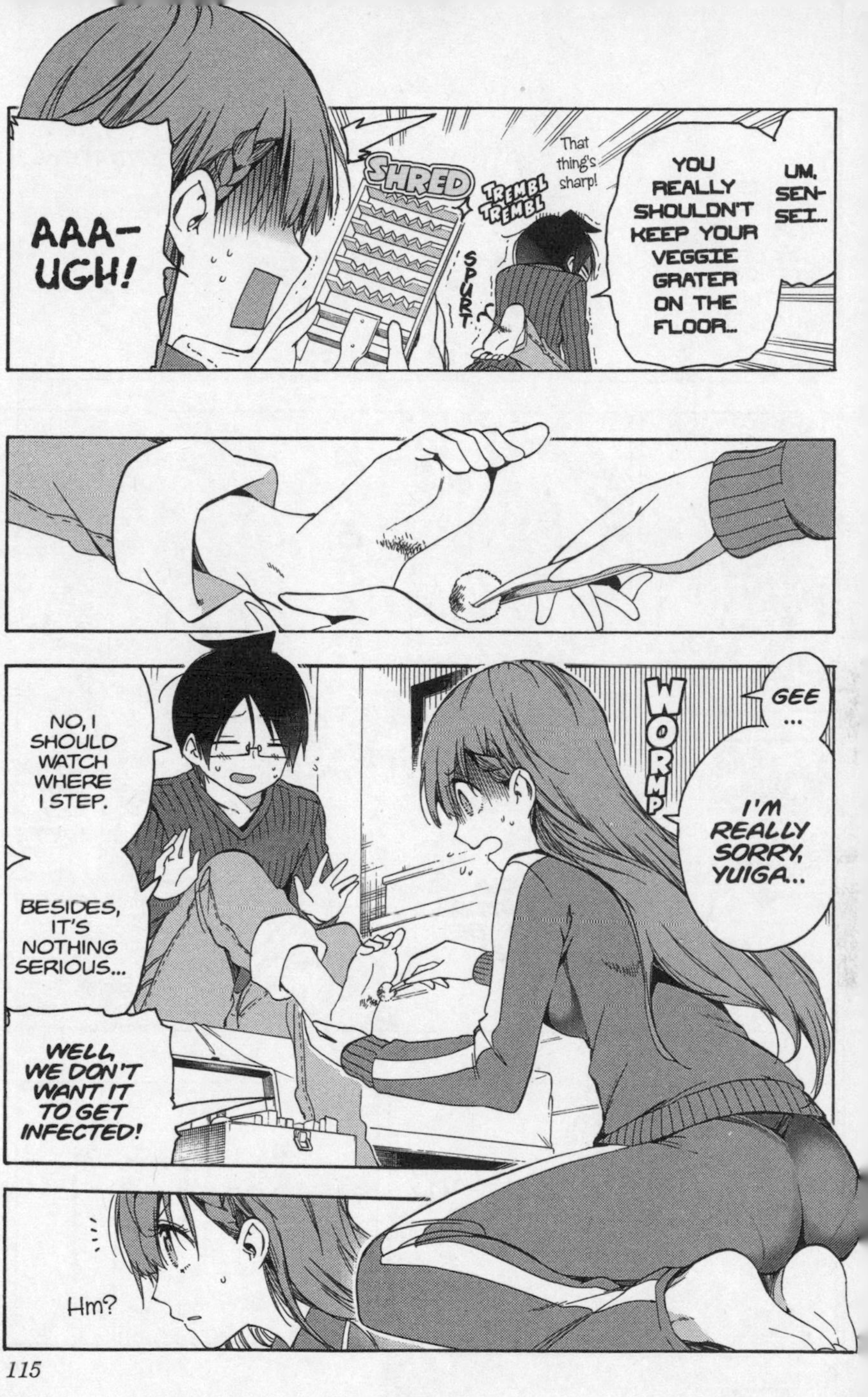
UM, SEN-SEI...
YOU REALLY SHOULDN'T KEEP YOUR VEGGIE GRATER ON THE FLOOR...
That thing's sharp!
TREMBL TREMBL
SPURT
SHRED
AAA-UGH!
GEE ...
I'M REALLY SORRY, YUIGA...
WORMP
NO, I SHOULD WATCH WHERE I STEP.
BESIDES, IT'S NOTHING SERIOUS...
WELL, WE DON'T WANT IT TO GET INFECTED!
Hm?

THIS SITUATION...

...IS JUST LIKE THE SCENE FROM THAT MANGA...

Uncle!

FLAIL FLAIL

AIEEE!!

GRIND

FOR REAL?!

STUFF LIKE THIS ACTUALLY HAPPENS?!

YEOWCH! THAT HURTS, SENSEI!! BE GENTLE!!

FLAIL FLAIL

Aiieee!

IMPOS-SIBLE.

NAH...

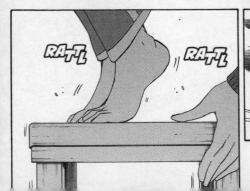

RATTL

RATTL

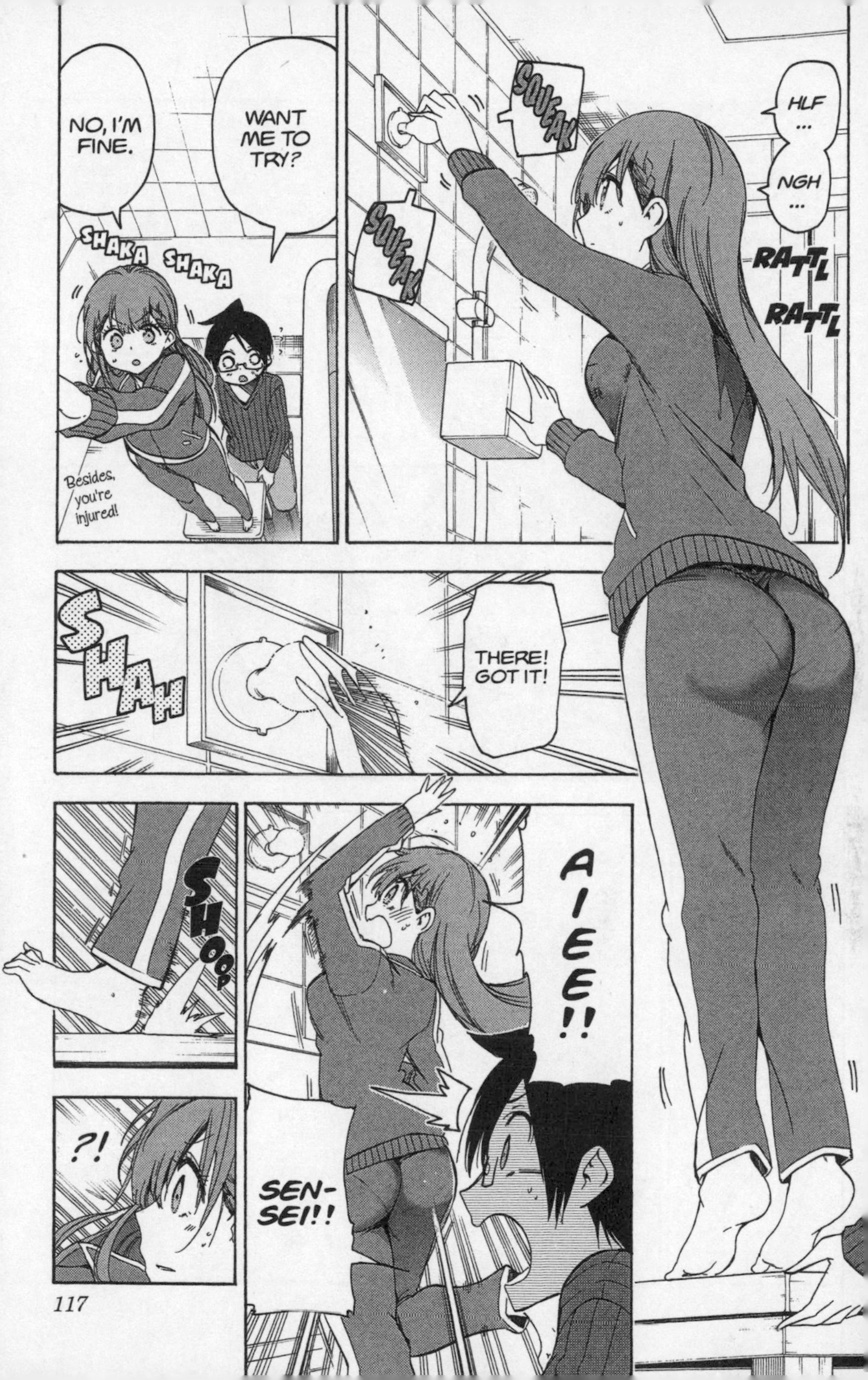
HLF ...
NGH ...
RATTL
RATTL
SQUEAK
SQUEAK
WANT ME TO TRY?
NO, I'M FINE.
SHAKA SHAKA
Besides, you're injured!
THERE! GOT IT!
SHAH
AIEE!!
SEN-SEI!!
SHOOP
?!

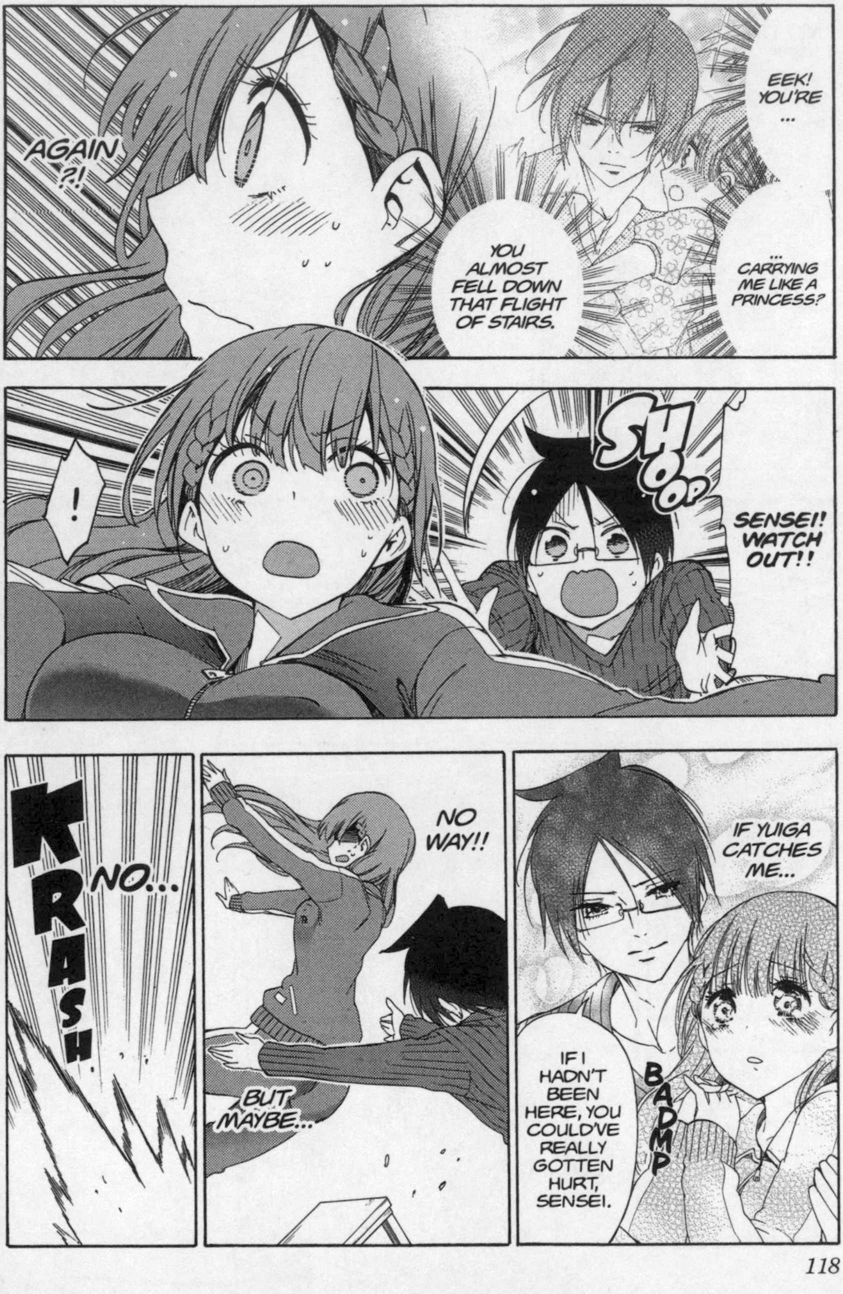
EEK! YOU'RE ...
... CARRYING ME LIKE A PRINCESS?
YOU ALMOST FELL DOWN THAT FLIGHT OF STAIRS.
AGAIN ?!
SHOOP
SENSEI! WATCH OUT!!
!
IF YUIGA CATCHES ME...
BADMP
IF I HADN'T BEEN HERE, YOU COULD'VE REALLY GOTTEN HURT, SENSEI.
NO WAY!!
BUT MAYBE...
NO...
KRASH

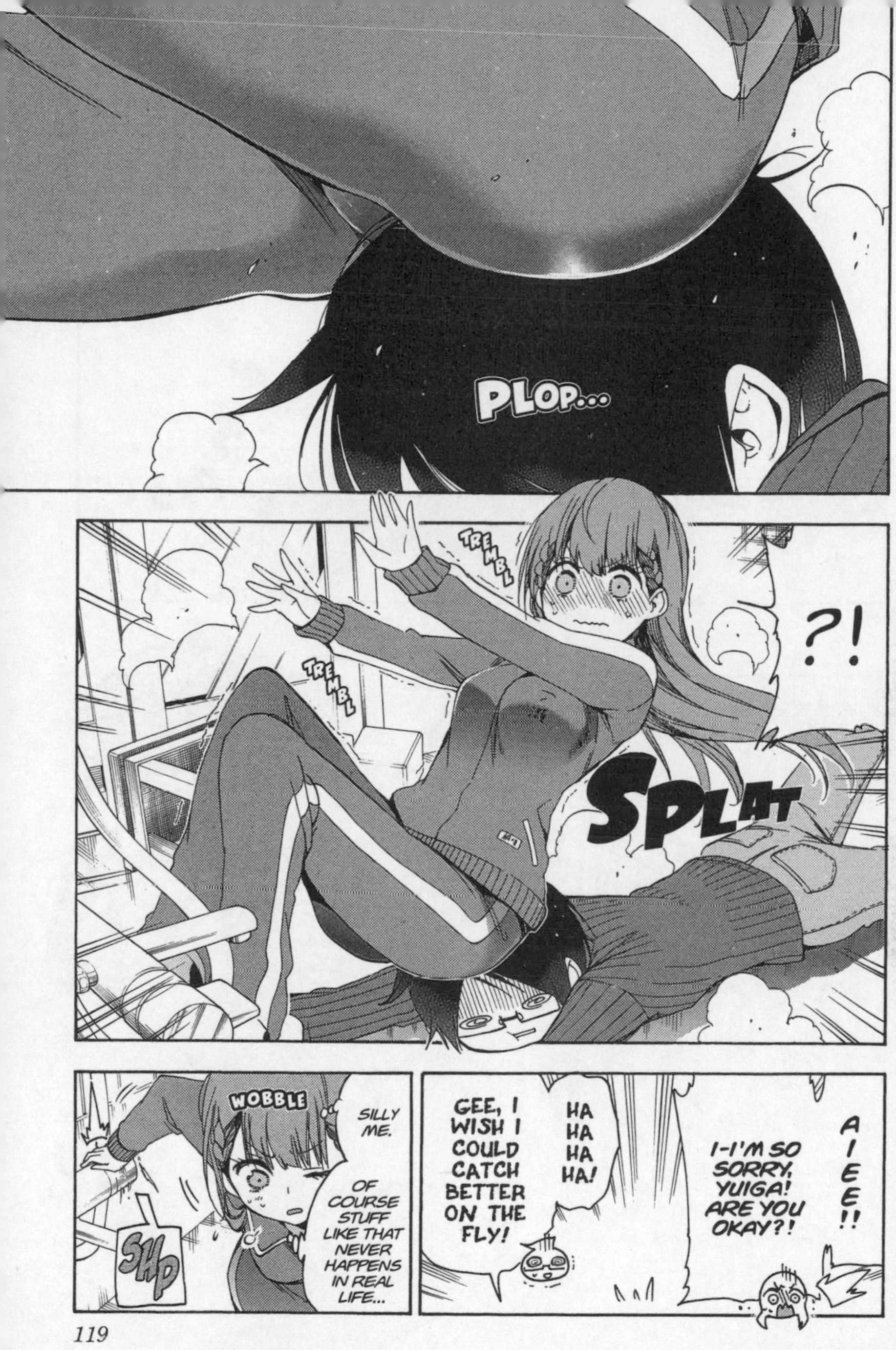
PLOP...
?!
SPLAT
TREMBL
TREMBL
AIEE!!
I-I'M SO SORRY, YUIGA! ARE YOU OKAY?!
HA HA HA HA!
GEE, I WISH I COULD CATCH BETTER ON THE FLY!
SILLY ME.
OF COURSE STUFF LIKE THAT NEVER HAPPENS IN REAL LIFE...
WOBBLE
SHP

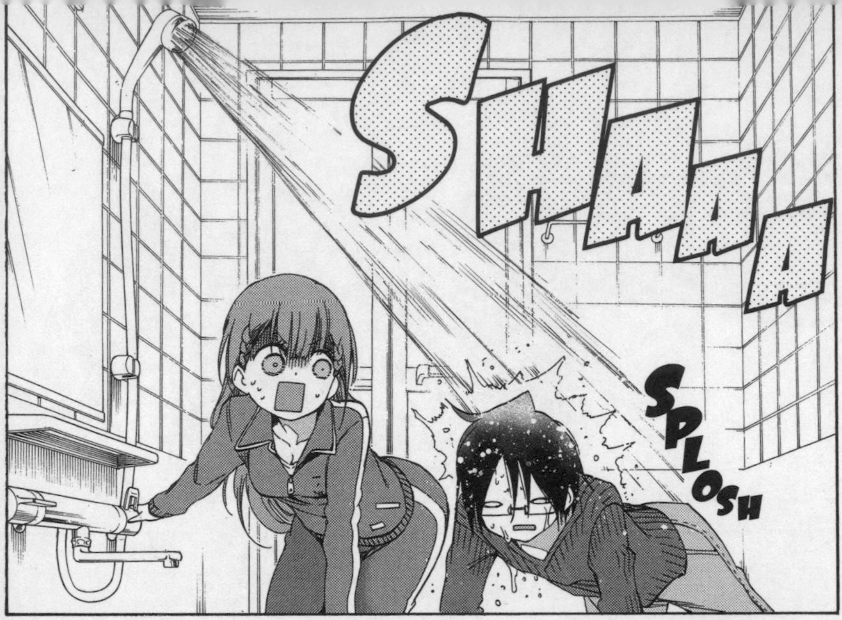
SHAAAA
SPLOSH

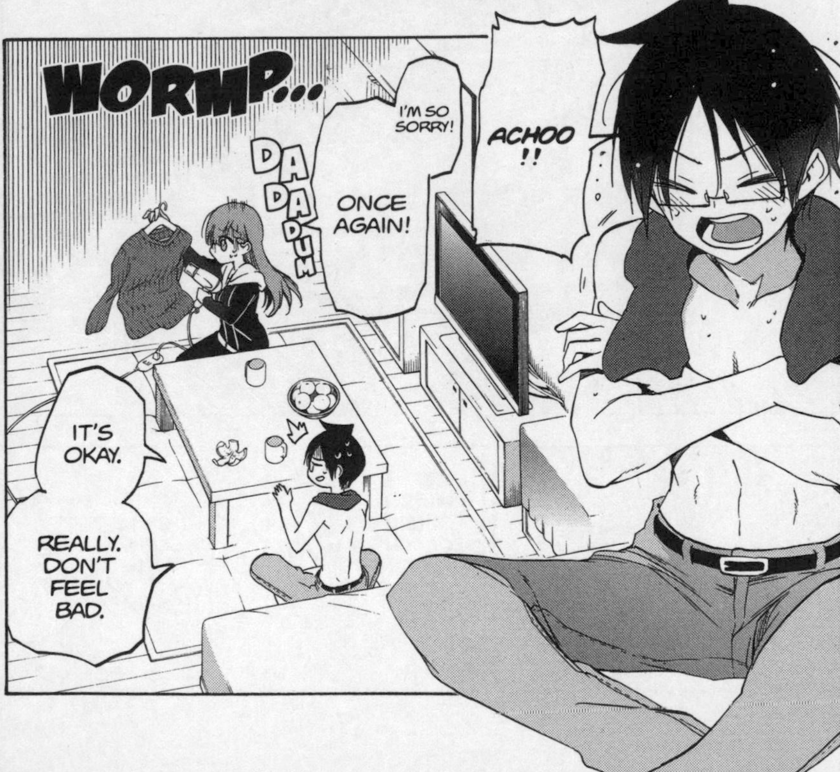
ACHOO!!
I'M SO SORRY!
ONCE AGAIN!
DADADUM
WORMP...
IT'S OKAY.
REALLY. DON'T FEEL BAD.

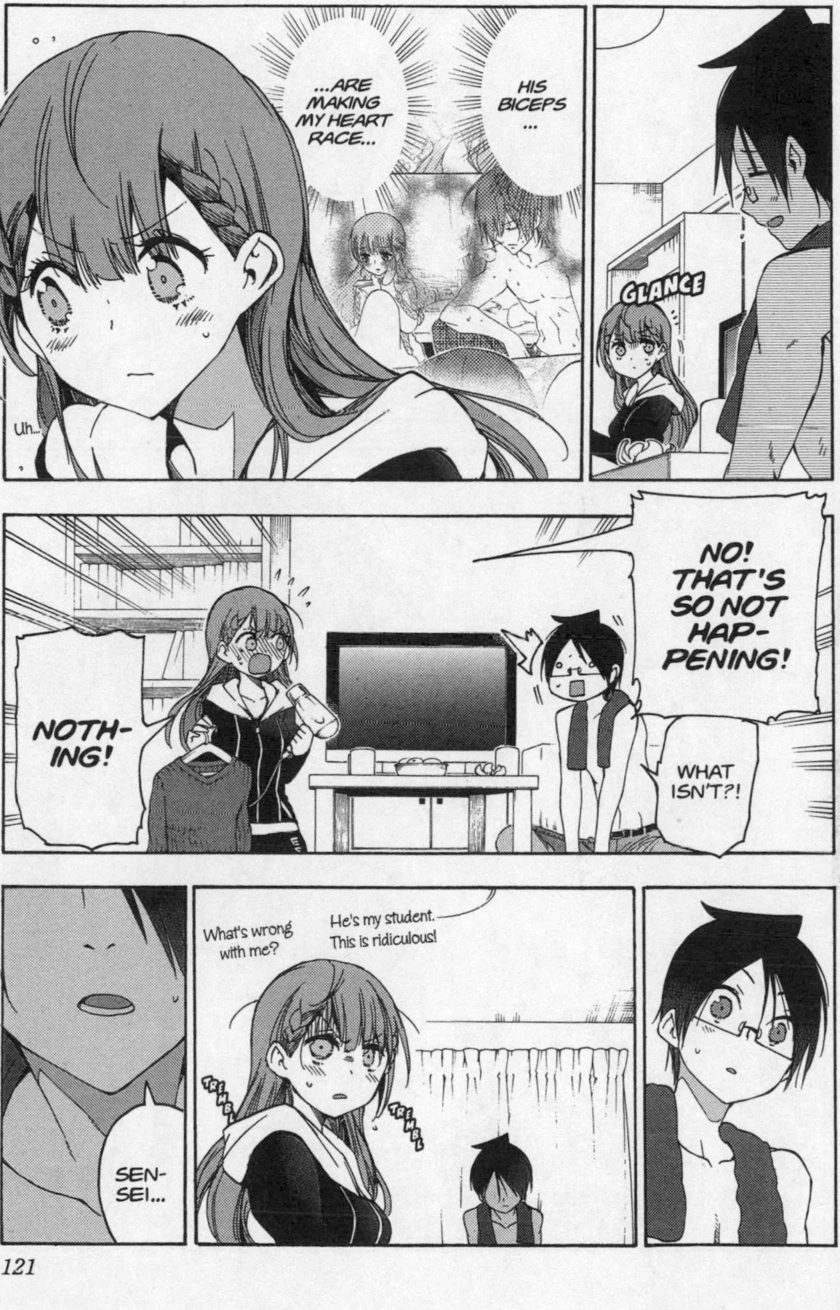
GLANCE
HIS BICEPS ...
...ARE MAKING MY HEART RACE...
Uh...
NO! THAT'S SO NOT HAP-PENING!
WHAT ISN'T?!
NOTH-ING!
He's my student. This is ridiculous!
What's wrong with me?
TREMBL
TREMBL
SEN-SEI...

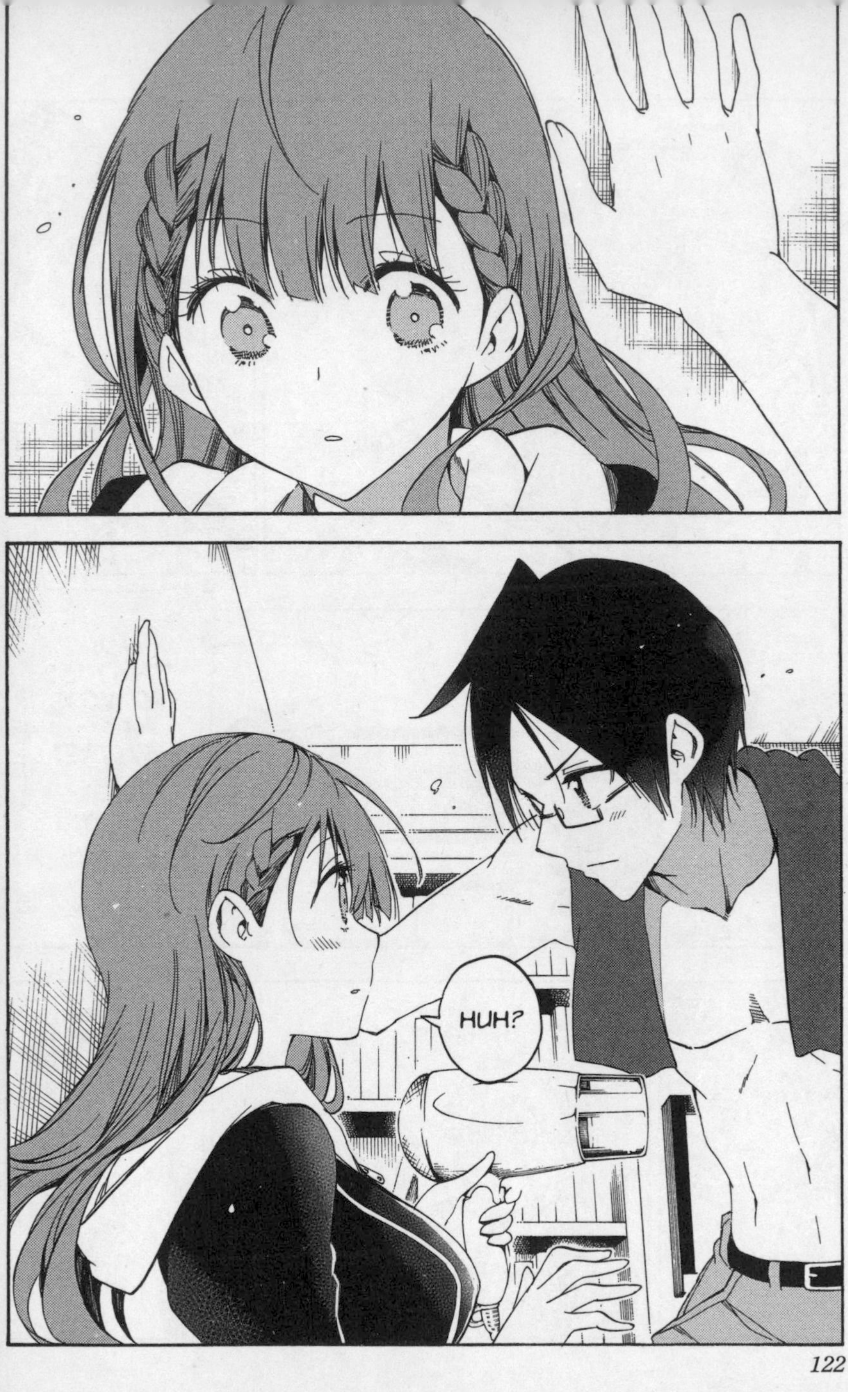
HUH?

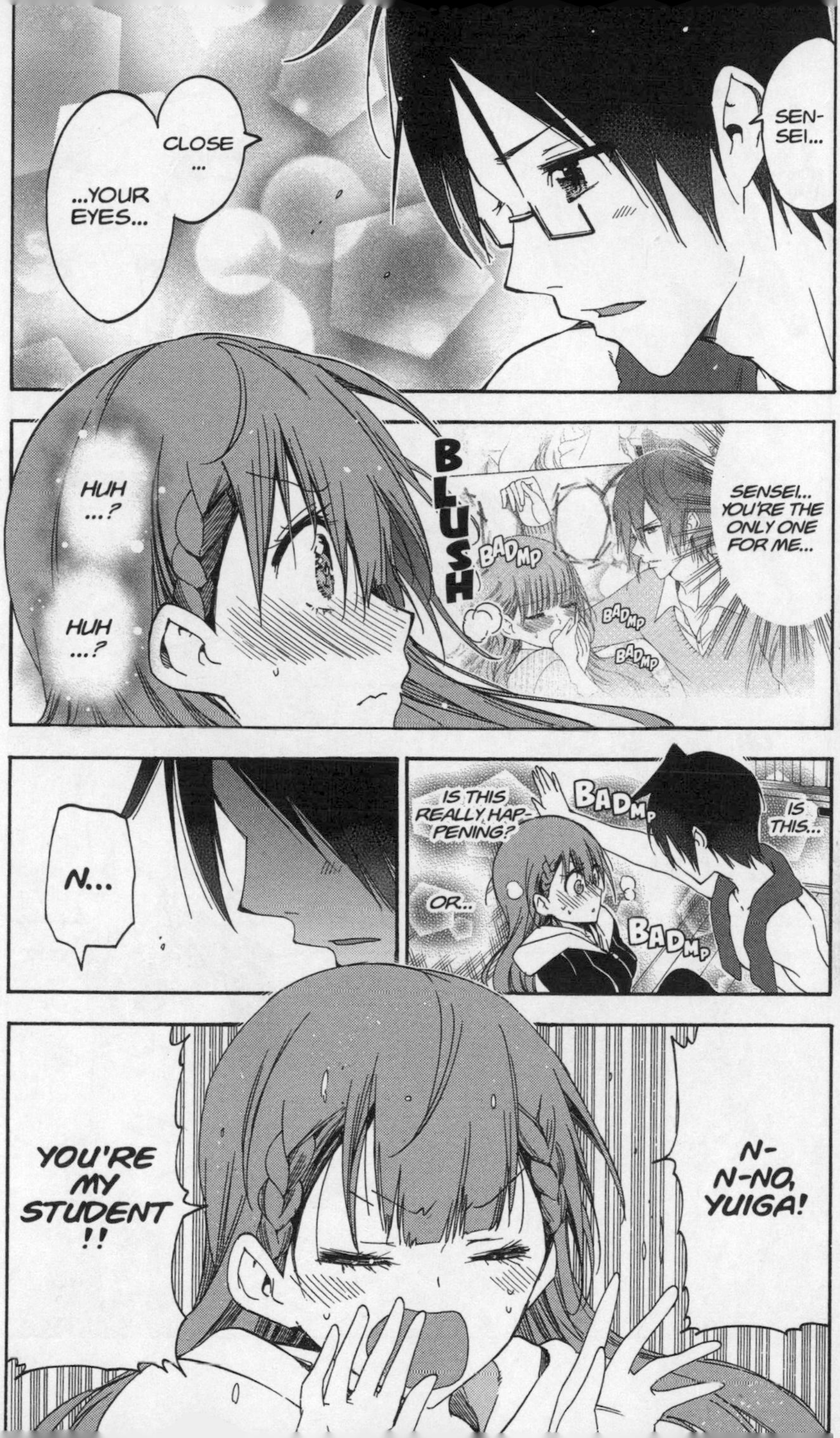
SEN-SEI...
CLOSE ... ...YOUR EYES...
SENSEI... YOU'RE THE ONLY ONE FOR ME...
BADMP
BADMP
BADMP
BLUSH
HUH ...?
HUH ...?
IS THIS...
BADMP
IS THIS REALLY HAPPENING?
OR..
BADMP
N...
N-N-NO, YUIGA!
YOU'RE MY STUDENT !!

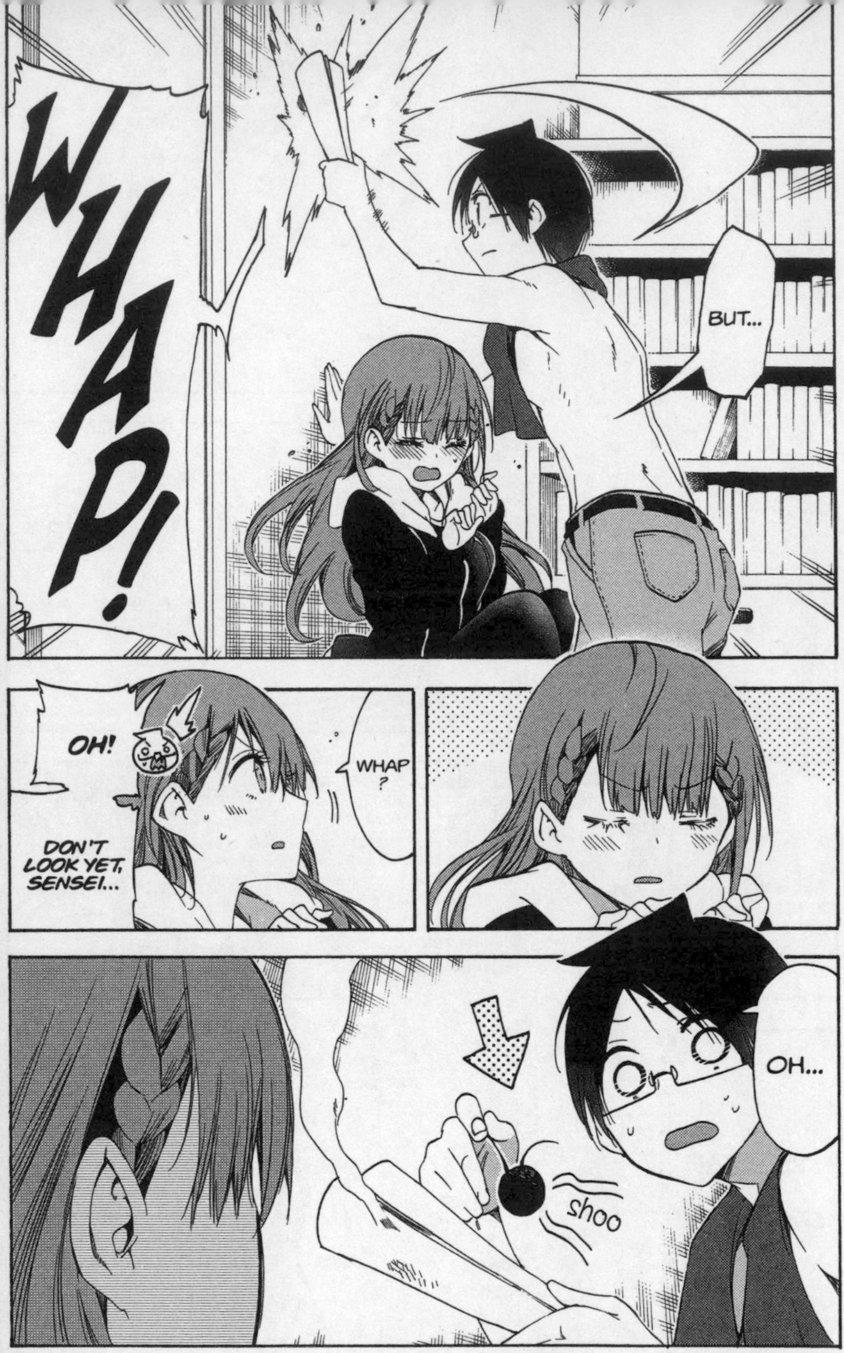
BUT...
WHAP!
WHAP?
OH!
DON'T LOOK YET, SENSEI...
OH...
shoo

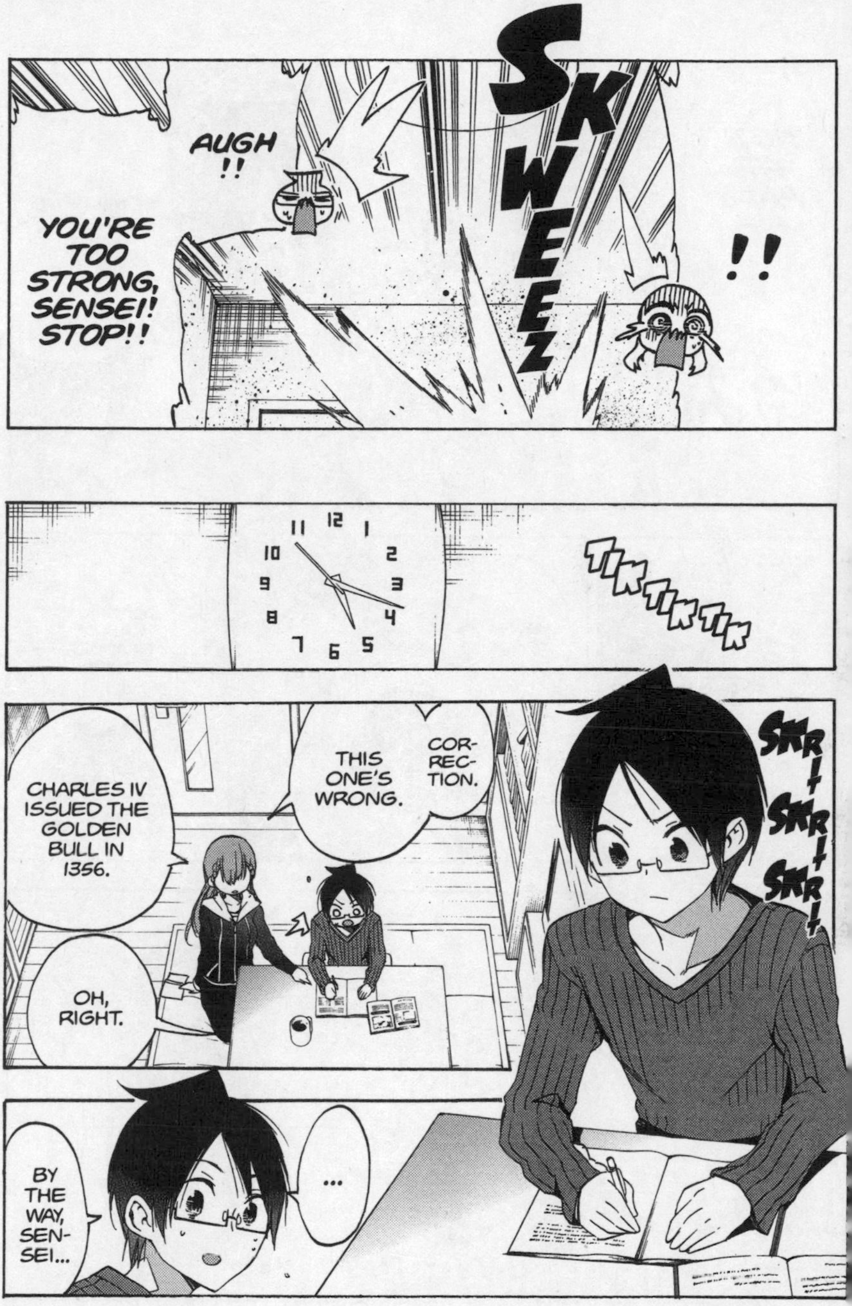
SKWEEZ
!!
AUGH!!
YOU'RE TOO STRONG, SENSEI! STOP!!
TIK TIK TIK
SKRIT SKRIT SKRIT
CORRECTION.
THIS ONE'S WRONG.
CHARLES IV ISSUED THE GOLDEN BULL IN 1356.
OH, RIGHT.
...
BY THE WAY, SENSEI...

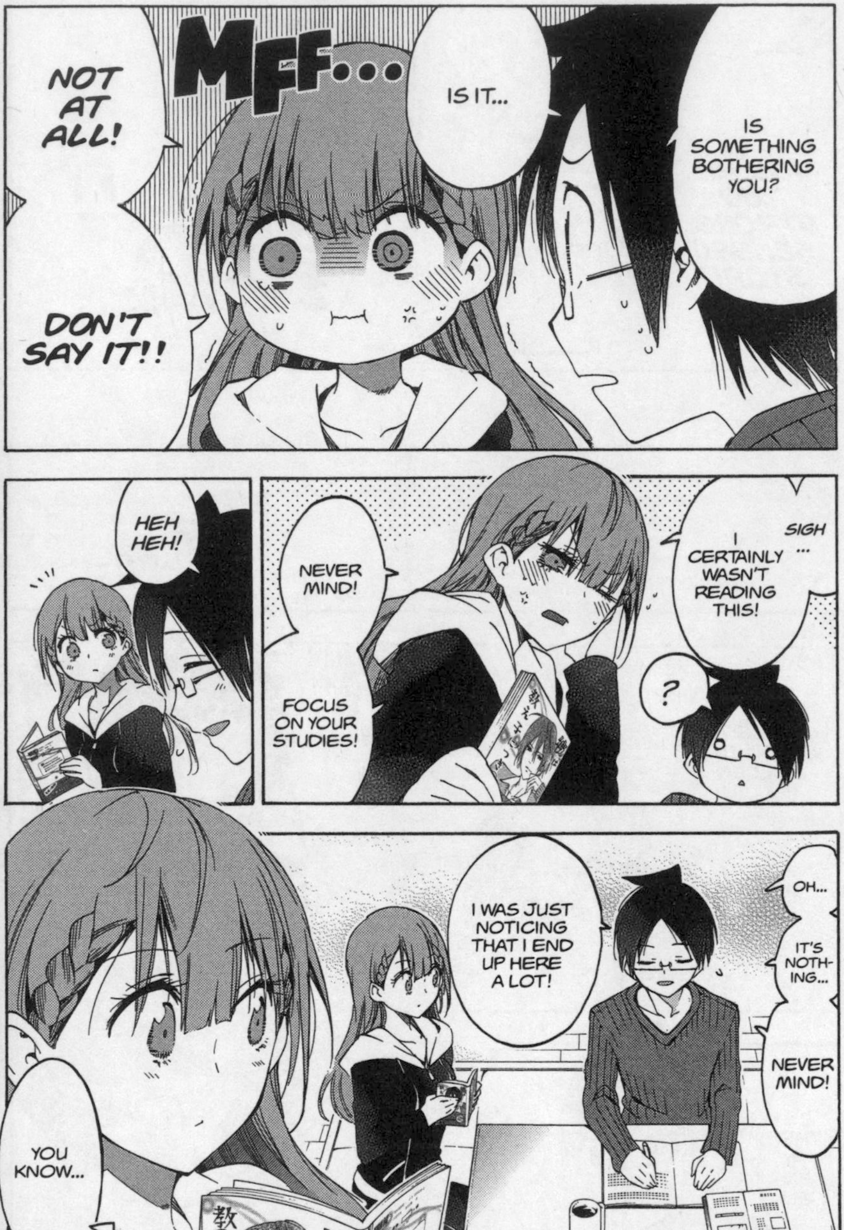
IS SOMETHING BOTHERING YOU?
IS IT...
MFF...
NOT AT ALL!
DON'T SAY IT!!
SIGH ...
I CERTAINLY WASN'T READING THIS!
?
NEVER MIND!
FOCUS ON YOUR STUDIES!
HEH HEH!
OH...
IT'S NOTHING...
NEVER MIND!
I WAS JUST NOTICING THAT I END UP HERE A LOT!
YOU KNOW...

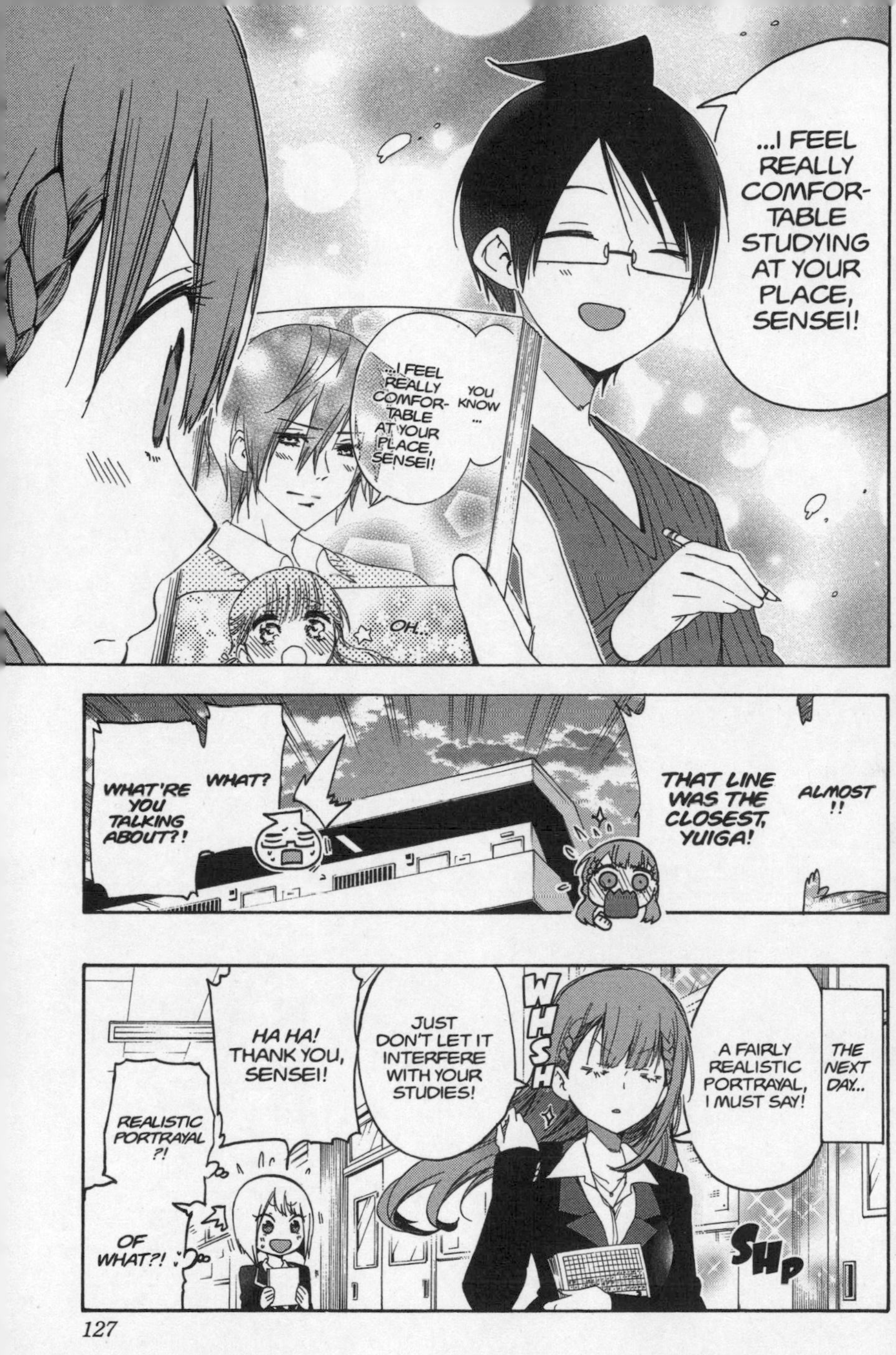
...I FEEL REALLY COMFORTABLE STUDYING AT YOUR PLACE, SENSEI!
YOU KNOW ...
...I FEEL REALLY COMFORTABLE AT YOUR PLACE, SENSEI!
OH...
ALMOST!!
THAT LINE WAS THE CLOSEST, YUIGA!
WHAT?
WHAT'RE YOU TALKING ABOUT?!
THE NEXT DAY...
A FAIRLY REALISTIC PORTRAYAL, I MUST SAY!
WHSH
SHP
JUST DON'T LET IT INTERFERE WITH YOUR STUDIES!
HA HA! THANK YOU, SENSEI!
REALISTIC PORTRAYAL ?!
OF WHAT?!

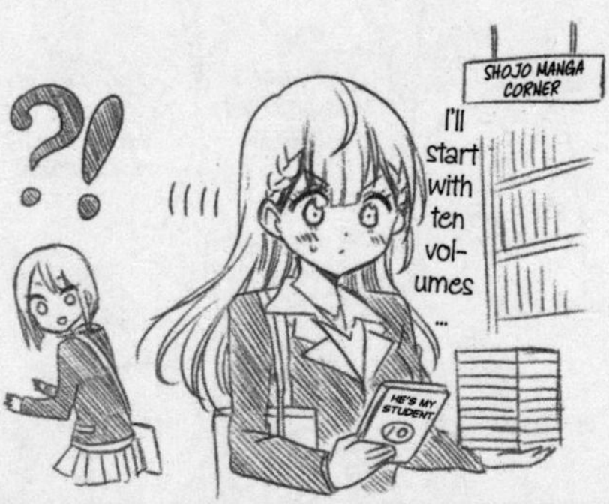

SHOJO MANGA CORNER
I'll start with ten vol-umes ...
?!
HE'S MY STUDENT
10

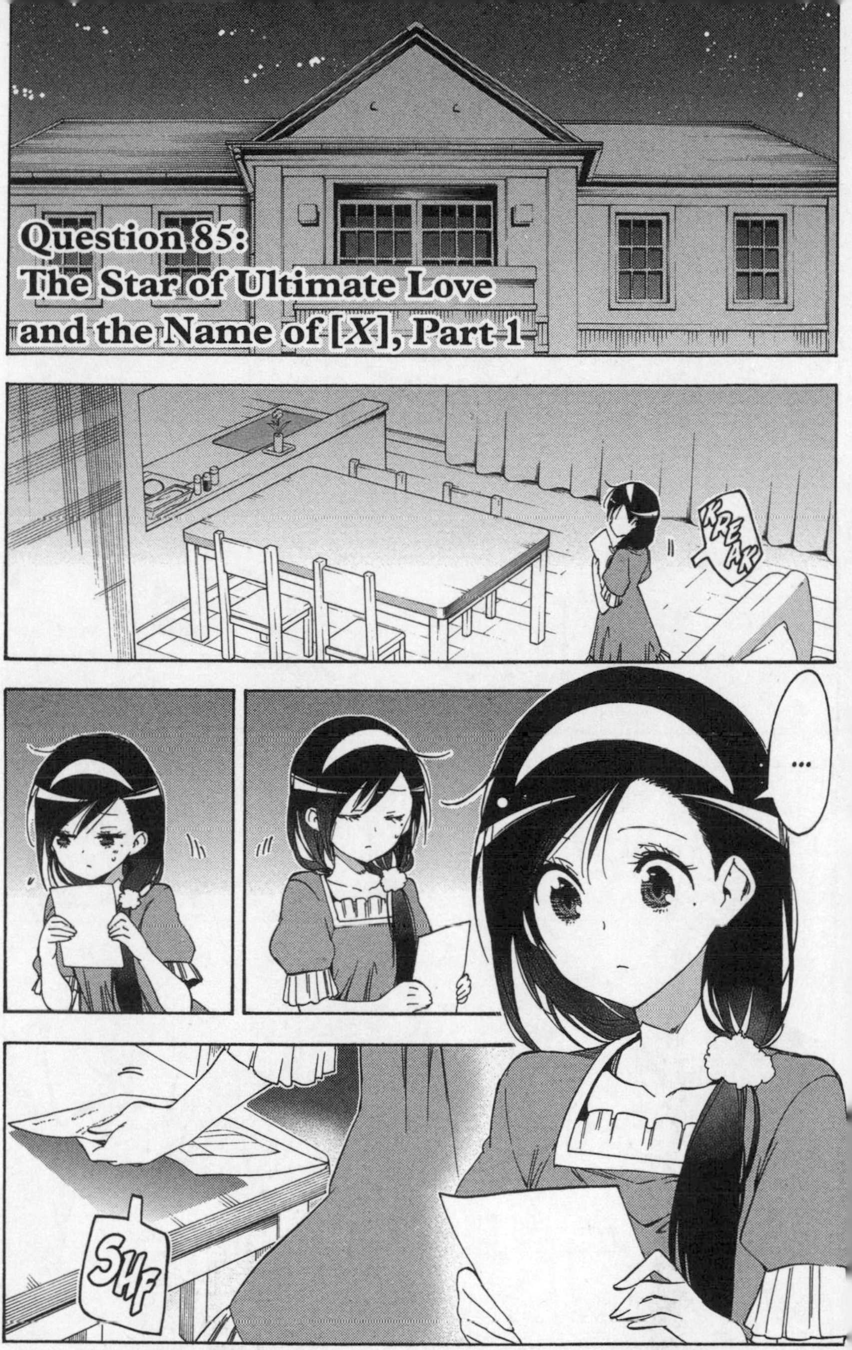
Question 85:
The Star of Ultimate Love
and the Name of [X], Part 1
KREAK
...
SHF

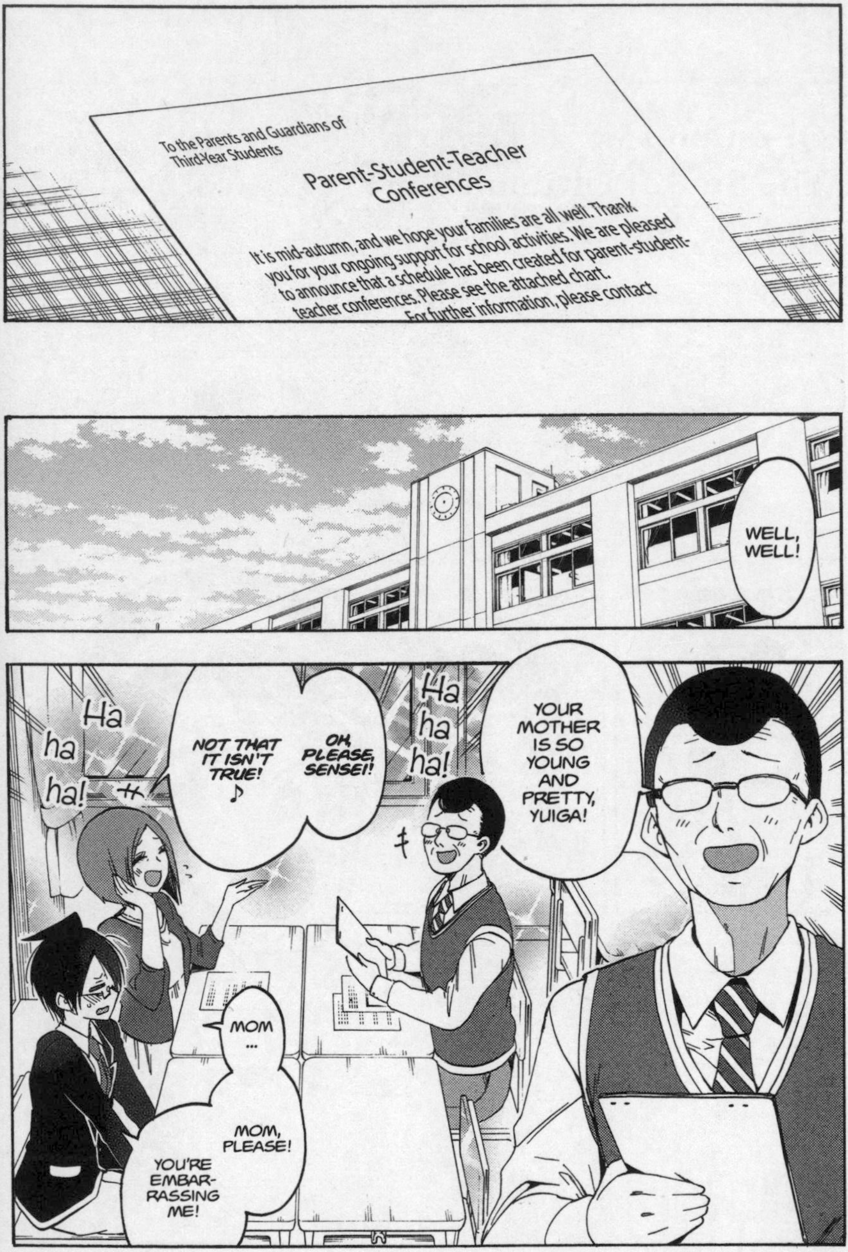
To the Parents and Guardians of Third-Year Students
Parent-Student-Teacher Conferences
It is mid-autumn, and we hope your families are all well. Thank you for your ongoing support for school activities. We are pleased to announce that a schedule has been created for parent-student-teacher conferences. Please see the attached chart.
For further information, please contact
WELL, WELL!
YOUR MOTHER IS SO YOUNG AND PRETTY, YUIGA!
Ha ha ha!
OH, PLEASE, SENSEI!
NOT THAT IT ISN'T TRUE! ♪
Ha ha ha!
MOM...
MOM, PLEASE!
YOU'RE EMBARRASSING ME!

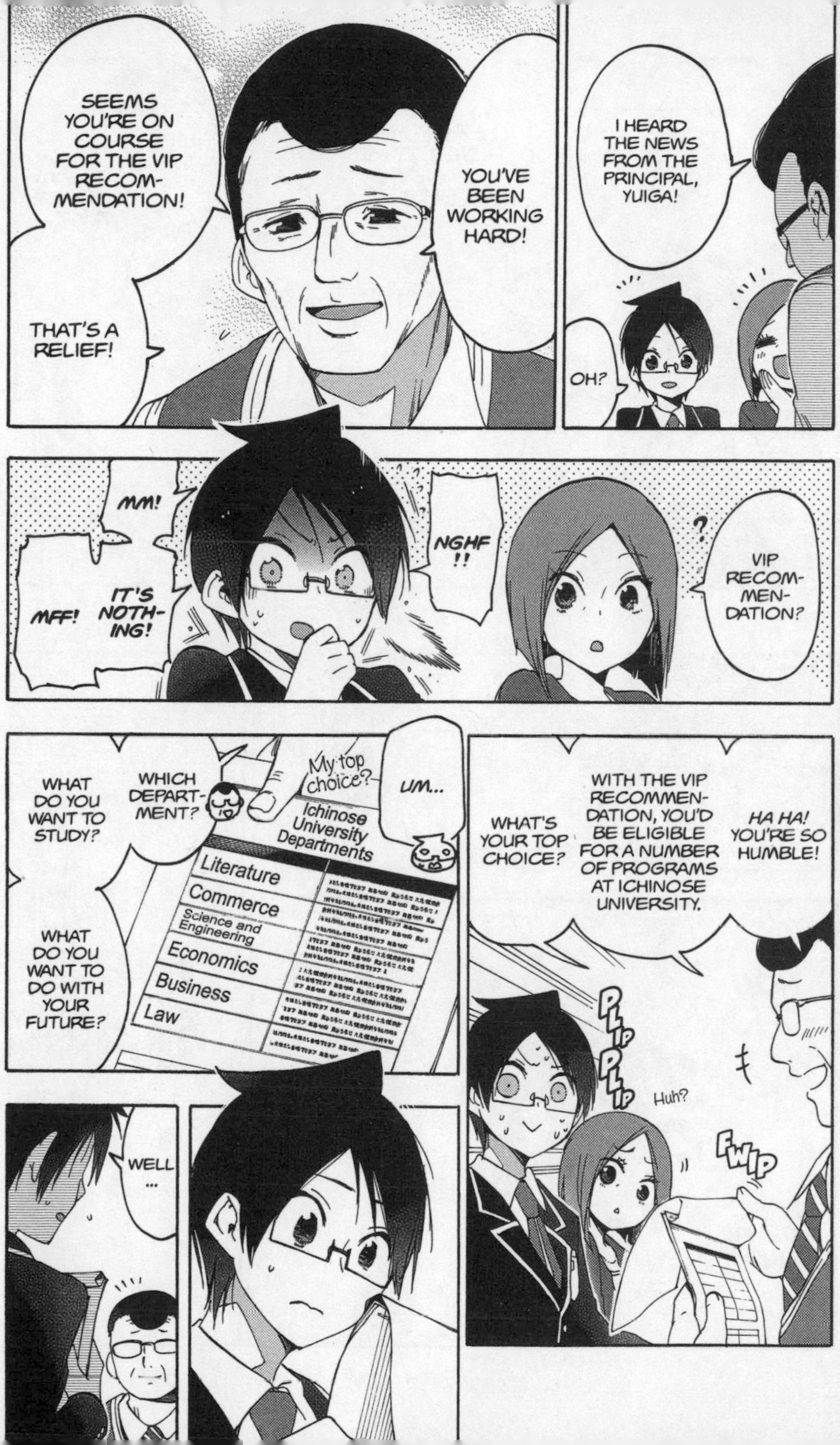
I HEARD THE NEWS FROM THE PRINCIPAL, YUIGA!
OH?
YOU'VE BEEN WORKING HARD!
SEEMS YOU'RE ON COURSE FOR THE VIP RECOMMENDATION!
THAT'S A RELIEF!
VIP RECOMMENDATION?
NGHF!!
MM!
IT'S NOTHING!
MFF!
HA HA! YOU'RE SO HUMBLE!
WITH THE VIP RECOMMENDATION, YOU'D BE ELIGIBLE FOR A NUMBER OF PROGRAMS AT ICHINOSE UNIVERSITY.
WHAT'S YOUR TOP CHOICE?
PLIP PLIP
Huh?
FWIP
UM...
My top choice?
WHICH DEPARTMENT?
WHAT DO YOU WANT TO STUDY?
WHAT DO YOU WANT TO DO WITH YOUR FUTURE?
Ichinose University Departments
Literature
Commerce
Science and Engineering
Economics
Business
Law
WELL...

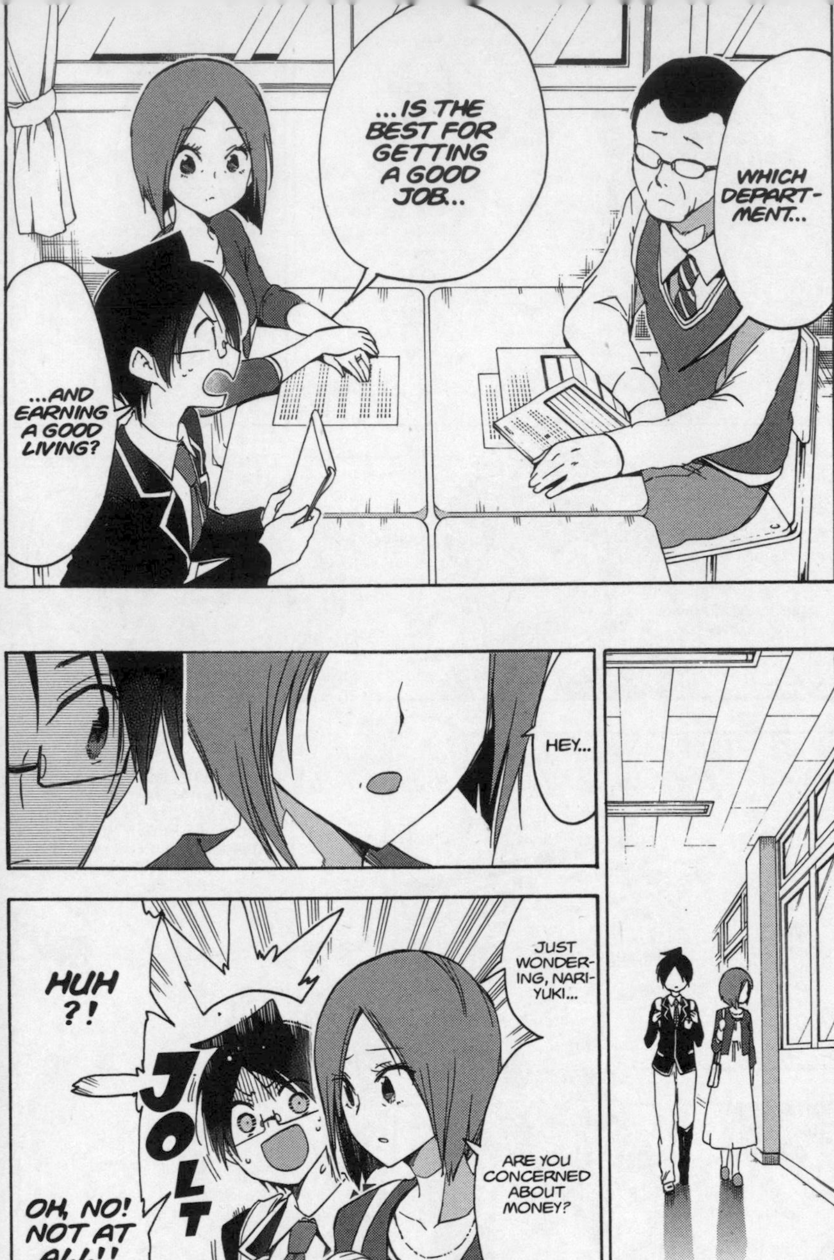
WHICH DEPARTMENT...
...IS THE BEST FOR GETTING A GOOD JOB...
...AND EARNING A GOOD LIVING?
HEY...
JUST WONDERING, NARIYUKI...
ARE YOU CONCERNED ABOUT MONEY?
HUH?!
JOLT
OH, NO! NOT AT ALL!!

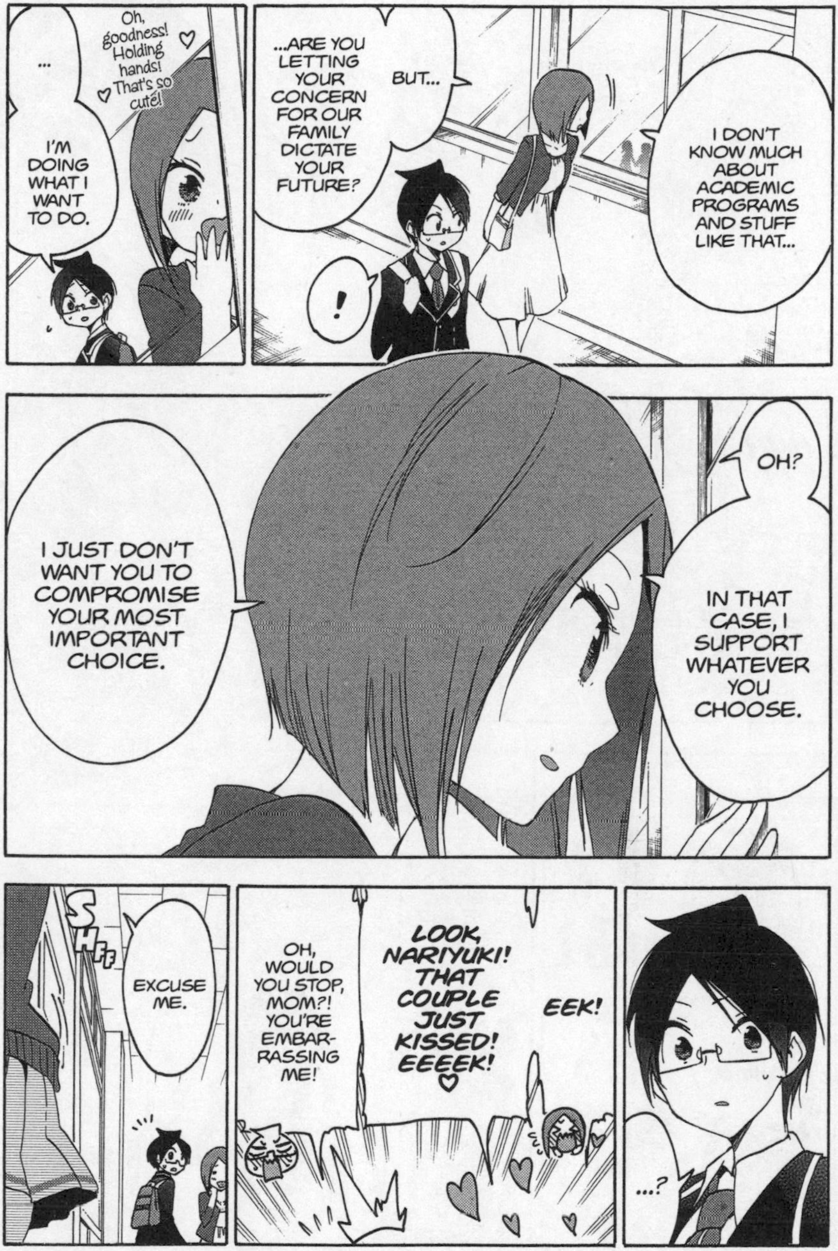

I DON'T KNOW MUCH ABOUT ACADEMIC PROGRAMS AND STUFF LIKE THAT...
BUT...
...ARE YOU LETTING YOUR CONCERN FOR OUR FAMILY DICTATE YOUR FUTURE?
!
Oh, goodness! Holding hands! That's so cute!
...
I'M DOING WHAT I WANT TO DO.
OH?
IN THAT CASE, I SUPPORT WHATEVER YOU CHOOSE.
I JUST DON'T WANT YOU TO COMPROMISE YOUR MOST IMPORTANT CHOICE.
...?
EEK!
LOOK, NARIYUKI! THAT COUPLE JUST KISSED! EEEEK!
OH, WOULD YOU STOP, MOM?! YOU'RE EMBARRASSING ME!
SHFF
EXCUSE ME.

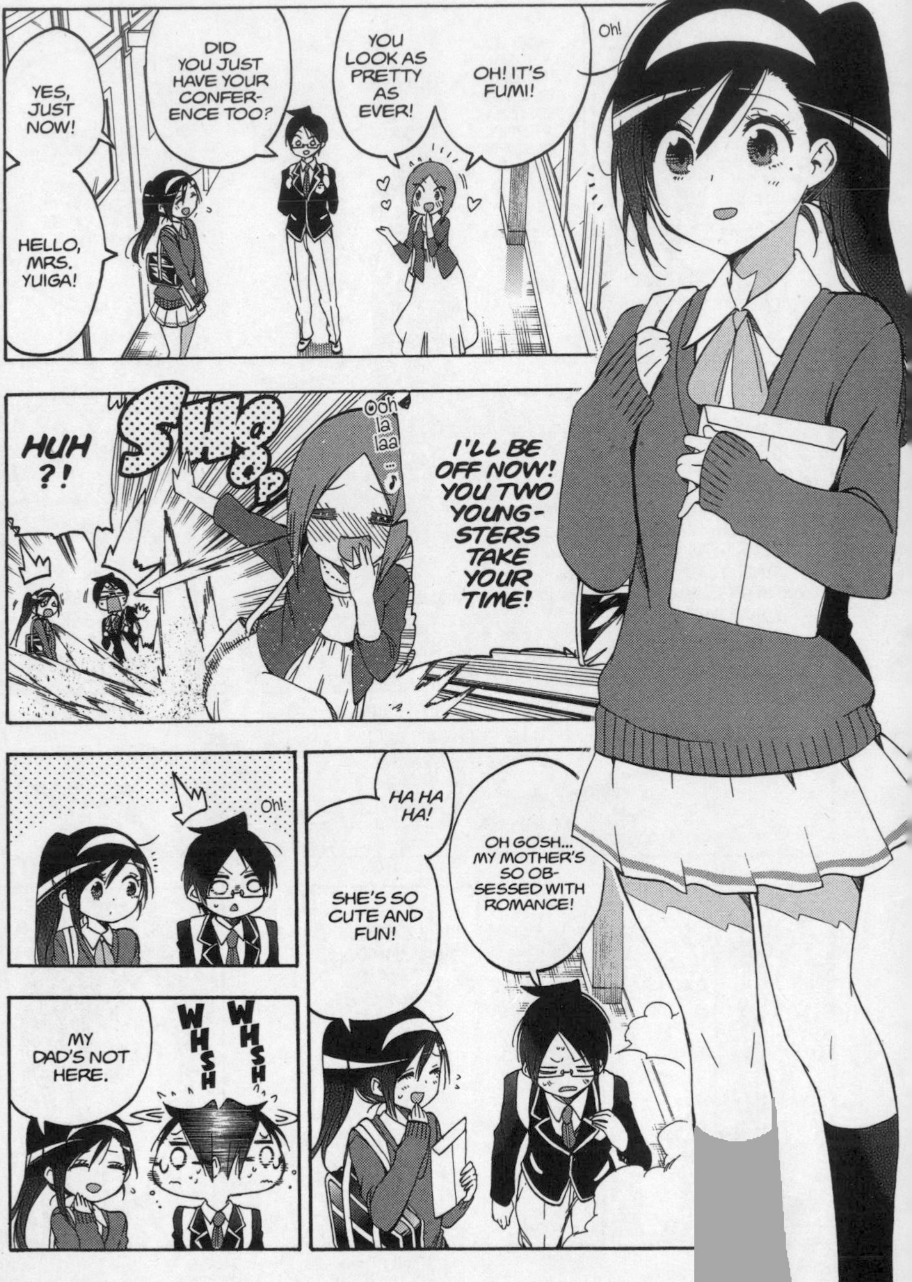
Oh!
OH! IT'S FUMI!
YOU LOOK AS PRETTY AS EVER!
DID YOU JUST HAVE YOUR CONFERENCE TOO?
YES, JUST NOW!
HELLO, MRS. YUIGA!
I'LL BE OFF NOW! YOU TWO YOUNGSTERS TAKE YOUR TIME!
Ooh la laa...♪
SHOO
HUH?!
OH GOSH... MY MOTHER'S SO OBSESSED WITH ROMANCE!
HA HA HA!
SHE'S SO CUTE AND FUN!
Oh!
MY DAD'S NOT HERE.
WHSH
WHSH

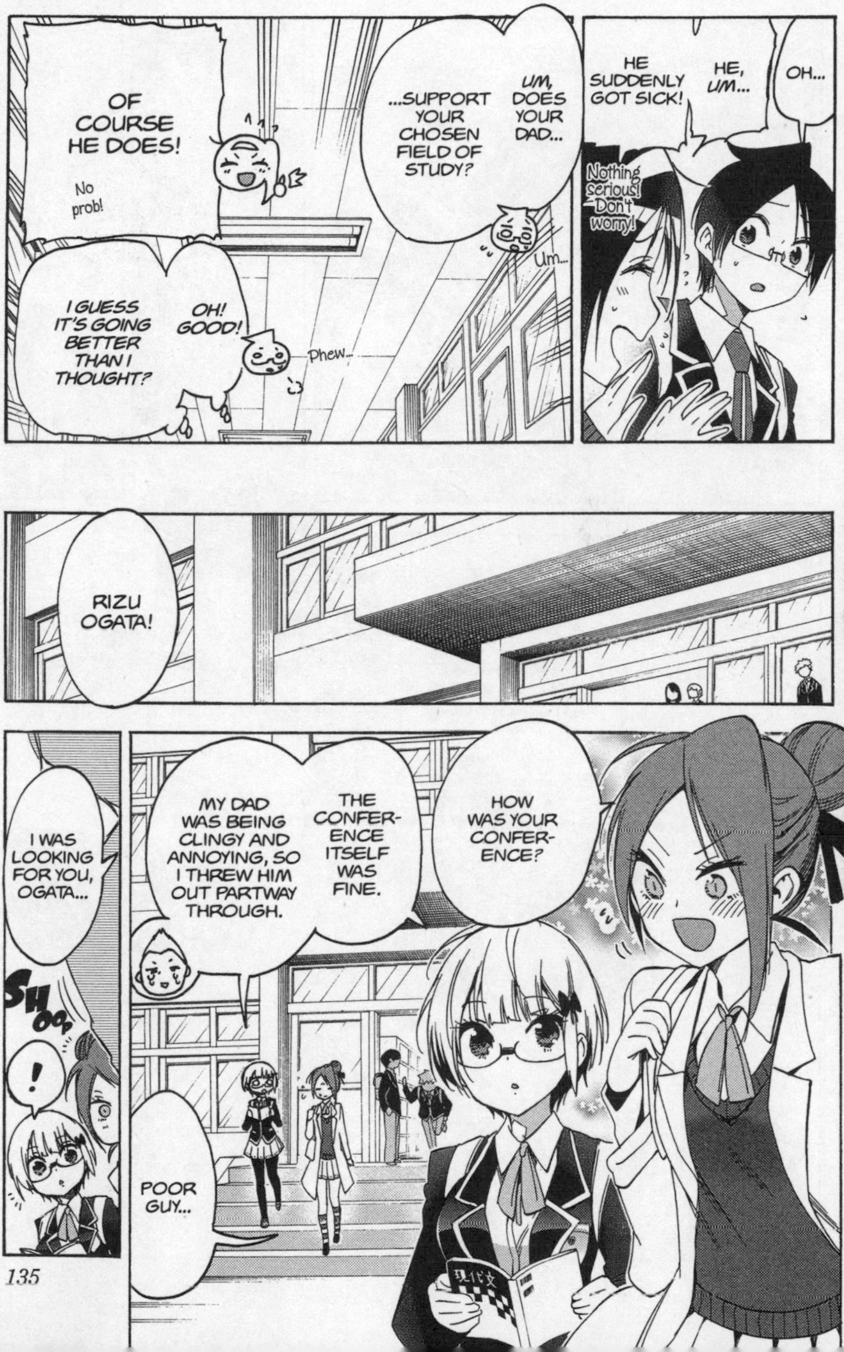

OH...
HE, UM...
HE SUDDENLY GOT SICK!
Nothing serious! Don't worry!
UM, DOES YOUR DAD...
...SUPPORT YOUR CHOSEN FIELD OF STUDY?
Um...
OF COURSE HE DOES!
No prob!
OH! GOOD!
I GUESS IT'S GOING BETTER THAN I THOUGHT?
Phew...
RIZU OGATA!
HOW WAS YOUR CONFERENCE?
THE CONFERENCE ITSELF WAS FINE.
MY DAD WAS BEING CLINGY AND ANNOYING, SO I THREW HIM OUT PARTWAY THROUGH.
POOR GUY...
I WAS LOOKING FOR YOU, OGATA...
SHOOP
!

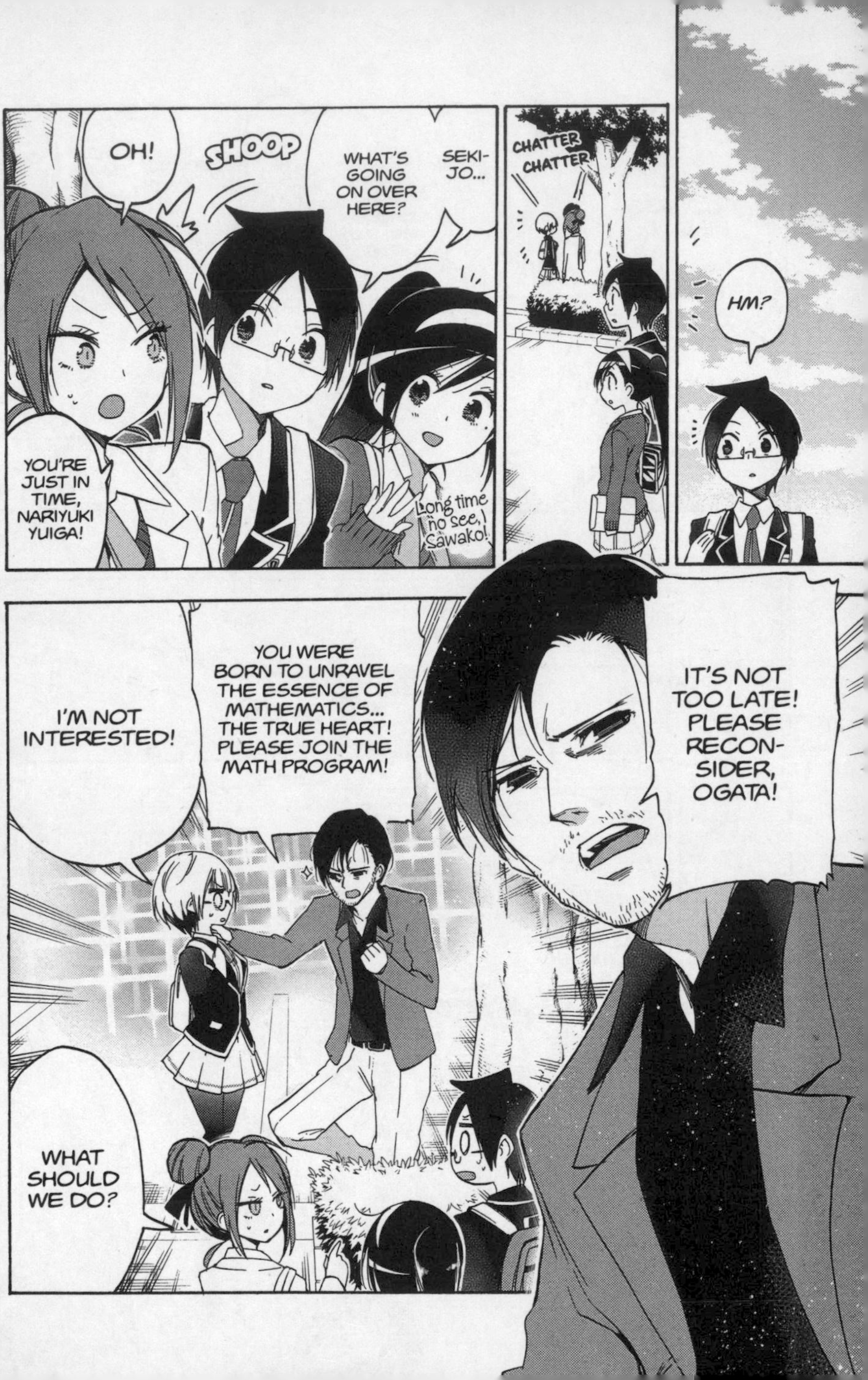
HM?
CHATTER CHATTER
SEKI-JO...
WHAT'S GOING ON OVER HERE?
SHOOP
OH!
Long time no see, Sawako!
YOU'RE JUST IN TIME, NARIYUKI YUIGA!
IT'S NOT TOO LATE! PLEASE RECON-SIDER, OGATA!
YOU WERE BORN TO UNRAVEL THE ESSENCE OF MATHEMATICS... THE TRUE HEART! PLEASE JOIN THE MATH PROGRAM!
I'M NOT INTERESTED!
WHAT SHOULD WE DO?

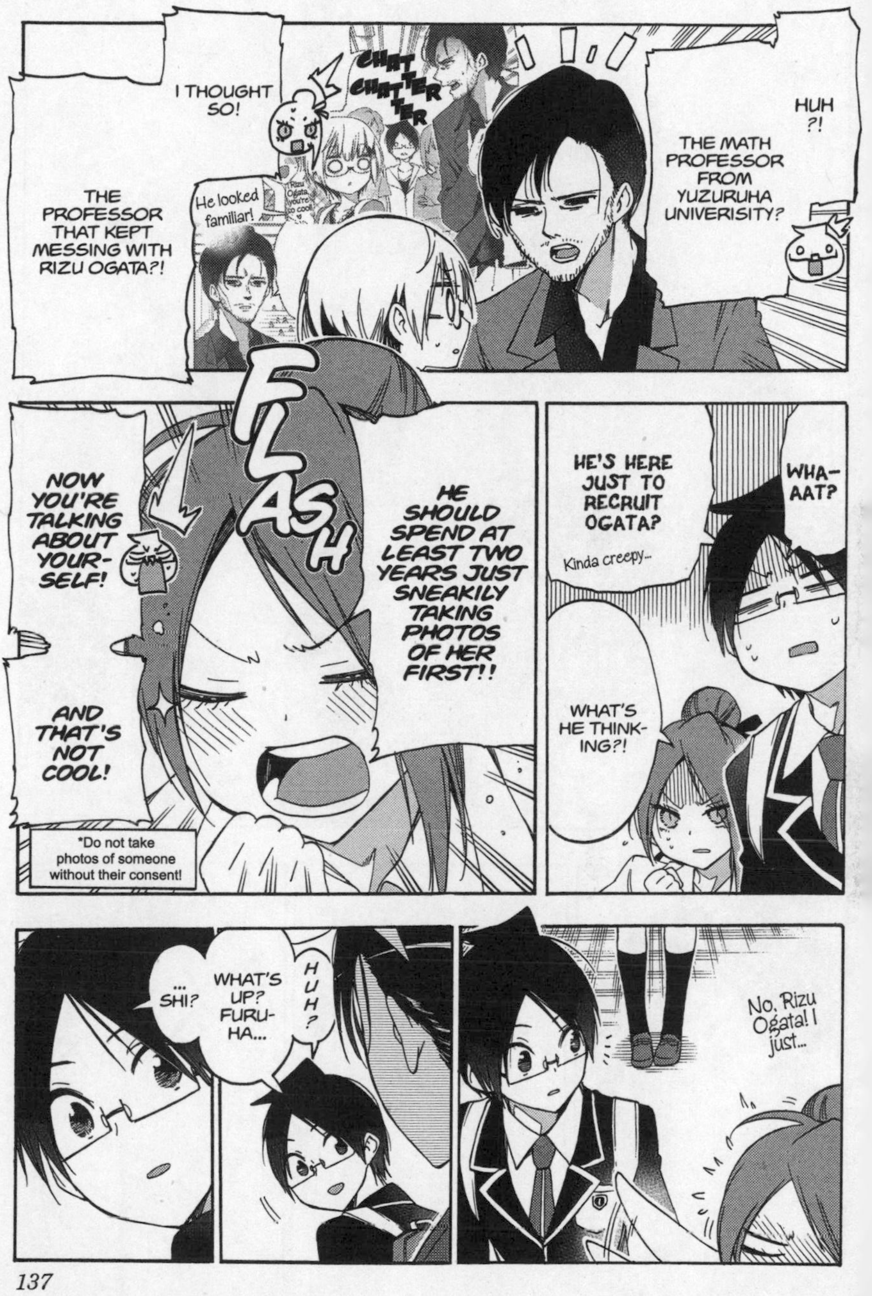
HUH ?!
THE MATH PROFESSOR FROM YUZURUHA UNIVERISITY?
CHATTER CHATTER
I THOUGHT SO!
Rizu Ogata, you're so cool!
He looked familiar!
THE PROFESSOR THAT KEPT MESSING WITH RIZU OGATA?!
WHA-AAT?
HE'S HERE JUST TO RECRUIT OGATA?
Kinda creepy...
WHAT'S HE THINKING?!
FLASH
HE SHOULD SPEND AT LEAST TWO YEARS JUST SNEAKILY TAKING PHOTOS OF HER FIRST!!
NOW YOU'RE TALKING ABOUT YOURSELF!
AND THAT'S NOT COOL!
*Do not take photos of someone without their consent!
No, Rizu Ogata! I just...
HUH?
WHAT'S UP? FURUHA...
...SHI?

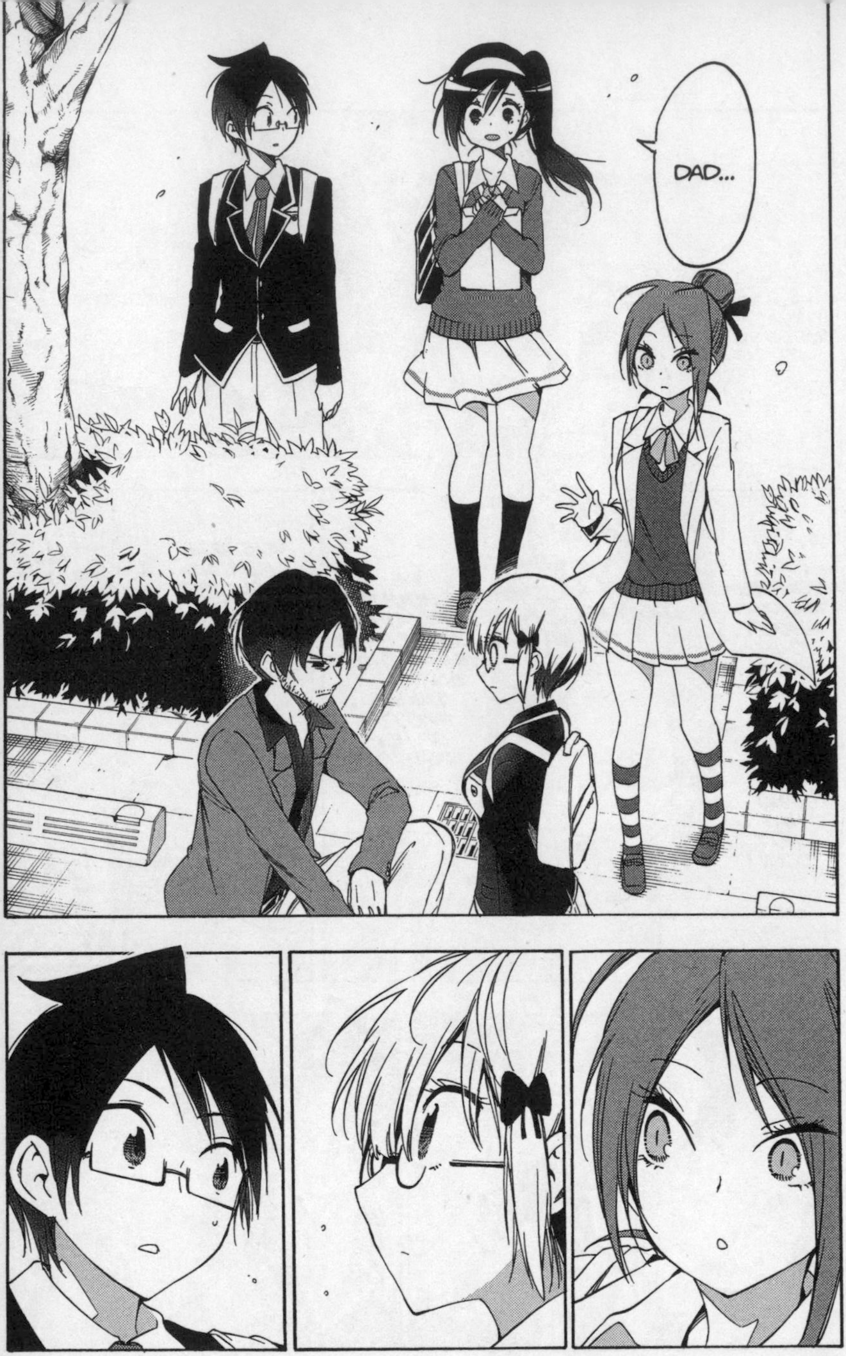
DAD...

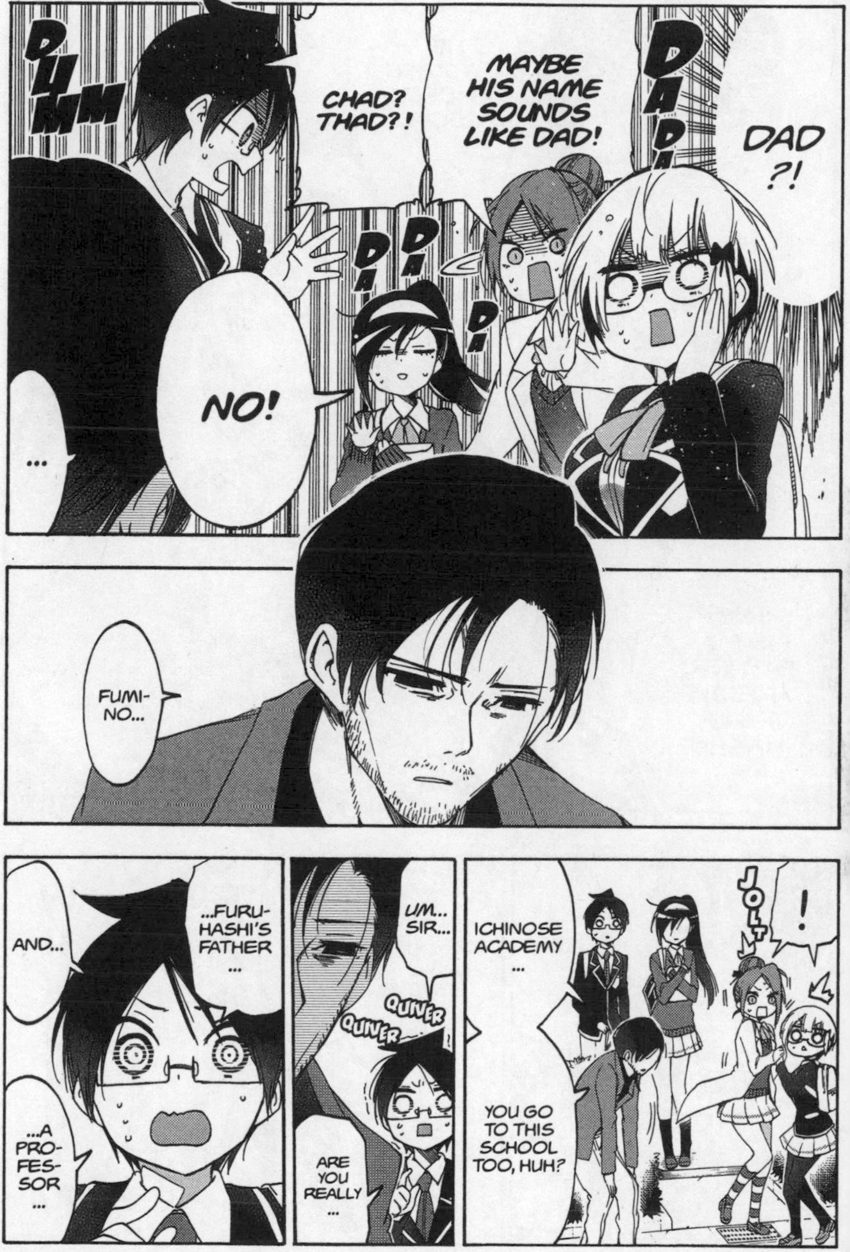
DAD?!
DA DA
MAYBE HIS NAME SOUNDS LIKE DAD!
CHAD? THAD?!
DA DA DA
DUMM
NO!
...
FUMINO...
!
JOLT
ICHINOSE ACADEMY...
YOU GO TO THIS SCHOOL TOO, HUH?
UM... SIR...
QUIVER QUIVER
ARE YOU REALLY...
...FURUHASHI'S FATHER...
AND...
...A PROFESSOR...

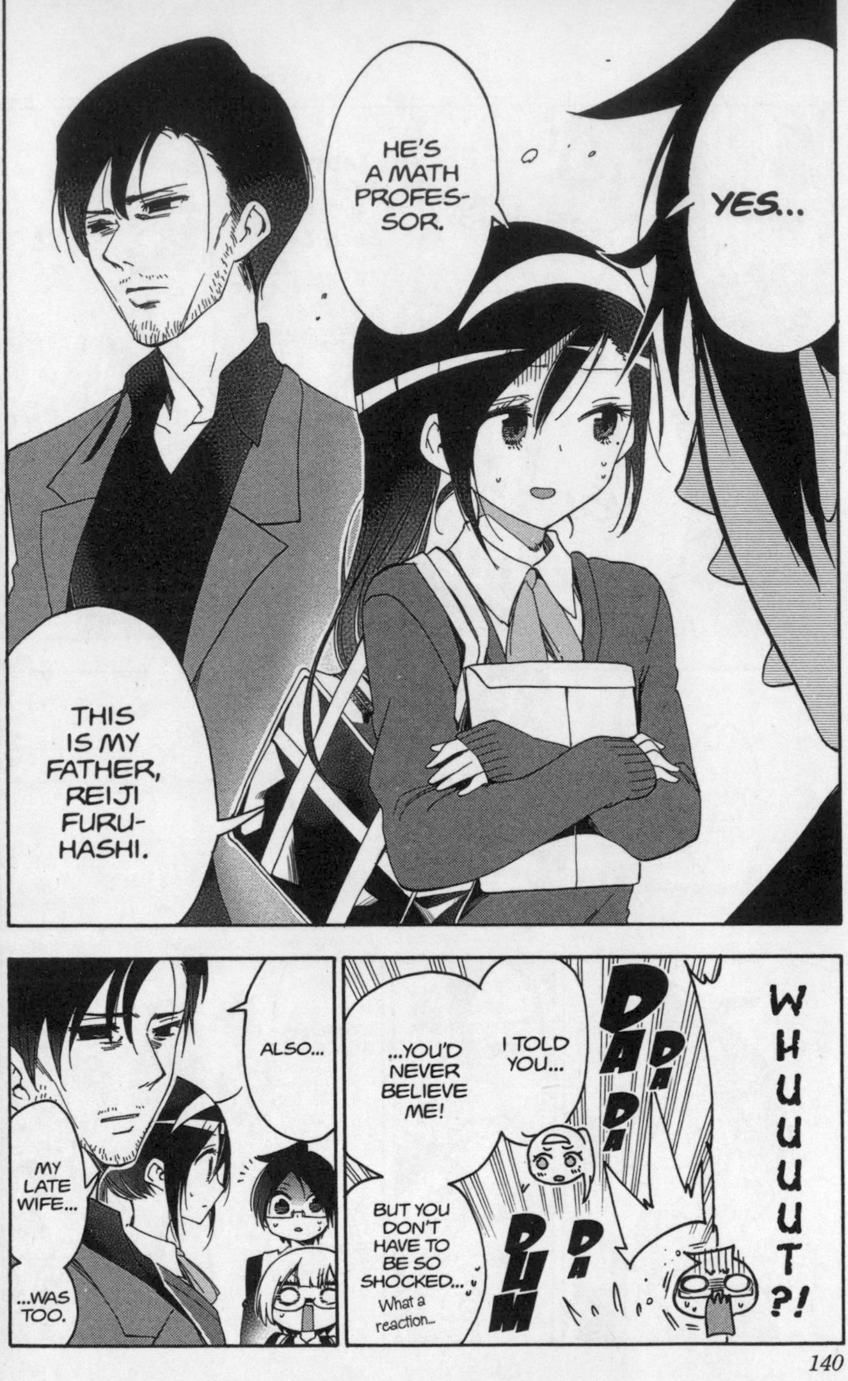
YES...
HE'S A MATH PROFESSOR.
THIS IS MY FATHER, REIJI FURUHASHI.
WHUUUUUT?!
DADADA
I TOLD YOU...
...YOU'D NEVER BELIEVE ME!
DA DA DUM
BUT YOU DON'T HAVE TO BE SO SHOCKED...
What a reaction...
ALSO...
MY LATE WIFE...
...WAS TOO.

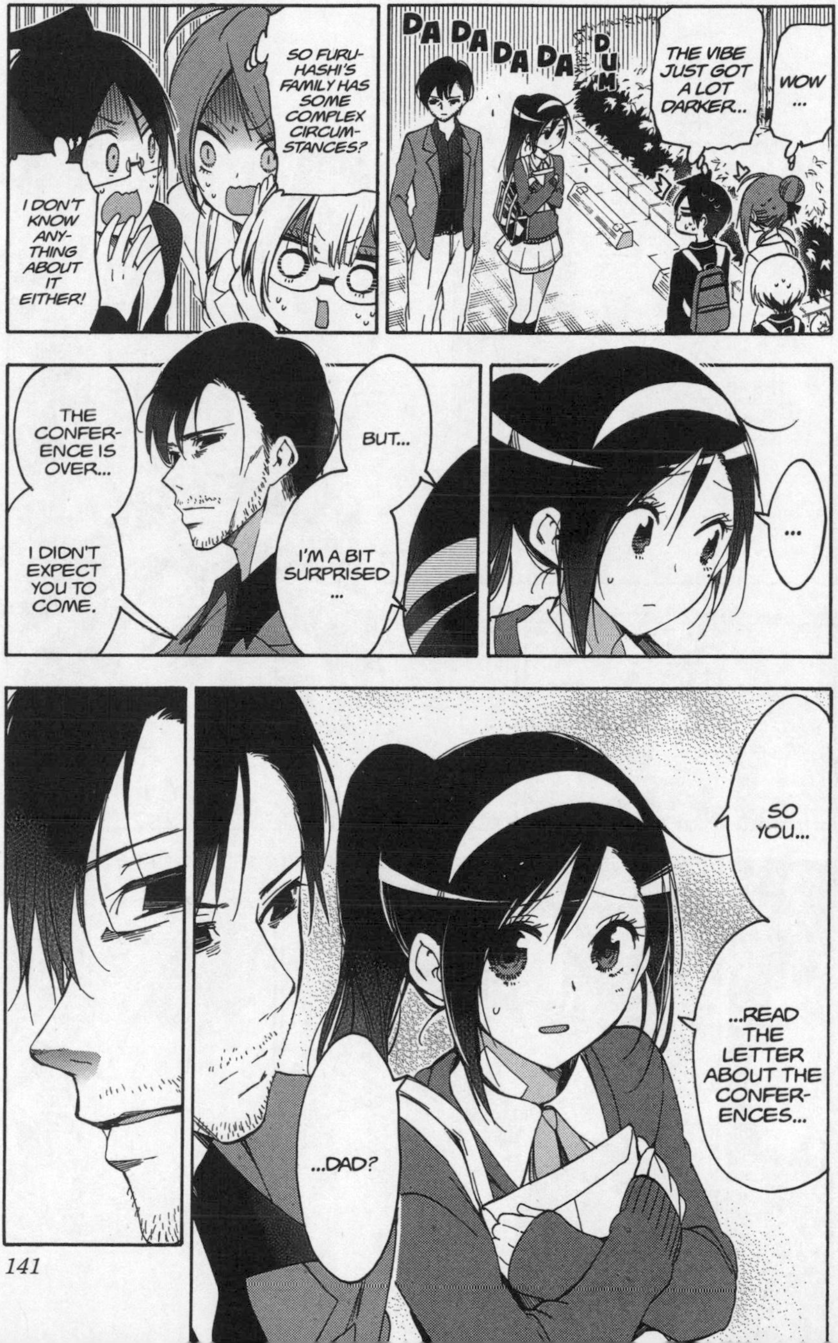
WOW ...
THE VIBE JUST GOT A LOT DARKER...
DA DA DA DA DA DUM
SO FURU-HASHI'S FAMILY HAS SOME COMPLEX CIRCUM-STANCES?
I DON'T KNOW ANY-THING ABOUT IT EITHER!
...
BUT... I'M A BIT SURPRISED ...
THE CONFER-ENCE IS OVER... I DIDN'T EXPECT YOU TO COME.
SO YOU... ...READ THE LETTER ABOUT THE CONFER-ENCES...
...DAD?

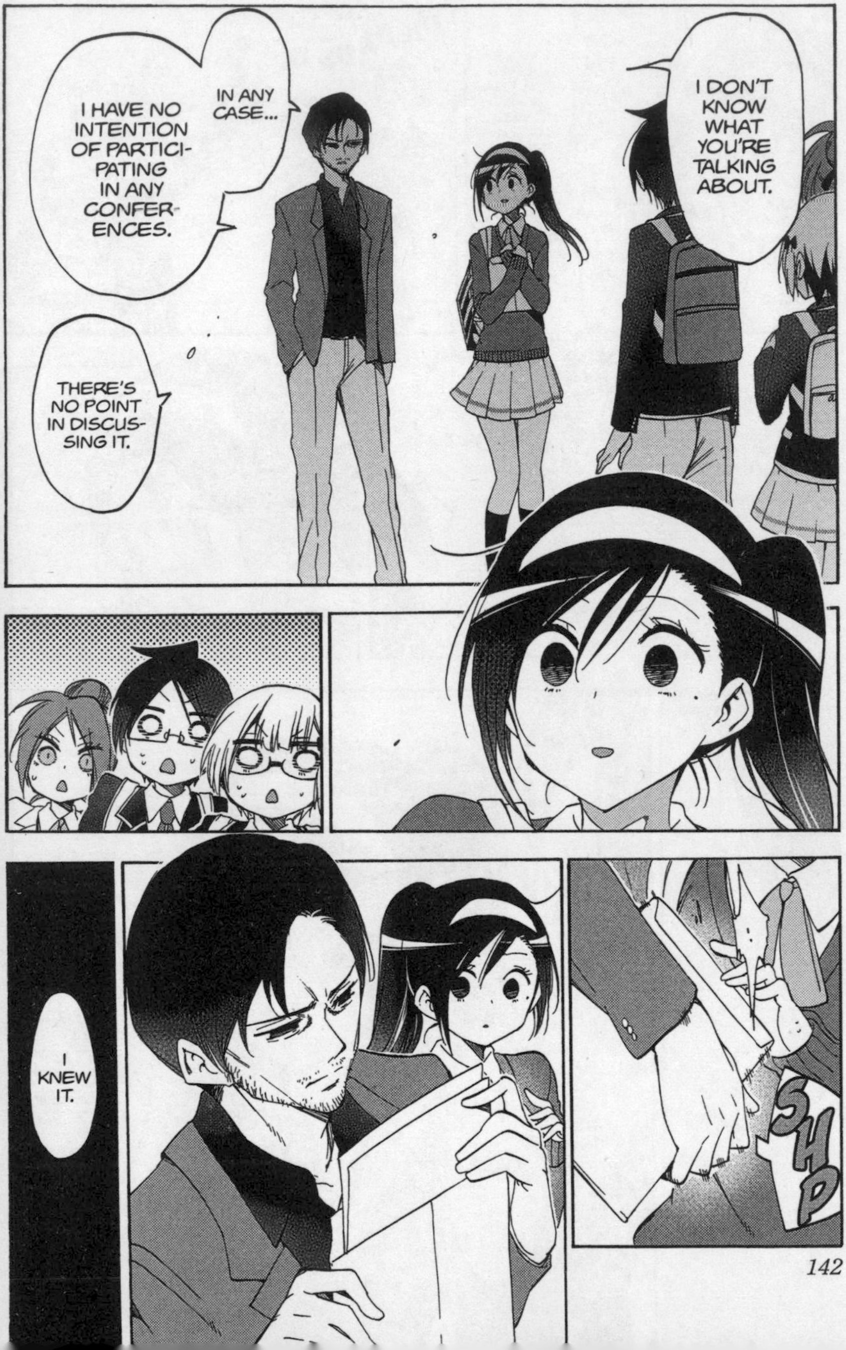
I DON'T KNOW WHAT YOU'RE TALKING ABOUT.
IN ANY CASE...
I HAVE NO INTENTION OF PARTICIPATING IN ANY CONFERENCES.
THERE'S NO POINT IN DISCUSSING IT.
SHP
I KNEW IT.

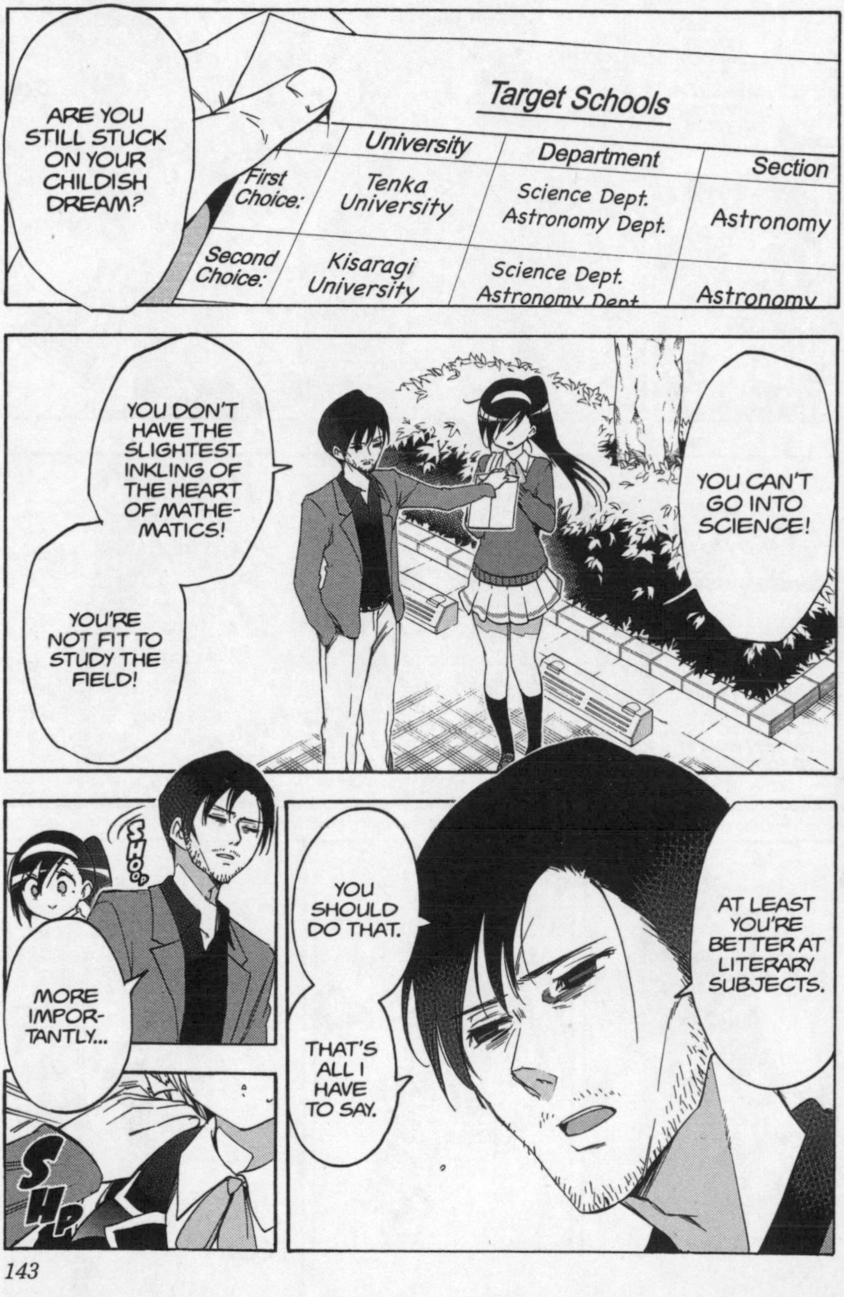
Target Schools
University
Department
Section
First Choice:
Tenka University
Science Dept. Astronomy Dept.
Astronomy
Second Choice:
Kisaragi University
Science Dept. Astronomy Dept
Astronomy
ARE YOU STILL STUCK ON YOUR CHILDISH DREAM?
YOU CAN'T GO INTO SCIENCE!
YOU DON'T HAVE THE SLIGHTEST INKLING OF THE HEART OF MATHE-MATICS!
YOU'RE NOT FIT TO STUDY THE FIELD!
AT LEAST YOU'RE BETTER AT LITERARY SUBJECTS.
YOU SHOULD DO THAT.
THAT'S ALL I HAVE TO SAY.
SHOOP
MORE IMPOR-TANTLY...
SHP

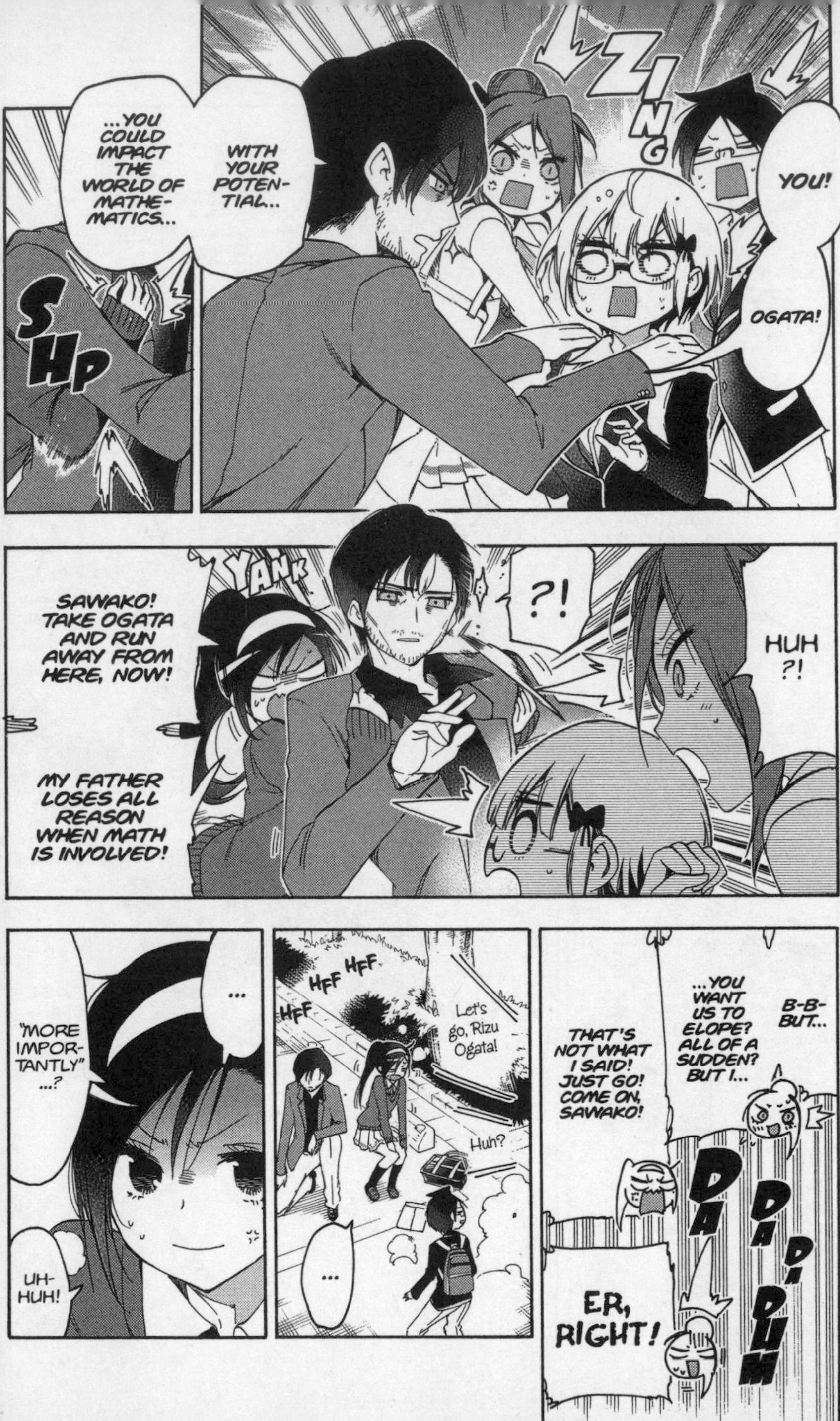
ZING
YOU! OGATA!
WITH YOUR POTENTIAL...
...YOU COULD IMPACT THE WORLD OF MATHEMATICS...
SHP
HUH ?!
?!
YANK
SAWAKO! TAKE OGATA AND RUN AWAY FROM HERE, NOW!
MY FATHER LOSES ALL REASON WHEN MATH IS INVOLVED!
B-B-BUT...
...YOU WANT US TO ELOPE? ALL OF A SUDDEN? BUT I...
THAT'S NOT WHAT I SAID! JUST GO! COME ON, SAWAKO!
DA DA DI DUM
ER, RIGHT!
HFF HFF HFF
Let's go, Rizu Ogata!
Huh?
...
...
"MORE IMPORTANTLY" ...?
UH-HUH!

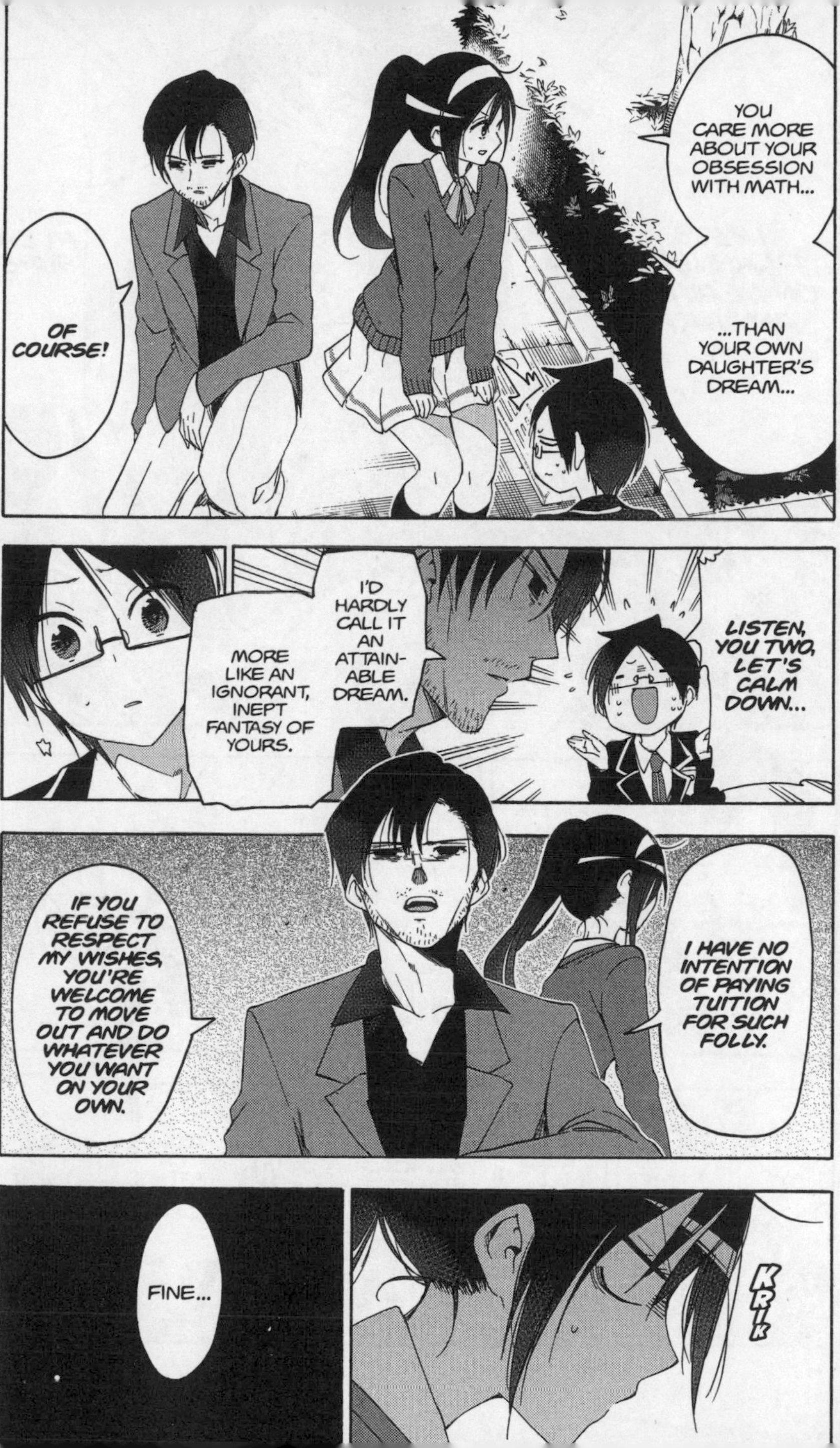
YOU CARE MORE ABOUT YOUR OBSESSION WITH MATH...
...THAN YOUR OWN DAUGHTER'S DREAM...
OF COURSE!
LISTEN, YOU TWO, LET'S CALM DOWN...
I'D HARDLY CALL IT AN ATTAIN-ABLE DREAM.
MORE LIKE AN IGNORANT, INEPT FANTASY OF YOURS.
I HAVE NO INTENTION OF PAYING TUITION FOR SUCH FOLLY.
IF YOU REFUSE TO RESPECT MY WISHES, YOU'RE WELCOME TO MOVE OUT AND DO WHATEVER YOU WANT ON YOUR OWN.
KRIK
FINE...

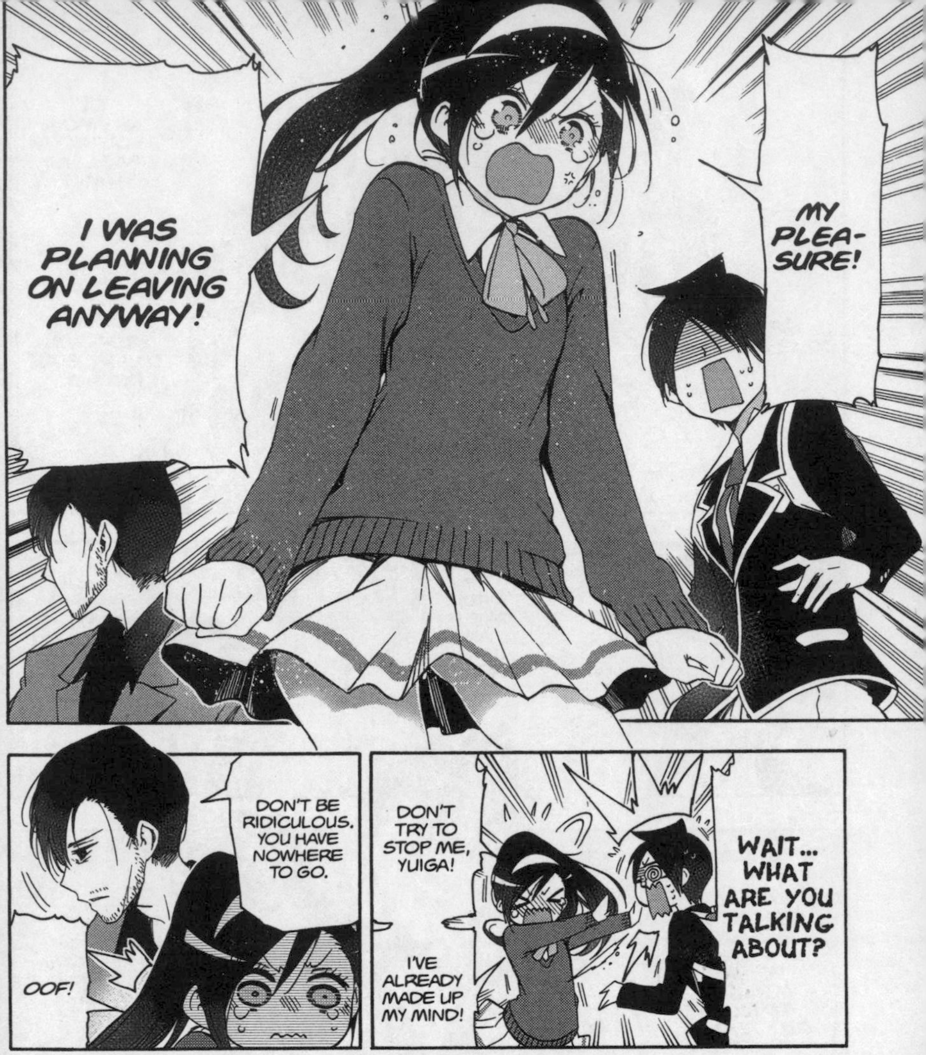
MY PLEA-SURE!
I WAS PLANNING ON LEAVING ANYWAY!
WAIT... WHAT ARE YOU TALKING ABOUT?
DON'T TRY TO STOP ME, YUIGA!
I'VE ALREADY MADE UP MY MIND!
DON'T BE RIDICULOUS. YOU HAVE NOWHERE TO GO.
OOF!
WILL YOU RENT AN APARTMENT? HOW WILL YOU PAY FOR IT?
I'LL GET A PART-TIME JOB!
WHSH
WHO WILL BE YOUR GUARANTOR? NOBODY WILL VOUCH FOR YOU IF YOU HAVE NO INCOME!
I'LL... WELL... UM...
Mumble Mumble
WHSH
WHSH
EX-CUSE ME!!
SHOOO
?!

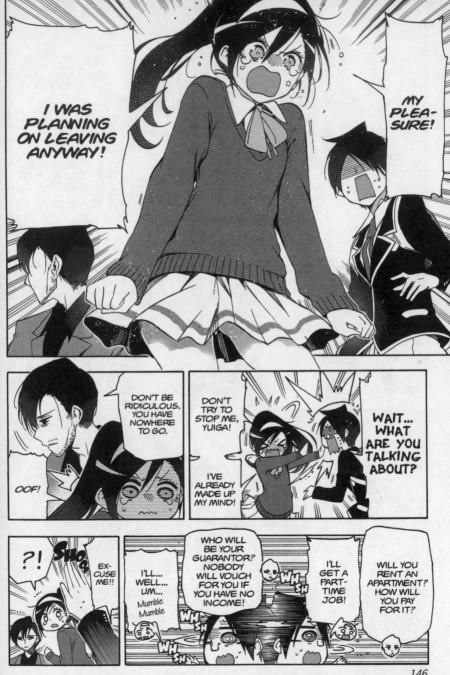

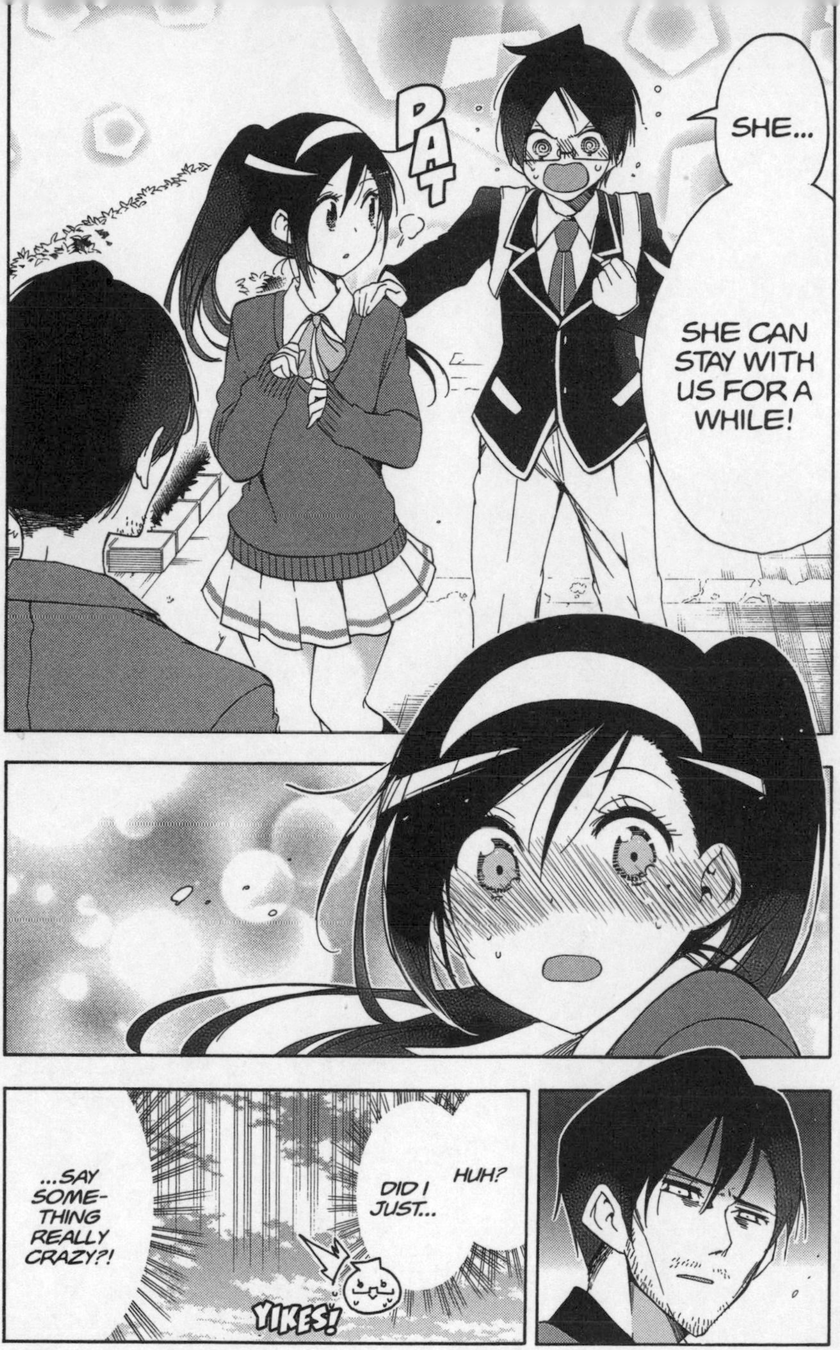
SHE...
SHE CAN STAY WITH US FOR A WHILE!
PAT
HUH?
DID I JUST...
...SAY SOMETHING REALLY CRAZY?!
YIKES!

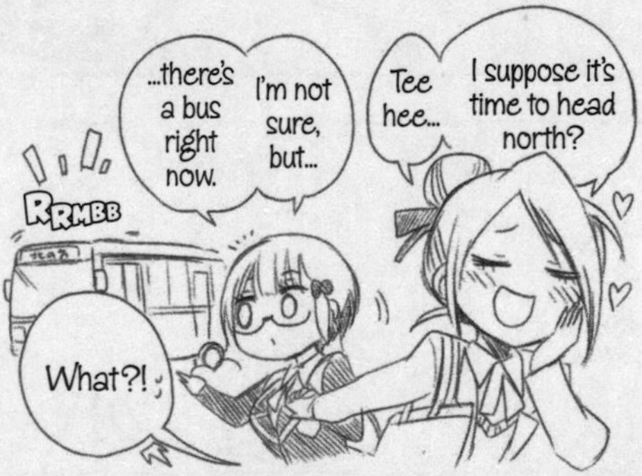
I suppose it's time to head north?
Tee hee...
I'm not sure, but...
...there's a bus right now.
RRMBB
What?!

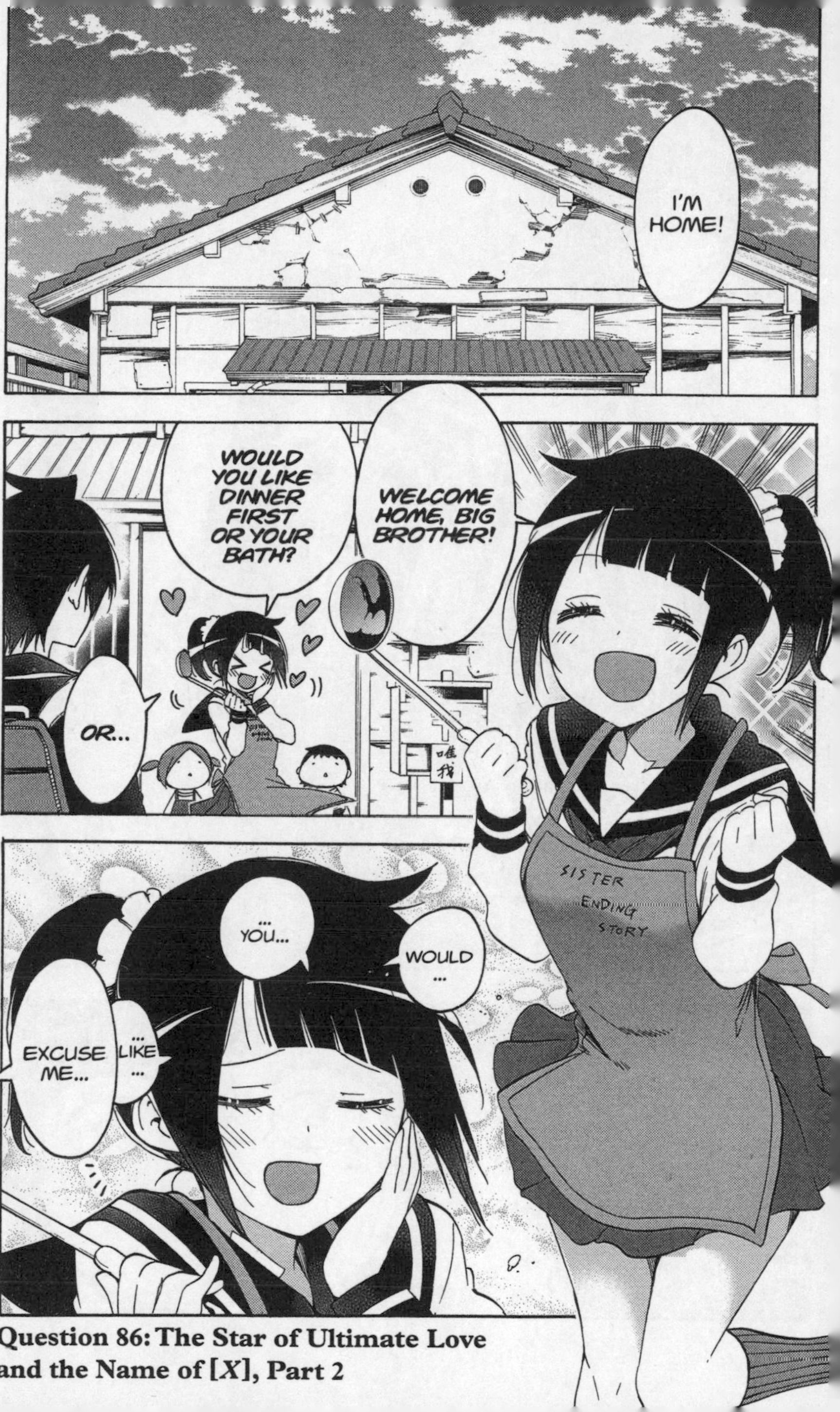
I'M HOME!
WELCOME HOME, BIG BROTHER!
WOULD YOU LIKE DINNER FIRST OR YOUR BATH?
OR...
SISTER ENDING STORY
WOULD ...
... YOU...
... LIKE ...
EXCUSE ME...

Question 86: The Star of Ultimate Love and the Name of [X], Part 2

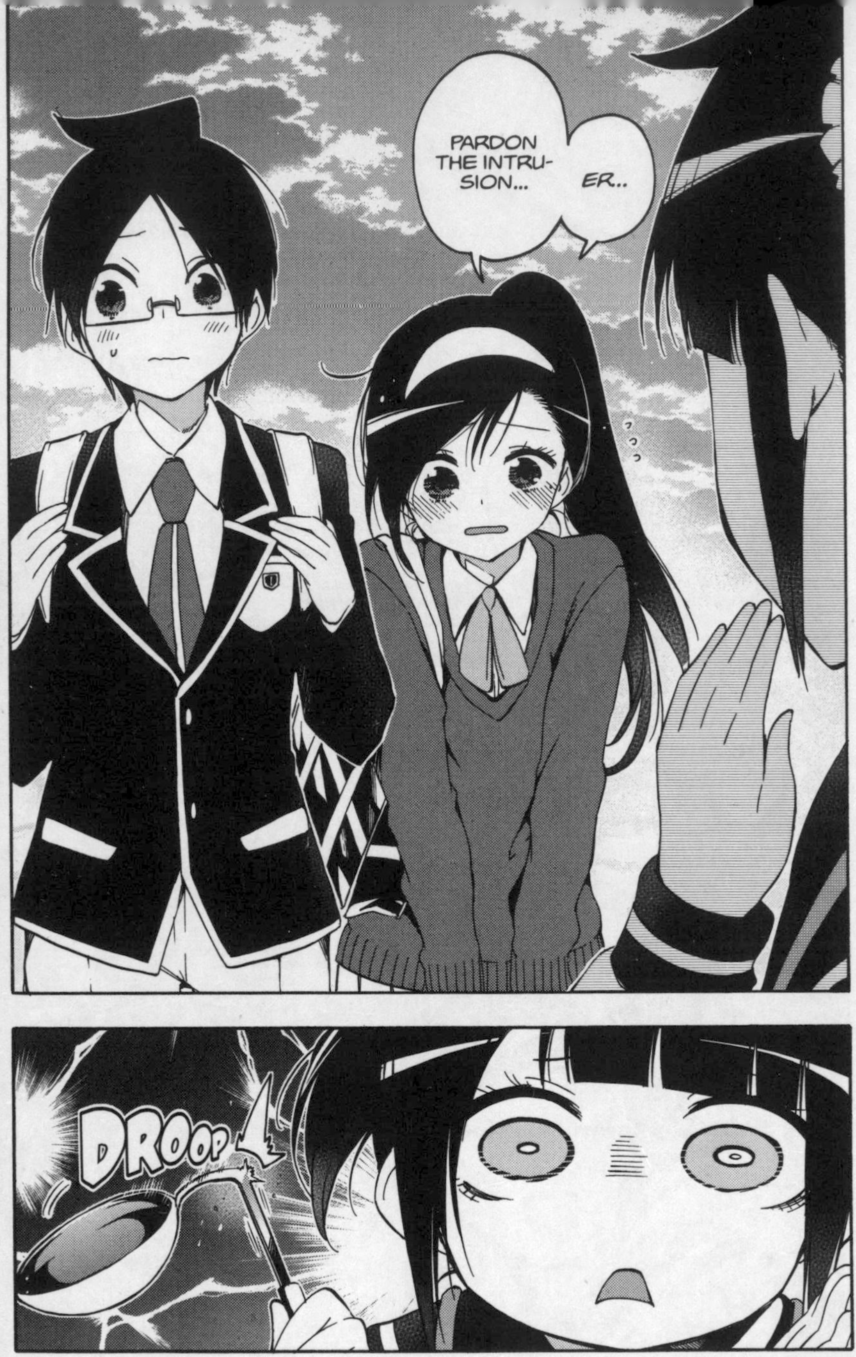
PARDON THE INTRU-SION...
ER...
DROOP

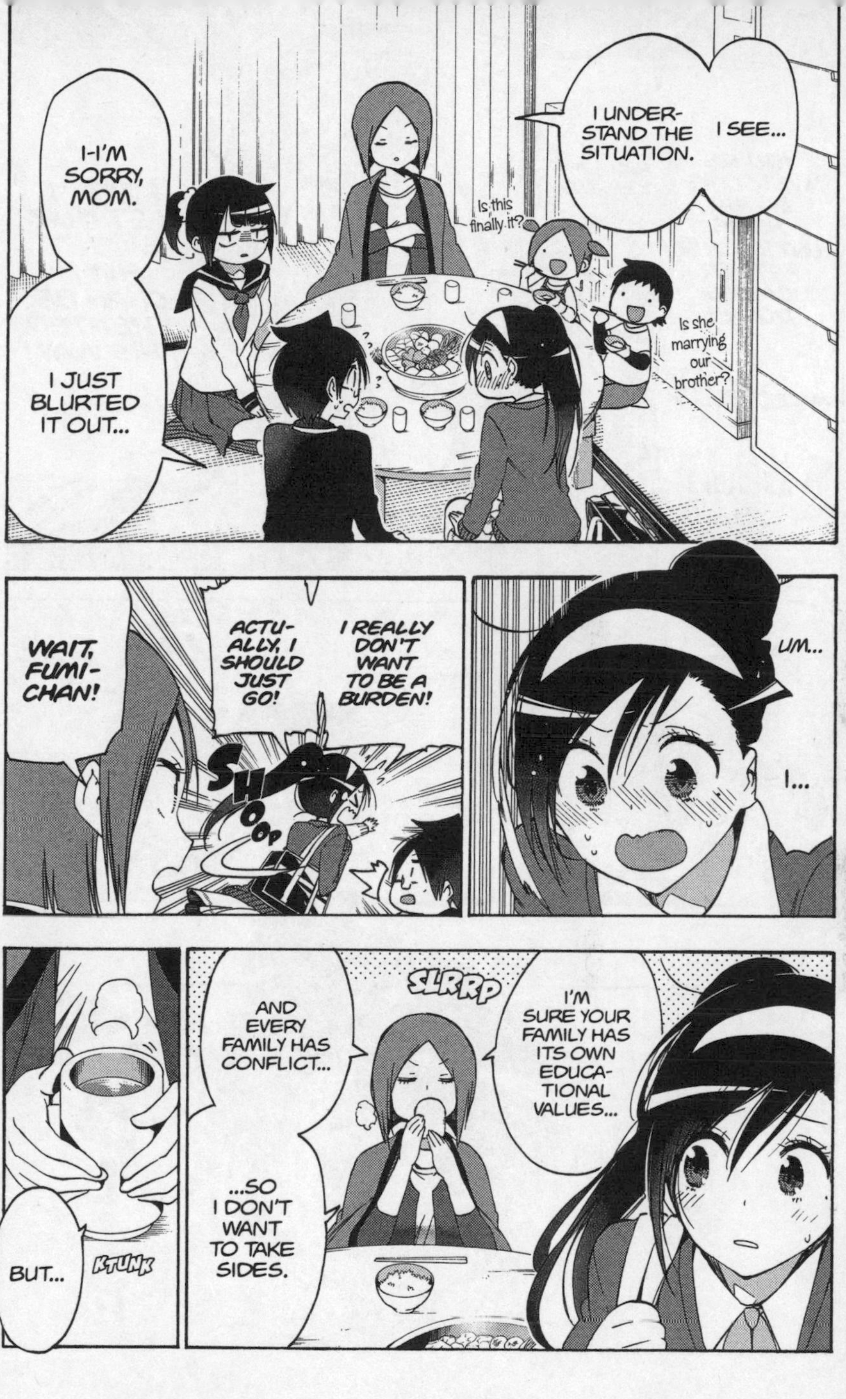

I SEE...
I UNDERSTAND THE SITUATION.
Is she marrying our brother?
Is this finally it?
I-I'M SORRY, MOM.
I JUST BLURTED IT OUT...
UM...
I...
I REALLY DON'T WANT TO BE A BURDEN!
ACTUALLY, I SHOULD JUST GO!
SHOOOP
WAIT, FUMI-CHAN!
I'M SURE YOUR FAMILY HAS ITS OWN EDUCATIONAL VALUES...
SLRRP
AND EVERY FAMILY HAS CONFLICT...
...SO I DON'T WANT TO TAKE SIDES.
KTUNK
BUT...

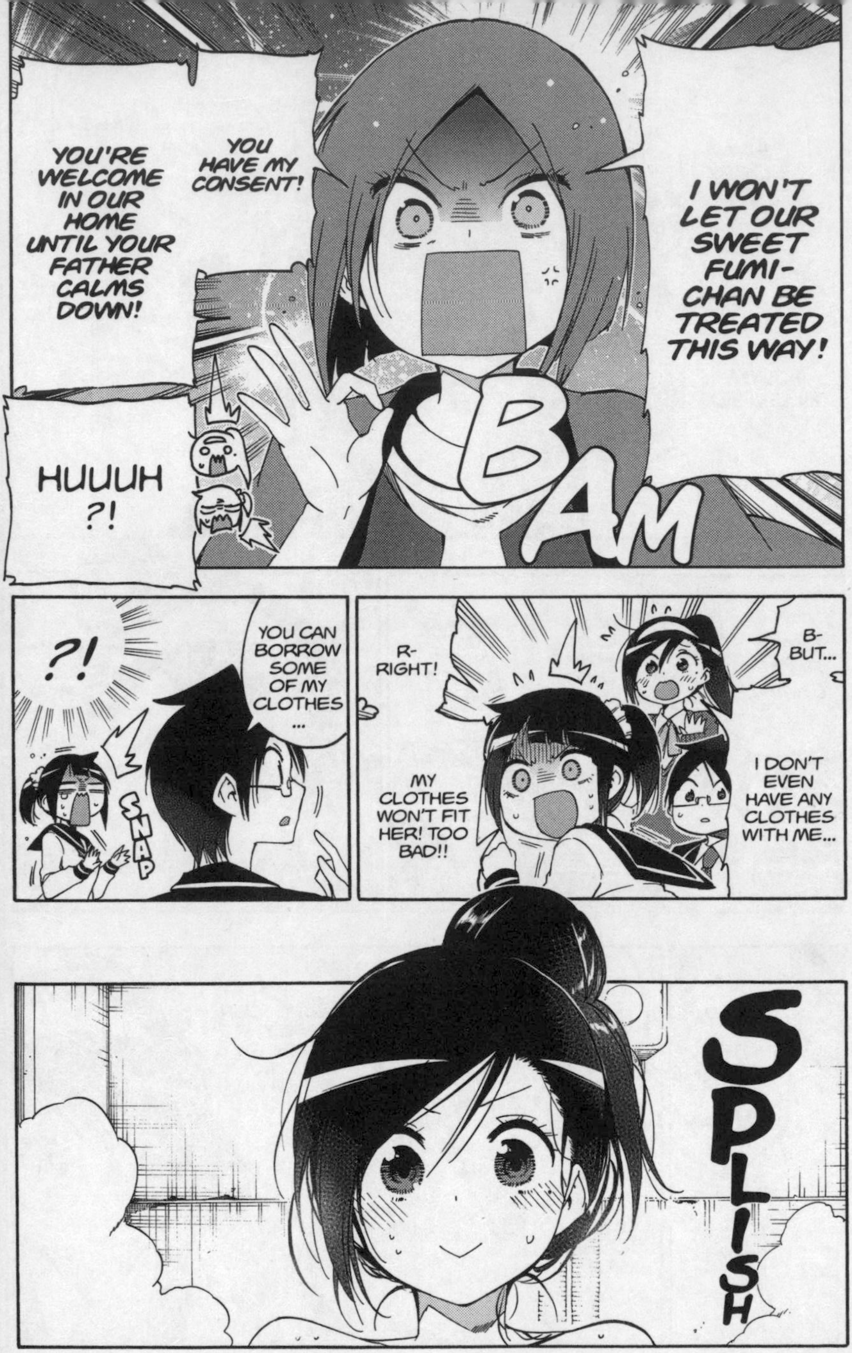
I WON'T LET OUR SWEET FUMI-CHAN BE TREATED THIS WAY!
BAM
YOU HAVE MY CONSENT!
YOU'RE WELCOME IN OUR HOME UNTIL YOUR FATHER CALMS DOWN!
HUUUH ?!
B- BUT...
I DON'T EVEN HAVE ANY CLOTHES WITH ME...
R- RIGHT!
MY CLOTHES WON'T FIT HER! TOO BAD!!
YOU CAN BORROW SOME OF MY CLOTHES ...
?!
SNAP
SPLISH

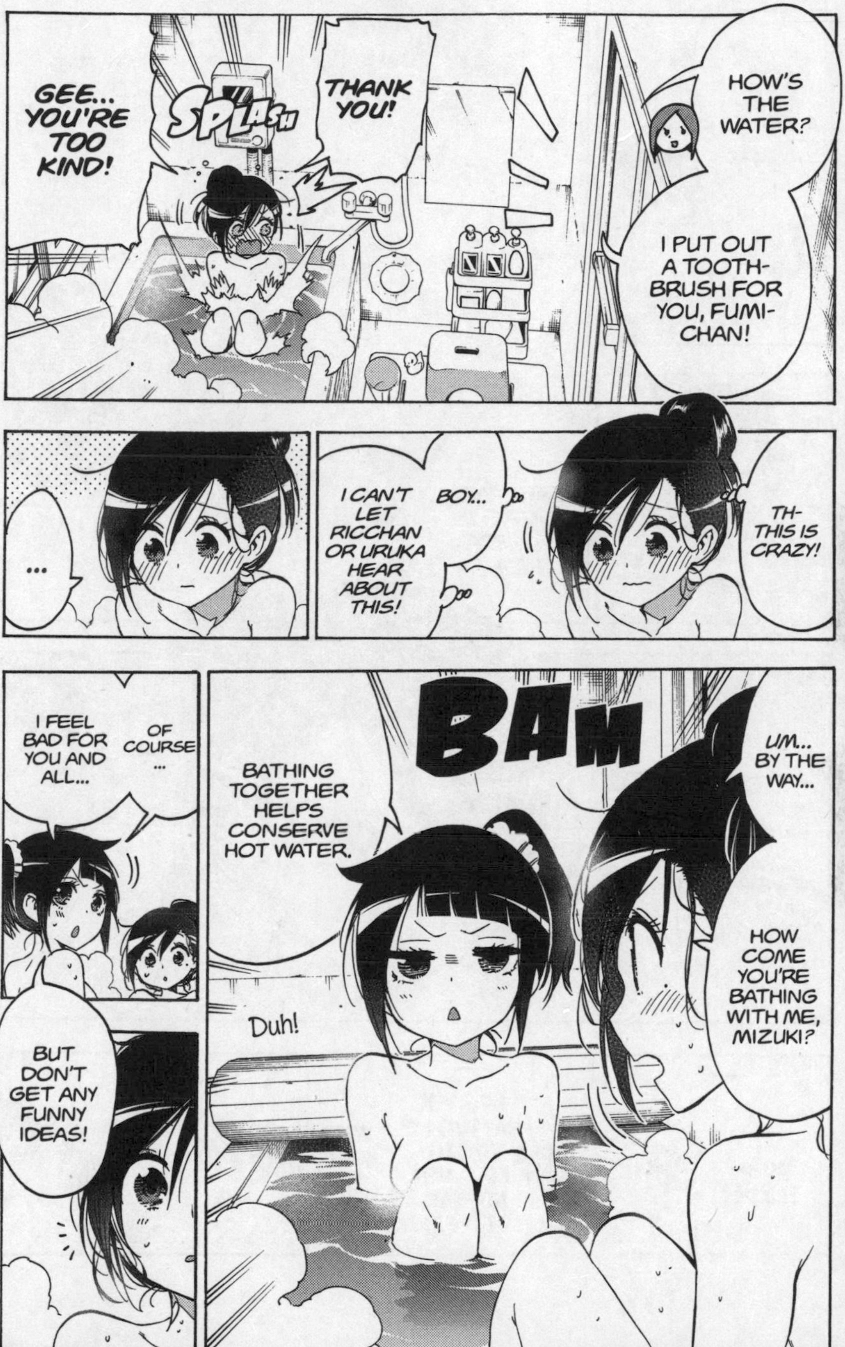
HOW'S THE WATER?
I PUT OUT A TOOTH-BRUSH FOR YOU, FUMI-CHAN!
THANK YOU!
SPLASH
GEE... YOU'RE TOO KIND!
TH- THIS IS CRAZY!
BOY...
I CAN'T LET RICCHAN OR URUKA HEAR ABOUT THIS!
...
UM... BY THE WAY...
HOW COME YOU'RE BATHING WITH ME, MIZUKI?
BAM
BATHING TOGETHER HELPS CONSERVE HOT WATER.
Duh!
OF COURSE...
I FEEL BAD FOR YOU AND ALL...
BUT DON'T GET ANY FUNNY IDEAS!

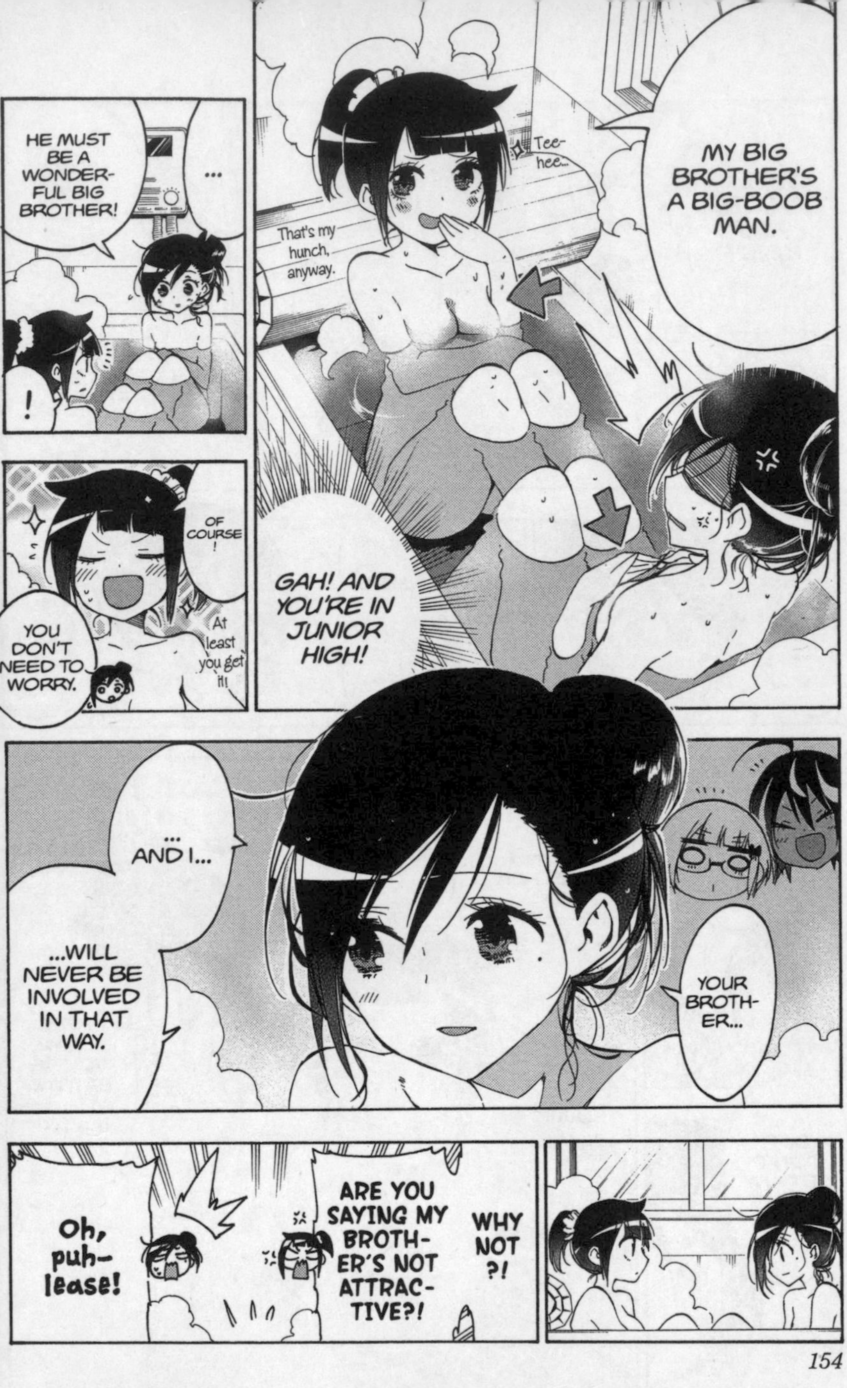
MY BIG BROTHER'S A BIG-BOOB MAN.
Tee-hee...
That's my hunch, anyway.
GAH! AND YOU'RE IN JUNIOR HIGH!
HE MUST BE A WONDERFUL BIG BROTHER!
...
!
OF COURSE!
At least you get it!
YOU DON'T NEED TO WORRY.
YOUR BROTHER...
... AND I...
...WILL NEVER BE INVOLVED IN THAT WAY.
WHY NOT?!
ARE YOU SAYING MY BROTHER'S NOT ATTRACTIVE?!
Oh, puh-lease!

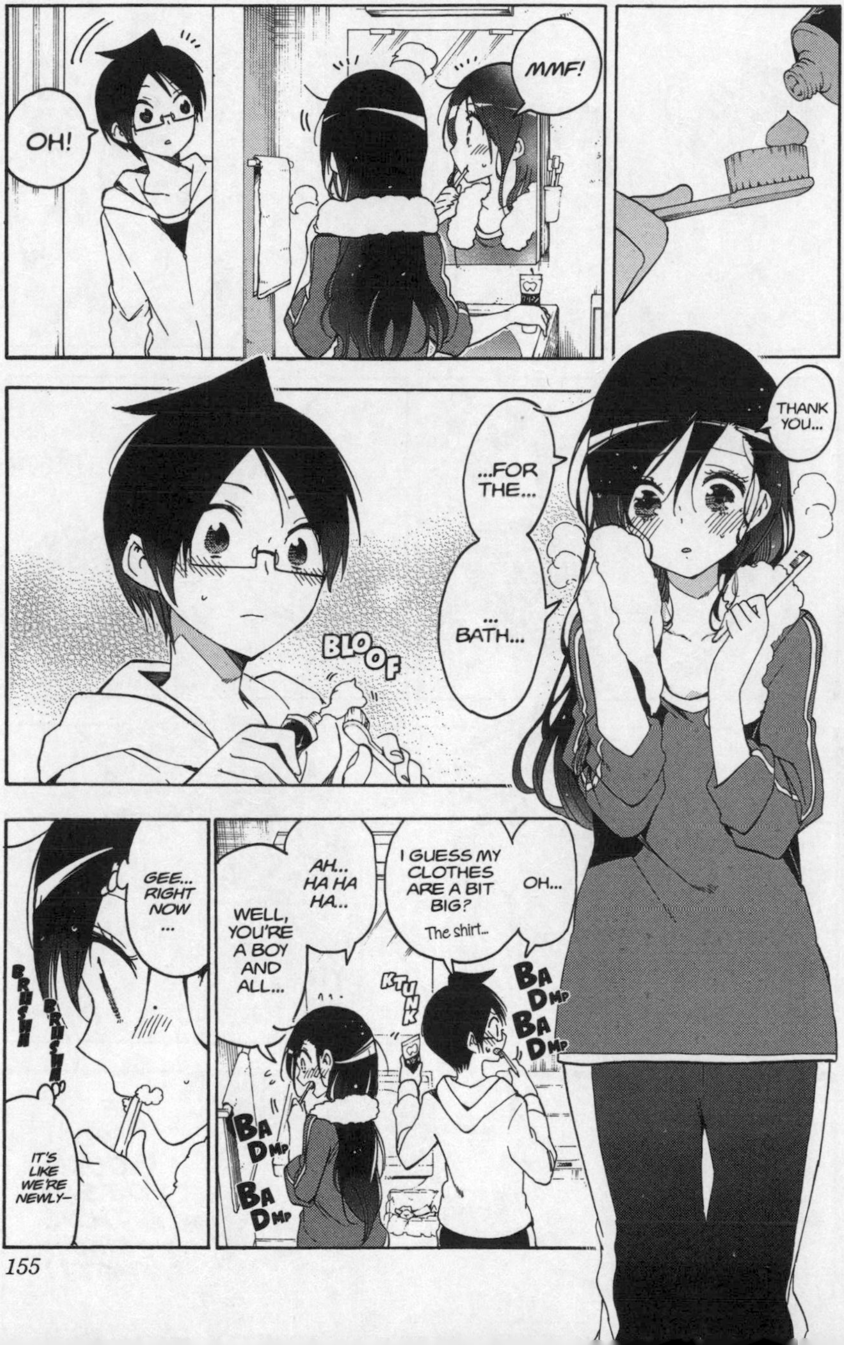
MMF!
OH!
THANK YOU...
...FOR THE...
... BATH...
BLOOF
OH...
I GUESS MY CLOTHES ARE A BIT BIG?
The shirt...
AH.. HA HA HA..
WELL, YOU'RE A BOY AND ALL...
KTUNK
BADMP BADMP
BADMP BADMP
GEE... RIGHT NOW ...
BRUSH BRUSH
IT'S LIKE WE'RE NEWLY-

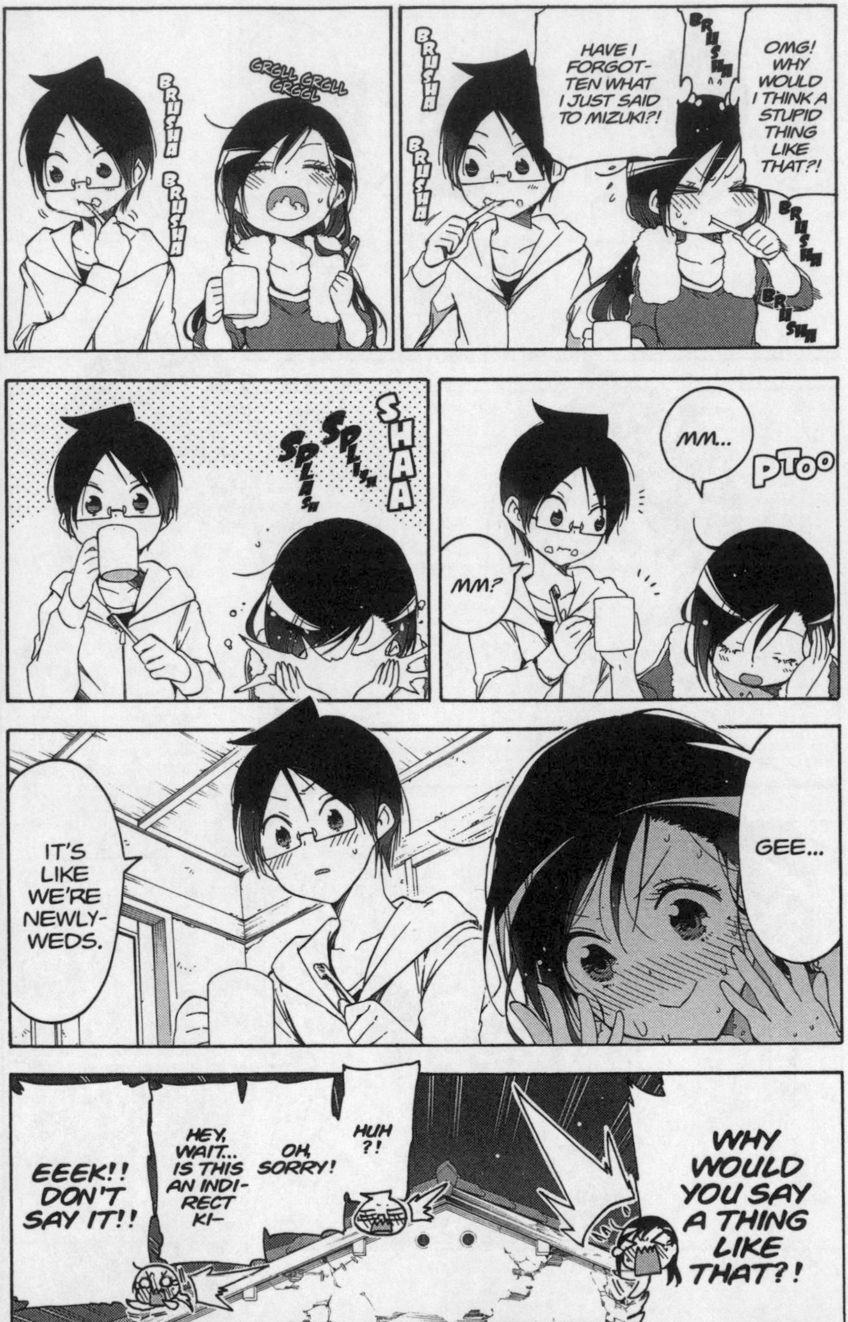
OMG! WHY WOULD I THINK A STUPID THING LIKE THAT?!
BRUSH
BRUSH
BRUSH
HAVE I FORGOT-TEN WHAT I JUST SAID TO MIZUKI?!
BRUSHA
BRUSHA
GRGLL GRGLL GRGGL
BRUSHA
BRUSHA
BRUSHA
MM...
PTOO
MM?
SHAA
SPLISH
SPLASH
GEE...
IT'S LIKE WE'RE NEWLY-WEDS.
WHY WOULD YOU SAY A THING LIKE THAT?!
HUH?!
OH, SORRY!
HEY, WAIT... IS THIS AN INDI-RECT KI-
EEEK!! DON'T SAY IT!!

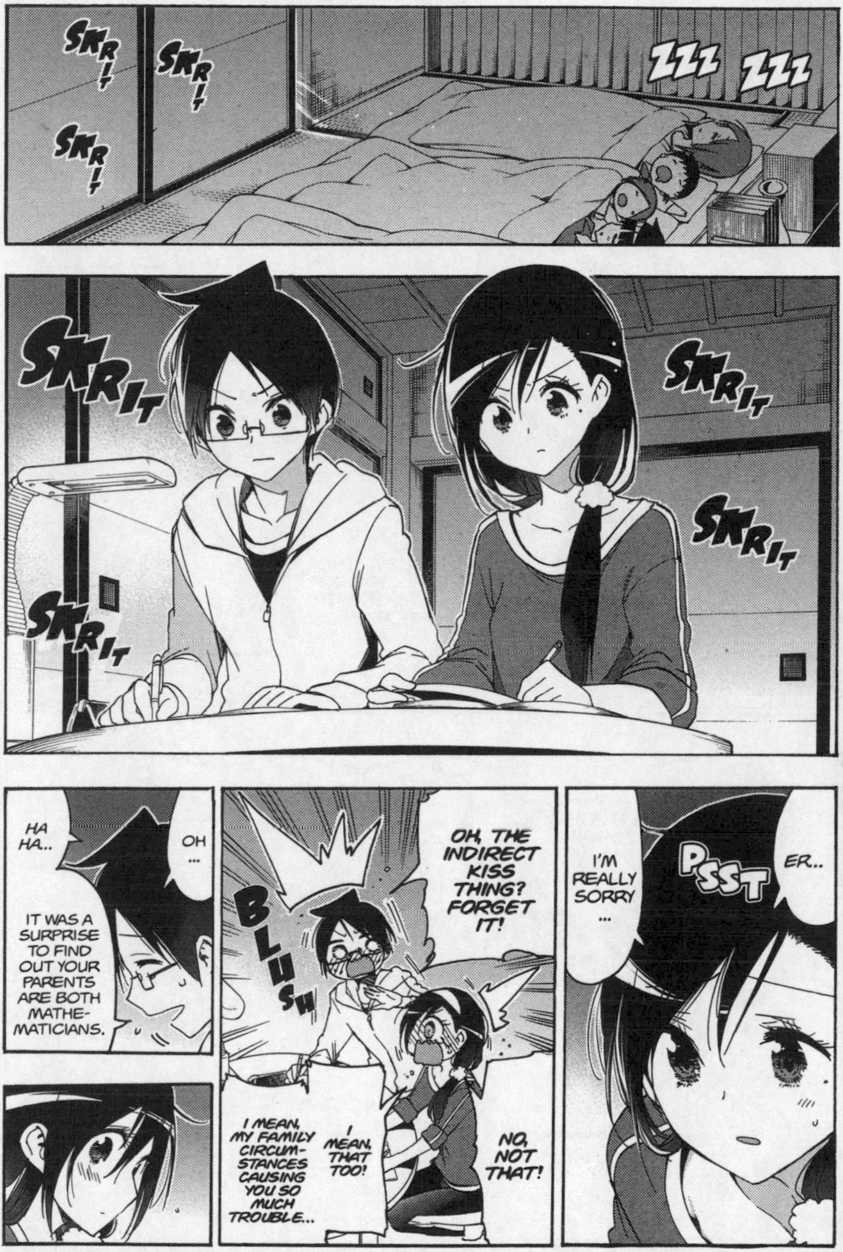
ZZZ
ZZZ
SKRIT
SKRIT
SKRIT
SKRIT
SKRIT
SKRIT
SKRIT
ER...
PSST
I'M REALLY SORRY ...
OH, THE INDIRECT KISS THING? FORGET IT!
BLUSH
NO, NOT THAT!
I MEAN, THAT TOO!
I MEAN, MY FAMILY CIRCUM-STANCES CAUSING YOU SO MUCH TROUBLE...
OH ...
HA HA...
IT WAS A SURPRISE TO FIND OUT YOUR PARENTS ARE BOTH MATHE-MATICIANS.

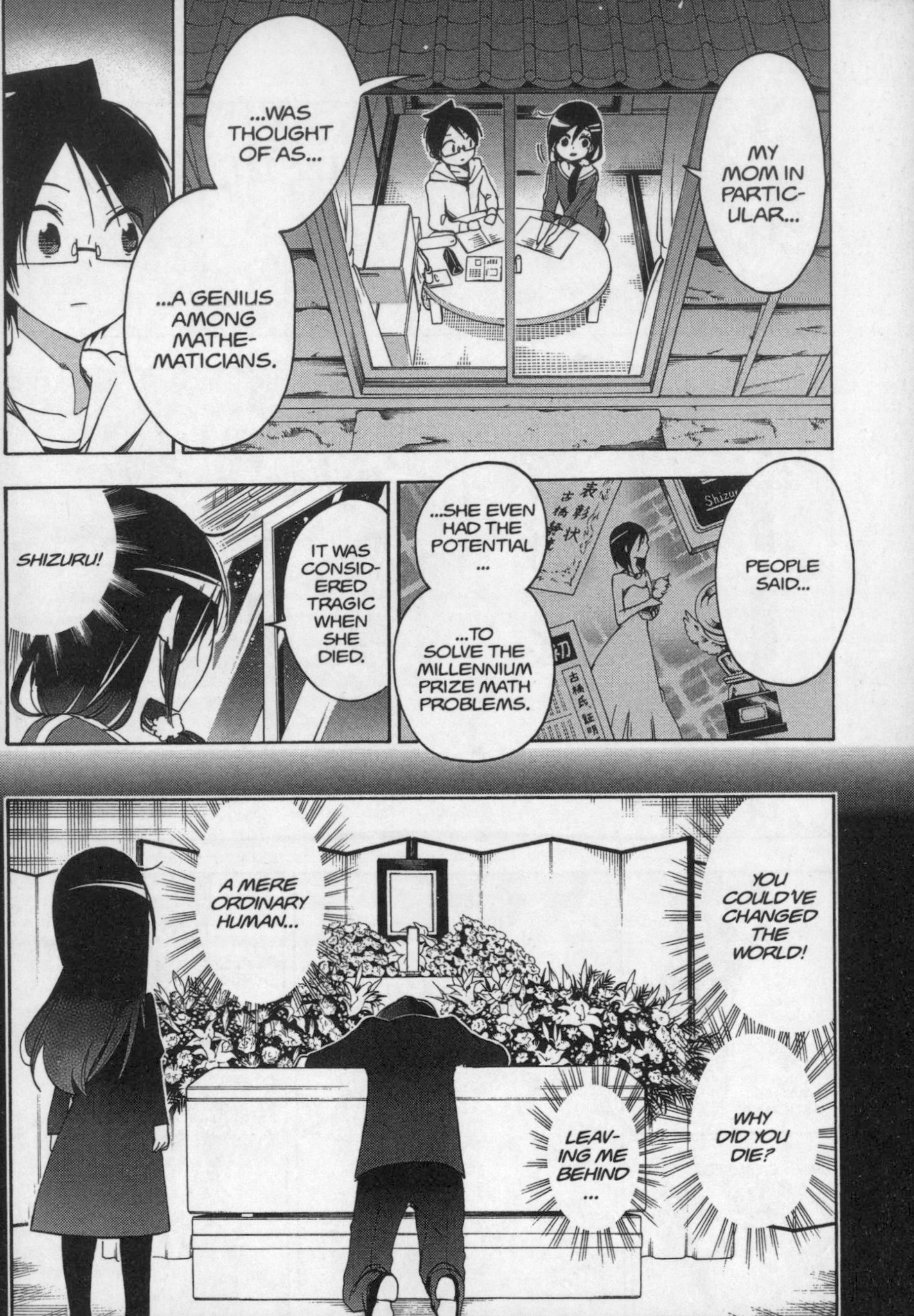
MY MOM IN PARTICULAR...
...WAS THOUGHT OF AS...
...A GENIUS AMONG MATHEMATICIANS.
PEOPLE SAID...
...SHE EVEN HAD THE POTENTIAL ...
...TO SOLVE THE MILLENNIUM PRIZE MATH PROBLEMS.
IT WAS CONSIDERED TRAGIC WHEN SHE DIED.
SHIZURU!
YOU COULD'VE CHANGED THE WORLD!
A MERE ORDINARY HUMAN...
WHY DID YOU DIE?
LEAVING ME BEHIND ...

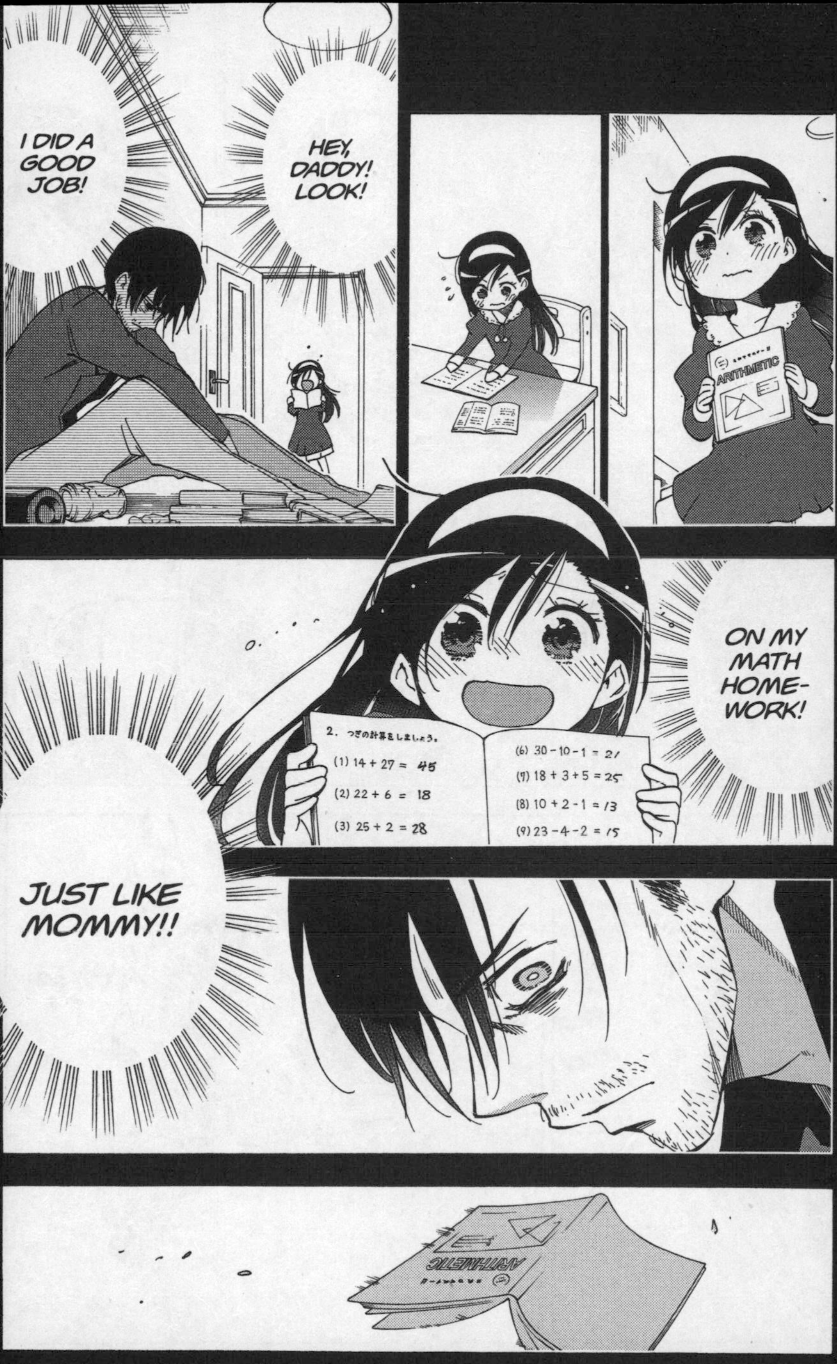
ARITHMETIC
HEY, DADDY! LOOK!
I DID A GOOD JOB!
ON MY MATH HOME-WORK!
2. つぎの計算をしましょう。
(1) 14 + 27 = 45
(2) 22 + 6 = 18
(3) 25 + 2 = 28
(6) 30 − 10 − 1 = 21
(7) 18 + 3 + 5 = 25
(8) 10 + 2 − 1 = 13
(9) 23 − 4 − 2 = 15
JUST LIKE MOMMY!!
ARITHMETIC

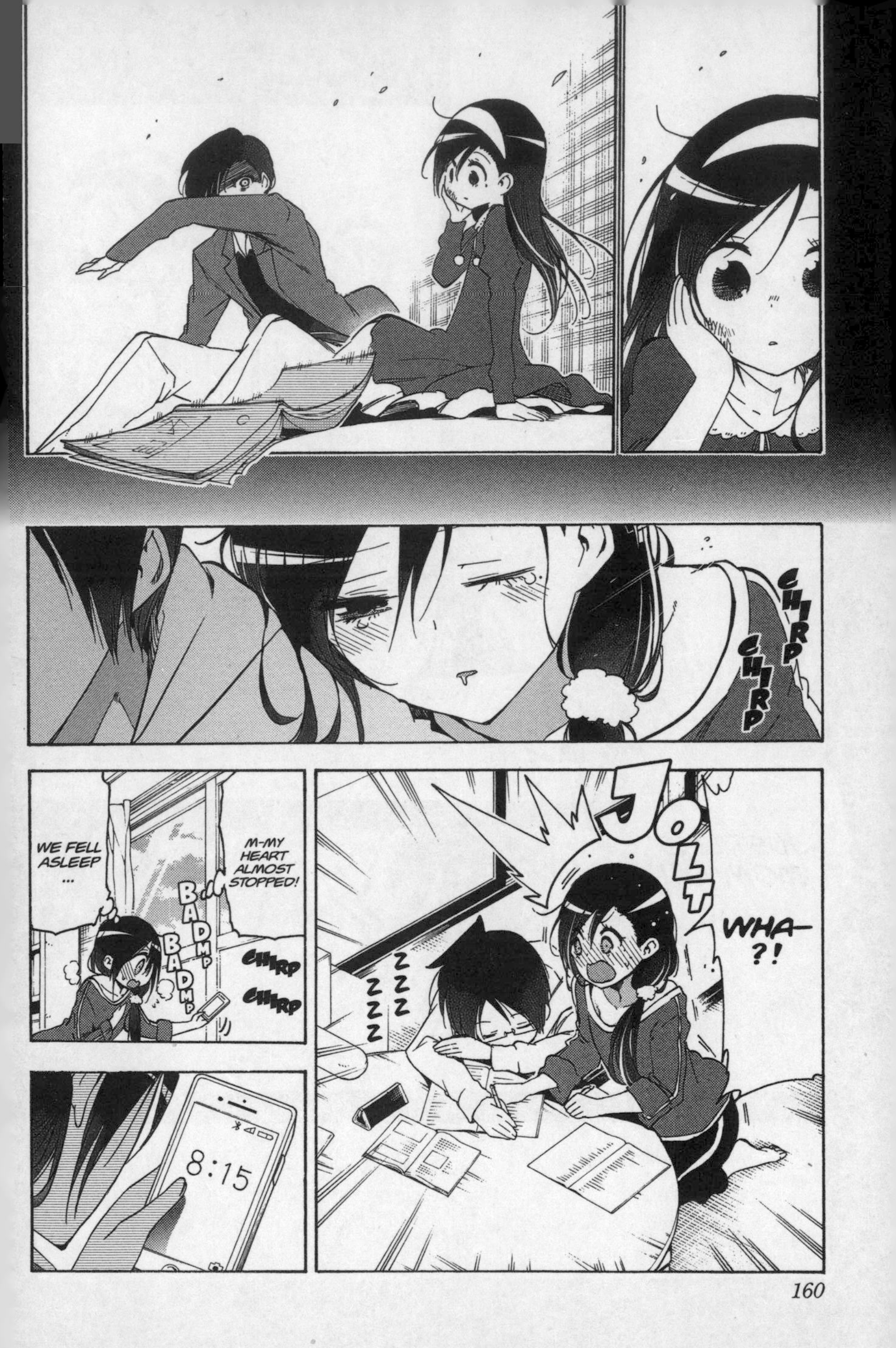
CHIRP
CHIRP
JOLT
WHA-?!
ZZZ
ZZZ
M-MY HEART ALMOST STOPPED!
WE FELL ASLEEP ...
BADMP
BADMP
CHIRP
CHIRP
8:15

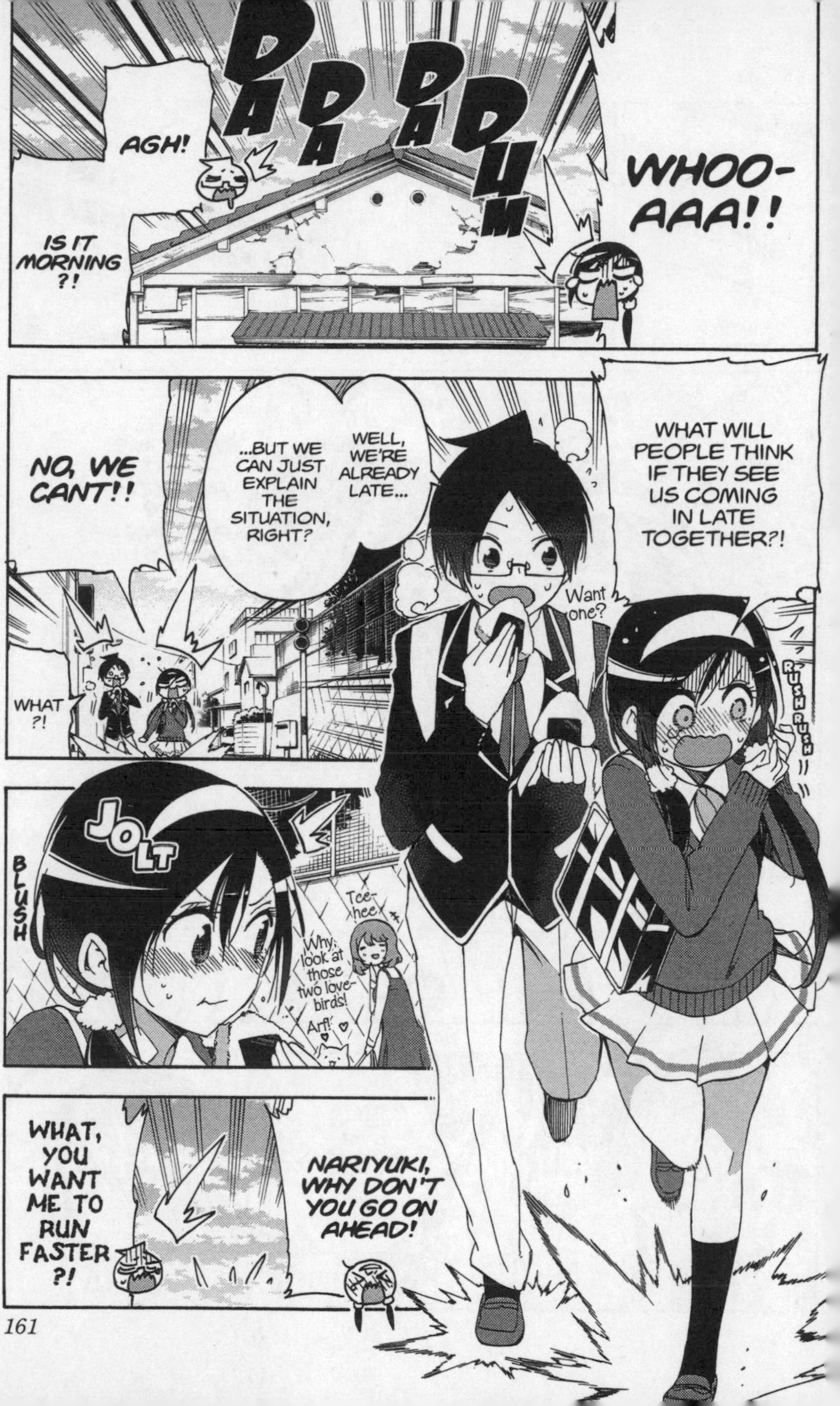
WHOO-AAA!!
DA DA DA DA DUM
AGH!
IS IT MORNING?!
WHAT WILL PEOPLE THINK IF THEY SEE US COMING IN LATE TOGETHER?!
Want one?
RUSH RUSH
WELL, WE'RE ALREADY LATE...
...BUT WE CAN JUST EXPLAIN THE SITUATION, RIGHT?
NO, WE CANT!!
WHAT?!
JOLT
Tee-hee
Why, look at those two love-birds!
Arf!
BLUSH
NARIYUKI, WHY DON'T YOU GO ON AHEAD!
WHAT, YOU WANT ME TO RUN FASTER?!

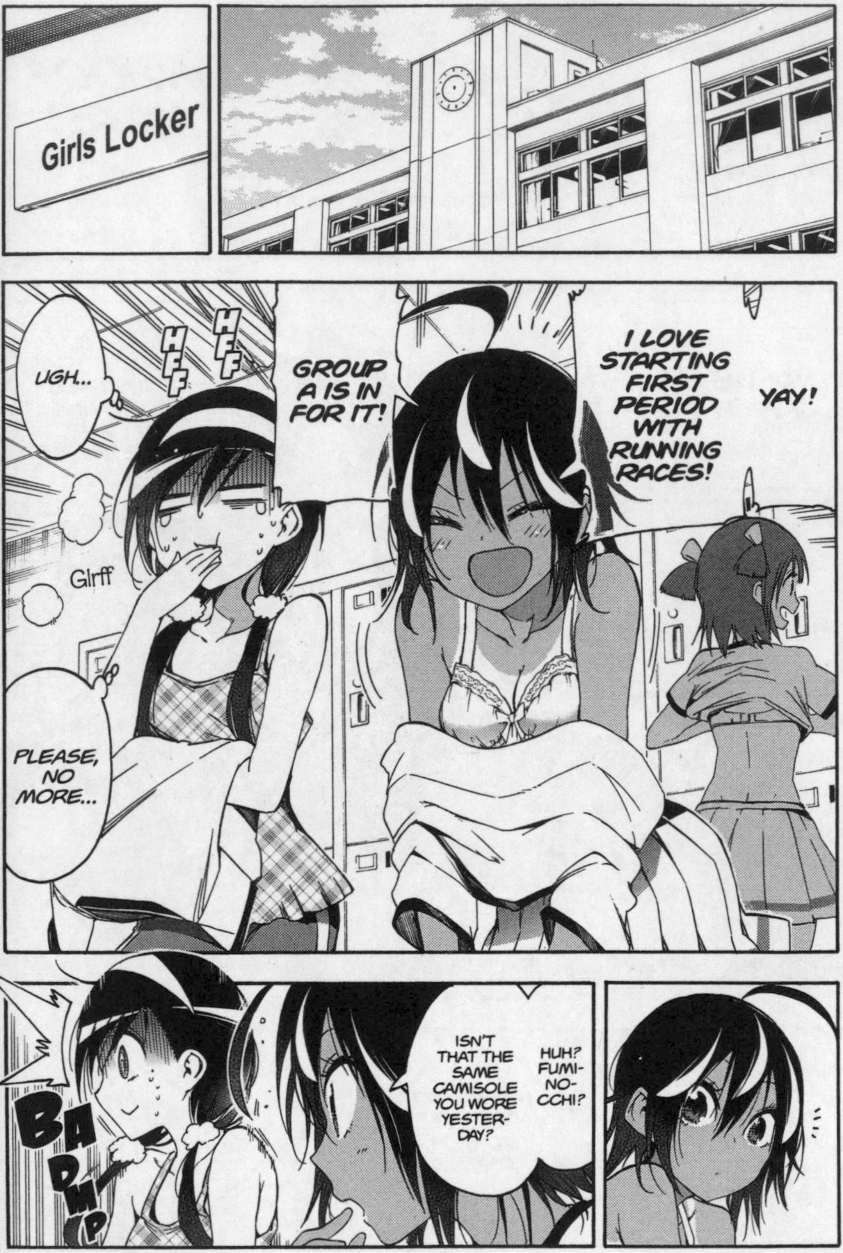
Girls Locker
YAY!
I LOVE STARTING FIRST PERIOD WITH RUNNING RACES!
GROUP A IS IN FOR IT!
HFF HFF
UGH...
Glrff
PLEASE, NO MORE...
HUH? FUMI-NO-CCHI?
ISN'T THAT THE SAME CAMISOLE YOU WORE YESTER-DAY?
BADUMP

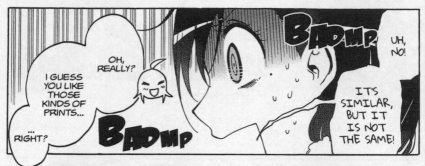

BADMP
UH, NO!
IT'S SIMILAR, BUT IT IS NOT THE SAME!
OH, REALLY?
I GUESS YOU LIKE THOSE KINDS OF PRINTS...
...RIGHT?
BADMP
HEY, YOU SMELL DIFFERENT TOO!
SNFF SNFF
EEK!
ER, UM... YEAH!
DID YOU CHANGE YOUR SHAMPOO?
I KNEW IT!
I REALLY LOVE THIS SMELL!
C'MON, TELL ME!
WHAT'S IT CALLED?
HEY, FUMINOCCHI?
KSHHH
FUMINOCCHI?!
ARE YOU DEAD?!
THIS IS NOT GOOD...
NOT GOOD... BUT...
BAM

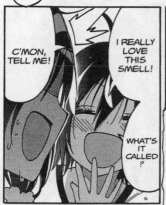

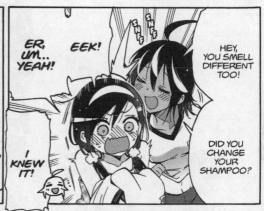

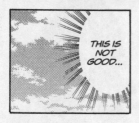

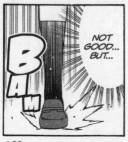

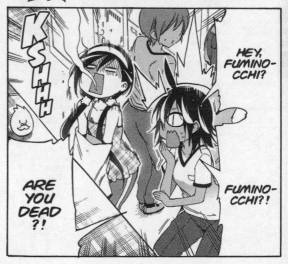

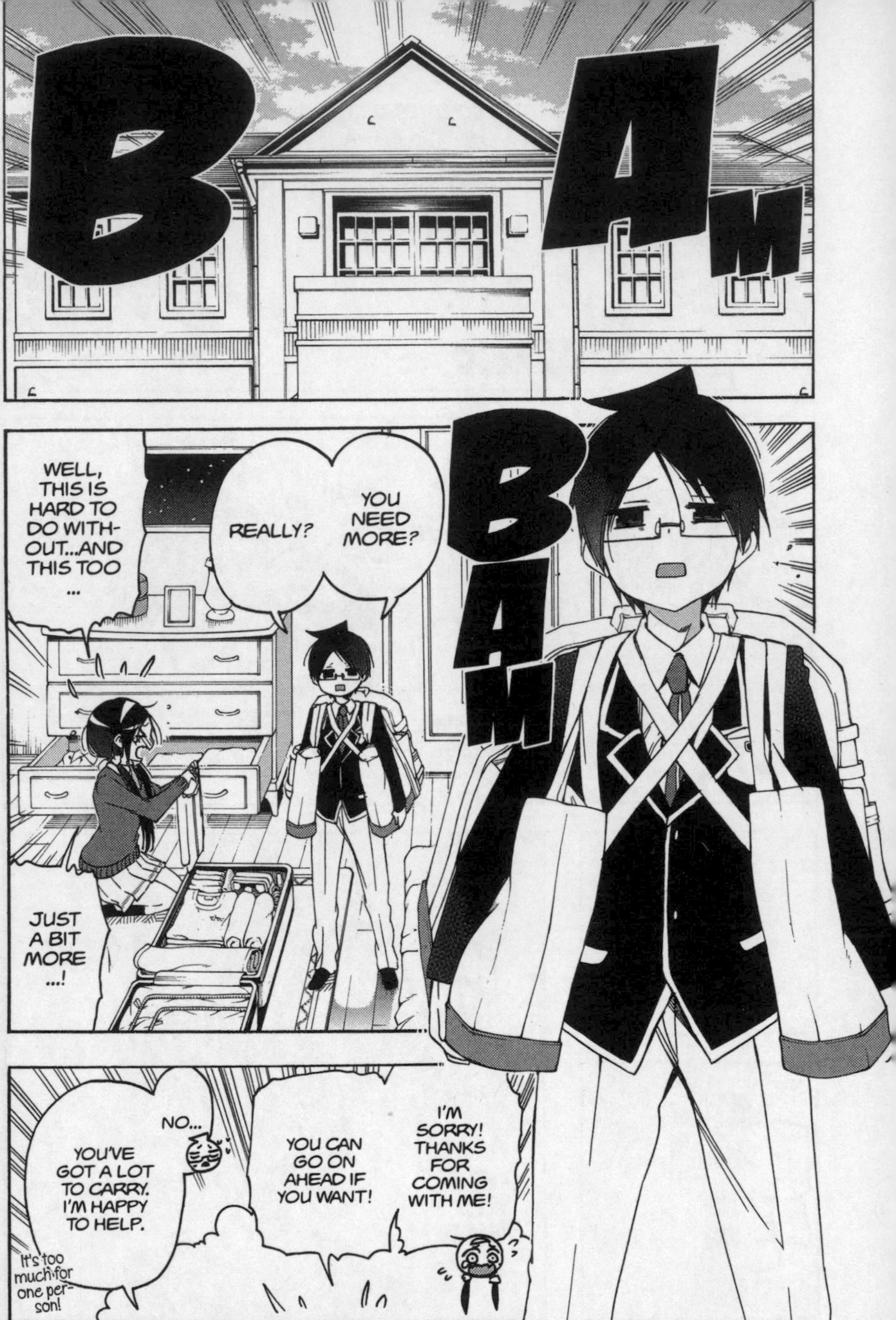
BAM
BAM
YOU NEED MORE?
REALLY?
WELL, THIS IS HARD TO DO WITH-OUT...AND THIS TOO ...
JUST A BIT MORE ...!
I'M SORRY! THANKS FOR COMING WITH ME!
YOU CAN GO ON AHEAD IF YOU WANT!
NO...
YOU'VE GOT A LOT TO CARRY. I'M HAPPY TO HELP.
It's too much for one per-son!

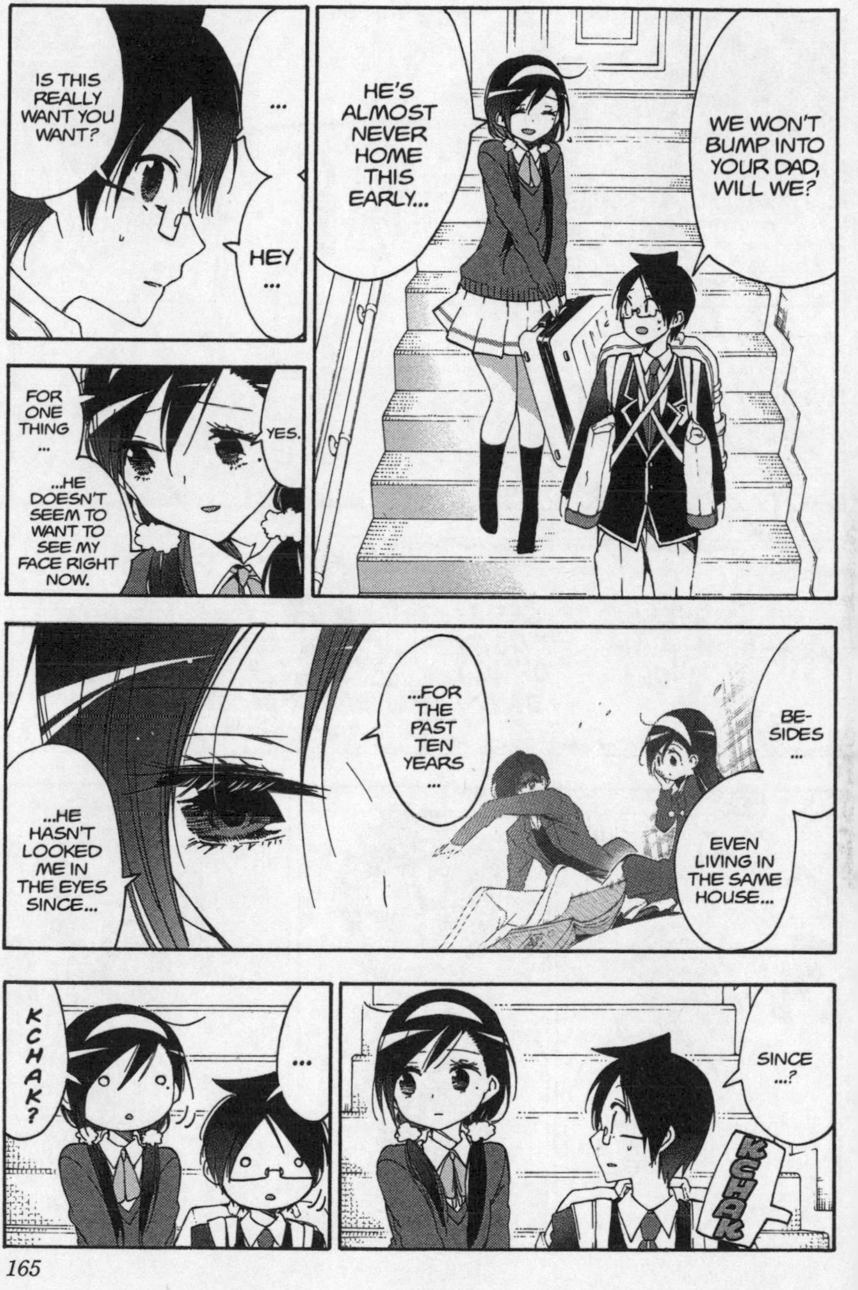
WE WON'T BUMP INTO YOUR DAD, WILL WE?
HE'S ALMOST NEVER HOME THIS EARLY...
...
HEY ...
IS THIS REALLY WANT YOU WANT?
YES.
FOR ONE THING ...
...HE DOESN'T SEEM TO WANT TO SEE MY FACE RIGHT NOW.
BE-SIDES ...
EVEN LIVING IN THE SAME HOUSE...
...FOR THE PAST TEN YEARS ...
...HE HASN'T LOOKED ME IN THE EYES SINCE...
SINCE ...?
KCHAK
...
KCHAK?

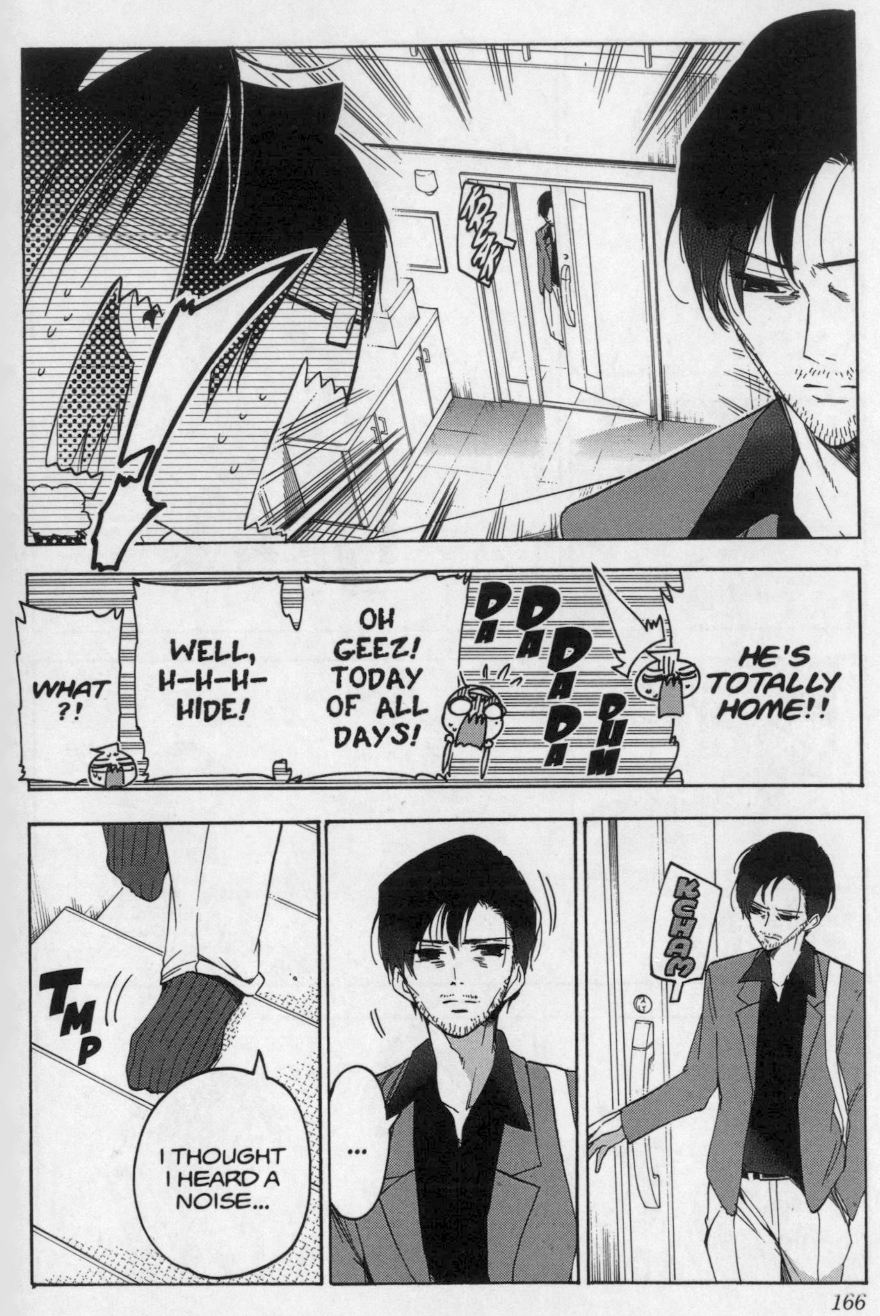
KRAK
HE'S TOTALLY HOME!!
DA DA DA DA DUM
OH GEEZ! TODAY OF ALL DAYS!
WELL, H-H-H-HIDE!
WHAT?!
KCHAM!
...
TMP
I THOUGHT I HEARD A NOISE...

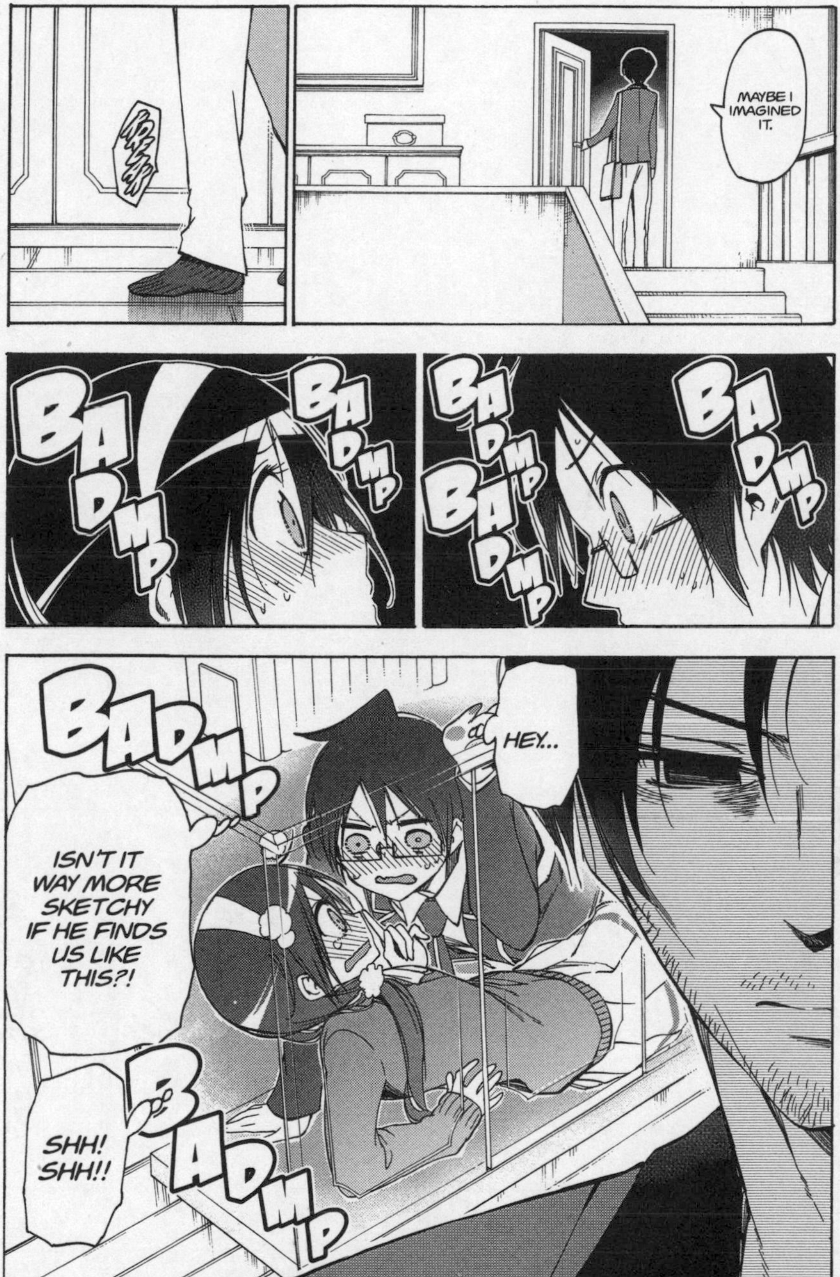
MAYBE I IMAGINED IT.
BADMP
BADMP
BADMP
BADMP
BADMP
HEY...
BADMP
ISN'T IT WAY MORE SKETCHY IF HE FINDS US LIKE THIS?!
SHH! SHH!!
BADMP

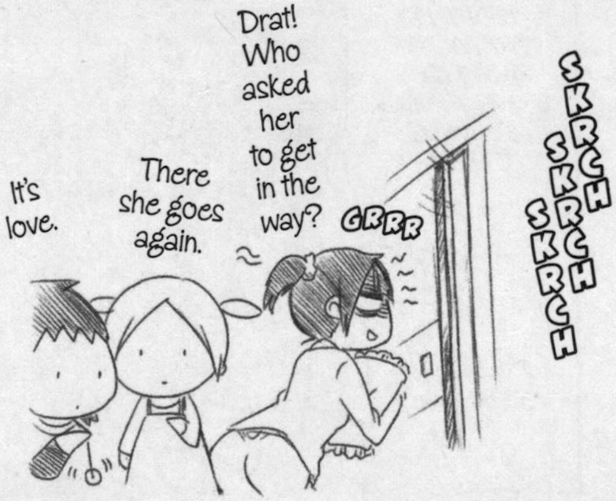
SKRCH SKRCH SKRCH
GRRR
Drat! Who asked her to get in the way?
There she goes again.
It's love.

Question 87: The Star of Ultimate Love and the Name of [X], Part 3

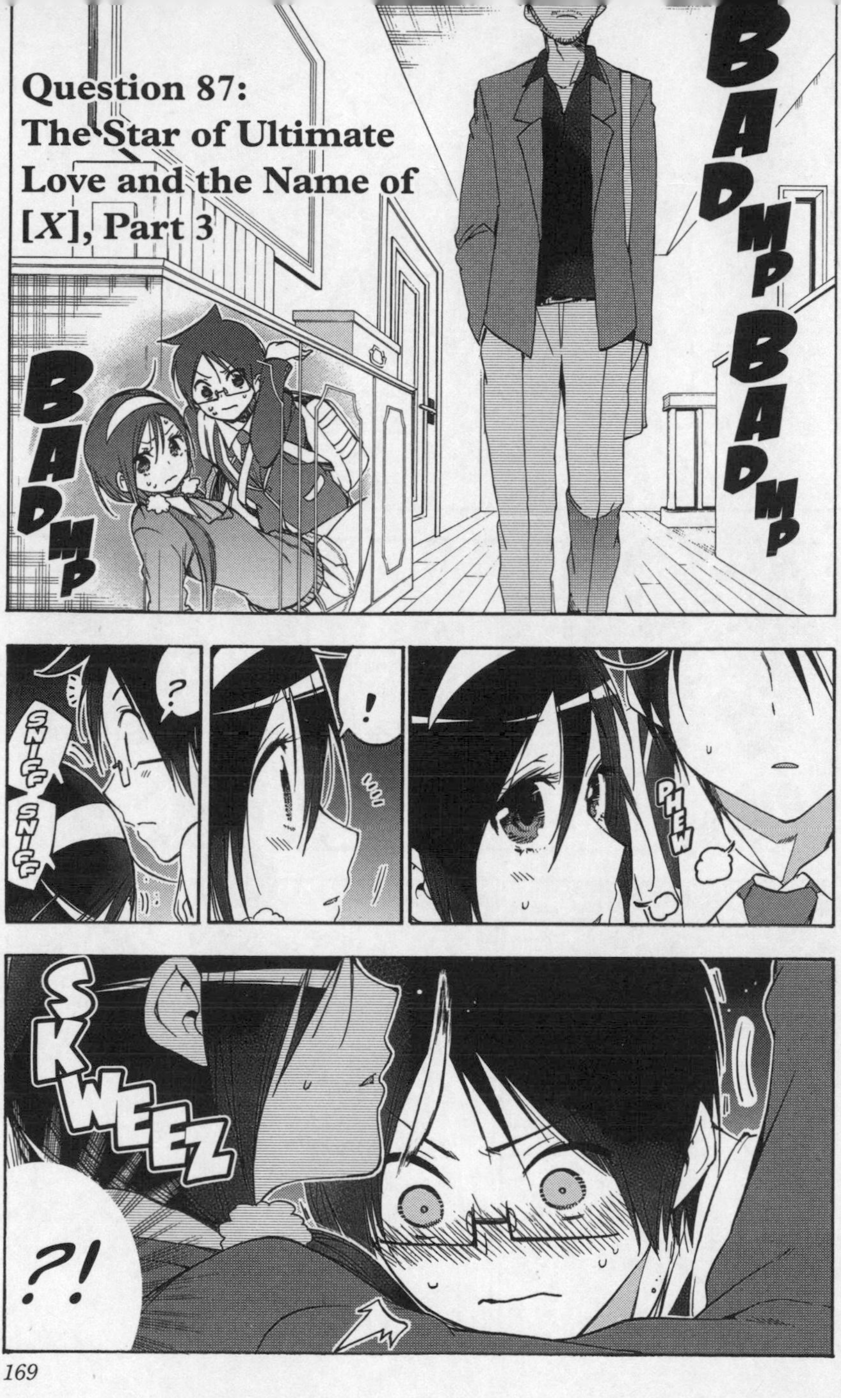
BADUMP BADUMP BADUMP
BADUMP
PHEW
!
?
SNIFF SNIFF SNIFF
SKWEEZ
?!

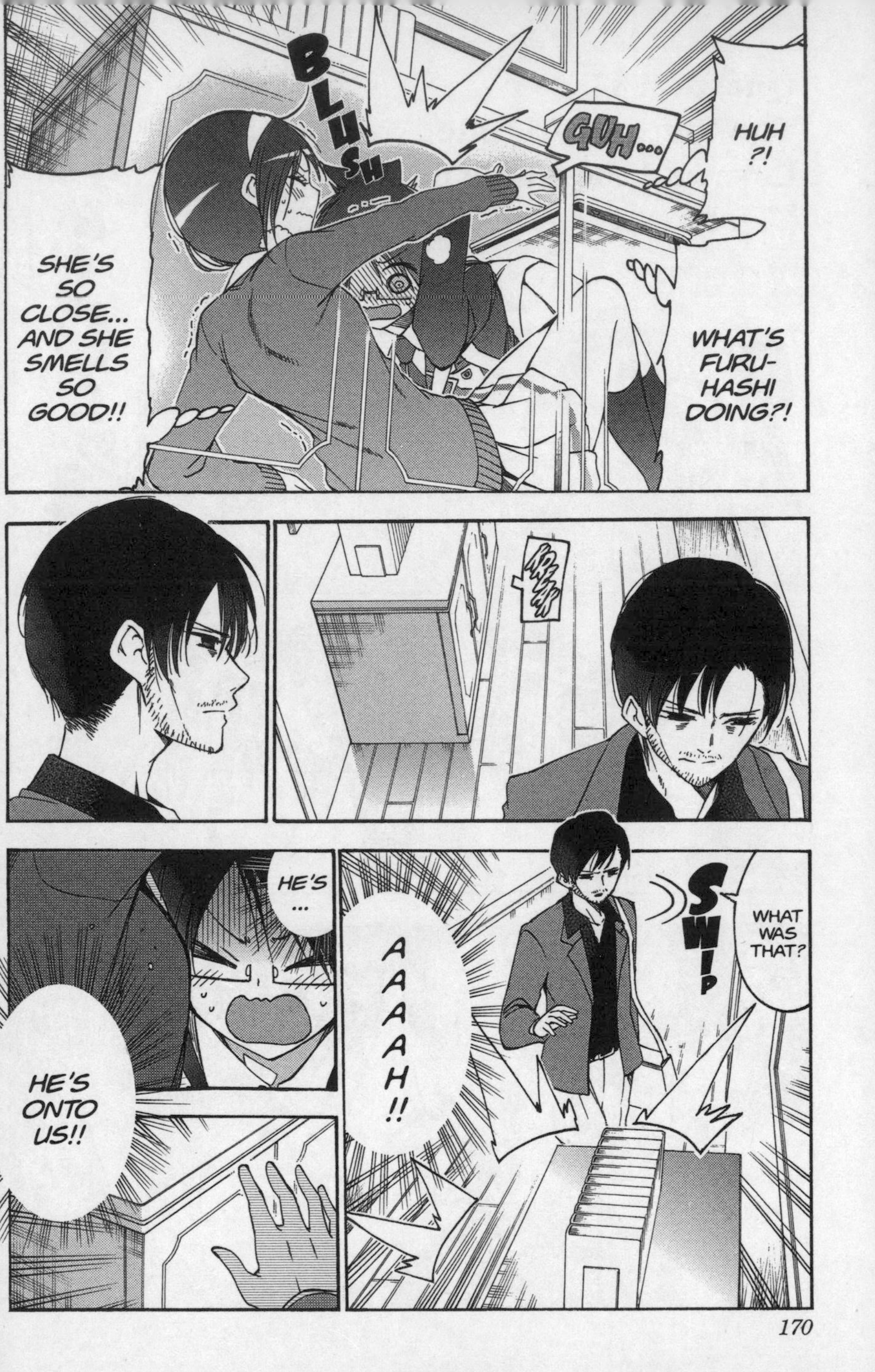
HUH ?!
GUH...
WHAT'S FURU-HASHI DOING?!
BLUSH
SHE'S SO CLOSE... AND SHE SMELLS SO GOOD!!
KREAK
SWIP
WHAT WAS THAT?
AAAAAH!!
HE'S ...
HE'S ONTO US!!

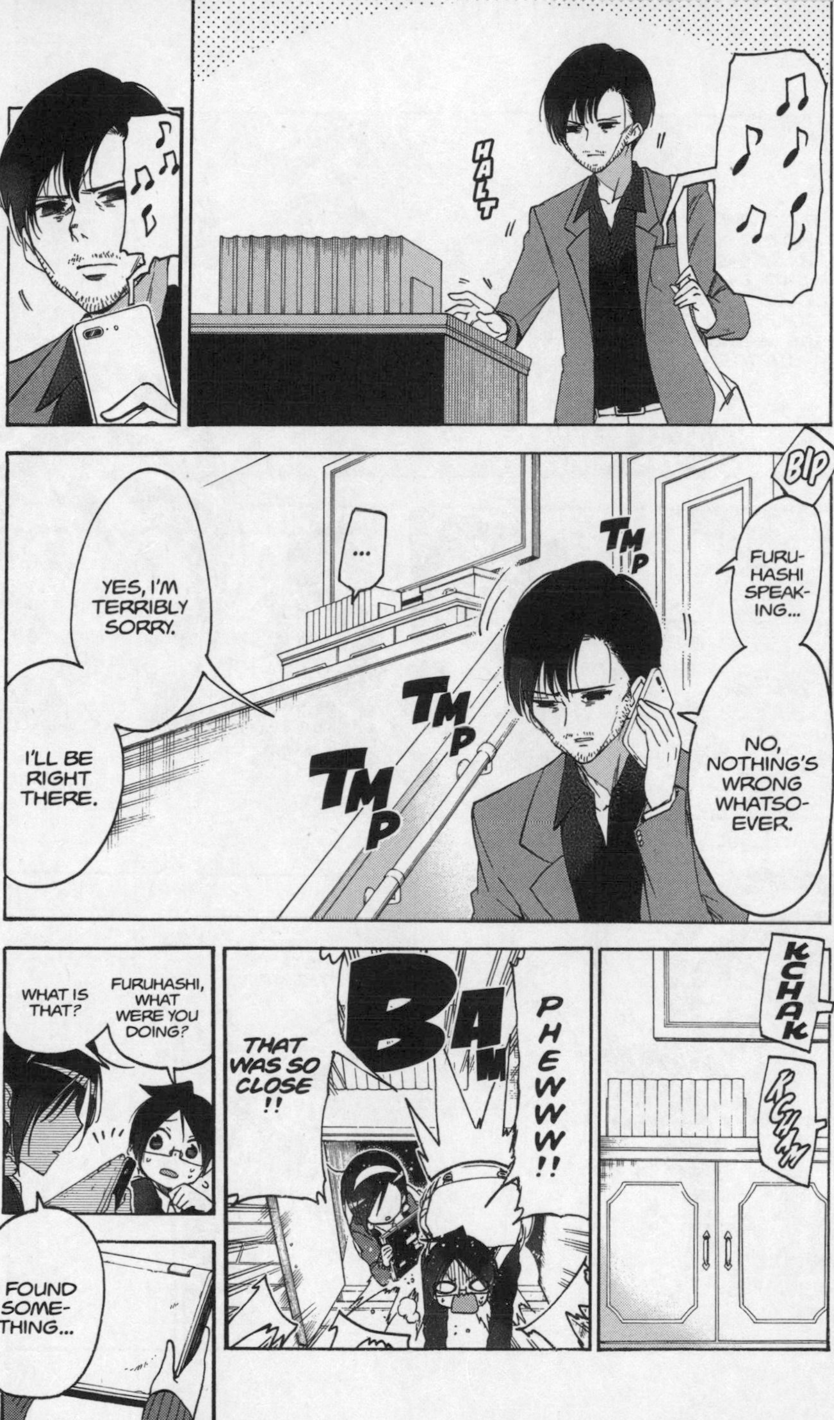
HALT
BIP
TMP
FURUHASHI SPEAKING...
NO, NOTHING'S WRONG WHATSOEVER.
...
TMP
TMP
YES, I'M TERRIBLY SORRY.
I'LL BE RIGHT THERE.
KCHAK
KCHAK
BAM
PHEWWW!!
THAT WAS SO CLOSE!!
FURUHASHI, WHAT WERE YOU DOING?
WHAT IS THAT?
I FOUND SOMETHING...

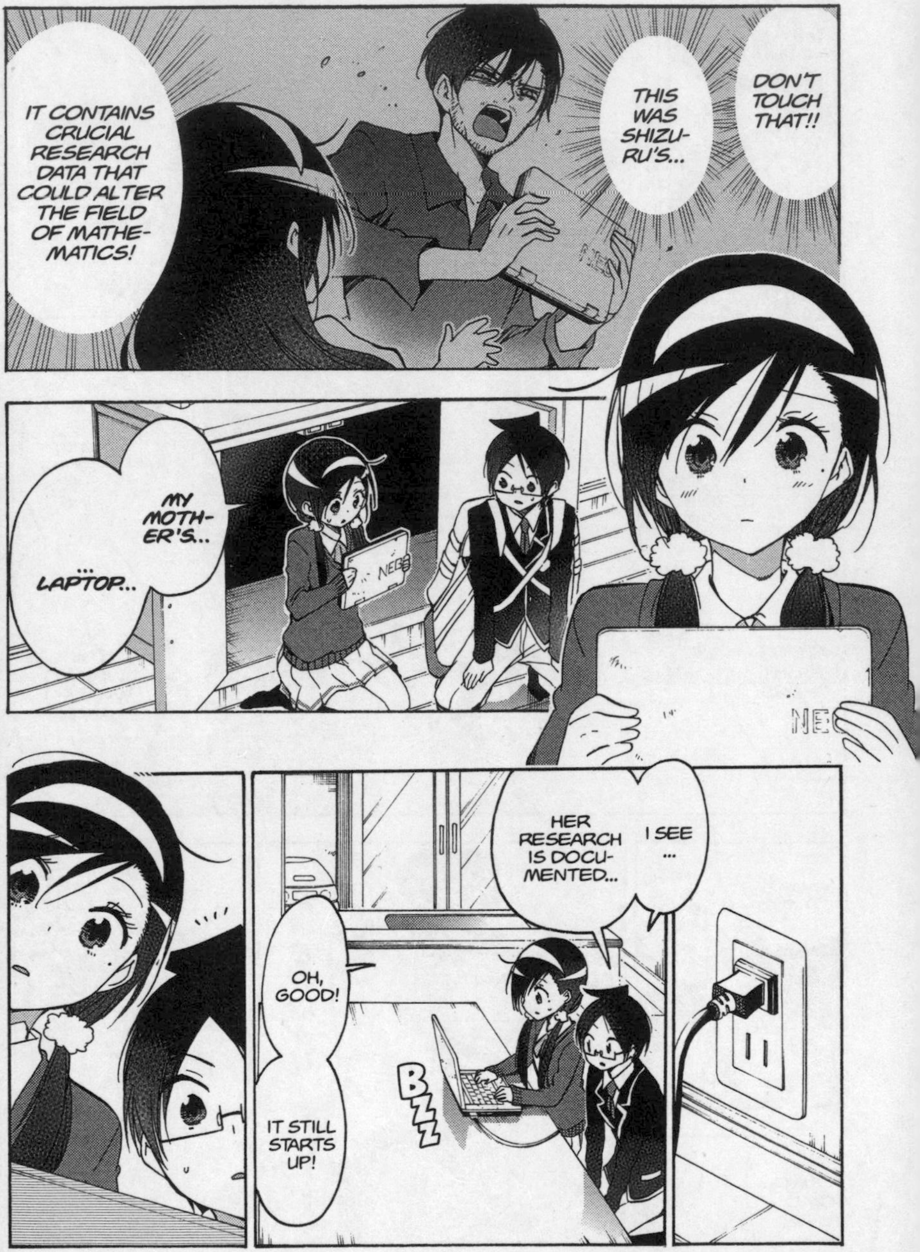
DON'T TOUCH THAT!!
THIS WAS SHIZU-RU'S...
IT CONTAINS CRUCIAL RESEARCH DATA THAT COULD ALTER THE FIELD OF MATHE-MATICS!
MY MOTH-ER'S...
... LAPTOP...
I SEE ...
HER RESEARCH IS DOCU-MENTED...
OH, GOOD!
BZZ
IT STILL STARTS UP!

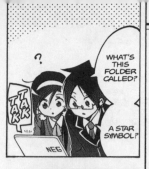

「☆」
スタート
WHAT'S THIS FOLDER CALLED?
A STAR SYMBOL?
?
TAK TAK
NEG
!
[☆] Requires a password to open. All data will be deleted if a wrong password is entered one more time.
PASSWORD:
ACCEPT
CANCEL
EVERY-THING WILL BE DELETED IF A WRONG PASS-WORD IS ENTERED ONE MORE TIME?!
THAT'S SO EXTREME!
DOES THIS MEAN...
...EVEN DAD HASN'T SEEN WHAT'S INSIDE?
I BET MY DAD'S BEEN DYING TO GET INTO THIS FOLDER...
I FEEL KINDA SORRY FOR HIM...
NO, THERE'S NOTHING WRONG WHATSO-EVER.
KRIK

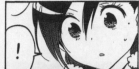

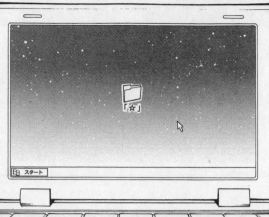

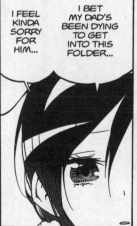

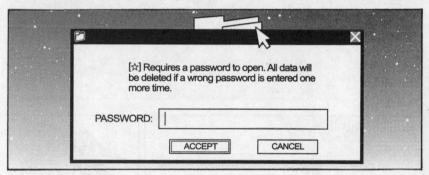

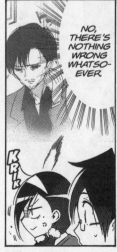

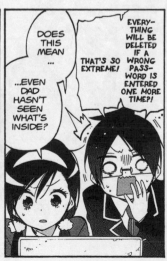

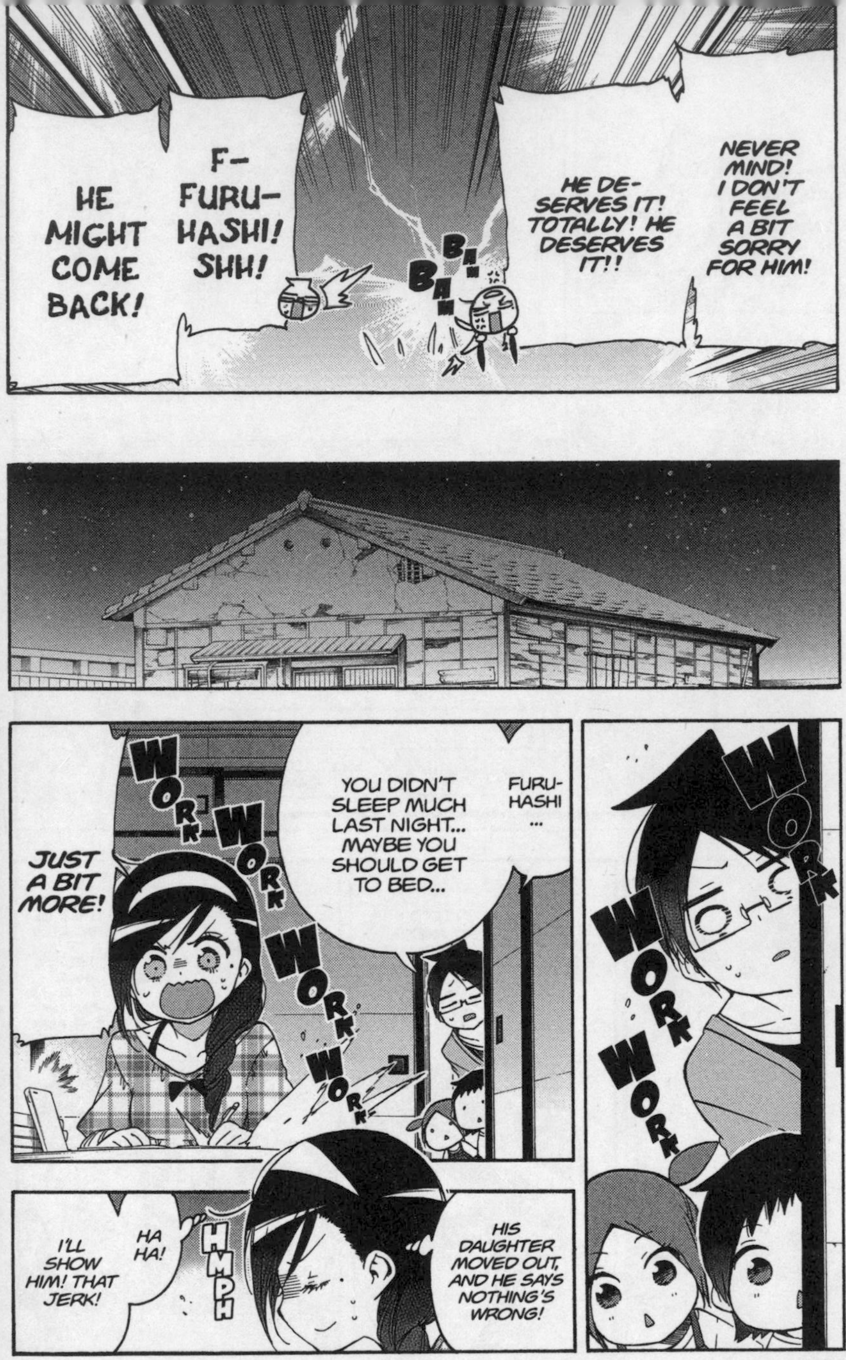
NEVER MIND! I DON'T FEEL A BIT SORRY FOR HIM!
HE DE-SERVES IT! TOTALLY! HE DESERVES IT!!
BAM BAM
F-FURU-HASHI! SHH!
HE MIGHT COME BACK!
WORK WORK WORK
FURU-HASHI ...
YOU DIDN'T SLEEP MUCH LAST NIGHT... MAYBE YOU SHOULD GET TO BED...
JUST A BIT MORE!
WORK WORK WORK WORK WORK
HIS DAUGHTER MOVED OUT, AND HE SAYS NOTHING'S WRONG!
HMPH
HA HA!
I'LL SHOW HIM! THAT JERK!

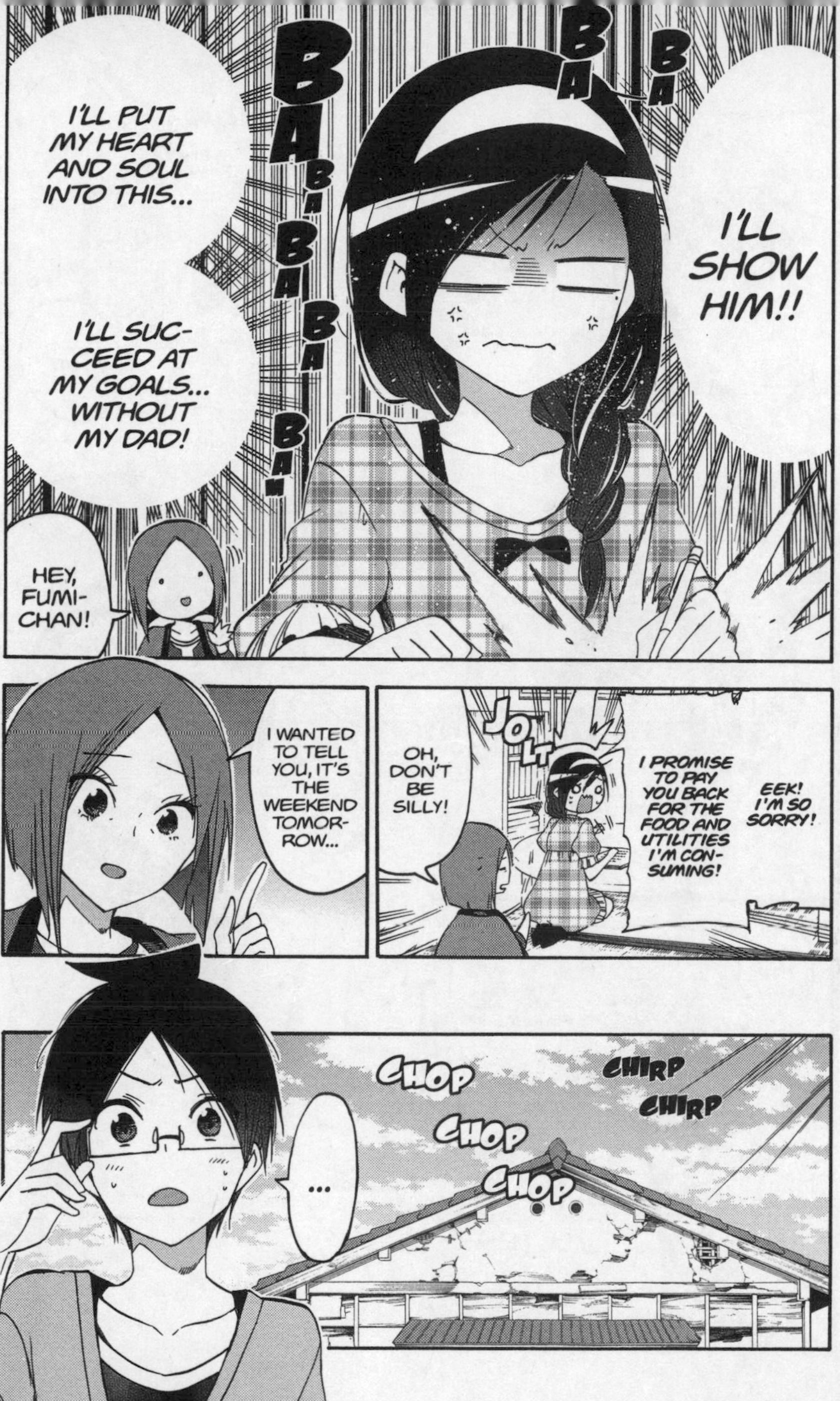
BA BA
I'LL SHOW HIM!!
BABABABABABA BAM
I'LL PUT MY HEART AND SOUL INTO THIS...
I'LL SUC-CEED AT MY GOALS... WITHOUT MY DAD!
HEY, FUMI-CHAN!
EEK! I'M SO SORRY!
I PROMISE TO PAY YOU BACK FOR THE FOOD AND UTILITIES I'M CON-SUMING!
JOLT
OH, DON'T BE SILLY!
I WANTED TO TELL YOU, IT'S THE WEEKEND TOMOR-ROW...
CHIRP CHIRP
CHOP CHOP CHOP
...

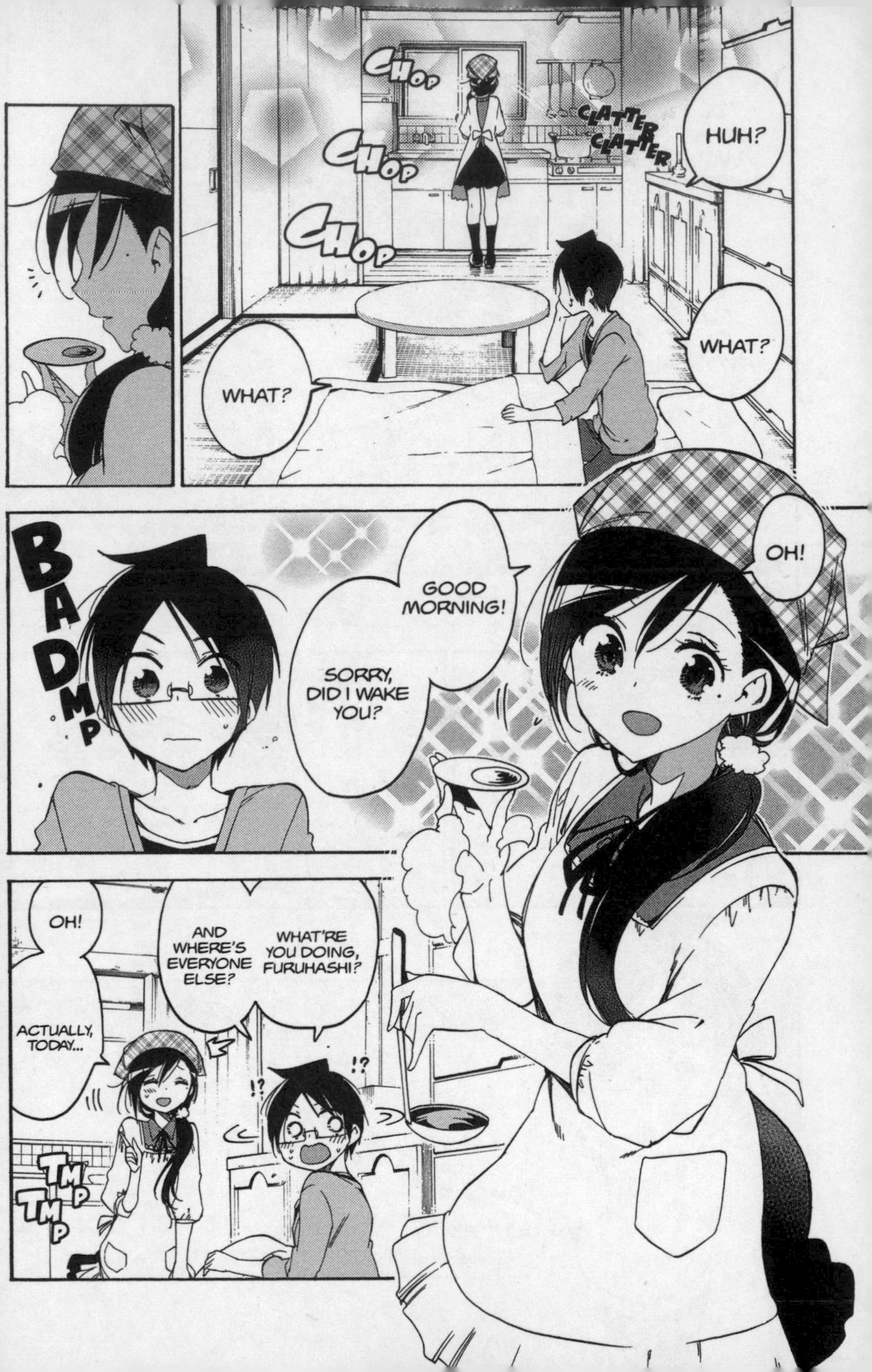
HUH?
CLATTER CLATTER
CHOP CHOP CHOP
WHAT?
WHAT?
OH!
GOOD MORNING!
SORRY, DID I WAKE YOU?
BADMP
WHAT'RE YOU DOING, FURUHASHI?
AND WHERE'S EVERYONE ELSE?
!?
!?
OH!
ACTUALLY, TODAY...
TMP TMP

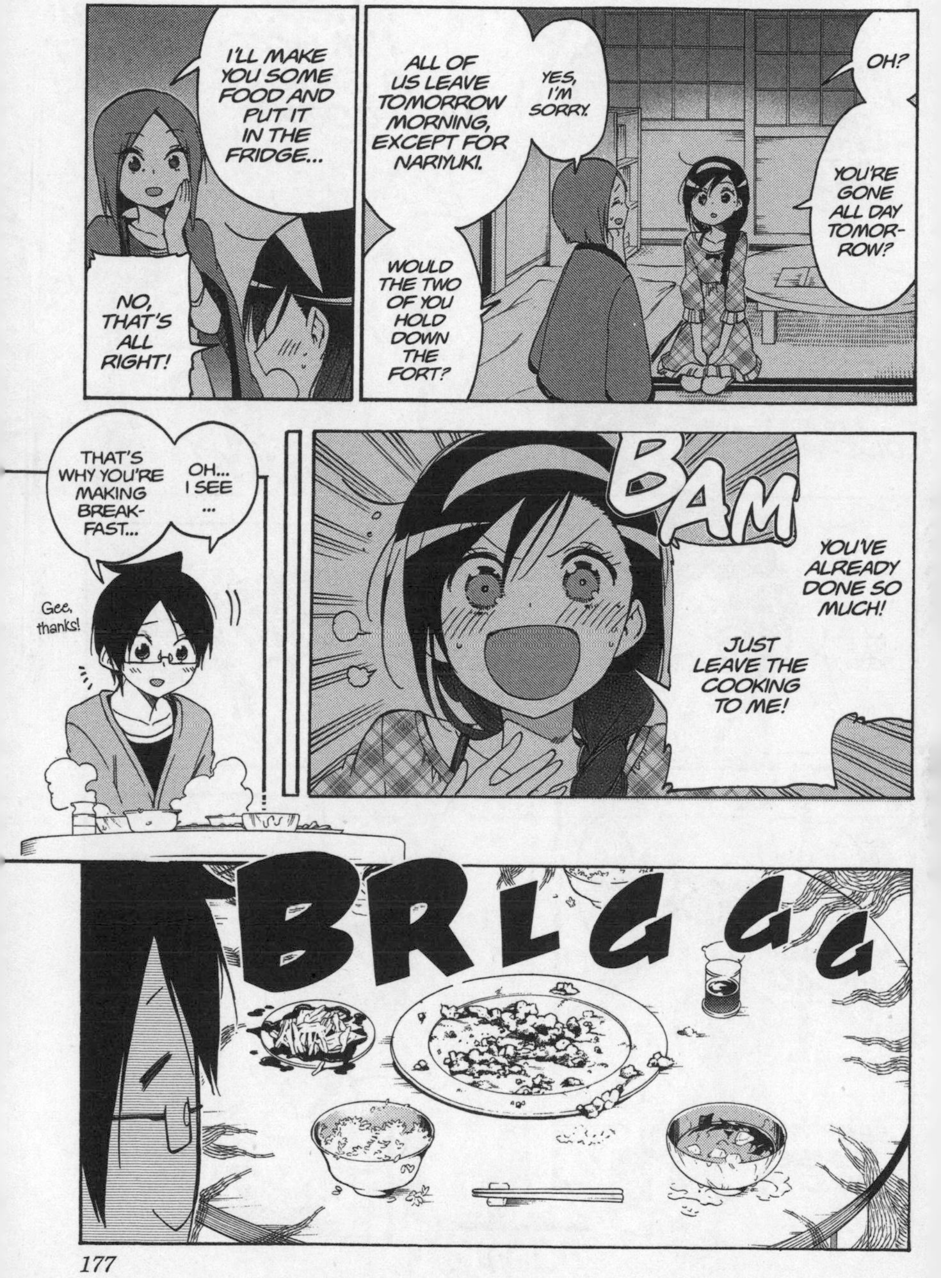
OH?
YOU'RE GONE ALL DAY TOMORROW?
YES, I'M SORRY.
ALL OF US LEAVE TOMORROW MORNING, EXCEPT FOR NARIYUKI.
WOULD THE TWO OF YOU HOLD DOWN THE FORT?
I'LL MAKE YOU SOME FOOD AND PUT IT IN THE FRIDGE...
NO, THAT'S ALL RIGHT!
BAM
YOU'VE ALREADY DONE SO MUCH!
JUST LEAVE THE COOKING TO ME!
OH... I SEE ...
THAT'S WHY YOU'RE MAKING BREAK-FAST...
Gee, thanks!
BRLGGG

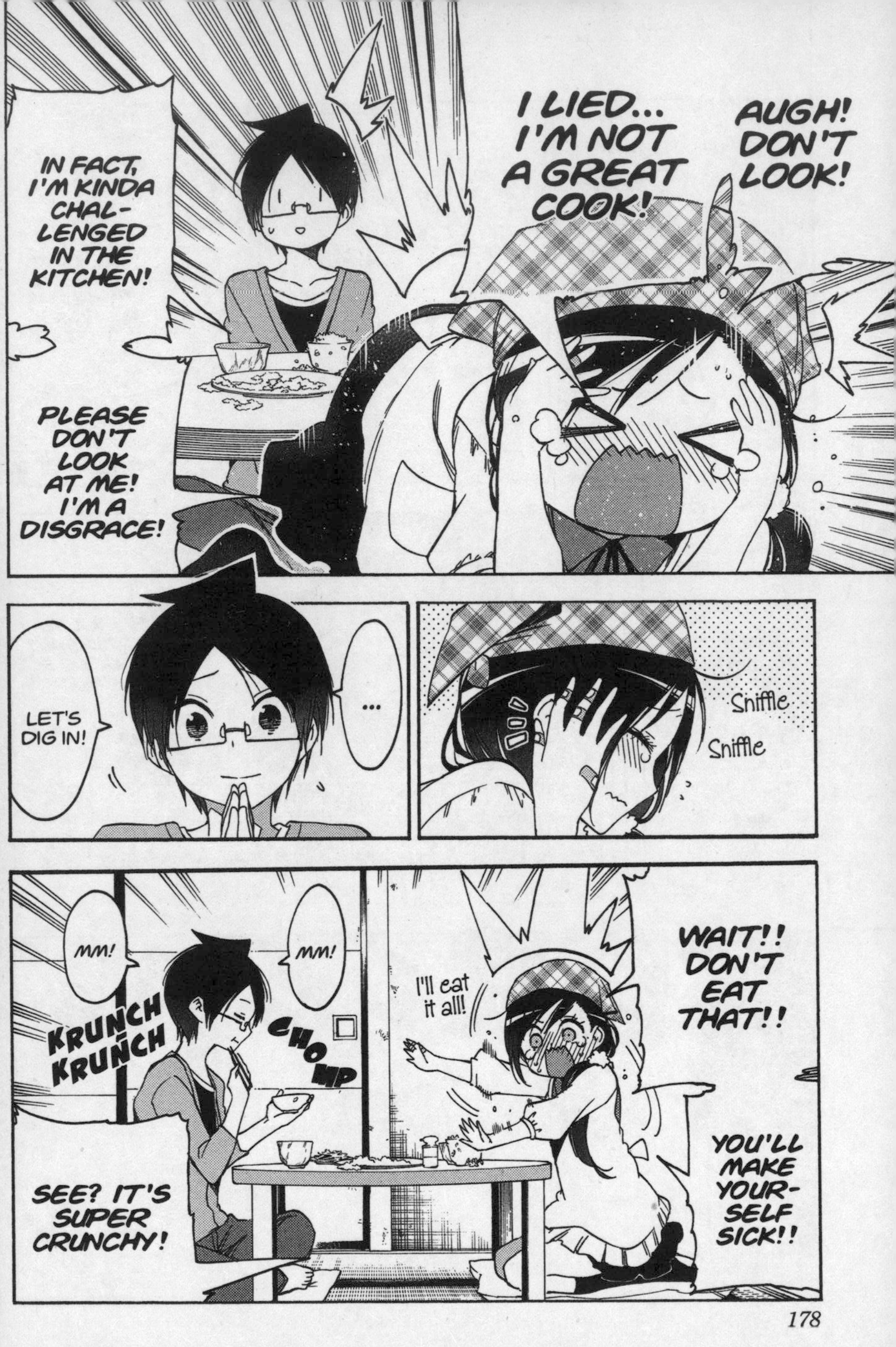
AUGH! DON'T LOOK!
I LIED... I'M NOT A GREAT COOK!
IN FACT, I'M KINDA CHAL-LENGED IN THE KITCHEN!
PLEASE DON'T LOOK AT ME! I'M A DISGRACE!
Sniffle
Sniffle
...
LET'S DIG IN!
WAIT!! DON'T EAT THAT!!
YOU'LL MAKE YOUR-SELF SICK!!
I'll eat it all!
MM!
MM!
CHOMP
KRUNCH KRUNCH
SEE? IT'S SUPER CRUNCHY!

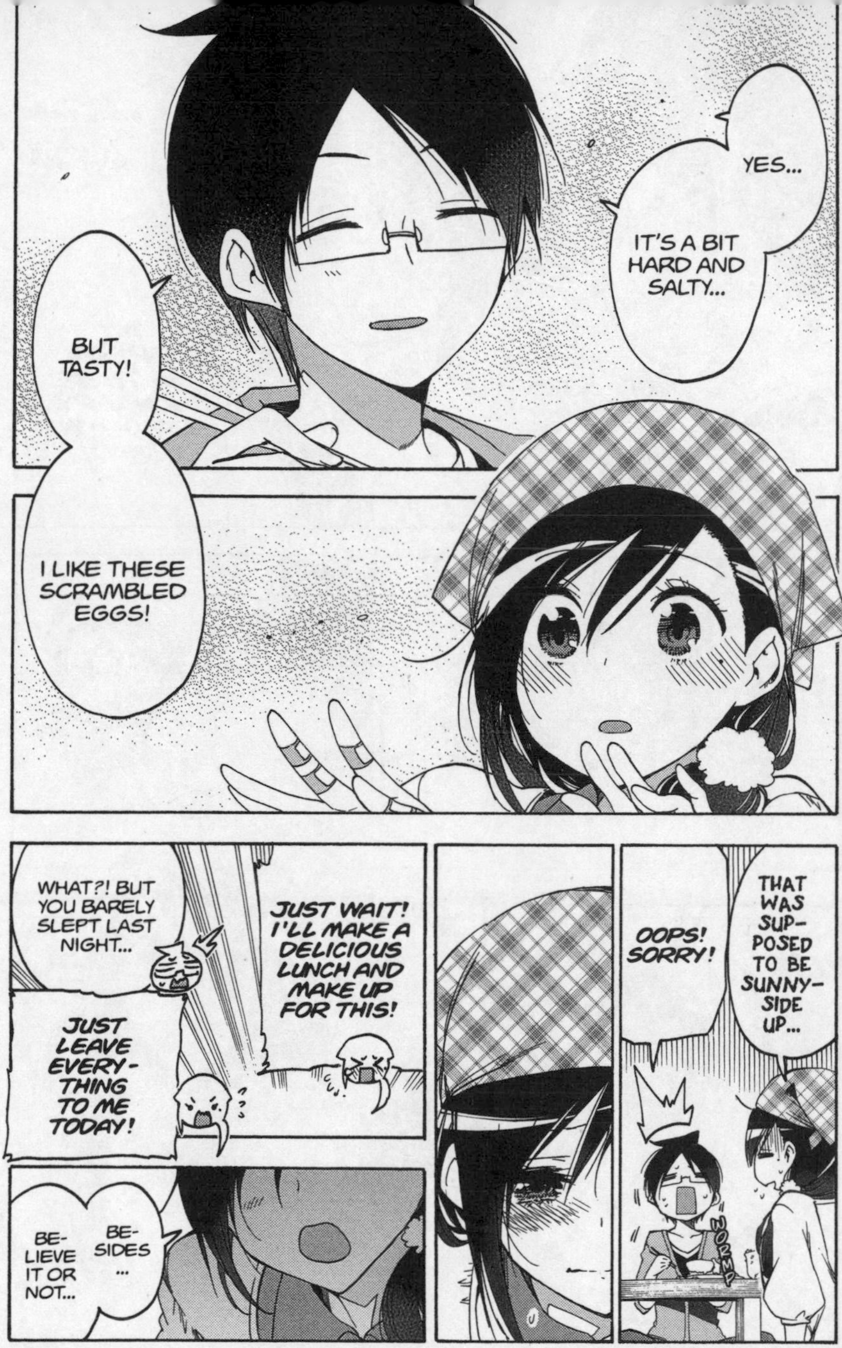
YES...
IT'S A BIT HARD AND SALTY...
BUT TASTY!
I LIKE THESE SCRAMBLED EGGS!
THAT WAS SUP-POSED TO BE SUNNY-SIDE UP...
OOPS! SORRY!
JUST WAIT! I'LL MAKE A DELICIOUS LUNCH AND MAKE UP FOR THIS!
WHAT?! BUT YOU BARELY SLEPT LAST NIGHT...
JUST LEAVE EVERY-THING TO ME TODAY!
BE-SIDES ...
BE-LIEVE IT OR NOT...

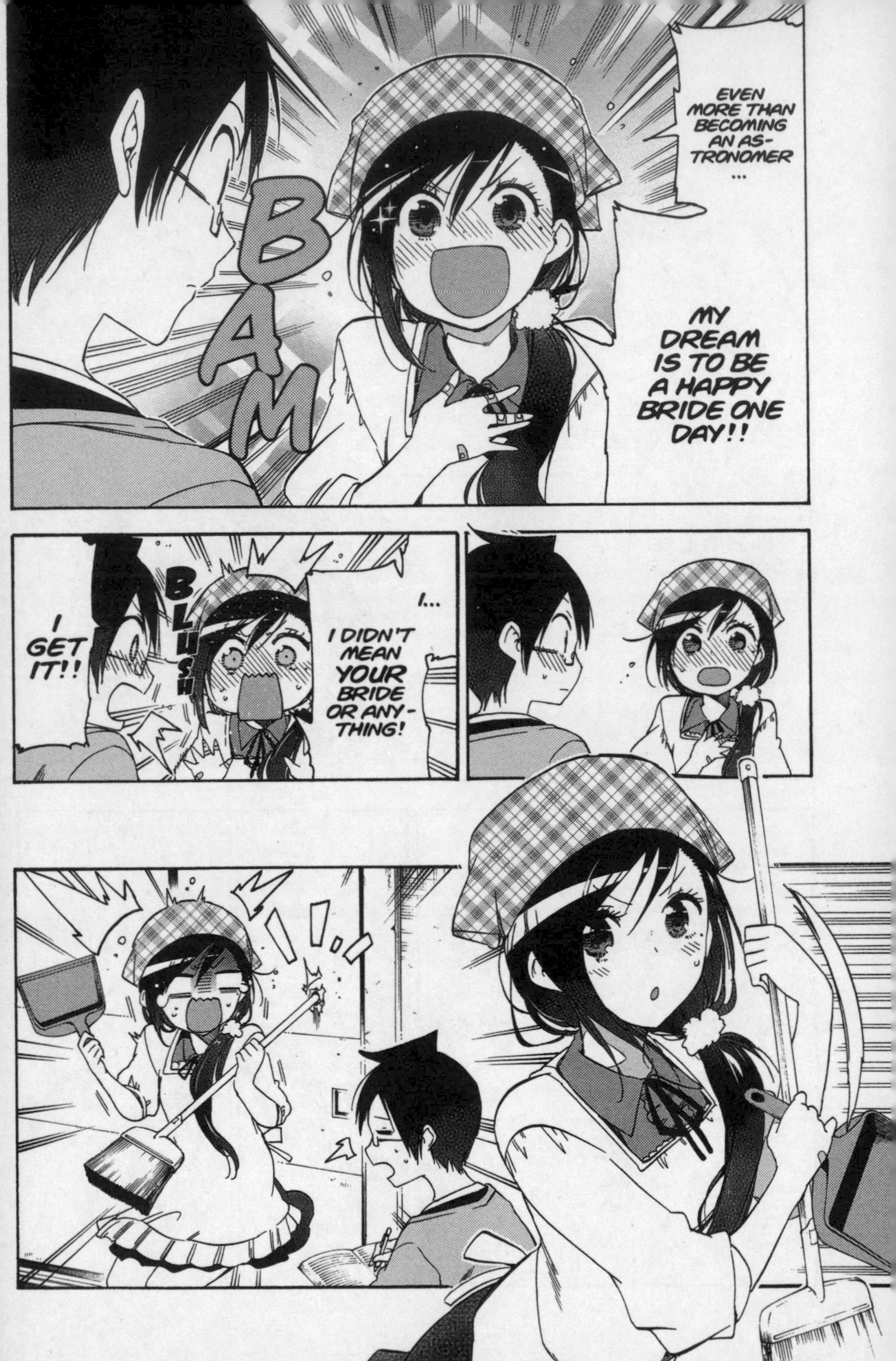
EVEN MORE THAN BECOMING AN AS-TRONOMER ...
BAM
MY DREAM IS TO BE A HAPPY BRIDE ONE DAY!!
I...
I DIDN'T MEAN YOUR BRIDE OR ANY-THING!
BLUSH
I GET IT!!

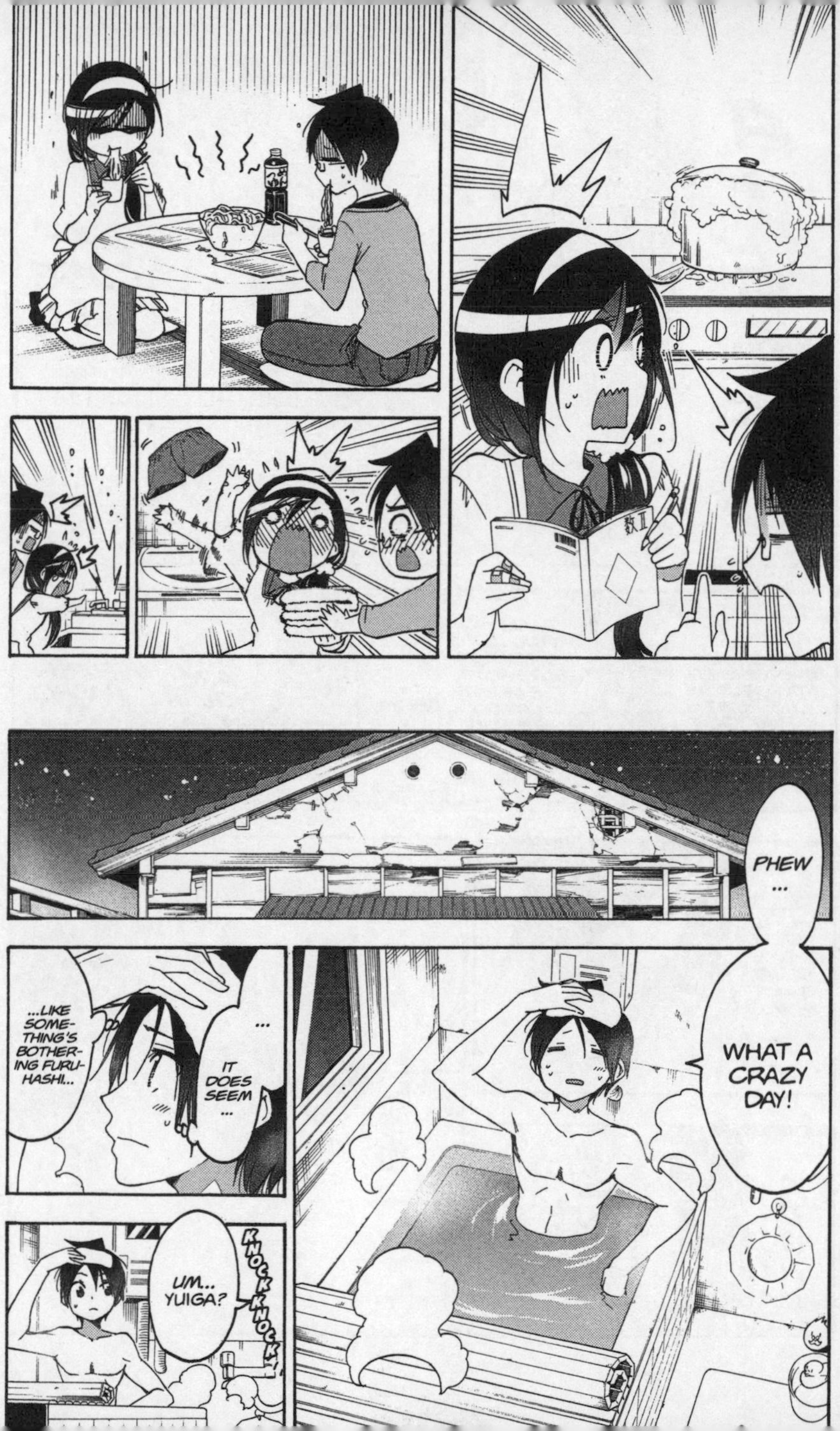
数II
PHEW ...
WHAT A CRAZY DAY!
... IT DOES SEEM ...
...LIKE SOME-THING'S BOTHER-ING FURU-HASHI...
KNOCK KNOCK
UM... YUIGA?

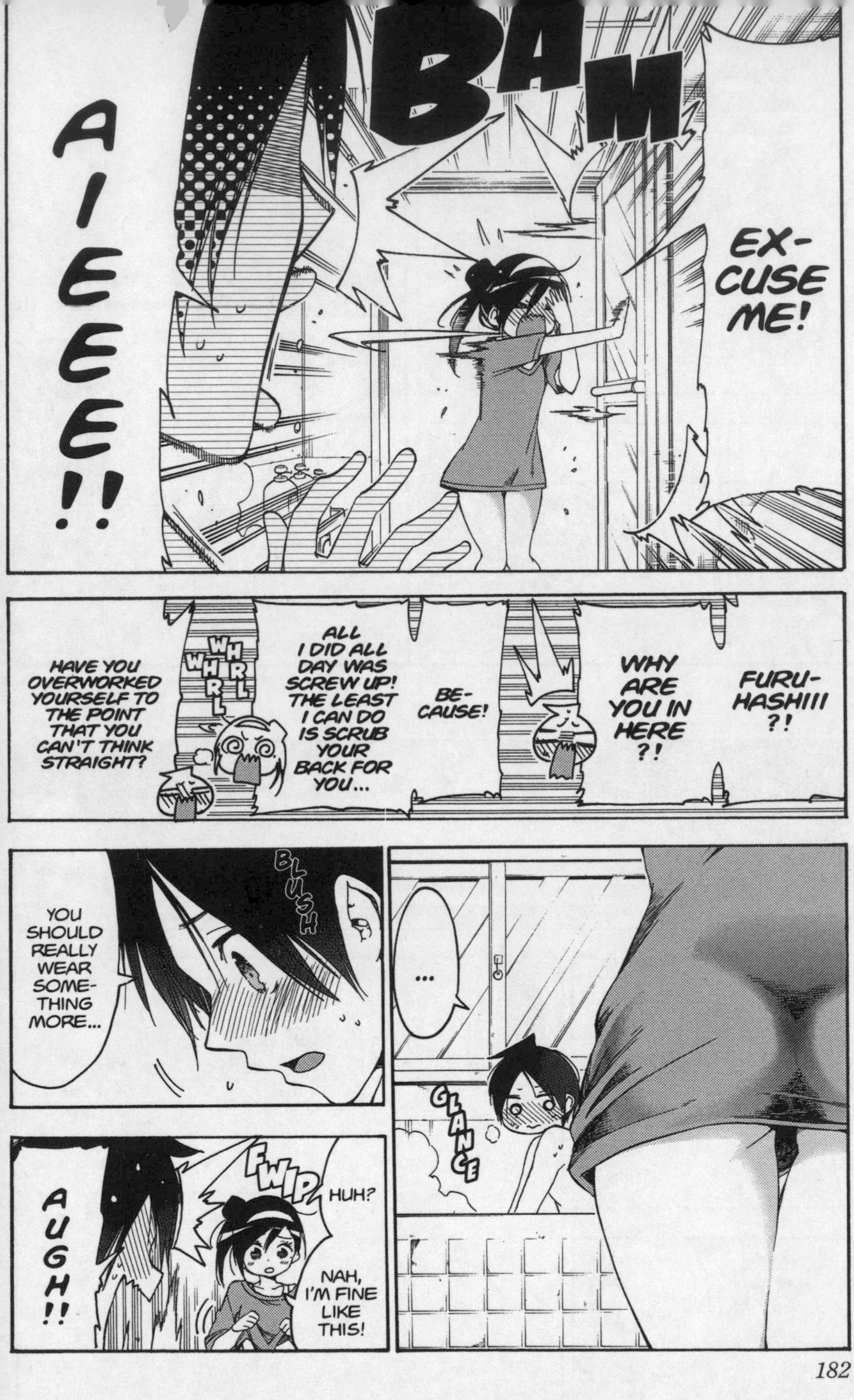

BAM
EX-CUSE ME!
AIEEEE!!
FURU-HASHIII?!
WHY ARE YOU IN HERE?!
BE-CAUSE!
ALL I DID ALL DAY WAS SCREW UP! THE LEAST I CAN DO IS SCRUB YOUR BACK FOR YOU...
WHRL WHRL
HAVE YOU OVERWORKED YOURSELF TO THE POINT THAT YOU CAN'T THINK STRAIGHT?
...
GLANCE
BLUSH
YOU SHOULD REALLY WEAR SOME-THING MORE...
FWIP
HUH?
NAH, I'M FINE LIKE THIS!
AUGH!!

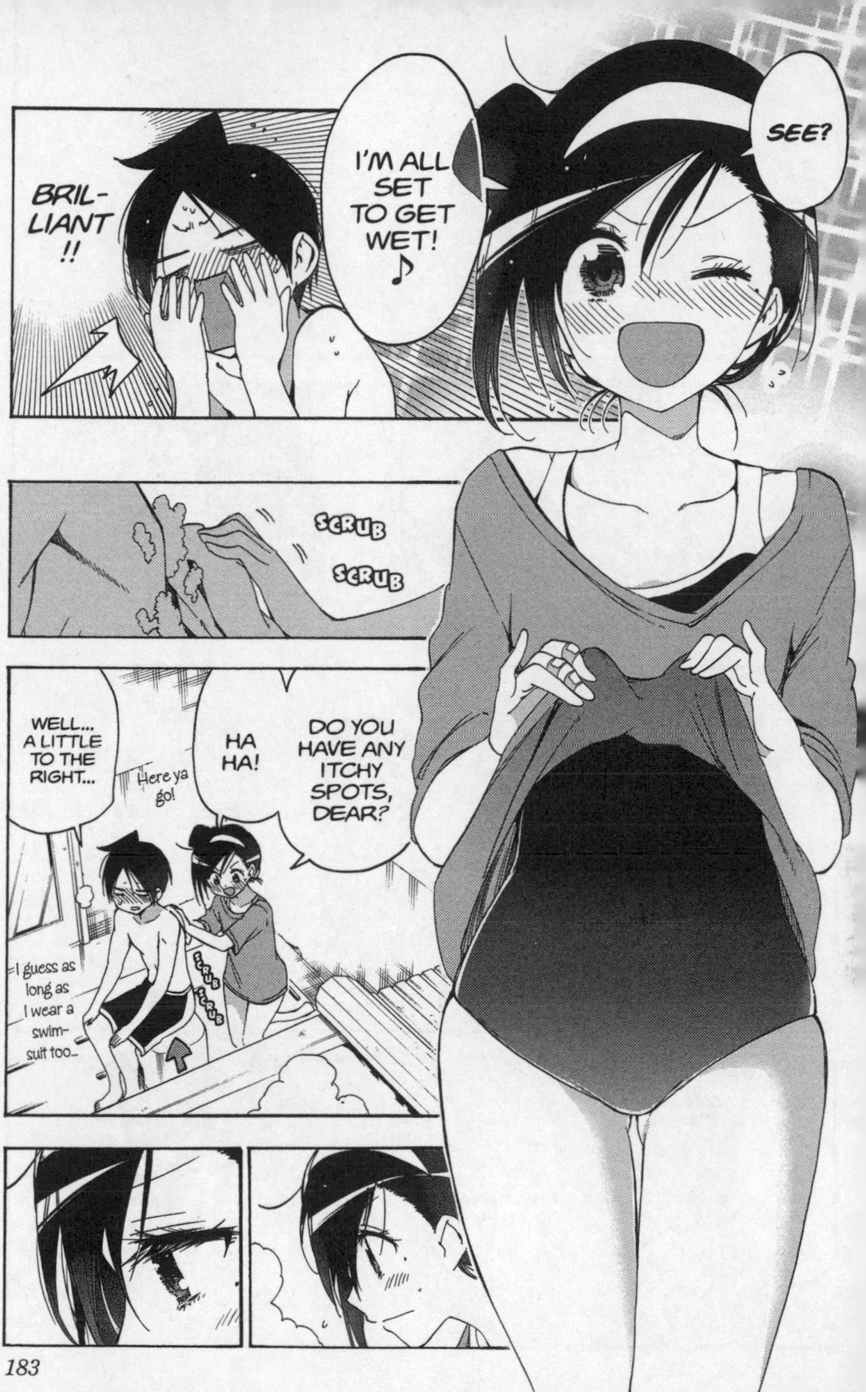
SEE?
I'M ALL SET TO GET WET! ♪
BRIL-LIANT!!
SCRUB
SCRUB
DO YOU HAVE ANY ITCHY SPOTS, DEAR?
HA HA!
WELL... A LITTLE TO THE RIGHT...
Here ya go!
SCRUB SCRUB
I guess as long as I wear a swim-suit too...

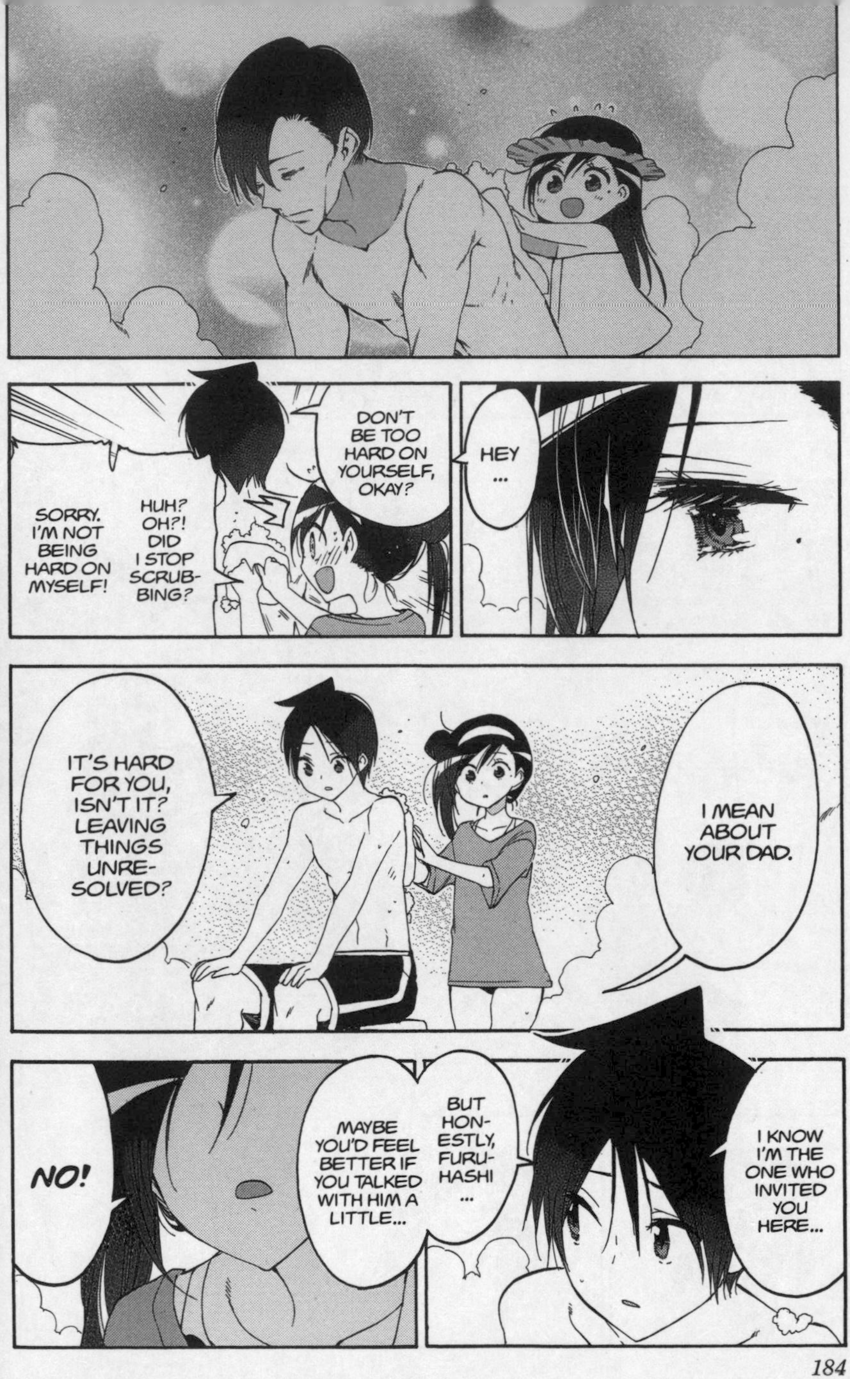
HEY ...
DON'T BE TOO HARD ON YOURSELF, OKAY?
HUH? OH?! DID I STOP SCRUB-BING?
SORRY. I'M NOT BEING HARD ON MYSELF!
I MEAN ABOUT YOUR DAD.
IT'S HARD FOR YOU, ISN'T IT? LEAVING THINGS UNRE-SOLVED?
I KNOW I'M THE ONE WHO INVITED YOU HERE...
BUT HON-ESTLY, FURU-HASHI ...
MAYBE YOU'D FEEL BETTER IF YOU TALKED WITH HIM A LITTLE...
NO!

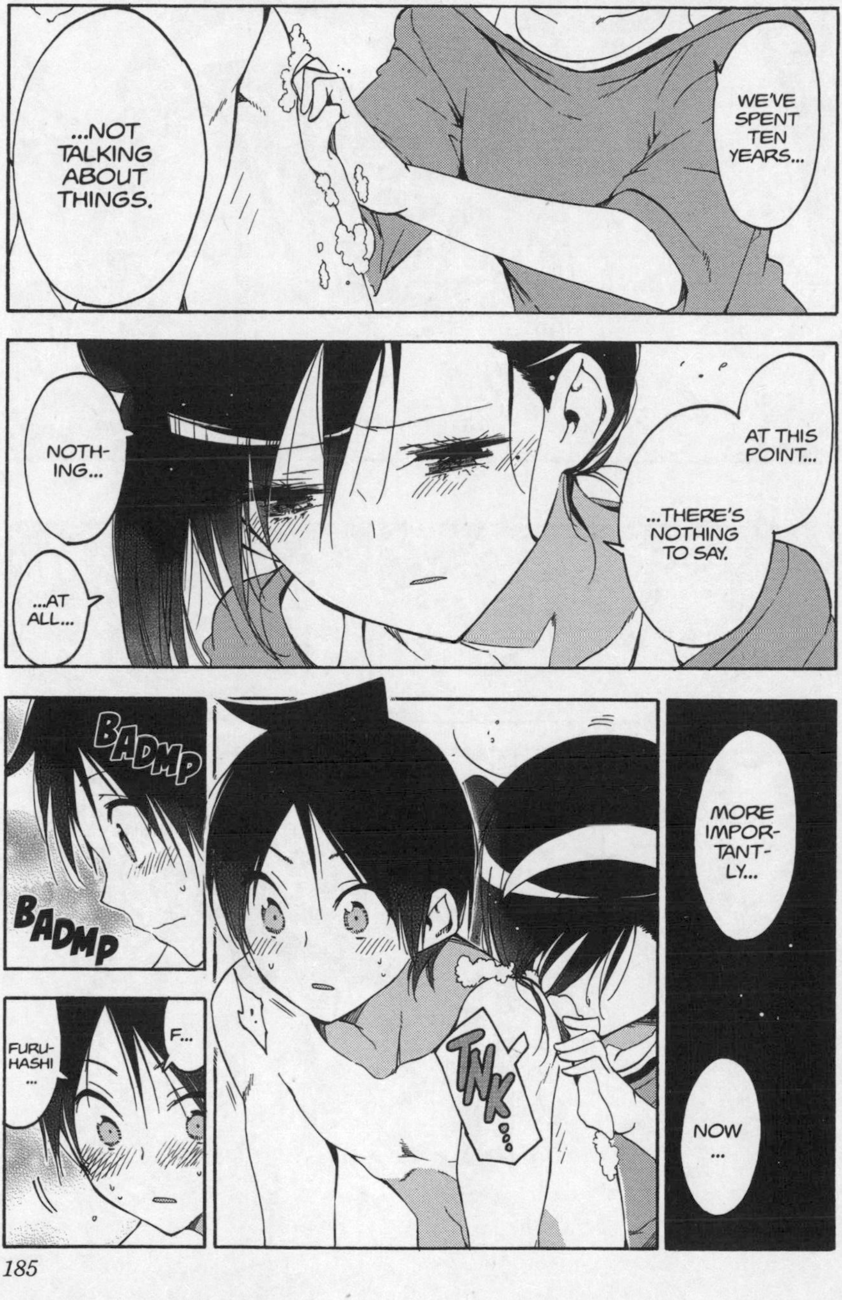
WE'VE SPENT TEN YEARS...
...NOT TALKING ABOUT THINGS.
AT THIS POINT...
...THERE'S NOTHING TO SAY.
NOTH-ING...
...AT ALL...
MORE IMPOR-TANT-LY...
NOW ...
TNK...
BADMP
BADMP
F...
FURU-HASHI ...

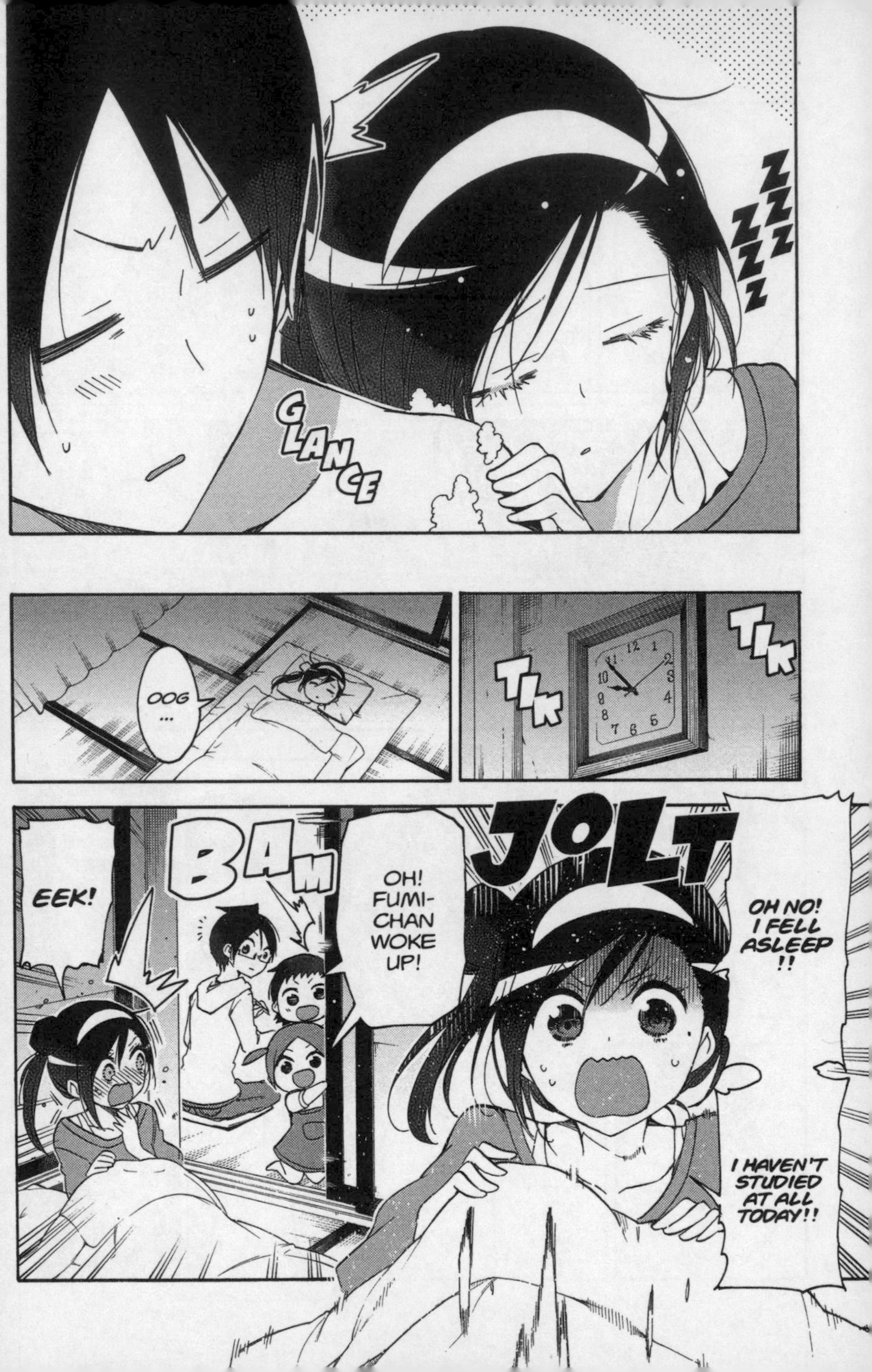
ZZZZZZZ
GLANCE
TIK TIK
OOG ...
JOLT
OH NO! I FELL ASLEEP!!
I HAVEN'T STUDIED AT ALL TODAY!!
OH! FUMI-CHAN WOKE UP!
BAM
EEK!

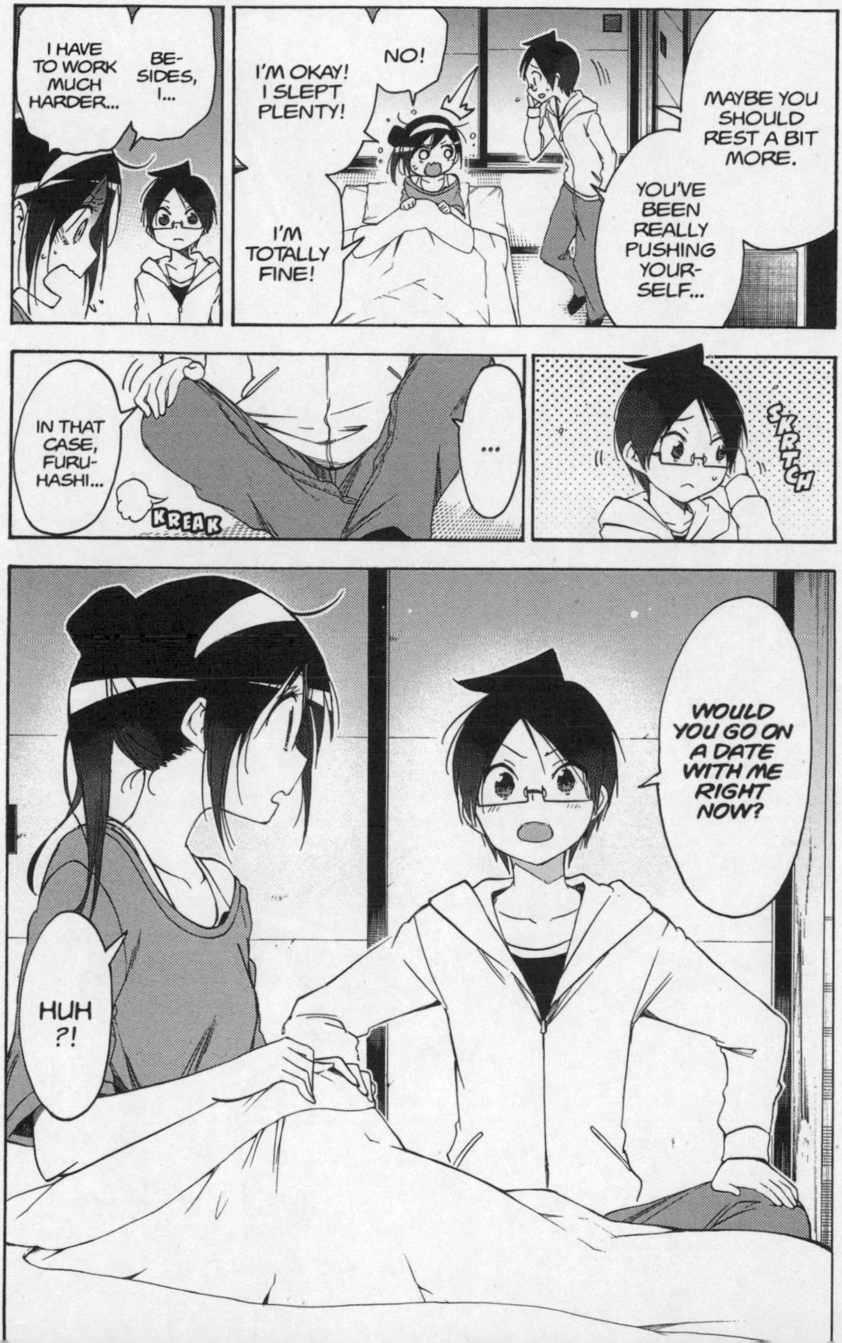
MAYBE YOU SHOULD REST A BIT MORE.
YOU'VE BEEN REALLY PUSHING YOUR-SELF...
NO!
I'M OKAY! I SLEPT PLENTY!
I'M TOTALLY FINE!
BE-SIDES, I...
I HAVE TO WORK MUCH HARDER...
SKRTCH
...
IN THAT CASE, FURU-HASHI...
KREAK
WOULD YOU GO ON A DATE WITH ME RIGHT NOW?
HUH ?!

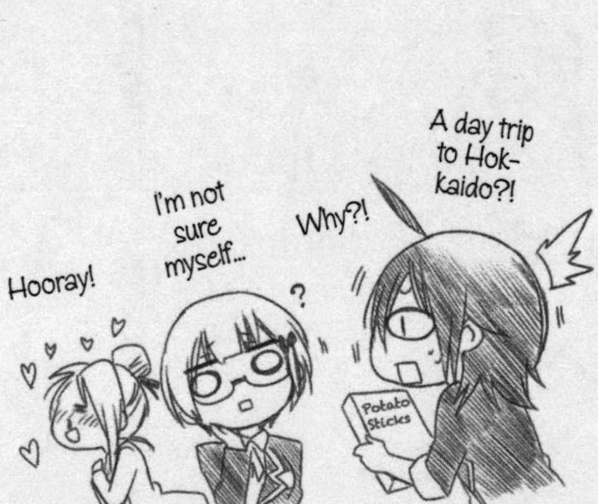
A day trip to Hok-kaido?!
Why?!
Potato Sticks
I'm not sure myself...
?
Hooray!

We Never Learn 10

STAFF LIST

STAFF

Taishi Tsutsui

Yu Kato

Naoki Ochiai

Sachiko

Yukki

Satoshi Okazaki

HELP

Paripoi

Fuka Toma

Shinobu Irooki

Chikomichi

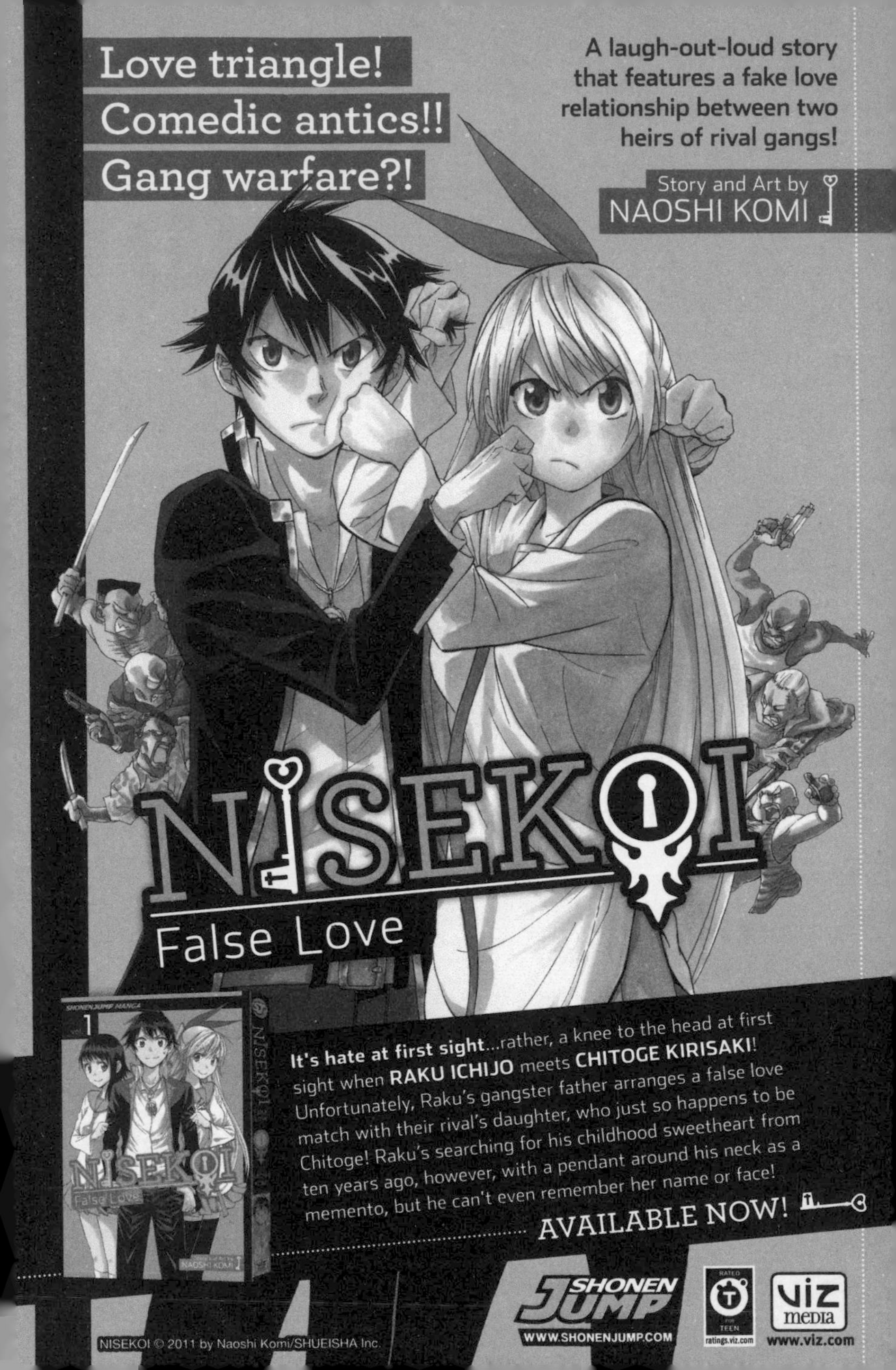
Love triangle!
Comedic antics!!
Gang warfare?!
A laugh-out-loud story that features a fake love relationship between two heirs of rival gangs!
Story and Art by
NAOSHI KOMI
NISEKOI
False Love
SHONEN JUMP MANGA
vol. 1
NISEKOI
False Love
NAOSHI KOMI
It's hate at first sight...rather, a knee to the head at first sight when RAKU ICHIJO meets CHITOGE KIRISAKI! Unfortunately, Raku's gangster father arranges a false love match with their rival's daughter, who just so happens to be Chitoge! Raku's searching for his childhood sweetheart from ten years ago, however, with a pendant around his neck as a memento, but he can't even remember her name or face!
AVAILABLE NOW!
SHONEN JUMP
WWW.SHONENJUMP.COM
RATED T FOR TEEN
ratings.viz.com
VIZ media
www.viz.com
NISEKOI © 2011 by Naoshi Komi/SHUEISHA Inc.

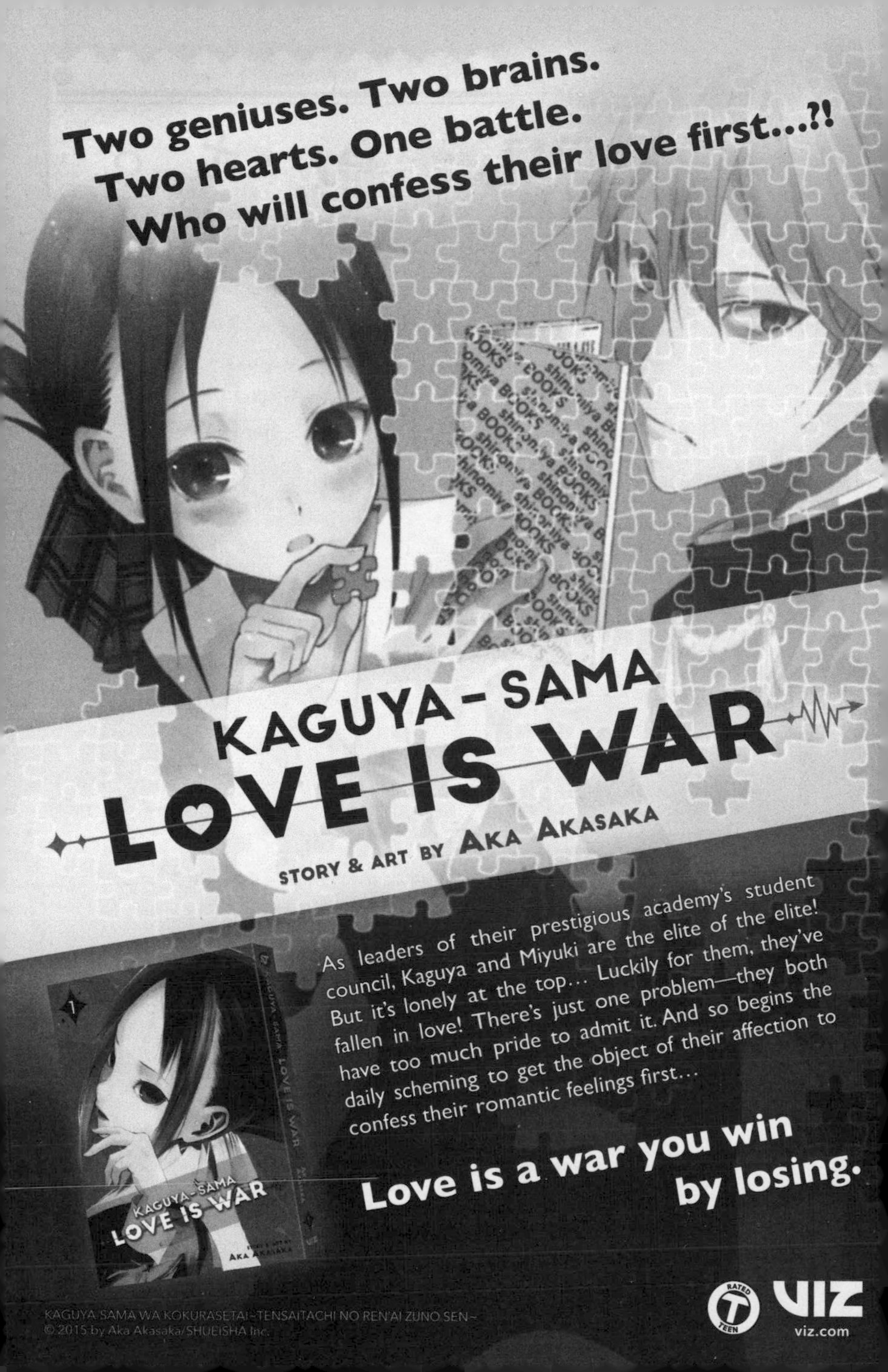

Two geniuses. Two brains.
Two hearts. One battle.
Who will confess their love first...?!
KAGUYA-SAMA
LOVE IS WAR
STORY & ART BY AKA AKASAKA
As leaders of their prestigious academy's student council, Kaguya and Miyuki are the elite of the elite! But it's lonely at the top... Luckily for them, they've fallen in love! There's just one problem—they both have too much pride to admit it. And so begins the daily scheming to get the object of their affection to confess their romantic feelings first...
Love is a war you win by losing.
KAGUYA-SAMA WA KOKURASETAI~TENSAITACHI NO REN'AI ZUNO SEN~
© 2015 by Aka Akasaka/SHUEISHA Inc.
RATED T TEEN
VIZ
viz.com

We Ne

from right to left, starting in the upper-right corner. Japanese is read from right to left, meaning that action, sound effects and word-balloon order are completely reversed from English order.

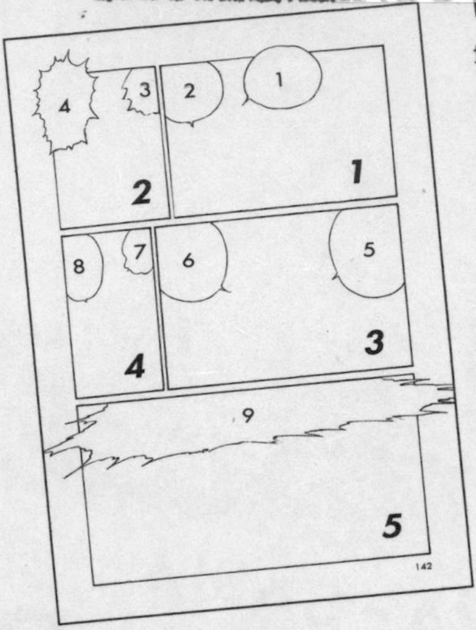
1
2
3
4
5
6
7
8
9
142

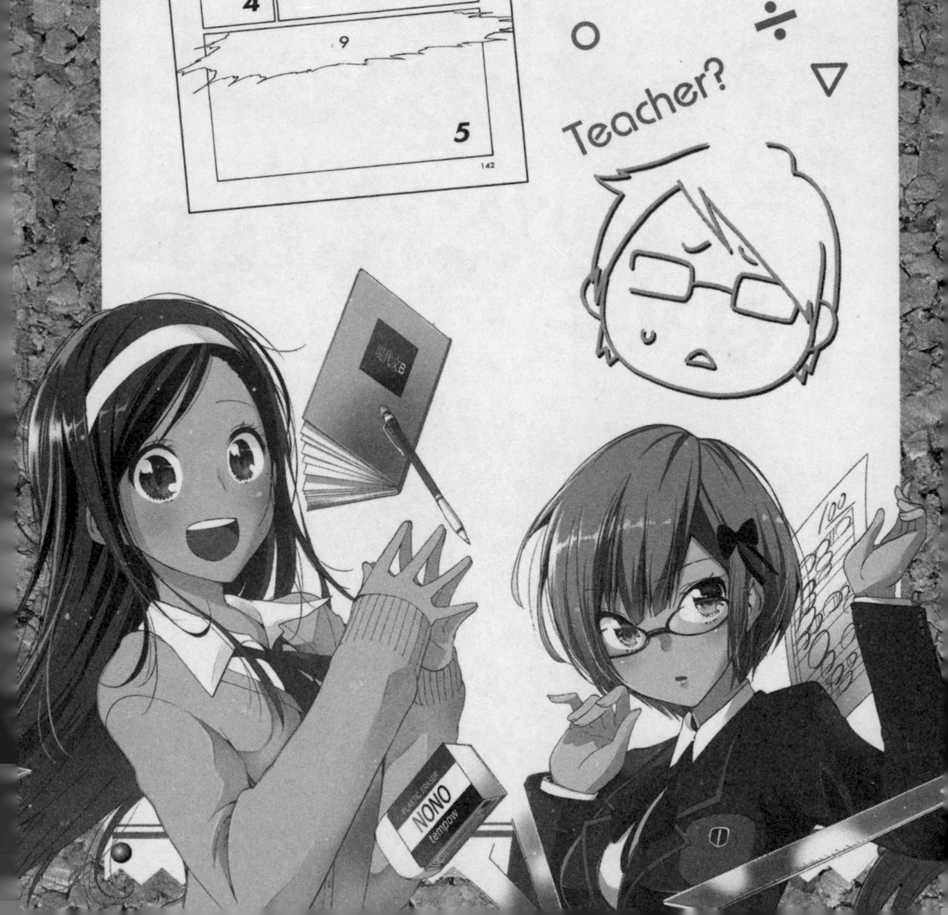
Teacher?
NONO
tempow